Turning to Nature in Germany

A group of *bündische* hikers in the early 1920s. By permission of Archiv der deutschen Jugendbewegung.

Turning to Nature in Germany

Hiking, Nudism, and Conservation, 1900–1940

John Alexander Williams

Stanford University Press

Stanford, California

Stanford University Press
Stanford, California

Printed in the United States of America on acid-free, archival-quality paper

Library of Congress Cataloging-in-Publication Data

Williams, John A. (John Alexander), 1962-
   Turning to nature in Germany : hiking, nudism, and conservation, 1900-1940 /
John Alexander Williams.
       p. cm.
   Includes bibliographical references and index.
   ISBN 978-0-8047-0015-3 (cloth : alk. paper)
   1. Social movements--Germany--History. 2. Hiking--Germany--History. 3.
Nudism--Germany--History. 4. Nature conservation--Germany--History. I.
Title.

HN445.W55 2007
304.20943'0904--dc22

                                2007023694

Designed by Bruce Lundquist
Typeset at Stanford University Press in 11/13.5 Adobe Garamond

For my parents, Sarah and Max,
and for Olaf

Contents

Part III   Conservation

Acknowledgments

THIS BOOK HAS BEEN LONG IN THE MAKING, and I have many colleagues and friends to thank. I owe a special debt of gratitude to my mentors at the University of Michigan, Geoff Eley and Kathleen Canning, who have helped me tremendously to develop my skills. I hope that they will recognize in this book the powerful influence they have had on my thinking. Heartfelt thanks also to the following for their constructive criticism and encouragement: Celia Applegate, Kenneth Barkin, David Blackbourn, Brad Brown, Robert Buffington, Peter Carmichael, Sandra Chaney, David Crew, Raymond Dominick, David Dorondo, Heather Fowler-Salamini, Atina Grossmann, Greg Guzman, Konrad Jarausch, Philip Jones, Thomas Lekan, Cliff Lovin, Khalil Marrar, Leisa Meier, Stacey Robertson, Adelheid von Saldern, Annette Timm, Corinna Treitel, Frank Uekötter, Gretchen Van Dyke, Max Williams, Sarah Williams, and Thomas Zeller.

My colleagues at Bradley University asked probing questions and made typically brilliant remarks about an early version of the nudism chapter; and my department has been wonderfully supportive. Special thanks to Audrey Redpath and Gina Meeks for their able assistance. The smart students whom I have had the pleasure of teaching have helped me clarify my thinking and writing. Two terrific research assistants, Sarah Carey and Peter Quigg, shared their time and talent.

I am grateful as well to the skillful archivists who helped me so patiently in Augsburg, Baunatal, Berlin, Bonn, Burg Ludwigstein, Hamburg, Hannover, Kassel, Koblenz, Leipzig, and Munich. Norris Pope,

Carolyn Brown, and Cynthia Lindlof at Stanford have been a pleasure to work with as they ably guided the book toward completion.

My family and friends have kept me alive to the "real world," especially Christine Blouch, Brad Brown and Stacey Robertson, Martha Craig, Kerry Ferris, Marianne Fischbach, Emily Gill and Jim Temples, Joseph Heine, Daniela Groger, Hanne Hermann and Odile Lemonnier, Harald Kolze, Tom Kuehler, Hiddy and Ron Morgan, Walter Pretz and Alex Miklosy, Andreas Ruell, Bärbel Schröter, Catherine and Pongracz Sennyey, Joan and John Tricamo, Gretchen Van Dyke, Larry Vielhak, Liza Williams and Taylor and John Heise, and Ray Williams.

Finally, this book would never have come about if it had not been for three special people. My parents, Max and Sarah Williams, have inspired and encouraged me all my life. My partner, Olaf Griese, has kept me going with his unfailing patience and love. This is for them.

John Alexander Williams
Berlin, June 2007

Turning to Nature in Germany

Introduction

The Ideology of Naturism
in Early Twentieth-Century Germany

IN 1924 ADOLF KOCH, a young elementary schoolteacher in Berlin, declared, "The misery of our times, the monotony of work, the world war and its legacies have made us into disturbed human beings, both internally and externally."[1] To help working-class Germans of all ages overcome this condition, Koch founded a network of thirteen exercise schools in industrial cities throughout Germany. There he and his colleagues put workers and their children through a rigorous program of group exercises in the nude. Members of a Koch School partook of at least two hours of nude training per week, attended lectures and group discussions on matters of importance to the socialist labor movement, and received advice about physical health and sexuality from resident medical experts. The cost for most adults was 5 percent of their yearly income; but the schools were free to children, the unemployed, pregnant women, and mothers of infants. During the warmer months, Adolf Koch's organization set up nudist camps in wooded areas outside cities. There people exercised, played games, and talked about political issues. The Koch Schools won the support of prominent Social Democratic parliamentarians, educators, sociologists, and physicians. By 1930 several thousand men, women, and children had attended these schools.

Socialist nudists aimed to compensate for the harsh working and living conditions of an urban, industrial society. They saw health in holistic terms—that is, as simultaneously a matter of the body, of the mind, and even of the political consciousness. Nudism was a way for the working class to turn to nature for strength and inspiration. The concept of "nature" in nudist ideology was twofold—nature was manifested in both the nonhuman rural environment and the naked human body. Moreover, the socialist nudists saw nature as egalitarian. They declared that there was no class hierarchy in nature and banned the formal pronoun for "you" from their discourse. The motto "We are nude and call each other *Du*" (rather than *Sie*) made plain this commitment to working-class solidarity. It was also a proud statement of their political superiority to the traditional, elitist, and status-conscious bourgeois nudist organizations.

Socialist nudism was only one of many organized efforts to bring the German people into closer contact with nature during the early twentieth century. This book investigates three of the most interesting and significant movements—hiking, nudism, and conservation. Although these movements differed in many ways, they were all galvanized by a new ideology that I call *naturism*.[2] This is not to be confused with ecological thought. Although proponents of naturism were deeply concerned with the consequences of industrialization and urbanization, their main concern was not with pollution, natural diversity, or sustainability but with social and cultural crisis. Naturist movements believed that Germany was beset by a number of crises, including the threat of urban living conditions to the body, psyche, moral character, and political consciousness; the capitalist exploitation of industrial workers; the moral and sexual waywardness of adolescents, particularly young males; and the decline in popular devotion to the regional and national "homeland" (*Heimat*). Organized naturists attempted to reorient the German people toward nature, and they hoped thereby to find solutions to the problems of modern society.

The history of naturist movements shows how politically charged popular culture became in early twentieth-century Germany. Not only were naturist perceptions of crisis shot through with political ideologies, but the more controversial ideas and practices of these movements caught the attention of the public, sparking loud debates and moral panics. Adolf Koch's nudist schools, for example, faced a barrage of attacks from conservative politicians, morality leagues, and clergymen. These enemies of nudism accused Koch and his colleagues of conspiring to rob people of their God-given sense of shame. Nudism, they warned, was encouraging sexual license in the shape of premarital sex, pedophilia, prostitution, and homosexuality.

In part because of such controversies, naturist movements gained considerable cultural influence. Prominent politicians and intellectuals, including Kaiser Wilhelm II, Friedrich Ebert, Karl Liebknecht, Gertrud Bäumer, and many others, lent their support to projects of turning to nature. Hundreds of thousands of less famous Germans participated directly in organized naturism. The large majority were city dwellers who chose naturist activities over countless other ways to spend their leisure time. The available sources, most of which were written by naturist leaders and functionaries, do not allow definite conclusions about the motives of rank-and-file members. Some inferences can be made, however. First, many city dwellers were seeking relief from the crowds, noise, and dirt of everyday urban life; and hiking and other forms of exercise in a rural setting gave them a sense of escape and rejuvenation. One young metalworker put it this way in a 1912 survey of working-class attitudes and desires: "In the woods I feel myself freer and lighter, and I admire for hours . . . the movement and life of organic nature. But when I think of returning to the treadmill of the human struggle for existence with all its untold miseries, tears of outrage fill my eyes."[3] Second, many people were no doubt attracted by the promise of collective sociability offered by naturist organizations. It was a common desire among city dwellers throughout the urbanizing world to overcome feelings of anonymity by seeking new forms of community. Third, many members of naturist movements probably agreed with the notions of social crisis and ideologies of progress that were expressed by their leaders. Supporting this assertion is the fact that rank-and-file membership in any given naturist movement was highest when there was ideological consensus among leaders, whereas the number of members dropped markedly when that consensus broke down.[4]

The desire to turn to nature as an antidote to the problems of urban-industrial modernity was not at all unique to Germany. Throughout the nineteenth and twentieth centuries, deep-seated ambivalence toward industrialization and urbanization has been a powerful undercurrent in Western intellectual life. We need only recall such writers as Charles Dickens, George Eliot, Thomas Hardy, Joseph Conrad, D. H. Lawrence, Virginia Woolf, and F. Scott Fitzgerald, as well as a host of painters, poets, philosophers, and politicians. A tendency of some German naturists—the drawing of parallels between the rural landscape and national identity—has been omnipresent in nationalist discourse since the nineteenth century. Theodore Roosevelt's celebration of the American wilderness is one of many examples. Moreover, organized naturist movements have been relatively common beyond Germany. Adult-sponsored youth movements, for instance, tried to use the nature experience to "cure" adolescent wayward-ness in Britain, the United States, and elsewhere. The American conserva-tion movement predated the German one; and hiking and even nudist groups have been fairly common in Western Europe and North America.[5]

However, in the years 1900–1940, naturism became more popu-lar and better organized in Germany than elsewhere. What was it about Germany in the early twentieth century that made naturism such an im-portant current in popular culture? At the heart of this development lay an unusually strong perception of crisis. Social and political uncertainty, as well as the desire to overcome it, was intense and enduring in Impe-rial, Weimar, and Nazi Germany. In their book *Shattered Past*, Konrad Jarausch and Michael Geyer call upon historians to study "the extraordi-nary upheavals that ripped apart a nation, and all the exertions required to allow a people to pull itself back together" through the "processes of the making and unmaking of the German nation."[6] Although the authors are referring primarily to the upheavals of war and revolution, we should also look to longer-term instabilities, both real and imagined, if we want to understand this era. Organized naturism is a clear example of the general perception among cultural activists that everyday social instabilities were causing an ongoing crisis of the nation.

Until recently, those few historians who paid any attention to natur-ism tended to condemn it as antirationalist, antimodern, and illiberal. Hans Kohn, George Mosse, and others argued that these characteristics made naturist thought a precursor of Nazism. Taking an intellectual his-tory approach, they asserted that German intellectuals had become pecu-liarly obsessed with nature in the Romantic era. Because of Romanticism, leading intellectuals had also turned away from Enlightenment values—particularly rationalism and the liberal ideology of progress through more individuality and freedom vis-à-vis the state. This historical misdevelop-ment persisted into the late nineteenth and twentieth centuries, when the uncertainties that accompanied rapid industrialization and urbanization caused many ordinary Germans to follow the intellectuals in rejecting modernity. As George Mosse put it, many people in the upper and middle classes underwent a "chaos of experience," which in turn gave rise to a desire to "escape from reality into a dream world where time stood still, a world that pointed back to the past rather than forward to the future." The result was a naively "romantic" belief in the "healing power of na-ture, symbolizing the genuine and the immutable, [which] could serve to reinforce human control over a world forever on the brink of chaos." This vision of nature appealed to "the need of men and women to annex a piece of eternity in order to keep their bearings." According to Mosse and others, "folkish" naturist movements such as the *Wandervögel* and the bourgeois conservationists helped to transmit reactionary "agrarian romanticism" to an even broader audience. This outlook was allegedly both nationalist and racist, and it ultimately helped to set the ideological stage for many Germans' support of Nazism.[7]

This thesis of a peculiarly Teutonic, protofascist agrarian romanticism has been quite influential in the historiography of modern German culture. Yet it fails to explain adequately the origins, ideological complexity, and influence of mass naturist movements. There are several basic flaws. First, these historians derive their claims about deep-seated popular attitudes from a very narrow source base indeed. Texts written primarily by intellectual, artistic, and political elites are juxtaposed to prove the Germans' rejection of industrial modernity and obsession with nature. In truth, elite texts can tell us little about popular attitudes—they can only tell us about elites.

Second, in seeking the ideological origins of Nazism, these historians take a myopic and teleological view of pre-Nazi German culture. Thus, they tend to ignore the moderate, reformist currents in naturism and exaggerate the influence of the small, far-right-wing "folkish" fringe. A good example is nudism, which began in the pre–World War I era as a fanatically racist fringe movement of the middle class but became a much more popular movement of industrial workers committed to democratic ideals in the 1920s. Only the bizarre racial theories of the bourgeois nudists receive adequate attention in these historians' studies. The result of this myopia is the incorrect but oft-repeated claim that the only critics of industrialization and urbanization were elite conservatives and/or radical nationalists. In fact, moderate bourgeois reformers and liberal Social Democrats led the way in organizing the popular turn to nature. The most conservative movement, bourgeois conservationism, was also the smallest in terms of membership.

Other flaws in the "naturism to Nazism" argument stem from ideological bias. These historians simply assume that any critique of industrial capitalism and the burgeoning industrial metropolis was irrational. There has been an ongoing struggle between intellectual advocates of the Enlightenment and of Romanticism that has endured to the present; and clearly these historians are on the side of Enlightenment values. But proponents of the Enlightenment have often exaggerated the ideological differences between the two movements. They have cast rationalism as the sole motor of progress at odds with an allegedly naive, backward-looking, and illiberal romantic worldview. A good example in German history is Thomas Mann. In a 1924 speech calling on his listeners to adopt a rationalist commitment to the Weimar Republic, Mann declared, "All that within us that is opposed to life and the future is romanticism. Romanticism is the siren song of nostalgia for the past, the song of death."[8] After World War II many historians of Germany adopted a similarly derogatory concept of romantic ideology to try to explain the Nazi project of imperialism, war, and genocide. In so doing, they reduced the multifaceted philosophical, aesthetic, and political tradition of Romanticism, which was neither simply antimodern nor simply antirationalist—and certainly not genocidal.[9]

Another ideological source of these historians' critique of naturism lies in their commitment to modernization theory. Originating early in the cold war, this normative model of social and political development offers an ideal narrative of progress from traditional agrarian society to modern industrial society. The avant-garde of progress in this theory is the capitalist middle class working within the liberal-democratic state. Rationalism, in the form of science, industrial technology, and the domination of nature, is a key motor of modernization. These historians' commitment to a specific capitalist model of progress creates a scholarly bias against any historical attempt to construct a different, less exploitative relationship between humanity and the natural environment. It also leads them to underestimate how Nazism was, in its own way, committed to an ideology of progress that combined pseudoscientific rationalism, industrial technology, and the domination of nature.[10]

In short, those historians who cast German naturism as simply irrational and antimodern greatly underestimate the variety of historical responses to urban, industrial modernity. Since the 1990s, however, a number of scholars have begun to challenge this thesis. They have undertaken a rethinking of historical attitudes toward nature in Germany. Using the methods of cultural history, they are analyzing a wide range of nonelite sources in search of evidence about everyday attitudes and practices. Their research is revealing that German cultural attitudes toward urban-industrial modernity were always ambiguous and that there was no direct line of continuity between the naturist critique of modern life and the Nazi attempt to radically overhaul it.[11]

This newer scholarship on naturism is related to a broader shift in the historiography of Germany under way since the 1980s. At the center of this transformation is an ongoing effort to reevaluate modernity itself. The older thesis of German misdevelopment has given way to a paradigm of Germany as a prime example of Western modernity. A new view has taken shape of modern society as complex and multifaceted, with both emancipatory and oppressive potentials.[12] Historians since the 1980s have also developed a broader concept of culture as a set of concepts, perceptions, and ideologies that are created and put into practice in everyday life. One of the most fruitful results of this "cultural turn" has been a growing body of research into how categories of social identity—class, gender, sexual, religious, ethnic, racial, generational—are defined, standardized, and made normative through language and imagery.[13]

Another important development is the strong focus on the ways in which people created a realm of cultural activism in the late nineteenth and early twentieth centuries. During the Second Empire, hundreds of activist organizations were founded that ranged in membership from under one hundred to several hundred thousand. They included such varied initiatives as radical nationalist and anti-Semitic pressure groups, Social Democratic and Catholic subcultural organizations, women's movements, projects of bourgeois reformism, and the naturist groups that are the subjects of this book. All of these movements took popular culture very seriously, trying to bring about change in the mentalities and lives of the German people. By expanding the public discourse on modern life, the popular ferment in this era brought with it the politicization of all those Germans who were concerned about the future of the collective to which they felt they belonged, be it the class, the confession, the gender, the generation, or the nation as a whole. These movements spread their perceptions of Germany's problems to the masses; but they also propagated notions of how to move the nation forward by confronting those problems. Millions were seized with an activist desire to have some influence over the nation's evolution, and the extent to which they organized themselves only increased in the pluralistic atmosphere of the Weimar Republic. Indeed, cultural activism outside the formal political system was the primary way in which both elites and ordinary people carved out a thriving civil society.[14] It took the determined efforts of the Nazis and their supporters to put an end to this diversity in the public sphere.

Thus, we now have a much more open-ended discussion of the early twentieth century. Historians no longer view Germans' perceptions of the difficulties of modern life as simple expressions of antimodern "cultural despair" but as the very thing that prompted people to seek ways to overcome crisis and reform their society.[15] The new paradigm of a heterogeneous modernity has liberated the field of German history from deterministic narratives of linear continuity from the Kaiserreich to the Third Reich. Modernity is no longer seen as lacking or peculiar in Germany, nor is it identified automatically with a progressive increase in reason and human rights.

Movements for hiking, nudism, and conservation in the early twentieth century were at the forefront of popular cultural efforts to diagnose and solve the problems of urban-industrial society. Naturists focused in particular on the city and everything that it seemed to say about modern life. Their discussions exemplified the typical ambivalence toward urban life that characterized German culture from the late nineteenth century onward. Discussions of the city among intellectuals, for example, nearly always presented it as the pinnacle of modernity; and these discussions were nearly always full of contradiction and unease. To take one example from pre–World War I social thought, the economist Werner Sombart wrote in 1906 that urban conditions were leading to a frightening loss of empathy and indifference to life among the proletariat. Yet elsewhere he wrote of city life as liberating: "The freedom that earlier resided in the mountains has today moved into the cities, and the masses follow after it. . . . It is above all the freedom of personality in the broadest sense that appears to be attractive; negatively expressed, liberation from the bonds of clan, of neighborhood, and of class domination."[16]

Such contradictory views of the city are not surprising when we consider the extremely rapid industrialization and urbanization of Germany. Unification in 1871 gave a tremendous push to industrial capitalism. A remarkably fast-paced urbanization commenced. While the entire population increased 58 percent between 1871 and 1914 (from 41 to 65 million), the number of people living in towns with over 5,000 residents increased by 229 percent (from 9.7 to 31.7 million). Meanwhile, the percentage of the population living in villages with fewer than 2,000 fell to 40 percent. The growth of metropolitan areas with over 100,000 residents is just as striking. In 1871 there were only eight such large cities containing a mere 4.8 percent of the population. By 1914 there were forty-eight, and 20 percent of Germans lived there. Certain industrial cities like Duisburg grew in population by nearly 2,000 percent. And urban sprawl was rapid and unstoppable. The average area of larger cities doubled between 1850 and 1910 from twenty-one to forty-two square kilometers. In 1895 the population of Berlin's suburbs was only 17 percent of that city's total population. By 1910 the suburban population of Berlin composed 45 percent of the total.[17]

Mass internal migration to the cities meant that every second German left his or her place of birth for an urban life during the Second Empire. Imagine the new city dwellers' sense of strangeness and dislocation! Alienation compelled many people from smaller towns and villages to build new communities within the city ranging from neighborhood associations, to social and political subcultures, to organized movements. By 1914 the city had become the locus of civil society in which even social outsiders could carve a niche for themselves with others of their ilk.[18] And cities were the source of most economic growth, technological advancement, and cultural innovation. This was one positive side of the expansion of urban life.

The negative side was plain to every city dweller. Miserable living conditions in the industrial city spawned anxieties about public health and fears for the future of the nation. Even though advances in health and sanitation were gradually lowering the urban death rate, the urban environment for the vast majority remained terribly unhealthy and polluted. Air pollution increased dramatically in every city and in rapidly industrializing regions of the Rhineland and Silesia. Water pollution was equally dire. Everyday experiences of the industrial city included pestilent air spewing from factory smokestacks and rivers that were little more than sewers. Consider the following 1903 report on the Ruhr Valley by a state-affiliated agricultural expert:

At many places, what is flowing there is not so much water as a viscous black mass sluggishly pushing itself forward. The thick settlement of the entire southern part of the area with industrial installations, the densely populated cities and towns, the extensive fortified network of roads, and the countless railway embankments have completely erased the formerly agrarian character of the region. . . . [E]very last drop of water, after traveling only a short way from its origin, is changed into intensely fermenting liquid manure.[19]

Crowded living conditions in the city also caused a great sense of foreboding and spawned a movement to combat the "housing emergency" (*Wohnungsnot*). The population density in Germany increased from an average of 76 people per square kilometer in 1871 to 120 in 1911. Expanding cities like Berlin, Breslau, Hamburg, Aachen, Hannover, and the towns of the Ruhr had up to seven times this average density by 1911. Older neighborhoods saw the construction of rental barracks (*Mietskaserne*), cheap buildings that encompassed up to 80 two- or three-room apartments with very little natural lighting. These were intended for unskilled and semiskilled workers; yet even better-off industrial workers were crowded into ramshackle housing. In Hannover, for instance, some 50 percent of the population lived in apartments with only one heated room. Working-class housing conditions in smaller and medium-sized towns were not significantly better than in the metropolis. In Augsburg, an inspection in 1909 of 1,625 apartments found that over 70 percent were afflicted with construction flaws, overcrowding, or other problems. Nor did the rapidly expanding suburbs, where many skilled and organized workers lived, offer any real relief from overcrowding.[20]

This situation, in which housing in working-class districts was smaller and much more crowded than in upper-class residential areas, was as true of the Weimar era as it was of the late Empire. Article 155 of the Weimar constitution guaranteed healthy living quarters to all citizens. Yet the migration of laborers to the cities had increased during the war, and a stream of refugees came from territories lost in the war's aftermath. Given the wartime hiatus in apartment construction, there was an estimated deficit of 1.5 million apartments by 1920.[21] Not until a state-sponsored program of small-apartment construction began in 1925 did the situation improve somewhat, albeit only for better-off workers with steady jobs.[22]

Even though cultural standards of adequate living space for an individual were lower than they are now, most socially aware Germans saw urban housing as a serious threat to national health. Beginning around 1900, a movement for housing reform began to undertake statistical surveys of urban living. This movement's diagnosis and suggestions for reform offer yet another example of ambivalent, even contradictory, attitudes toward the city. Typical was a 1912 speech by the housing reformer Dr. Von Mangoldt. The speaker warned that "being housed like animals" was endangering the physical and moral health of the urban poor. This crisis was hurting the power of the nation vis-à-vis its competitors by reducing the birth rate and increasing infant mortality. The result would be the limited military fitness of the urban populace. Moreover, the lower classes' love of the *Heimat* and loyalty to the German state were waning. Mangoldt moved easily from a social problem of the city to a cultural and a political problem. The solution that he offered was to reform the city itself. Young people above all must be removed from these ruinous living conditions, he declared, and the entire layout of Germany's cities would have to be "more expansive and natural."[23]

Mangoldt's solution was characteristic of most bourgeois criticism of the industrial metropolis. These commentators saw no way for the nation to return to agrarianism if it were to thrive in the modern world of intense international competition. They wanted to reform, rather than reject, urban modernity. The large city in the competitive nation-state was the paradigm of modernity within which attempts at reforming Germany had to stand or fall. Yet within this nationalist mind-set, there were also possibilities for the projects of social justice that were developed by socialists and liberals. Attempts to counter the negative effects of the industrial city were complex, forward looking, and ideologically multivalent—far more than mere "agrarian romanticism." Indeed, reformers of the moderate left and right who criticized the city took pains to distance themselves from the reactionary antiurbanist fringe. Their problem-solving efforts grew out of a "basic 'yes' to the city."[24]

The same may be said of a larger and more influential movement for "life reform" (*Lebensreform*) out of which emerged organized nudism. *Lebensreform* ideas were not original to Germany, but they had arrived there by the mid-nineteenth century, when a handful of urban intellectuals began to found tiny vegetarian and homeopathic organizations. The doctor Theodor Hahn coined the term *Lebensreform* in 1870, and by 1900 this had become a full-fledged popular movement, the "most holy duty" of which was to convert "mistaken fellow creatures."[25] Life reformers aimed to improve urban-industrial society by exposing the body to more "natural" ways of living, which ranged from vegetarianism, abstinence from alcohol and nicotine, dress reform, and nudism to natural healing through sunlight, water, and fresh air (*Naturheilkunde*) and the building of rural communes and "garden cities." *Lebensreform* associations were extraordinarily active, promoting their causes in countless public lectures, magazines, pamphlets, and books. The popularity of life reform ideas and practices grew rapidly in the Wilhelmine era. The abstinence movement, for example, published no fewer than sixty-seven journals with a combined circulation of 400,000 by 1909; and the German League of Associations for Natural Living and Healing experienced a steady growth in membership from 19,000 in 1889 to 148,000 in 1913.[26]

Lebensreform had an appeal that transcended class differences and political ideologies. From the beginning, *Lebensreformer* interpreted sickness as holistic—that is, common to the body, the mind, and the spirit. Sickness was caused by the disrupted relation of the individual to nature brought by industrialization and urbanization. Yet most *Lebensreformer* saw their project not as a rejection of the modern world but as an alternative path for society. Indeed, this critique of industrial capitalism helped make these ideas attractive to urban workers.

The example of garden cities reveals how *Lebensreform* attracted conservative, liberal, and socialist reformers alike. The aim of the Garden City Society (founded 1902) was to create a synthesis between city and country. The many proponents of the garden city believed that new, "greener" settlements should be built on the outskirts to alleviate the housing shortage, create better living conditions for workers, and promote a more efficient interaction between urban and rural economies. The garden city concept was also popular among leading labor movement figures. Karl Liebknecht, for instance, said in 1912 that urban dwellers were mentally, morally, and physically crippled and called for cities to be turned into garden cities.[27] No doubt the idea also intrigued poor city dwellers who were plagued by poverty and overcrowding. In Munich, for instance, the local branch of the Garden City Society planned a garden city on the urban outskirts in which every family would own between 80 and 150 square meters of garden. The claim that the garden city would create a sense of community in the citizen sold well to municipal authorities. Nine garden cities and four garden suburbs were built before the First World War, with three more planned.[28]

An overtly socialist branch of the *Lebensreform* movement began to develop after 1900 and went on to become a mass proletarian movement in the 1920s. The first Social Democratic organization was the German Workers' Abstinence League (*Deutscher Arbeiter-Abstinenten Bund*), which was founded in 1903 "to further the liberationist struggle of the working class, to raise the proletariat's living standard, and to prevent the degeneration caused by the enjoyment of alcohol." In 1911 the group declared alcohol a great hindrance to the labor movement and a boon to capitalism that could only be overcome through full abstinence.[29]

The Abstinence League paved the way for other prewar socialist *Lebensreform* organizations. The Federation for People's Health (*Verband Volksgesundheit*), for example, was formed in 1908 to promote natural healing and vegetarianism. The organization elaborated a trenchant critique of urban physical and cultural conditions under capitalism.[30] The president of the *Verband Volksgesundheit* beginning in 1920 was the secondary schoolteacher Hermann Wolf. He came from a large lower-middle-class family; his mother had died giving birth to her thirteenth child. He never forgot the terrible hygienic conditions of his childhood, a situation that he saw repeating itself again and again among his students in eastern Germany; and in 1887 he founded a local organization, the Association for Health and Non-Medicinal Healing. Wolf's experience of dire living conditions, and his growing awareness that this was endemic in the working class, seems to have been typical of many socialist *Lebensreform* leaders.[31] Under his watch, the *Verband Volksgesundheit* became the best example of a deeply politicized version of *Lebensreform*, dedicating itself to strengthening Germany's industrial workers and fighting social inequality. The *Verband* announced that it was "above all determined to awaken the working class to the fact that our current miserable health conditions are intertwined with our social relations."[32] As we will see in Chapters 1 and 2, the Social Democratic naturist movements took this central political tenet of left-wing *Lebensreform* very seriously indeed.

In the 1920s and 1930s, naturist-influenced projects of cultural activism remained intensely committed to solving the perceived crises of modern urban-industrial society. As Andrew Lees points out, by contrast to France and Great Britain, "Germany produced more and more writing about urban life with every passing year."[33] The First World War and its disruptive legacies no doubt perpetuated this obsession with the city. Total war brought mass death on a scale that was unprecedented. Over 2 million soldiers were killed on the battlefront, and the nearly eight hundred thousand injured men who returned became a constant reminder of the cost for the young male generation and their families. On the home front, exhaustion, malnutrition, and epidemics led to an estimated three hundred thousand civilian fatalities, not including those who perished in the 1918–19 flu epidemic.[34] In bringing a general collapse of traditional institutions of authority, the war worsened the long-standing sense of social crisis among moderates and conservatives. In the revolutionary phase that began late in the war, Germans on the home front directly experienced the rapid breakdown of established hierarchical relationships of authority—adults over youth, men over women and children, bourgeoisie over proletariat, party leaders over rank and file, the state over civil society.

The trauma of mass death and rapid social and political transformation greatly intensified preexisting fears that the moral, physical, and social health of the nation was in danger. In the Weimar Republic chronic structural weakness in the economy, political instability, and the wounded sense of national pride further deepened popular anxieties about the nation's well-being. As Detlev Peukert put it, the one certainty about the Weimar years is that they were fraught with *un*certainty:

The hectic sequence of events, the depths of the crisis shocks, and the innovative power of the social-cultural and political changes were not marginal; they were central characteristics of the epoch. From them grew an underlying sense of insecurity and absence of bearings—of changes in the framework of everyday life and of the calling into question of traditional generational and gender roles. Insecurity was the mark of the epoch.[35]

Ironically, insecurities that often hindered the popular acceptance of democracy could be more freely expressed than ever before within the democratic context of civic pluralism. Cultural representations of the metropolis in the 1920s therefore remained just as ambivalent as they had been before the war. Berlin in particular came to symbolize for many the uninhibited spirit of a restless modernity. Some, particularly those who might well have been shunned as outsiders in a smaller town, idealized the capital as a liberating Eldorado. Conservative moralists, on the other hand, fiercely attacked Berlin as a new Sodom. Most typical, however, was an attitude in which fears and hopes were intermingled.[36] For example, the most famous Weimar vision of the urban future, Fritz Lang's 1927 movie *Metropolis*, begins by representing the city as a dystopia of class exploitation and technological dehumanization. Yet the film concludes with a reassertion of human control over technology and a utopian promise of social harmony.

The Nazi movement that took power in 1933 was fully within the mainstream of concerns about the health and future of the nation. Despite their extreme critique of the city as the fount of liberal and "Jewish" modernity and their professed commitment to the peasantry at the expense of the metropolis, the Nazis were just as oriented to the industrial city as their predecessors were. Prior to taking Germany to war in 1939, Hitler's regime put into practice its own racist diagnoses and uniquely brutal "therapies." In their prewar efforts to bring homogeneity, health, and military prowess to the "racial-national community," the Nazis focused much of their energy on "cleansing" the city and its inhabitants.

My overarching goal in this study is to investigate how nature and modernity became intertwined in early twentieth-century German culture. The organizations at hand left many published and archival sources. Desiring support from both the populace and the state bureaucracies, naturist leaders and publicists produced a veritable avalanche of periodicals, pamphlets, books, requests for funding, and statements of intent. I take a twofold approach in analyzing these documents. One guiding theme is the organizational history of naturist movements, with attention paid to questions of sociological composition, the building of institutional frameworks, and the everyday practices that were intended to bring people into contact with rural nature.

My second main focus is the ideological history of hiking, nudism, and conservation. I trace the ways in which leaders and spokespersons collectively developed *ideal narratives of turning to nature*. Even though these ideal narratives were mutable and diverse, each followed a basic pattern. Each narrative began with a detailed diagnosis of a particular social crisis (or crises). The next step involved advocating and describing ideal ways of turning to nature. Each narrative concluded with a vision of improvement for the individual, for the membership of the organization, and ultimately for the entire nation.

Some additional general points should be made about these ideal narratives. First, naturists asserted that the nation was suffering primarily because of rapid industrialization and urbanization. Those developments had alienated the German people from rural nature. Furthermore, naturists nearly always expressed this theme of alienation through the language of health. Their concept of health was holistic, for they saw physical, mental, moral, and political health as intertwined. In other words, naturist diagnoses of Germany's crises were always also warnings about failing health. However, by taking the form of narratives that offered ways toward a better future, naturist discourse was forward looking in its attitude toward modern life.

Second, narratives of turning to nature were intertwined with notions of social identity. Class, gender, and generation were unstable identities in early twentieth-century Germany. The benefits of turning to nature promised by naturist writers included the stabilization and strengthening of these social categories. Class formation, for instance, was of great importance to naturists. For Social Democratic hiking and nudist leaders, the working class needed to reach a higher degree of collective solidarity. For middle-class naturists, the educated bourgeoisie had to be strengthened in order to maintain their respectability and status as cultural leaders.

Third, theories of human nature played a large role in these narratives. Socialist nudists, for example, wanted to guide German workers toward liberation from what they saw as the outdated and unnatural tradition of shame about the naked body. There was a sufficient store of reason in human nature, they argued, to enable people to control any sexual drives that might surface during group nudity. But for the enemies of nudism, the problem was that human reason could never prevail over desire. Thus, any unconventional attempt to liberate the body would open the Pandora's box of rampant sexuality.

Fourth, at the same time that leading naturists were creating ideal narratives of the turn to nature, they were also generating their own specific visions of the natural world itself. There was a dialectical relationship between naturist ideologies of human progress and nature itself. All naturist ideologues represented nature as a realm in which their followers could improve their health in a holistic way. But the ultimate, higher goals of turning to nature varied among the different movements; and these goals were reflected in differing visions of nature. Socialist movements, for example, desired a more rational and just society. They envisioned nature as a realm governed by rational laws that, if observed and adopted by human beings, would lead to greater justice.

There is nothing unusual about this process of constructing nature through culture. People have often conceived of a "nature" that corresponded to their own goals and desires. This is one way in which human beings have appropriated the nonhuman material world, and different groups within any given historical context have developed competing visions of nature. As the environmental historian William Cronon writes, "[B]ecause people differ in their beliefs, because their visions of the true, the good, and the beautiful are not always the same, they inevitably differ as well in their understanding of what nature means and how it should be used—because nature is so often the place where we go searching for the fulfillment of our desires."[37] Historians have uncovered how cultural representations of landscapes and natural phenomena came to legitimize social inequality and imperialism in such varied settings as Britain, France, the Americas, Asia, and Australia. They have shown how essentialist concepts of "the natural" have been used to buttress self-aggrandizing claims about gender, racial, and sexual identities. Environmental historians have also demonstrated that visions of nature both reflect and further motivate human exploitation of the environment.[38] Naturist movements in early twentieth-century Germany, then, are yet another example of the age-old process of appropriating the natural world by means of culture.

German naturists' concepts of nature were nearly always anthropocentric, for the nature that they envisioned existed primarily to help human beings progress. Moreover, they lacked the preoccupation with "untouched" wilderness that characterized American initiatives like the Sierra Club, simply because there was very little such wilderness left in Germany by 1900. Aside from the wilder parts of the Alps, the landscape was thoroughly populated, characterized by agriculture, cultivated woodlands, and rapidly growing urban areas. In terms of location and membership, naturist organizations were primarily urban in character. Theirs was a reformist project, and they made no attempt to wrench the nation backward toward the preindustrial past. They were maneuvering within an increasingly industrial society, striving to forge a path toward a brighter future. The naturist goal was both pastoral and thoroughly modern. The turn to nature, they hoped, would bring about harmony between the industrial city and the rural countryside.

This book is divided into three parts, each dealing with a sector within organized naturism. Part I (Chapters 1 and 2) focuses on naturism within the Social Democratic labor movement subculture. Chapter 1 investigates socialist nudism, tracing how the nudists attempted to counter attacks from conservative politicians and moralists. Influenced by the contemporary discourse of sex reform, the nudists defended themselves by fashioning a narrative of turning to nature in which group nudity would lead to a more rational sexuality.

Chapter 2 addresses the socialist Tourist Association "Friends of Nature" (*Touristenverein "Die Naturfreunde"*), a mass organization for working-class hiking. Founded in Austria in 1898, the *Naturfreunde* had by 1914 won a following among German workers. The German membership reached a high point of some 116,000 during the 1920s. The *Naturfreunde* offered urban workers the opportunity for physical and mental recuperation, as well as a new kind of class solidarity in rural nature and a sharp critique of capitalist exploitation. The leaders of this movement attempted to anchor progressive republican values in the minds of the working class through the turn to nature. Their notion of "social hiking" demanded that workers look at other working people within both the rural and the urban landscape in a socialist way, observing and learning about the everyday injustices of capitalist society. This effort to use hiking as a way to raise political consciousness did not, however, preclude a reverent attitude toward nature among the *Naturfreunde*, which manifested itself in both an ethos and an actual practice of conservation.

Both the nudist movement and the *Naturfreunde* reached the zenith of their popularity during the Weimar era, spreading naturist ideas to tens of thousands of industrial workers. Soon after the Nazis came to power in 1933, they outlawed socialist hiking and socialist nudism as antipathetic to the "racial-national community" (*Volksgemeinschaft*). This was in part due to the regime's general hatred of socialism and in part to its understanding of how attractive naturist activities had become to many Germans. Although the new regime encouraged politically innocuous hiking for workers through its "Strength Through Joy" program, it heavily circumscribed even the "politically correct" remnants of the small bourgeois nudist movement.

Part II (Chapters 3, 4, and 5) concerns the youth hiking movement, focusing primarily on organizations of the educated middle class. Chapter 3 is a case study in the late Wilhelmine conflict between the generations over the human nature of the adolescent and the best path to adult citizenship. On one side of this struggle over Germany's bourgeois youth were educated adolescents and young adults in the Rambler (*Wandervogel*) movement, who were seeking liberation from the institutions of adult control through group hiking. On the other side were adult "youth cultivators" (*Jugendpfleger*), a growing group of educators and professional youth specialists, who aimed to guide Germany's teenagers along the path toward rational and self-disciplined citizenship. The two sides clashed for the first time in 1913–14 over the theme of adolescent sexuality; and in the course of a nationwide moral panic over the allegedly irrational nature of adolescence, hiking itself came under critical scrutiny. One result was that youth cultivators came to see the appropriation and retooling of the *Wandervogel* hiking tradition as necessary in order to win the consent of young people to their project of discipline.

Chapter 4 shows that fears of a "crisis of youth" persisted in the wake of the war and revolution. It traces how youth cultivators tried to turn hiking to the purpose of teaching adolescents self-discipline. They successfully won state and civic support for youth hiking, propagating the activity through such organizations as the National Federation of Youth Hostels. Recognizing the need to win the consent of as many young people as possible, they incorporated into their project some of the liberationist ideas that had been so central to the *Wandervogel* hiking tradition. In so doing they ensured that organized youth hiking never lost its aura of individuality and autonomy, the disciplinary intent of youth cultivation notwithstanding.

Chapter 5 concerns the problems of both youth cultivation and youth hiking that arose in the late Weimar years of economic depression and political strife. It traces how after 1933 the Nazi youth organization tried to turn hiking into a method of "steeling" young people. The Hitler Youth soon realized, however, that *Wandervogel*-style hiking was fundamentally at odds with their totalitarian goals. By 1937 the Hitler Youth had purged all remnants of the early hiking tradition, replacing them with regimented camps and marching for the purpose of premilitary training. However, some young people clung to their vision of nature as a realm of liberty and persisted in illegal "wild hiking" in defiance of the regime.

Part III (Chapter 6) is a study of organized conservation (*Naturschutz*), a movement largely dominated by educated middle-class male elites. *Naturschutz* ideology was intertwined with the concept of *Heimat* from the beginning. This gave the movement a pronounced cultural and aesthetic bent in the Second Empire. During the 1920s leading conservationists attempted with only limited success to popularize their project among young people and industrial workers, whom they saw as dangerously impulsive and "rootless." After 1925 many conservationists placed racial nationalism at the center of their discussions of the landscape. They also demonstrated a marked willingness to compromise with industrial engineers in order to "create new beauties in the landscape where old ones are destroyed." Most leaders in the conservation movement welcomed the Nazi takeover, hoping that Hitler would both restore social order and use the state to enforce conservation on a national scale. The regime's promulgation of the first national conservation law in 1935 clinched the conservationists' support, and they embarked on a phase of intense activism. Although the Nazis themselves were not genuinely "green" in their thinking—Hitler's goals of economic autarky and war preparation were fundamentally at odds with protecting the rural environment—the conservationists' active support of the regime ultimately intensified their own racism and made some of them complicit in the regime's crimes during the war.

The concluding chapter draws together the varied threads of German naturism, summarizing the similarities and differences between the pre-1933 movements. It also addresses the question of continuities between Wilhelmine-, Weimar-, and Nazi-era naturism. Both pre-1933 and Nazi naturism shared the aim of defining and solving social crises. However, the Nazis divested naturism of all its liberationist and critical impulses, perverting it to the purpose of exerting physical and psychological control over the population. Far from subscribing to a reverent, romantic vision of the natural world, most Nazi ideologues had a reductive, social darwinist concept of nature. Hitler called nature "the cruel queen of all wisdom" and saw himself as her executor.[39] The Nazis referred to this deterministic vision of nature in their efforts to justify the murderous "cleansing" of the racial-national community. In another sense Hitler recognized early in the war that popular enjoyment of nature might serve as something of a compensation for "Aryan" Germans. In a decree of the Reich Forestry Department on July 9, 1940, the Führer let it be known that he wanted all "woods, conservation areas, parks, and landscape areas of particular beauty that are popular destinations for hikes and outings" to remain open to the public.[40] Nevertheless, the everyday policies of the regime regarding nature enjoyment were relentlessly totalitarian. The state heavily regulated adult hiking with the Strength Through Joy program and forbade all independent youth hiking in favor of marching in the Hitler Youth. Nudists and conservationists were tolerated as long as they clearly supported the regime's racist goals. The Nazi turn to nature, combining "natural law" ideas to justify genocide with the systematic control of everyday activities in nature, gutted the naturist tradition of all its emancipatory potential.

The fact that a minority of naturist thinkers and functionaries were willing to cast their lot with the Nazi regime discredited organized naturism for years after the war, rendering it "beyond the pale" in the eyes of most historians. This is unfortunate, for the history of naturist ideology and practice from the turn of the century to the beginning of the Second World War reveals in microcosm some of the ways in which Germans perceived modernity, confronted their fears, and imagined ways toward a better future. Naturists shared with most other critics of urban-industrial life a desire not to turn the clock back on modernity but to find a way toward a society that would be able to overcome its problems. Their path toward that future society lay in nature.

Part I   Socialists and Nature

1

"The Body Demands Its Rights"
The Workers' Nudist Movement

NO OTHER NATURIST MOVEMENT was more concerned with the body than the practitioners of "Free Body Culture" (*Freikörperkultur*—FKK), or nudism. Nudist ideology offers a clear example of the naturists' holistic goal of simultaneously healing the mind, the body, and the soul. Typical was one bourgeois nudist's optimistic announcement in 1926: "The body is entering into an organic relationship with the soul. . . . The human body-soul (*Körperseele*) is unfurling and blooming once again."[1] For the socialist nudist Adolf Koch, "Education raises the consciousness of both body and mind."[2] Therefore, physical and mental education had to be combined. The nudists set out to achieve this holistic process of healing the nation.

Nudism originated before the First World War as an extremely elitist middle-class branch of the diverse and loosely organized *Lebensreform* movement. Organizations were composed of just a few hundred intellectuals, artists, businesspeople, professionals, employees, civil servants, and students. The movement's prewar ideology was formed by reactionary "folkish" thinkers who propagated nudism as a bulwark against the supposed decline of the German nation's racial health. Their ideas were thoroughly reactionary, racist, and anti-Semitic, and they have drawn the attention of historians searching for precursors of the Nazis in German culture. George Mosse, for instance, argued that proto-Nazi "blood and soil" rhetoric was at the heart of nudist ideology from the beginning. For Mosse and others, the movement helped prepare the German public to accept the Nazis' racist ideal of health as represented by the blond, blue-eyed Aryan.[3]

Of all the naturist movements that emerged before the First World War, bourgeois nudism was the most radically right-wing in its ideology. Yet the generalization that all nudists were racists, still prominent in even the most recent studies, is simply not valid—especially for the Weimar Republic. The result has been an extremely distorted view of nudism that largely ignores the left wing of the movement that emerged in the 1920s.[4] That socialist faction was in the majority in the Weimar years. By the early 1930s there were an estimated eighty thousand practicing nudists, only twenty thousand of whom belonged to the bourgeois camp. The rest were closely affiliated with socialist nudist groups.[5]

The socialist nudists conceived of the worker's body—both male and female—as a symbol of the health of the working class. "Health" in this discourse meant not only physical but also moral and political health; and it became a metaphor for the potential of industrial workers to take hold of their own fate collectively. Weimar socialist nudists thought that the health of the proletariat was in very dire straits indeed. Thus, one goal of socialist nudism was to restore the body, the worker's only real capital. More generally, the movement's leaders argued that liberating the body would also ennoble the mind and raise political consciousness: "If we want justice within our nation, then we must help the subjugated to throw off their yoke."[6] This emphasis on class solidarity, consciousness raising, and social justice took socialist nudism far beyond the conservative ideology of the bourgeois nudists. They aimed to "rattle the foundations of bourgeois state and society." For this branch of nudism, creating the "new human being" (*der neue Mensch*) was an issue of human rights. The battle cry of socialist nudism became, "The body demands its rights, even within the proletarian movement."[7]

In my view socialist nudism is the most interesting branch of the *Lebensreform* movement, for it serves as a case study of the culture wars surrounding the body and its sexuality and the ways in which moral panic affected an essentially emancipatory project. The history of nudism was influenced in large part by a constant stream of attacks from conservative political parties, morality leagues, and Catholic and Protestant clergy. These antinudist elements accused the movement of indecency, sexual license, and the "planned and deliberate corruption of our children."[8] The nudists were thus obliged more than any other socialist cultural organization to convince their more moderate observers, including the Social Democratic labor movement leadership, that they were engaged in a politically and morally significant attempt to help the working class. Influenced by the language of social hygiene and sex reform, nudist leaders focused increasingly on a project of disciplining the proletarian body and rationalizing its sexuality. Shamefaced petit bourgeois and religious attitudes toward the body had to be discarded, they announced, and sexual behavior had to be liberated from mystification, ignorance, and irrationality.

The ideal narrative of socialist nudism asserted that nudism was both a way to liberate the worker and a method of controlling sexual drives. On the surface this seems to involve a basic contradiction regarding individual liberty. How can one be both liberated and controlled? The answer lay in the socialist nudist definition of freedom, which was derived from the liberal Enlightenment emphasis on civic virtue and *self*-control found most prominently in Rousseau's *Social Contract*. There was an element of being "forced to be free" in socialist nudist ideology. In practice this led to the exclusion of some sexual "deviants" and increasing medical advisement along eugenicist lines in the later Weimar years. Nonetheless, socialist nudists rejected the aesthetic of the ideal body that was prominent in the bourgeois movement and that excluded older, less-than-ideal individuals both from their photographs and their clubs. Instead, they celebrated the diversity of workers' bodies. They defined the body as the working-class's conduit to a nature that would strengthen workers, making them into "new human beings" who would guide Germany toward a just, democratic, and socialist future.

The Organization of Nudism

The founders of German nudism in the late nineteenth century were bourgeois artists and *Lebensreformer*. The painters Karl Diefenbach and Hugo Höppener (a.k.a. Fidus) and the natural healing practitioners Heinrich Pudor and Richard Ungewitter initially found little support in the prudish society of early Wilhelmine Germany, leading Pudor to complain in 1893 that "a naked human being is for the people of our times an offense, a slap in the face—so unnatural have we become."[9] However, by 1900 the notion that "air and light baths" taken outdoors in the nude had great health benefits began to find favor with some municipal authorities. They established fenced-in bathing areas that typically consisted of open showers and exercise equipment. Berlin established the first such location in 1901. By 1906, about 230 such establishments existed throughout Germany; and by 1912, there were about 380. There was also growing official tolerance for periodicals whose sole purpose was to present arty photographs of tastefully posed nudes.[10]

Yet nudism as an organized movement remained tiny and marginal in Wilhelmine Germany. Nudists published a number of journals and ideological tracts and founded secretive groups modeled after the Masonic lodge. The earliest such "lodges" were Heinrich Pudor's Freya-League (*Freyabund*) and Richard Ungewitter's League for Ascendant Life (*Treubund für aufsteigendes Leben*), both of which were founded in 1909. Pudor and Ungewitter propagated nudism as the solution to the supposed moral and racial decline of the German people. They used populist arguments to try to win converts. Pudor called for a republican political system founded upon nudism. Clothing, he thundered, was one way that the aristocracy of "the upper 10,000" held the nation down: "The church keeps them subordinate, the police enforces obedience, and the culture of clothing causes them to repress themselves." Clothing was a "peel" made of a "dead, lifeless material" unnatural and foreign to the human being: "Where clothes begin, so does death. . . . A clothed person is interred alive, standing with one foot already in the grave."[11] Pudor also offered a slightly enigmatic theory about the sexual temptations of clothing. Clothing fashions, he wrote, were invented by prostitutes—women's fashion by "sluts," and men's fashion by male prostitutes. Women flirted by wearing clothes that accentuated the rear, because they wanted to appeal to the innate homosexual tendencies of men. Furthermore, the modern bathing suit was the "least respectable piece of clothing" because it directed attention to "that certain place and points a finger at it."

[T]here is something secret, something hidden, like an Easter egg, something very remarkable, something that one should be ashamed of—sin, or that with which one sins or should sin or wants to sin. . . . "Cultured people" do something similar when they adorn museum statues with fig leaves. That always reminds me of a murderer shouting in the street, "I didn't murder him, not I, definitely not!"[12]

Richard Ungewitter was, like Pudor, a racist and anti-Semite. His "statement of purpose" includes points that reflect a eugenic emphasis on nudity as a means of weeding out the unfit from reproduction:

6. Prevention of "degenerate offspring" by means of marriage bans or castration in the case of the insane, alcoholics, tuberculars, the venereally diseased, criminals, and so on.

7. Preservation of racial purity by means of a ban on marriage between Germanic racial types and Latin, Slavic, Jewish, and other racial types, and by means of a ban on the immigration of Italians, Czechs, Poles, Jews, and so on.

8. Improvement of the Germanic race through a breeding policy favoring the blond and blue-eyed and including the Scandinavians.[13]

Such rhetoric clearly placed Wilhelmine nudist leaders in the radically right-wing nationalist camp. Yet this early nudism barely survived on the fringes of Wilhelmine culture. Ungewitter's organization had no more than four hundred members scattered throughout Germany, Austria, and Switzerland; and Pudor's organization was even smaller.[14] The bizarre theories and hysterical tone of the literature, along with the secretive character of the organizations, help explain the relative inconsequentiality of prewar nudism. Most significant in hindering the movement's growth, however, was the puritanical character of Wilhelmine society. The Catholic Church and conservative morality leagues constantly accused nudists of obscenity and immorality. The church declared in 1910 that nudism was "hygienically unnecessary and aesthetically worthless" and in moral terms "extremely dangerous and thus absolutely reprehensible."[15] Franz Walter, the Catholic author of the 1910 book *The Body and Its Rights in Christianity*, wrote that organized nudism was one of the most pernicious results of secularism and modern "pagan-naturalistic" morality. "The last dams are being torn down, and the muddy floods of sexual decadence threaten to rush out into the nation."[16] When Catholic publications began to identify the term "nude culture" with strip tease, nudist leaders felt pressured to describe their goal as "Free Body Culture" (*Freikörperkultur*) instead. The Wilhelmine state sometimes put nudists on trial for obscenity. Richard Ungewitter, for example, underwent a two-year trial following the publication of his book *Culture and Nudity* in 1911. He was acquitted, apparently having convinced the court of his organization's value.[17]

In the far more liberal atmosphere of the early Weimar years, the nudist movement grew rapidly. By 1930 an estimated one hundred thousand people took part in organizations that were either dedicated wholeheartedly to nudism or practiced it regularly. The movement of some eighty thousand hard-core nudists also became more ideologically diverse, splitting into bourgeois and socialist sectors. An umbrella organization for bourgeois nudists, the Reich Federation for Free Body Culture (*Reichsverband für Freikörperkultur*), was founded in Leipzig in 1924. It encompassed twenty-six organizations and some twenty thousand members by 1931.[18] The Federation's stated aims included nude group gymnastics in a natural, rural setting as an "educational method for moral strictness"; nature conservation; abstinence from alcohol and nicotine and the rejection of makeup and jewelry; and the building of group meeting houses.[19] But the *Reichsverband* was only a loose confederation, and there were several small independent groups on the local level in central and northern Germany.[20]

The bourgeois branch of nudism became more politically diverse in the 1920s. Ungewitter's radically folkish League for Ascendant Life survived, but Joseph Seitz led a secession of its Badenese members to form the first significant southern German organization, the League of the Friends of Light (*Bund der Lichtfreunde*). Seitz was determined to make nudism respectable by toning down confrontational aspects such as the demand for everyday nakedness outside designated nude bathing areas.[21] The best-known nudist leader on the right was the physical educator Hans Surén. In 1924 Surén became commander of the Army School for Physical Exercise in Berlin-Wunsdorf, where he made changes in the army's physical education along *Lebensreform* lines. He introduced mud baths, nude cross-country running, and strength training with medicine balls and tree trunks. In 1925 he left the army school and began to hold his own courses for young men and women. Surén made a name for himself by publishing his ideas in fourteen profusely illustrated and popular books between 1924 and 1932.[22]

For Surén, the conventional focus on educating the mind was unbalanced and unnatural. There should be a new type of physical education based on the kind of rhythmic gymnastic exercises that, he asserted, the ancient Greeks had practiced. Only in this way could the physical and mental emergency of the time be overcome.[23] As we will see, Hans Surén eventually became one of the most important leaders of the Nazi physical culture movement. In his Weimar writings, his language tended to the nationalist right, but at least until 1933, he was more of a conservative monarchist than a fascist.[24] In any case, it was probably not his vaguely and confusingly expressed political ideology but his practical directions on activities like boxing and gymnastics that won Surén a substantial readership.[25]

Another new organization in the early 1920s, the League for Free Life Formation (*Liga für freie Lebensgestaltung*), was founded near Hamburg. Benefiting from the relative abatement of censorship, the League

Hans Surén and students at his camp in Birkenheide in 1925. By permission of
Archiv der deutschen Jugendbewegung.

published many books and journals filled with photographs of people
carrying out daily family activities in the nude.[26] Most such bourgeois
nudist groups demonstratively avoided taking a strong political position,
even an antisocialist one. Like many moderate middle-class movements
for cultural reform, they believed that cultural activity and politics should
not mix. The 1926 statutes of one small local organization, the League for
Free Body Culture in Leipzig, were typical. They pledged to make people
"more resistant to contemporary dangers" by emancipating them from
"the imperative to wear clothes" (*Kleiderzwang*). They promised also to
overturn the common prejudice against the nude body as immoral. The
group welcomed anyone to its ranks, regardless of profession or age (although minors needed a guardian's permission), as long as the applicant
was "morally irreproachable." I have found no racial or religious restrictions in any group's statutes before 1933. In fact, the revised 1928 statutes
of this same Leipzig group explicitly forbade every political activity having
to do with parties, religious confessions, or race.[27]

The avoidance of political rhetoric and the relative inclusiveness
stemmed from the bourgeois nudists' attempt to gain a mass following

in the Weimar years. In this they were relatively successful considering that there cannot have been more than two thousand organized nudists before the war. Yet it was the socialist labor movement that most successfully popularized nudism in the Weimar years. By the early 1930s, some seventy-five thousand working-class people either practiced nudism casually in youth and hiking associations (such as the *Sozialistische Arbeiterjugend* and the *Touristenverein "Die Naturfreunde"*) or belonged to one of the two left-wing organizations dedicated exclusively to nudism. The leaders of this branch of nudism, moreover, were anything but reticent about their political stance.

The founder of organized socialist nudism was Adolf Koch, who was born in 1879 in Berlin to a working-class family. Koch had suffered terribly as a volunteer soldier in the war. He was wounded several times, was once nearly buried alive, and contracted cholera while in a field hospital. His wounds, sickness, and medical treatment left him with a limp, as well as allergies and near-constant fever during the warmer months. Following the war he earned his teaching certificate and took a job in 1923 at an elementary school in Moabit, a working-class neighborhood in Berlin. In his free time Koch studied psychology, medicine, massage, exercise techniques, and sexology (the latter through contact with the new Prussian Institute for Sexual Sciences). He became deeply concerned about the poor health of proletarian children, who suffered from the legacies of wartime poverty and, for many, the loss of their fathers. With the assistance of a group of parents, he began taking some of these children on hikes and teaching them orthopedic exercises. He also arranged reading and discussion groups and engaged informally in psychological counseling for his charges.[28]

Koch was a classic example of a socialist *Lebensreformer* who saw the physical, mental, and psychological health of industrial workers as a matter of social justice. His own physical problems no doubt strengthened his sense of common cause with the urban proletariat. In a manifesto that he published in 1923 as a flyer and distributed to labor movement organizations, Koch urged workers to struggle for a new world:

The misery of our times, the monotony of work, the world war and its legacies have made us into disturbed human beings, both internally and externally. . . . "No more war" should not be just an empty slogan but rather should be the real result of each person's reverence for the bodies of others. Our lives should be based on love for others, on the principle of mutual aid and understanding. Our children must be made to feel at home in this view of the world at an early age. . . . One way to achieve this is by educating them to be proud of their own bodies.[29]

Koch's deep concern about the mental and physical crisis of postwar Germany, combined with his commitment to social justice for all Germans, became the ideological foundation of the socialist nudist movement. A number of Leagues of Free People (*Bünde freier Menschen*) emerged in various working-class neighborhoods throughout northern and central Germany in the early 1920s. In 1926 these leagues united to form the Group of Free People (*Gruppe freier Menschen*) and collectively joined the Federation for People's Health (*Verband Volksgesundheit*), the umbrella organization of the socialist *Lebensreform* movement. By early 1933 there were thirty-three such local groups of working-class nudists in the Group of Free People. Although it never had more than three thousand members, the Group under the guidance of eloquent propagandist Hermann Schmidt communicated the ideals of socialist nudism to a wide readership through the cultural journal *Urania*.[30] Influenced by Koch's ideas, the Group practiced nude exercise and bathing, hikes, discussions of health and hygiene, and medical counseling as a way to help save Germany's industrial workers.[31]

In the early 1920s Koch undertook on his own time to teach bodily hygiene and exercises to his young students at the elementary school in Berlin-Moabit. He believed that they learned more about their and others' physical condition if the exercises were carried out in the nude. The school director allowed him to use a schoolroom in the afternoon for sex-segregated nude exercises, and he had the written support of the children's parents. When his teaching colleagues from other schools expressed interest in the program, Koch invited several of them, along with representatives from parents' councils, to a demonstration in late October 1923.[32] Apparently they approved of the program, but their support could not prevent a scandal from erupting.

According to the Social Democratic Party (*Sozialdemokratische Partei Deutschlands*—SPD) newspaper *Vorwärts*, a Catholic cleaning woman in the school one day "happened to catch sight through a keyhole" of the naked children during their exercises. She alerted her priest, who then informed the press. Koch was subjected to attacks from the political right in both the municipal government and the Berlin press. The Nationalist Party city councilor Kunze announced that Koch had "misused two hundred female pupils for nude dancing," hinted that he had abused both boys and girls sexually, and demanded that he be sent to an asylum. The real culprits behind all this degeneration, Kunze added, were the Jews—even though Koch himself was not Jewish.[33] Other right-wing enemies of the republic voiced their disgust at "the young child molester" in the press. As one wrote, "[T]he new republican romanticism is bearing fruit. . . . The bubbles rising out of the revolutionary swamp smell foul, very foul—and there are more and more new boils on the infected body."[34] Only the SPD defended Koch in the press and the parliament. Eventually the Berlin school board fired Koch not for immorality but on a technicality—according to an 1852 law, the school board had to be consulted about the private use of a schoolroom, and this had not occurred.[35]

Koch, a dedicated member of the SPD who rejected all radical politics, was inspired to a more radical kind of cultural activism by the scandal. In 1924 he founded his own private school for nude exercise, the School for Health Pedagogy and Body Culture, which became known simply as the Koch School. The famed sex reformer Magnus Hirschfeld, founder of the Institute for Sexual Science was helpful in this endeavor, for he allowed Koch to use a room in the Institute for the school's first year. Within two years the project had gained sufficient popularity and financial clout to enable Koch to establish branches in other cities. By the late 1920s there was a network of thirteen Koch Schools for workers of all ages in Berlin, Hamburg, Dresden, Mannheim, Breslau, Barmen-Elberfeld, and Ludwigshafen.

These Koch Schools attracted an illustrious group of voluntary assistants and supporters that included teachers, school reformers, sociologists, and physicians, as well as Social Democratic members of the Prussian, Hamburg, and national parliaments. Such prominent figures helped the schools carry out an extensive educational program, with between eight and sixteen lectures each month on science and current political and sociological subjects. Some of Koch's most important supporters were women, including Dr. Hildegard Wegscheider and Clara Bohm-Schuch, SPD delegates to the Prussian Diet and the Reichstag, respectively, and Ilke Dieball and the Jewish sculptor Ruthild Hahne, who became exercise instructors at the Berlin Koch School.[36] The support of the prominent sex reformers Friedrich Wolf, Max Hodann, and Magnus Hirschfeld helps explain the strong emphasis on rational sexuality in the movement, which will be discussed later. Dr. Hans Graaz was the organization's medical director and Koch's closest colleague; he contributed heavily to the shaping of socialist nudist ideology through copious articles and speeches. The Koch Schools were also fairly well known outside Germany. At a conference held at the Berlin school in November 1929, two hundred delegates were present from France, England, Austria, and Switzerland.[37]

The individual members of the Koch School participated in at least two hours of group nude gymnastics weekly, took part in lectures and group discussions, and received advice in physical health and sexual pedagogy from the schools' resident medical experts. Each individual received a medical checkup every three months. The schools' offerings cost 5 percent of one's yearly income, though the schools were free to children, the unemployed, pregnant women, and mothers with infants less than one year old. There is little surviving information on the class, gender, generational, religious, and ethnic makeup of Koch's movement. We do know that about 78 percent of Koch's pupils in Berlin were unmarried.[38] Scattered bits of evidence suggest that the rank-and-file membership was composed of better-off industrial workers and lower-middle-class employees. This would be in keeping with what we know of other cultural and exercise organizations in the socialist labor movement. The Koch Schools appear to have been attended by a roughly equal number of men and women. In terms of religious affiliation, both the leadership and rank and file included Christians, Jews, and atheists, although we have no information on the percentages.[39]

Also helpful is the impressionistic report of two American nudists, Frances and Mason Merrill, who visited socialist nudist facilities in and around Hamburg in the early 1930s. At a small suburban camp used by the Koch School, they found persons both young and old, as well as pregnant women. In Hamburg the Merrills observed a Koch School class of eleven young men and women. The director of the school was a woman, although the teacher of this particular course was a man. The number of male and female students was roughly equal, and there appeared to be an attitude of respect between the sexes. The showers were coed. "Everything is as clean and neat as in the most up-to-date hospital clinic," wrote the Merrills enthusiastically.[40]

The extent to which the socialist nudists accepted less than young and healthy-looking people into their organizations is difficult to determine from the movement's published sources, which provide no information on age or body types. Certainly the ideal body celebrated in the journals' photographs belonged to healthy, athletic young men and women, just as in the photographic iconography of nonsocialist nudism.[41] Yet the Merrills reported older people and "a dark-skinned woman [with a] big stomach and fat thighs" at a socialist camp near Hamburg.[42] Those whose bodies did not fit the ideal were apparently absent only in the movement's iconography, not from its everyday activity. It is also probable that younger people were more likely to take part in the demanding exercise classes, whereas older members would have preferred more relaxing and less conspicuously celebrated alternatives.

In 1928 Koch brought his organization into the *Verband Volksgesundheit*. Socialist nudists were now so influential that the Federation's leadership decided to form a new Branch for Proletarian *Lebensreform* and Free Body Culture. By early 1933 thousands of men, women, and children had attended the Koch Schools. The school in Berlin alone had 3,947 members on January 1, 1933. Koch placed an upper limit on attendance, concerned that otherwise the movement would lose its focus on small groups and individuals.[43] Koch's ideas and methods were generally well respected not only among the SPD party leadership but also in the liberal press. He was good at cultivating courteous relations with more moderate members of the bourgeois nudist community, who sometimes wrote favorably of his work in their journals. Bourgeois and socialist nudist groups even socialized and played sports together in an area on the north bank of Lake Motzensee near Berlin.[44] The Merrills reported that a nudist camp near Lübeck was patronized by visitors from all classes—students, workers, lawyers, architects, businesspeople, aristocrats—and that they were diverse in their political commitments, ranging from conservative monarchists to socialists and one communist.[45]

Although some historians have taken this friendly interaction between nudists from differing political positions as a sign that there were no real ideological differences between them, this interpretation is mistaken.[46] In fact, socialist nudism developed a relatively democratic concept of improving proletarian health that differed markedly from the aims and ideologies of the nonsocialist sector. Above all, their diagnosis and solutions centered on the question of proletarian health. In this their interests diverged markedly from those of the bourgeois nudists, who talked mostly in terms of aesthetics and aimed to raise people to certain ideal standards of beauty. Socialist nudism, as one sympathetic reporter put it, taught people to accept not just "beautiful bodies, but also the 'unbeautiful' bodies, whether they be deformed by nature or by work in the factory."[47]

The Ideology of Socialist Nudism

What diagnosis of Germany's problems did the socialist nudist movement offer? At the core of this ideology was the notion that physical, mental, and moral health were intertwined; thus the threat to health, particularly the health of the proletariat, was all encompassing. The nudists argued that the decline of proletarian health stemmed both from oppression by outside forces and from the natural, irrational human drives of the workers themselves. As Adolf Koch described it, part of the problem lay in structural economic inequalities, but responsibility lay also with the workers themselves:

We exercise in the nude because we can clearly recognize in the body the damages brought by contemporary life. Sagging breast, hanging shoulders, and bad posture are imperfections [that we encounter daily]. The cultural-political work of exercise begins here, and here we should ask the questions, "Why have I become so? Are the workplace and the apartment, or my own way of life, at fault? Does not my pale, anemic complexion reflect the fact that state welfare and health insurance institutions only intervene when sickness is obvious? Does not bad or unpractical nutrition also play a role? Can we fight the political and economic fight when our bodies are weakened?"[48]

According to the socialist nudists, the *external* oppressive force was industrial capitalism and the unjust social conditions that it created and sustained. Poor health was partly due, then, to poverty and poor nutrition. Rationalized, assembly-line factory work was also considered damaging to the worker's body and played an increasing role in nudist rhetoric in the mid-1920s era of relative economic stabilization. The socialist nudists wrote that work on assembly lines was well suited for machines but not for "the subtleties of the human organism"; argued that the rhythm of the machine was taking over society and subjugating human life; and asserted that rationalization was draining both the body and the soul of the worker.[49] The unity between body and mind that characterized the proper kind of factory work, wrote Koch, was being destroyed by the kind of alienation from the work process that rationalization wrought.[50]

Also central to the nudist diagnosis of capitalism's ills was the housing emergency (*Wohnungsnot*), which remained chronic in the Weimar Republic despite concerted efforts by the state to build new apartments. Socialist nudists believed that the *Wohnungsnot* weakened the ability of working parents to raise their children into morally and sexually healthy individuals. It caused "dark hatred" to grow within the family "out of this forced closeness, out of this invasion of each other's privacy, out of this overhearing, almost feeling, and nearly seeing."[51] Parents in this situation were neither able to cope with their own desires rationally, nor could they teach their children openly and honestly about sex.

The nudists were not alone in their concern about the housing emergency. Indeed, they were influenced by the many statistical and anecdotal studies of *Wohnungsnot* and its alleged sexual consequences that were published during the 1920s and early 1930s.[52] According to most of these commentators, too many people were being forced to live together in close quarters; too many health problems were being promoted by such a life; and too many young people were being exposed to the sexual activity of their parents. This allegedly had both physical and moral consequences. Housing conditions killed the "finer" sexual feelings of married couples and thus made "any more elevated way of life impossible."[53] But the youngest members of working-class families were most imperiled. As one writer on the *Wohnungsnot*, Victor Noack, imagined, "In the dim gray night, big, astounded child's eyes look over to the beds where those in heat embrace in sultry lust: the parents, the sister and brother-in-law. . . . A child's ears listen. The holy command to 'Be fruitful and multiply!' becomes a curse."[54] The direct physical result of this state of moral degeneration was a virulent epidemic of venereal disease: "Syphilis creeps from bed to rumpled bed, poisons the youth—slips through the door to the neighbors—down the steps—grips the street—conquers the city—contaminates the nation."[55] In this rhetoric, both the present and the future proletariat were under threat of succumbing to a collective kind of corruption that would be both physical and moral.

The socialist nudists were committed to a left-wing version of the early twentieth-century ideology of social hygiene. According to this ideology, the condition of the worker's body and mind stemmed in part from everyday living conditions that themselves reflected social inequalities.[56] Although social-hygienist doctors, welfare experts, and cultural activists on the left were genuinely concerned with alleviating social inequality and working-class poverty, they shifted part of the blame for proletarian misery to the proletariat itself. These elites represented the working masses as tending toward irrationality. Capitalism was playing to this weakness and encouraging it. In a typical argument that moves easily from the discourse of mass irrationality to an emphasis on sex, the author Helmut Wagner wrote that the reasoning capacity of workers had been befogged by living conditions and mass culture under industrial capitalism.

How should people [in urban housing], who have never had the opportunity to have biologically and emotionally valid sexual intercourse, attain a higher level of sexual culture within marriage? Moreover, the tension of the worker and his mental weariness cause the purely impulsive gratifications—eating, drinking, making love, and sleeping—to take on their most primitive forms. The large role that sexuality plays in the life of the manual laborer . . . is not at all surprising. Hard physical work simply makes a person incapable of any higher form of enjoyment. The striving for life in these bodily wrung-out and shamelessly overstressed workers concentrates itself in the bestial exhibition of the most elementary drives: hunger and sexuality.[57]

For Wagner there was a growing tendency toward promiscuity in which workers were "ever searching for the 'right' sexual partner, despite the fact that they lack the ability to have a sexual relationship with full biological value."[58]

This passage reflects another important ideological influence, sex reform, which increasingly pervaded socialist nudism in the latter years of the Weimar Republic. Organized sex reformers gained considerable influence in the 1920s, agitating for a number of more or less progressive causes, including gay and abortion rights and the protection of mothers. Like social hygiene, sex reform was a normative ideology that called on workers to transform themselves into more rational and disciplined human beings.[59] Together, social hygiene, sex reform, and anticapitalism were all founts of socialist nudist ideology—a set of intertwined influences that distinguished this branch of nudism from the nonsocialist branch.

Within this socialist discourse of mass irrationality, a more specific critique of popular proletarian culture took shape as well. Socialist nudist leaders in particular condemned the sexual repression, prudery, and shame that they believed characterized popular everyday culture among workers. Dr. Hans Graaz, the medical director of the Koch Schools, took the lead in criticizing typical ways of discussing reproduction within the working-class family:

When a baby is born . . . and its older, naive siblings observe this miracle that "the stork" has brought them, a rude awakening soon comes: they tell their older playmates about it, and then they are cruelly and spitefully enlightened. "Yeah, yeah,

the stork. Children aren't brought by the stork—they come from your parents doing swinish things in bed." This is how children learn about sex from parents who
answer all their questions [evasively]. Early on, children begin to associate sexuality
with filthy behavior. And then they discover that their beloved and honored parents,
their models for later life, are doing dirty, secretive deeds. And so the first ideals of
youth are toppled.[60]

In such writings, Graaz and others blasted working-class prudery and eva-
siveness as a manifestation of popular irrationality. The goal of socialist
nudist pedagogy was to end sexual repression and at the same time to allow workers to take greater responsibility for their own sexuality.

Socialist nudists also attacked conservative religious morality and
its influence in the working class. Koch's movement vehemently rejected
organized religion, positing a better future in which workers would have
learned that there could be no reconciliation between the church and the
"affirmation of the body."[61] Fritz Bauer of the Koch School attacked the
church's teachings on sexuality, writing that all mothers were insulted
by the "worthless fantasy" of the immaculate conception.[62] Above all the
nudists criticized the church for teaching the emotion of shame to the
masses at an early age. Teaching shame to children always backfired:

There is no such thing as an inborn sense of shame. . . . Shame is inculcated into the
child, thereby laying the groundwork for the theft of the child's original naturalness.
The child learns that there are forbidden fruits, and its imagination is tempted early
on by thoughts of picking them. The child is practically educated to be sexually curious from the very beginning.[63]

Hans Graaz, always the most determined advocate for secular progress
through rationalism among the nudist leadership, defined shame as a
form of primitive superstition. Graaz explained that the "wild peoples"
(Wilden) covered their private parts for the same reason they wore rings
through their noses and ears—to protect themselves from demons. People
in the Koch Schools had liberated themselves from such primitivism.[64]
Although this critique of backward religious morality was common to
all sectors of the nudist movement, the socialists combined it with an attack on capitalism. Koch argued that shame was "an artificial feeling of
inferiority" inculcated by the ruling class, which was "counting on stupid-
ity" to enforce "the emotional anchoring of bourgeois morality" in every
individual.[65]

Thus, although the threatened proletarian body in nudist rhetoric by and large reflected the social condition of class exploitation, the nudists shifted some of the blame directly to the workers themselves, representing the proletariat as basically irrational and thus susceptible to the influences of mass culture, popular myth, and traditional religion. How did the nudists propose to liberate workers from capitalist exploitation, and from their own unreason, in order to build a generation of new human beings? Hermann Schmidt of the *Gruppe freier Menschen* summarized the answer given again and again in nudist texts: "The liberation from external constraints must go hand in hand with internal, personal liberation."[66]

The nudists' solution was to turn to a nature that they saw as liberating. Their rhetoric and practice elaborated two complementary ways of turning to nature, one literal and the other more figurative. The first involved leaving the city temporarily to experience the rural landscape. During the warmer months, local groups rented plots of suburban parkland or forestland from sympathetic municipal governments. There the members played sports, exercised, danced, and socialized in the nude. The largest of such sites was no doubt a one thousand–acre plot in the suburb of Berlin-Selchow, which Koch rented at a low price from the city beginning in 1931.[67]

Koch and his colleagues promised both physical liberation and holistic health benefits to those workers who took part in this communal nature experience. "Out there in nature," announced Richard Bergner, "we will get rid of our last constraints—our clothing—and let air and sun work upon our naked bodies. . . . Air and sun are the worst enemies of all proletarian sickness." In such a setting workers could "[get used] to the naked body in light and water" and cast off the urban "cult of enjoyment and clothing."[68] Furthermore, the experience of nature in the nude would create a stronger sense of community and family. As Siegfried Kawerau of the Koch School wrote,

There the family can exult in their recovered purity in the shadows of beech trees, in the waters of a cool lake, or lying stretched out on the mossy forest floor. And the children will thank their parents for the trust and honesty they have shown. Out of this experience will come comradeship and community. This experience will be a holy grail that all will protect with their lives.[69]

Germany's chronically bad weather encouraged a second, more metaphorical concept of returning to nature in socialist nudism. During most of the year the nudists had to pursue their activities inside their facilities in the city. However, this too they represented as a turn to "nature," which in this case meant the human body itself. Two supporters of Koch's efforts, the socialist doctors Magnus Hirschfeld and Friedrich Wolf, wrote about their observation of one of his classes that "one had the definite feeling that the naked human being represents natural creation in a higher and purer form."[70] The turn to nature in this sense occurred through a training process by which the worker would learn to relate in a healthier way to his or her own body and to the bodies of fellow workers.

This second concept of turning to nature evolved in the everyday discourse and activities of the Koch Schools. A key aim of Koch's exercise classes was to present the body in movement to scrutiny. Not only doctors and trainers but also one's fellow workers would observe with a critical eye the nude proletarian body. Koch explained that he wanted his students to learn to "see the body" and mark the ways in which it was suffering from capitalist exploitation. His method involved taking groups of ten to twelve students through a series of practices that combined mental and physical exertion. First, discussion and hygienic activities (including communal washing and scrubbing in the nude) encouraged the students to overcome their sense of shame and learn respect for their own and other bodies. Next came education about anatomy, bodily flaws, skin conditions, and sexual reproduction. This stage entailed more discussions as well as visits to sanatoriums and hospitals. The course of study then moved on to a more physical phase with gymnastic exercises to develop strength and coordination. Swimming, ball games, and folk dancing were also included.

In the next phase of Koch's course, "pure gymnastics" became the focus of activity, by which Koch meant breathing and stretching exercises; group running and "expressive movements" such as imitations of animals; and free-style movements to music. This stage included a strong element of individual expression and diversity of movements within the group. Teachers and observing medical practitioners would always be on the scene to help cure individual bodies of their more "unnatural" movements; peers were also encouraged to help each other in this way. Always the "inhibitions" of the body in motion were explained as resulting from the physical and mental stress of the worker's everyday life.

Advanced stages of the course included directed group activities such as drawing and painting, speaking choirs, singing, and theatrical skits, much of which was no doubt politically critical. The ultimate goal of the course was an "awakened consciousness of the unity of body and mind" that would promote "changes in apartment living; the struggle for land and school reform; the battle against alcohol and nicotine and for natural living and healing; a new sense of morality and responsibility; the experience of community; and a new religion based on the unity of body and spirit." The final result of the course, Koch hoped, would be nothing less than a socialist new human being with the knowledge and desire to act politically.[71]

Regulating Sexuality: The Problem of Freedom

Despite the growth of nudism into a mass movement, Weimar nudists were still obliged to stake their claims to moral and political respectability. In the increasingly illiberal atmosphere of the late Weimar years, conservatives, morality associations, and Catholic clergy denounced nudism with ever greater fury. The police occasionally placed nudist groups under observation, expressing suspicion that nudism was not only morally but also politically subversive.[72]

Up until the late 1920s, the published attacks on nudism tended to be ideologically incoherent, based more on visceral feeling than a strong political or religious position. Nationalism generally played a strong role in antinudist rhetoric. When a meeting of a small bourgeois nudist group near a Bavarian town became known to the locals in 1925, the town newspaper wrote, "We would like to warn energetically and in public against the further dirtying of our shelters and mountains. Our nation sees this public 'naked culture' as pure swinishness."[73] Beginning around 1926 the attacks became more frequent and more ideologically direct. The trend was apparently related to a broader moral panic over "trash and smut" (*Schund und Schmutz*) in mass-produced literature and film. This *Schund und Schmutz* debate was essentially a battle over censorship that raged for several months in the press and legislative bodies.[74] A primary target of the conservative advocates of censorship was the erotic mass-produced literature that was allegedly intended to corrupt young people; and they categorized all nudist publications in this way. Catholic morality leagues such as the White Cross Association were particularly active denouncers of nudism, as was the ultraconservative press affiliated with the German National People's Party.

A 1927 essay in the morality journal *Weißes Kreuz* by a school superintendent, one Herr König, typified the Catholic moral panic over nudism. König began by announcing that God had given the sense of shame to human beings and even to the higher female animals, which hid their sex organs just like the "primitive natural peoples." Therefore, any attempt to break down the barrier of shame was both ungodly and unnatural. König continued with a discussion of sexual corruption among both adolescent boys and women. When boys and men bathe in the nude together, the ever-present (and increasing) "evil of homosexuality" had a chance to take hold. "Is there not a danger," König inquired rhetorically, "that some same-sexer (*Gleichgeschlechtlicher*) could exploit nude culture in order to indulge his desires, in order to choose and capture his prey?" Women were equally under threat from out-of-control male *hetero*sexuality. Nudist men were taking advantage of women by posing as liberators, fooling women into overlooking their true exploitative motives. The "anarchic women's movement" was also doing its part by erasing the natural boundaries between the sexes. Moreover, the nudist claim that activities in the nude helped the sexes get used to each other and thus reduced sexual temptation was a lie, given that the "strongest human drive, the sex drive" will always dominate. If "nude culture" is allowed to influence large numbers of people and the body cult takes over, König concluded, "then the end will come."[75] The apocalyptic tone was typical of these attacks, particularly when combined with nationalist fears of the German people's moral and physical decline. Other critics launched similar tirades in the leading Catholic youth cultivation journal, calling nudism "the keystone of a purely secular culture" whose god was nature and "the natural." The nudists' historical model was ancient Greek culture, but just look at the historical consequences of this ideal:

Unnatural fornication [of homosexual men] is now called "the Greek vice." The completely degenerate Greeks were easily conquered by the Romans. When the Romans then adopted this prized Greek culture, their power slowly wasted away, and they fell victim to the Germanic tribes. Must the Germans now go down the same path?[76]

The traditional moralism, fears of sexual degeneration, and nationalism that characterized this Catholic antinudist campaign took a more secular form in attacks by the right-wing political parties around this time. Essayists on the political right focused especially on the alleged pedophilic threat posed by leading nudists. The German Nationalist press in Hamburg accused the head doctor at the local Koch School of the "planned and determined corruption of our children."[77] Other Nationalist newspaper articles attacked nudism as "swinishness" that "made Germans living in foreign lands ashamed of their Fatherland."[78]

In light of this determined campaign against nudism, it is interesting to note that there is almost no evidence on the response of the broader public to nudism. Catholic and right-wing moralists were taking it upon themselves to speak for the silent majority of the German nation; but it seems probable that the general public viewed the movement with a mixture of shock and curiosity. The one bit of available evidence is an isolated newspaper article from Berlin-Teltow, which reported that a fenced-in area belonging to the Koch School had drawn curious people who had peeked through cracks in the fence.[79]

Socialist nudists could count on some support against these attacks. Adolf Koch had gained the backing of the more liberal leaders of non-socialist nudism. A joint statement in 1931 signed by Koch and a number of bourgeois organizations announced that the Koch Schools practiced "a strictly systematic method of helping the working populace under the guidance of expert doctors and pedagogues."[80] Leaders in the Social Democratic Party also came to Koch's aid. During a 1931 debate in the Prussian parliament on "trash and smut," the SPD Interior Minister Rudolf Severing spoke against the Nationalists, insisting that Koch's movement had become perfectly respectable.[81]

What of the socialist nudists' own efforts to counter the attacks on their morality? Beginning in the late 1920s, the movement's leaders augmented their ideal narrative of turning to nature with a stronger component of sexuality. Very much in keeping with the tenets of the sex reform movement, socialist nudists argued that nudism was a method of making the sexuality of industrial workers more rational. This revised narrative followed a rhetorical progression from the problem of uncontrolled, unclean, and unhealthy sexual behavior to an optimistic vision of a "clean," regulated, and eugenically purposeful sexuality aimed toward an improvement of the future working-class collective.

The problem as defined by socialist nudists was the powerful and irrational sex drive of the human being, which they, like their critics, saw as an essential part of human nature. When groups of proletarian men and women were naked together, they argued, the sex drive might indeed take over. At any moment a telltale symptom of renegade desire might make its appearance: "The man who gives himself over to lascivious, erotic thoughts in the presence of naked women would betray his dirty mind to all present through the erection of his member."[82] This feared regression from rational thought and activity to instinctual desires pervaded the socialist nudists' concentration on the specter of the out-of-control, instinct-driven body. Yet they combined this new emphasis on the sex drive with their long-standing critical diagnosis of capitalist culture.

According to nudist rhetoric, sexuality was such a problem because of the contemporary socioeconomic context. Raising the specter of a proletarian "sexual emergency" (*Sexualnot*), nudists increasingly emphasized the cheaply erotic side of capitalist mass culture. Urban night life with its "obscenities and lasciviousness"—strip joints, pubs, and prostitution—was worsening the pernicious effects of petit bourgeois culture on working-class sexuality.[83]

This rhetoric also began to demonize and call for the exclusion of human threats to sexual health. According to late Weimar socialist nudists, out-of-control, socially destructive sexuality was embodied in the promiscuous woman and the homosexual man. The prostitute, who was commonly associated with venereal disease, was the most readily available symbol of dangerous female sexuality. She "befouled" the male body with both her immorality and her disease. Graaz, in his discussion of the rules for forming local nudist groups, called for each prospective member to be investigated by a doctor for active or incompletely healed venereal diseases. Every member had to sign a promise not to have any intercourse with prostitutes "for fear of contaminating the group." Prostitutes were not the only symbol of female promiscuity. Another was the immoral bourgeois woman who "half undresses her body in order to stimulate the man with the suggestion of that which remains covered."[84] Such rhetoric sent a clear message to working-class women to avoid promiscuous behavior.

The other threatening stereotype that caused great concern among socialist nudists was the homosexual man. It should be noted that Adolf Koch himself, clearly influenced by the leader of the Weimar gay rights movement, Magnus Hirschfeld, had a relatively progressive attitude toward homosexuality. Attempting to "correct" homosexual behavior, he wrote, only resulted in "a crippling of the soul." He called for the "cultivation of the priceless resource of human individuality for the good of society."[85] However, other leading socialist nudists adopted the homophobia of their conservative and Catholic critics. Hans Graaz, who among the nudists was always most determined to control sexuality, warned of the dangers to respectability that might follow from the participation of homosexual men. All nudists in local groups should know each other well, he wrote, "in order to keep out all impure elements that may only be seeking out nudism for a new sexual thrill." Such people might bring disrepute to the fledgling movement.

It is also inadvisable to allow persons with abnormal sexual tendencies—namely, homosexuals—into such communities. Although such persons can be just as moral as and generally similar to normal people, their peculiar drives are frequently known to the police, and they are thus well suited, through no fault of their own, to damage the nudist community.[86]

This exclusion of homosexuals was one strategic way to counter the conservative attacks. No doubt it also reflected genuine worries about the participation of gay men. We do not know how many such men were present in nudist groups. Nor does evidence exist that would indicate whether Graaz's admonition was followed in everyday organizational practice. In any case the ideology of nudism was becoming more and more exclusive through its negative emphasis on overtly sexualized, stereotypical identities of loose women and homosexual men. The "sexual problem" in late Weimar nudist discourse thus amounted to a combination of capitalist conditions, the workers' own irrationality and cultural backwardness, and the threat of deviant sexual identities. The goal was now to overcome this problem and "raise" the identity of nudist workers toward strictly controlled heterosexuality.

As the "problem" part of the nudist narrative changed, so did the solution that socialist nudists offered. They began to assert ever more vigorously that their everyday turn to nature, either in a rural setting or in a Koch School, controlled sexual desire. Turning to nature "objectively" and rationally was the key to success. According to Koch, nudism taught a new kind of love more attuned to the whole person. Sexual love between men and women developed "more according to instinct, more deeply, and more nobly" because the harmonious sexuality of nudists was directed not to the sex organs but to "the loved one in his wholeness."[87] Nudist group bonding also inculcated a more "natural"—that is, objective and rational—gaze upon the body. He compared this aspect of nudist pedagogy to the artistic movement of New Objectivity (*Neue Sachlichkeit*): "All the kitsch, all the sentimentality and tastelessness that accompany watching someone of the opposite sex get undressed . . . ceases to be a problem."[88]

Another spokesman of the Koch School described more specifically how sexual desire was overcome by rational nudism. Objective observation of the nude body, he wrote, led to the kind of straightforward and relaxed atmosphere "in which a girl could talk of her period without fear."[89] The claim that exercise repressed sexual urges became de rigueur. Hermann Schmidt of the *Gruppe freier Menschen* asserted, "Through strong movements in air, sun, and water, through bodily exercises [and] through massage and skin care . . . circulation is stimulated, metabolism is promoted, and fluids no longer collect at certain points in the lower body."[90] Dr. Graaz announced that venereal disease and abortions were virtually unknown among Berlin workers in the movement, even though some two-thirds of the participants were young singles.[91] Koch proudly proclaimed, "*We* have overcome this element of the psychical emergency. . . . Never within the past decade has even one case of sexual arousal been observed."[92]

According to Koch's widow, the Berlin school's lectures on sexuality prompted the strongest interest among members.[93] This can be taken as evidence both for the popular success of sex reform efforts in the movement *and* for a general attraction to all things sexual. In any case, claims about the absence of erections and VD expressed Koch's concept of nudist practice as something that was thoroughly public and constantly under the scrutiny and control of rational experts. Specific activities in the Koch Schools and elsewhere were tailored to help people overcome their sexual drives, becoming a kind of performance of desexualized nude bodies. Working together, pubescent boys and girls learned to control the sexual urge through exercise, jumping, and romping (*Tollen*).[94] In so doing they would erase the boundaries between public and private and between male and female, manifesting socialist community and freeing themselves from sexual distractions.

Thus, in the later years of Weimar the way that socialist nudists proposed to turn to nature—through group nude exercise—took on the ultimate goal of elevating the working individual to a new status as a rational, sexually disciplined, and politically conscious new human being. Liberation from the external chains of capitalism and religious tradition had to go along with personal, internal liberation from one's physical and psychological rigidity (*Verkrampfung*); and "natural control of the drives" was a characteristic of truly free human beings.[95] This shift in nudist discourse was a reaction to right-wing attacks, and it involved adopting the language of the sex reform movement. That new movement offered a definition of freedom as rising above one's own irrational drives, learning to control them, and thus rising to a higher form of emancipation than mere individual liberation. By inculcating communal virtue, the reform of sexuality through group nudist activities would help lead to a virtuous socialism.[96]

In formulating this narrative of turning to nature, socialist nudist leaders and writers standardized two central concepts, nature and the body. As represented in socialist nudist rhetoric, nature was a simple place. It invited the human being to celebrate and partake of its power as a way to ennoble human culture. In this literal conception of nature, the natural world "stands above morality, reveals itself openly, is always as harmonious and magnificent as on the first day of creation, and is the sole fountain of health."[97] Nature was essentialized, eternalized, and turned into a beneficent helpmate of human beings. The individual body as the worker's own piece of nature was similarly essentialized in socialist nudist rhetoric. It became a metaphor for the collective body of the German working class. The individual body remained sexual in a thoroughly respectable and disciplined way, but its gendered character seemed to all but disappear. I have discovered no discussion of differing exercises according to sex. In fact, the body seems to lose most of its individual character in the rhetoric of late Weimar socialist nudism. What we have here is an ideology of progress based on concepts of both nature and the body that were standardized and made to seem universal and unchanging.

The nudists' holistic ideal of the new human being—body, mind, and political consciousness combined—turned the nude body into a site of political agency in the liberation of the German working class. The goal of rationalizing and controlling sexuality through "objective" attention to the nude body became central to the nudist ideology of progress. To what extent did the late Weimar nudists' ideology and practice of turning to nature contain authoritarian potentials? Did the body become *dis*embodied in the rhetoric of nudism—that is, did it become universalized and devoid of individual difference as norms of physical health and sexual rationality took hold? In other words, did socialist nudism subordinate the individual worker entirely to the collective, threatening the freedom of the individual and the diversity of the working class?

There is evidence both for and against a trend toward authoritarianism. Let us first consider ideology, particularly eugenics. The pseudoscience of eugenics increasingly pervaded socialist nudist rhetoric in the late 1920s; and it no doubt played a practical role in the reproductive counseling that was offered to Koch School participants. Some historians have argued that *all* nudists were motivated by racial nationalism and that eugenics in the socialist branch was identical to the eugenics of right-wing nudists.[98] This is quite mistaken. Overt nationalism and eugenics were both rare in socialist nudism before the late 1920s. Only after 1925 did the movement adopt sex reform language with its "motherhood-eugenics consensus."[99] By that time eugenics had become widely accepted throughout the West as a means of scientifically controlling human reproduction. In Germany left-wing eugenics was propagated in such venues as trade union and health journals and the traveling exhibitions of the German Hygiene Museum in Dresden.[100] Many socialists in the women's movement believed that eugenics would help women regain control over their sexuality.[101] This left-wing version of eugenics, far less nationalist and racist than conservative or fascist models, was a logical outgrowth of social hygiene with its emphasis on improving the everyday lives and mentalities of urban workers. It combined conventional norms of the heterosexual family with a forward-looking goal of human biological improvement.

Eugenics also served a strategic purpose for socialist nudists by buttressing their claim that they were helping to build the new human being. As Kurt Schadendorf wrote,

There is eugenic value to nudism. Here one recognizes true heredity in the body's form and bearing! Here only the strong and beautiful body inspires admiration, reverence, and love. And here the more valuable hereditary characteristics can come together [more easily] than in the duller realms of social life where convention dominates and where the body [remains covered].[102]

Adolf Koch himself rarely mentioned eugenics in anything but vaguely positive terms; but his chief medical colleague, Dr. Hans Graaz, spouted eugenicist ideas ceaselessly. Graaz believed that nudism could directly improve the genetic health of present-day generations. The proletariat of the city were currently of higher genetic value than agricultural workers, but their genetic value was being reduced by a lack of physical and mental education. Through nudism workers could be brought up to their potential, indeed up to the "performing capacity" (*Leistungsfähigkeit*) of the ruling class.[103] This was positive eugenics, dedicated to encouraging the physically and mentally healthy to reproduce. Unlike right-wing versions of eugenics in which the individual was destined by heredity and "race" to be either inferior or superior, Graaz's eugenicism allowed room for the individual to improve his or her health and reproductive value. For nudism produced a "hygienic" consciousness of the body by forcing one to compare one's own nude body with those of other, more perfectly developed and "valuable" specimens.[104]

At one point Graaz did write of improving the Germans for the "racial struggle."[105] Since there is no evidence that Graaz envisioned, Nazi-style, a future war of Germans against other "races," he probably meant the general struggle of Germany to survive as a nation in the wake of the lost war. Indeed, Graaz's colleague Dr. John Toeplitz took pains in a 1929 essay to distance himself from far right-wing, militarist concepts of race. Toeplitz wrote that Germany needed a new concept of race that would judge people according to their (naturally unequal) talents and heredity. In this way people could be shown that human development could occur not through aimless pairing but only through "bonding on the basis of biological knowledge." Toeplitz concluded by announcing that information about members' health collected in the Koch Schools was being analyzed and made available for use by the general public.[106]

The notion of eugenics, with its goal of improving humanity according to fixed norms of health, is by definition antipathetic to human diversity. As a theory eugenics was at cross-purposes with the individual diversity and rights of working-class nudists. However, positive eugenics as trumpeted in nudist rhetoric glorified the mentally and physically healthy; it had little to say about the "inferior." The socialist nudist version of eugenics optimistically held out hope for biological improvement of the individual within his or her lifetime, refusing to condemn individuals to an irrevocable hereditary fate. Perhaps most important is the issue of everyday policy. Despite the influx of eugenicist rhetoric in late Weimar, there is no evidence that the socialist nudists ever had a policy of excluding individuals who did not reach eugenicist norms of mental and physical health.

It is also important to consider other, more liberating currents within the movement that may well have counterbalanced the oppressive potential of eugenics. Genuinely progressive ideas of women's emancipation and antimilitarism abounded in the late Weimar discourse. For example, Hildegard Wegscheider-Ziegler, a member of the Prussian parliament and participant in one of Koch's nudist conferences in 1929, argued that the mass of producers had to be made conscious of their value and dignity.

Particularly women, with their double burden of work and family life, needed to become more self-assured, and nudism could help them in this endeavor.[107] A striking example of pacifism is an anonymous 1932 article that spoke eloquently of the proletarian male body endangered by the upsurge of militant nationalism. The author described watching the happily naked swimmers in a pool at the Koch School and gradually becoming aware of the scarred and partially dismembered bodies of the older men. He worried about the future of the younger swimmers in a Germany where right-wing parties were calling for a return to militarism. Without a strong commitment to pacifism among the nudists, he concluded, the much more terrible war of the future would enslave these youths in a "bath of steel," tearing apart their "suntanned and athletic limbs."[108] Neither feminism nor pacifism was anywhere to be found in the rhetoric of nonsocialist nudism, nor were either weakened by the growing emphasis on eugenics.

Turning to everyday practice we again find evidence both for and against oppressive potentials in socialist nudism. We have already seen that the movement's leaders chose to exclude homosexual and sexually active ("promiscuous") individuals, primarily for strategic reasons. This was a blow against diversity in the movement. What of the exercise regimen in the Koch Schools? Many exercises involved the physical and mental standardization of collective movement, leaving little room for individual physicality. The photograph on page 51 shows one exercise in which posture and movement were judged according to their correctness. For Koch such activities taught the individual to "choose discipline" and submit to the rest for the good of the socialist ideal. "Leaping, jogging, and breathing exercises work best en masse. What a wonderful mass rhythm can be found when everyone is leaping and jogging at once. The group seems to turn into just one body!"[109] Koch's goal for these particular exercises was to make the individual disappear into the collective body of a self-disciplining proletariat. As Norbert Elias pointed out, such "molding" of physical behavior "aims at making . . . behavior automatic, a matter of self control, causing it to appear in the consciousness of the individual as the result of his own free will, and in the interest of his own health and human dignity."[110] Yet other evidence suggests that participants in the Koch Schools had opportunities for less regimented, more individualistic movement. Free-style exercises played as important a role in the curriculum as did more regimented ones. They encouraged "training of personal idiosyncrasies (*Eigenarten*)" and let

Rückgrat- und Beckenbildung. (3.) (Richtig nur der einzelne Junge in der Mitte.)

An exercise in "backbone and pelvis strengthening" at an Adolf Koch School compound. The caption reads, "Only the boy in the middle is doing it correctly." From Adolf Koch, *Körperbildung, Nacktkultur* (Leipzig, 1924).

students find their own "reawakened natural rhythm." The teacher was forbidden from intervening during such activities.[111] Even the regimented activities may have been less pedantic and standardized than they seem in the teachers' pedagogic directions. The Merrills reported after observing a class at the Hamburg Koch School that the teacher used a drum and chanted instructions in rhythm. Students moved from slow circular walking to running in a circle. These activities were accompanied by much boisterous teasing and joking. The students playfully performed tricks like walking on their hands, doing splits, and so forth during the three-minute rest period.[112] It appears that regimented and free-style exercises alternated, and neither canceled the other out. The curriculum consciously varied between the self-subordination and the liberation of the individual body.

Did ideas of gender difference, which are always potentially oppressive, play a role in shaping the Koch Schools' exercise programs? As we have seen, the mingling of the sexes was a point of honor for nudist leaders and a key part of their efforts to make (hetero)sexuality more controlled and rational by bringing the genders together in a relaxed way. Exercise and communal activities usually brought males and females together. After exercise classes students of both sexes took showers communally. Although sexual counseling and discussions of contemporary political issues were no doubt shaped in part by ideas of gender difference, there is no evidence that the exercises themselves differentiated between the sexes, for instance, by reserving more strenuous exercises for men. This practice was in marked contrast to nonsocialist nudism, in which the exercises were oftentimes sex segregated, an ideology of protected motherhood prevailed, and the leaders were almost always male. The apparent gender equality of Koch's organization made it unusually progressive and egalitarian within the Social Democratic workers' cultural movement and within Weimar culture as a whole.

By the early 1930s, the socialist nudists seem to have attained equilibrium between the individual and the group. The new concept of freedom demanded that the individual sublimate his or her sexual desires through exercise in the interest of increased reason and discipline. Yet the individual also had opportunities within everyday practice for physical self-realization and creativity. The new human being of socialist nudism walked a fine line between personal freedom and subordination to the group; but on balance socialist nudism remained firmly committed to the tradition of egalitarian, emancipatory, and democratic socialism.

The *Gleichschaltung* of Nudism

Like all other naturist movements, organized nudism underwent a decline during the Depression and a political transformation after the Nazis took power. Tracing the history of *Gleichschaltung* under the Nazis is unusually difficult in the case of nudism, however, for two reasons. First, much of the source evidence about socialist nudism was apparently destroyed, probably by the Nazis. Thus, we cannot explain with any certainty the motives behind Adolf Koch's troubling strategies of dealing with the new regime, including his entry into the Nazi paramilitary SA (*Sturmabteilung*—Storm Troopers) in 1933. Second, the Nazi leaders had diverse attitudes about nudism that ranged from demonization to guarded acceptance. The regime's policy toward the nonsocialist nudist sector was confusing and contradictory throughout the 1930s. This was one example of the ambiguous role that sexuality in general played in the Third Reich.[113]

The Depression caused serious financial problems for the Koch Schools. To cover costs, each of the schools needed to take in an average of

5.5 marks from each member per month. But by 1932 the average payment per person was only 3.9 marks because 52 percent of all members were unemployed. In the Berlin school, the three full-time employees—Koch himself, Dr. Hans Graaz, and exercise instructor Ilke Dieball—received only half of their salary in 1931 and 1932. They survived in part by giving paid public talks on nudism and health.[114]

Much worse for the movement was the political clampdown that began as early as 1932. A long-standing, stable coalition government in Prussia composed of Social Democrats, left-liberals, and Catholics had upheld democratic-republican values there since 1920. In July 1932 President Paul von Hindenburg authorized the overthrow of the Prussian government by Chancellor Franz von Papen and the placement of Prussia under the direct jurisdiction of the Reich government. This blow against the last governmental bastion of the Social Democrats was also the beginning of a more general assault on liberal elements in Germany's largest state. A state offensive against nudism commenced. Franz Bracht, the former Catholic mayor of Essen and new Reich commissioner in charge of Prussia, issued a decree forbidding the "degenerate phenomenon" of public coed nude bathing. Bracht defined "public" as visible from public waters or paths. He demanded that women's bathing suits cover the entire front of the upper body and underarms, forbidding suits in which the back was open below the lower end of the shoulder blades. Men were required to wear shorts. These rules did not apply when men and women bathed separately.[115]

The new regime in Prussia enforced Bracht's decree only against socialist nudist groups; nonsocialists were generally left alone. In the fall of 1932 the state began to harass the Koch Schools throughout Prussia, threatening them with closure. Finally in mid-January 1933 the threats turned into a conclusive ban on the schools' activities. Once the Nazis were installed in the national government, they extended this reactionary attack to the entire nudist movement throughout Germany. Hermann Göring's directive of March 3, 1933, to the state police forces declared "the naked culture movement" to be one of the greatest dangers to healthy German morality because it "deadens women's natural feelings of shame and kills men's respect for women." He commanded the police in each state to take all measures to destroy the movement. They should place organizations under surveillance, ban public nudist events, and pressure the owners of municipal swimming pools, bathing areas, and wooded property to break all contracts with nudist groups.[116] This soon led to the dissolution of all FKK groups and the confiscation of their property. Nudist publications were burnt along with other "enemy literature" in German cities on May 10.[117]

However, there was considerable variety in the fates of nudist groups throughout Germany during 1933. Archival documents reveal a confusing array of repressive governmental and police directives, letters of protest by nudist leaders, and communiqués between Nazi leaders. One conclusion we can draw from these sources is that local socialist groups did whatever they could to survive the clampdown. The simplest and most common tactic was to change the group's name and statutes in order to make it appear politically and morally above suspicion. The Leipzig chapter of the *Gruppe freier Menschen*, for instance, changed its name to the Garden Allotment and Weekend Settlement and rewrote its statutes to claim political and religious neutrality. The promise to help working people was jettisoned.[118] Although this local chapter's strategy gained it a reprieve for several months, the police and Gestapo investigators were not fooled. All chapters of the *Gruppe freier Menschen* had been banned by fall of 1933.

Unfortunately, very little reliable evidence exists on the fate of the Koch Schools. What information we have is limited to the central school in Berlin; and there are significant factual gaps and questionable conclusions even in the one historical study of the Berlin school by Giselher Spitzer. For example, Spitzer neglects to point out that Adolf Koch joined the SA in the late spring of 1933. He tends to ignore or downplay such disturbing facts in favor of a very positive evaluation of Koch's dealings with the Nazis that is based on Koch's own writings published after the war. Given this problem of evidence, we can draw only very tentative conclusions.

Most striking is the length to which Koch was willing to go to save his school in Berlin. In April 1933 the SA plundered the building in the Friedrichstraße and damaged the school's furnishings. The police confiscated the tract of land in Berlin-Selchow and forbade Koch to teach any further. In an apparent effort to appease the authorities, Koch changed his organization's name in April to the Adolf Koch League for Social Hygiene, Physical Culture, and Exercise. Around this time he also joined the SA. I have found no sources that could explain Koch's motives for doing this or tell us what he did in the Nazi paramilitary organization. Given that Koch had never expressed any sympathy with Nazism in his writings, we can only assume that this was a drastic attempt to conform to the new regime by completely jettisoning affiliation with socialism. Koch may have even been able to justify this move in reference to the current of social egalitarianism in the SA. In any case, after a few weeks the Berlin school quietly resumed its training courses behind locked doors.[119] One must assume that Koch's membership in the SA helped his school to survive—at least for a time.

On May 28, 1934, the Gestapo finally dissolved Koch's organization on the grounds that it had provided Marxist "elements damaging to national health" with a "broad field of endeavor."[120] This accusation of subversion was the typical reason given for Nazi bans on Social Democratic organizations. During the following three months, Koch tried to convince the authorities to reconsider, assuring them of his allegiance to the new regime. He denied that his movement had anything to do with communism; this was more or less true given the prevalence of Social Democratic leaders, supporters, and members.[121] He also committed himself to Nazi ideology. On June 12, 1934, Koch sent to the Reich Interior Ministry a copy of an apparently eugenicist booklet by Hans Graaz entitled *Healthy Mothers, Beautiful Children*, as well as a statement from a Berlin SA group that his school was "valuable for the SA." Koch added that an unnamed "long-time colleague" was preparing a program of exercise for the SA to be presented personally to its leader, Ernst Röhm. All this was proof "that our pioneering work is having a beneficial effect for the nation."[122]

Unfortunately for Koch, his timing regarding the SA was poor. Roughly two weeks later, on June 30, the SS (*Schutzstaffel*—Protective Squad) rounded up and murdered the SA leadership in the "Night of the Long Knives." Hitler's propaganda cast the SA as subversive and homosexual. Thus, the SA recommendation and Koch's promise to advise them probably did him more harm than good. On August 21 the Gestapo informed Koch that they had no intention of allowing him to reform his organization and that the affair was over. Koch made a last-ditch effort to win over Reich Interior Minister Wilhelm Frick, complaining that both his honor and livelihood had been destroyed. He now tried appealing to Nazi anti-Catholicism, writing that Catholics were unjustly accusing him of communist activity. He further assured Frick that "since the beginning of 1933 I've worked seriously and honestly to win hundreds for the National Socialist idea." Koch ended by appropriating the Führer's very words, repeating Hitler's corporatist slogan of "reconciliation with all national comrades!"[123]

Also at some point in the course of 1934—the chronology is uncertain—Koch published at least one issue of a journal in which the school advertised training sessions "in white exercise clothes." I have been unable to locate this publication and must rely on Spitzer's quotations from it. Koch praised the new regime's fascist salute, since this "makes impossible a crooked or rounded back."[124] Spitzer interprets this statement not as real approval but as irony; he also interprets the inclusion of an article by a Nazi member of the Koch School as a mere sham to appease the authorities. Dietger Pforte, however, diverges from Spitzer's sanguine view of this publication, taking it as evidence that Koch conformed ideologically to the new regime.[125]

Did Adolf Koch's writings in 1934 reveal a genuine commitment to Nazism? And did nudist ideology enable Koch to make a relatively easy transition into the Third Reich? Or was this the same kind of opportunism practiced by most leaders of civic organizations during the *Gleichschaltung* phase, including socialists? It is impossible to say for certain. Spitzer's article claims that even after Koch failed to save the school in Berlin, he continued his activities. He moved to a new building in the Ritterstraße and renamed the school the Institute for Eubiotics, probably to signify a closer focus on eugenics. There, according to Spitzer, Koch not only taught exercise classes but also provided a meeting place for former SPD members and trade unionists. He continued "political education" and even hid Jews. Relying on Koch's own explanation, Spitzer explains Koch's eighteen-month "supporting membership" (*Fördermitgliedschaft*) in the SS as another devious measure to keep the authorities fooled. In 1939 Koch was drafted into the medical corps and served near Berlin for the duration of the war. He was allegedly able to continue teaching even then, until the school was bombed in 1945. Again according to Koch, the denazification authorities in 1947 declared that he "had not betrayed his political views and had been active against fascism." The indefatigable Koch built up his organization yet again after the war. Spitzer's discussion of these points is perfunctory and extremely vague; and his only source is a 1947 manuscript entitled "Report on the Rehabilitation of Adolf Koch" written by Koch himself.[126] I have located an essay written in 1953 by a former Koch School participant, Horst Naftaniel, that seems to corroborate some of Spitzer's narrative. Naftaniel writes:

After 1936 the Institute for "Eubiotik" was founded. No one knew what that was supposed to mean. On the surface it was a massage or cosmetic salon. The SS promptly confiscated this institute after a year. Unfazed, Adolf Koch built up something in its stead in the Ritterstraße, the "Places for Life Regulation" (*Stätte für Lebensre-gelung*). A very sympathetic landlord, a democrat—Dietrich, who like Koch hated Hitler—helped out. We did the same thing that we had done earlier—exercise. . . . With enthusiasm we sang mocking songs about Hitler and his regime. Here the people remained just as they had been, equal human beings! Bearers of the Jewish star hid it under their jackets, so as not to endanger "our Adolf" unnecessarily. To this day it is a mystery to me that we were able to be together, even with our Jewish sisters, without being disturbed.[127]

Because of the lack of sources not produced by Adolf Koch himself, Koch's motives and actions in the Third Reich will probably always remain a mystery. A genuine commitment to Nazism on his part would suggest that the positive eugenics of late Weimar socialist nudism could be recon-ciled to the Nazis' negative eugenics. This would not be surprising since both versions of eugenics propose that some human beings are more valu-able than others. On the other hand, Koch's behavior may have been yet another example of opportunistic efforts by moderate socialists to survive by adopting Nazi rhetoric. In Koch's case this would have meant abandon-ing a career based on bringing about a better life for Germany's industrial workers. In any case there is no reason to believe that Koch was truly able to preserve nudism in its socialist guise under the Third Reich.

What became of nudist groups that were not "tainted" by socialism? Most vegetarian, natural healing, and nudist organizations had not been part of the radical right-wing fringe during the Weimar era; they had tended toward the moderate right and reformist left. The majority hoped to emancipate the individual for the good of the collective; were commit-ted to grassroots change, not statism; and did not subscribe to militantly racist forms of nationalism. As Wolfgang Krabbe has argued, after shut-ting out all liberal and socialist elements of the *Lebensreform* tradition, the movement was only a shell of its former self. Paradoxically, Krabbe writes, "The continued existence of the movement spelled its destruction. . . . Its transformation made it unrecognizable."[128] The socialist nudist movement is a case in point, and its destruction spelled the end of the left-liberal current within organized nudism. In its place arose a synchronized move-ment that reverted to the folkish and racist tradition of Wilhelmine nud-ism. Even the name of the nudist project, "Free Body Culture," changed officially to "Bodily Discipline" (*Leibeszucht*) in the course of the 1930s.

Even though most nonsocialist nudists were not fascists in 1933, they did share a number of ideological tendencies with the National Socialists—a strong sense of national crisis, a focus on eugenic health, and the glorification of bodily stereotypes inherited from classical Greek iconography.[129] These points of agreement seem to have created uncertainty among the Nazi leaders on how to deal with organized nudism; and they enabled the nudist organizations to carve out a niche for themselves in the Third Reich.

Knowing that nudism was distasteful to some figures in the new regime, the bourgeois nudist movement undertook a process of self-synchronization. On April 23, 1933, Nazi members of nudist groups in Berlin founded a commission whose aim was to incorporate the movement into the Third Reich. This Fighting Ring for Folkish Free Body Culture (*Kampfring für völkische FKK*) began to purge the movement of politically suspect groups and individuals. The *Kampfring* called on every organization to submit exact membership lists with information on profession, age, and political affiliation; requested a brief summary of any problems the members had encountered with the authorities since January 30, 1933; and called on the police to ban socialist groups.[130] Nonsocialist groups were invited to join the *Kampfring* after revising their statutes according to the following formula:

The organization aims for the physical and mental education of its members in the spirit of the National Socialist people's state through the planned cultivation of exercise. In particular the organization aims to shape the German human being through a natural form of bodily education that is bound to blood and soil, race and landscape. It holds that exercise should be carried out without clothing. Exercise, hiking, and natural health are methods of disciplined living, and folk songs and dances are the basis of a new German sociability. Only Germans of Aryan origin can become members.[131]

By June 1933 no fewer than fifty-nine nudist clubs had adopted this new statement of purpose and excluded "non-Aryans." In joining the *Kampfring*, with its claim to be working for racial health and against "bolshevism," these associations now had some hope of preserving themselves.[132]

Bourgeois nudists benefited from two situational factors in this early stage of *Gleichschaltung*. First, there was as yet no nationwide policy on nudism; despite Göring's blanket decree against the movement in March 1933, it was not repressed in all states. Apparently the police in Saxony, for example, were determined to destroy socialist nudism but would tolerate other sectors of the nudist movement. Answering a letter from the

Kampfring that asked them why nudist clubs had been banned in Leipzig, the police explained that they had nothing against nudism per se but that Leipzig nudists were almost all Marxists. They were still waiting for a concrete policy from the new regime and would not stand in the way of a reorganization of nudism "upon a folkish foundation."[133]

Second, the nudists had support from some prominent Nazis, most notably Agricultural Minister Richard Walther Darré, whose book *The Farmer as Life-Source of the Nordic Race* claimed that the old Teutonic tribes had practiced nudity as a way to find the most valuable reproductive partners.[134] Another supporter was Reich Sport Commissioner Hans von Tschammer. On October 25 Tschammer allowed all member organizations of the *Kampfring* to enter into the new Reich Physical Exercise League (*Reichsbund für Leibesübungen.*).[135] Soon the movement won even more support from the Nazi leadership. In December 1933 Adolf Hitler and Rudolf Hess requested the *Kampfring* to send them films and pictures from the movement.[136] We do not know how Hitler reacted to that material, but Hess came to a positive conclusion. He declared that nudism was healthy and should be welcomed as a "natural movement of renewal."[137] In January 1934 the *Kampfring* was invited to join the Reich Committee for National Health Service (*Reichsausschuß für Volksgesundheitsdienst*) within the Interior Ministry. In March the *Kampfring* followed Tschammer's advice and changed its name to the League for Physical Discipline (*Bund für Leibeszucht*), dropping the term FKK in order to "avoid confusion with Marxist organizations." Tschammer then wrote to Frick that since the nudists had worked with him to purge their movement of socialism, there was no longer any reason to be suspicious of the ten thousand remaining German nudists.[138] Thus, by the spring of 1934 the regime had officially recognized the synchronized movement's right to exist. This put an end to Göring's sweeping decree of the previous spring.[139] The state's policy toward nudism in 1933–34, contradictory as it was, seems to have reflected the competing sites of power that characterized the Nazi dictatorship. In this case Göring lost out to other leaders who did not share his moralistic qualms about nudism.

Nevertheless, organized nudists suffered setbacks throughout the mid-1930s. Ongoing discussions among many different individuals within the state apparatus in 1934 and 1935 reflected confusion and uncertainty. There was considerable regional inconsistency in the state's dealings with the movement. The police in Leipzig, for example, lifted their ban on local groups in December 1933; yet only three months later, the Saxon Interior Minister issued a decree that was a word-for-word repetition of Göring's antinudist directive of March 1933. The police then called on the city government to cancel all its contracts with nudist groups that allowed them to use the municipal sport hall and swimming pool. The Leipzig city government complied.[140]

Similar inconsistency characterized the actions of the national party leadership. A number of high-ranking Nazi officials, including Darré, Tschammer, and Heinrich Himmler, lent their support to nudism in the mid-1930s. The Reich Health Minister, Dr. Gross, argued that the movement's secular ideology of racial health was the same as that of the Nazi Party; both rejected the "clerical defamation of the human body," and both promoted behavior that was "closer to nature."[141] But other Nazi leaders subjected the movement to their own whims. In July 1935 Interior Minister Frick, who was at the time helping to sharpen Paragraph 175 of the legal code against male homosexuality, suddenly extended the ban on coed nude bathing to include same-sex groups. "Circles" that practice same-sex bathing, he suspected, included persons with a "sick constitution" who might use it as a "prelude to violating Paragraph 175."[142]

This was indeed a blow to the nudist movement; and although it is unknown how many groups might have attempted to circumvent Frick's ruling, the nudists did begin to don bathing suits that provided a minimum of coverage. Even measures like these were destined to fall short in the eyes of some German citizens, as can be seen in a letter written by a P. Büsch directly to Adolf Hitler. Frau Büsch begged the chancellor to "please forbid the horrible bathing suits and the coed swimming pools. You need only say the word and these immoral antics will come to an end. Please do not allow our womanly honor to be stomped upon any longer. God will surely richly reward you for such a great deed. *Gott zum Gruss*, Yours faithfully, P. Büsch." There is no record of a reply from the Führer.[143]

Nudist leaders reinforced their strategy of appeasement by offering assurances of the nonerotic, rational character of their project. The leader of nudism in Bavaria declared that carefully practiced nudism overcame impure sensual feelings "by means of intellectual conduct through the cultivation of the body" (*durch geistige Haltung in der Pflege des Leibes*). Total nudity was not necessary, he argued; minimal clothing should be worn to cover the most intimate parts of the body. Nudism should be practiced out of the public eye, and the groups should thoroughly investigate and "strictly control" all participants.[144] Indeed, the *Bund für Leibeszucht* began carefully screening all prospective members, making them sign this statement: "My sensibility is folkish. . . . I am of Aryan origin and have never belonged to a Marxist, Communist, or anarchist party or organization. . . . I suffer from no physical, mental, or moral weaknesses, have a clean reputation, and have no contagious or disgusting diseases."[145]

Nudist leaders also took great pains to distance themselves irrevocably from the Marxist, liberal, and Jewish influences of the "Weimar system." Some attacked Adolf Koch for "discrediting" the movement. Others recast their ongoing attacks on Catholic moralism in the language of racial nationalism. For Karl Bückmann all the decrees against nudism reflected the influence of a foreign, racially inferior, anti-Nordic Catholicism; and they were intended to prevent the Nordic human being from "becoming aware of his unique value." Anne Marie Koeppen blamed the Jews for undermining the original Germanic admiration for the nude body. Those who condemned the body themselves had reason to be ashamed of their own, she proclaimed. Their foreignness made them ugly and disgusting in the eyes of the beautiful German People, which was why they wanted to overthrow the Germans and enslave them. Will Tschierschky maintained that the ancient Germanic tribes had practiced nude coed bathing for eugenic purposes. They had subjected weaklings to "natural selection" by refusing to reproduce with them. Clothing in the modern liberal age had prevented this eugenic judgment of one's fellow Germans, contributing to the nation's racial degeneration.[146]

Hans Surén had been one of the best-known popularizers of nudism during the 1920s, and he took the opportunity to further his career in the Third Reich. His rhetoric conflated the enemies of nudism and accused them of a conspiracy against the German race. In an essay on the benefits of nudism that he sent to the Gestapo, Surén wrote, "Sickly, racially impure (Jewish), unnatural, and twisted (clerical) views, inherited for generations, have opened pathways that are themselves sickly and racially impure."[147] Such effective appeals to the Nazi worldview no doubt helped earn him an appointment in 1935 to lead the physical education program within the Reich Work Service. In 1936 he became the plenipotentiary for physical education in Darré's regulatory agricultural bureau, the *Reichsnährstand*.[148]

Surén led the way in fashioning a new, racist narrative of improvement through eugenic nudism. He insisted that the bathing suit was a crime against racial health, since the reproductive organs of both sexes needed fresh air, light, and sunshine. If nudism were practiced among the Nordic peoples, hundreds of thousands of the most valuable racial specimens would "joyfully enter into the striving for national power and character."

This type of striving representative of the race simply cannot understand how the sexual features could be impure and unclean . . . for he knows—at least during the time of his training—that he is completely free of any sexual impulses. The German is no southerner and no Jew! . . . It needs hardly be said that racial discipline in the process of choosing a mate (*Gattenwahl*) will arise from this striving, more perfect and more promising for the future than we can even imagine.[149]

Surén's hyperbolic, utopian racism made little mention of "the inferior," although that group of racial "losers" was always inherently present in positive eugenic discourse. Other nudist ideologues stepped in to raise the specter of racial inferiors. Anne Marie Koeppen, for example, wrote:

Beauty is the highest perfection of all creatures, the goal of all creative works, and the fulfillment of the great natural laws to which we are all subject. Therefore, when we gaze upon a stunted human being, we sense that this must be the result of some violation of natural law, some disturbance of the holy harmonies, something that disturbs us more than we can explain.

The highest ethical imperative, then, is not pity and care for the sick and inferior but prevention and eradication of all hereditary diseases combined with cultivation and training of healthy, beautiful people.[150]

This Nazified ideal narrative of turning to nature diagnosed the nation's ills as a lack of adequately eugenicist reproduction and an overload of "disturbing," genetically inferior people. The method of bringing about improvement was nudist activity in which people could find eugenically fit partners. Nudism would thereby contribute to bringing about a stronger, more militarily fit Aryan race.

Apparently this new narrative finally convinced the Nazi regime of nudism's value. Beginning in 1936 there was a steady trend toward more official approval. That summer, Himmler directed the Gestapo to desist from doing anything that would hinder nudist groups. Nudist camps in wooded areas were allowed once again. It seems probable that Hans

Surén's popular writings were instrumental in making nudism seem politically correct to Himmler and the SS. In 1936 the Nazi Party's Racial Policy Office approved of Surén's revision of *Der Mensch und die Sonne*, which he retitled *Mensch und Sonne: Arisch-olympischer Geist*, and made sure that it was published. By the end of 1942 the book had gone through twelve printings totaling 175,000 copies.[151] Surén made photographs of naked people permissible again, and the volume of publishing by the nudist movement rose in the late 1930s. It is also likely that the monumental nude statues and paintings of "Aryan" bodies by such artists as Arno Breker and Josef Thorak influenced the Nazi leadership to accept actual nudist practice—as long as they were convinced that it was racially and politically clean.[152]

What caused the regime to dismiss the fears of nudism as a site of homoerotic attraction? This is a mystery, especially since SS leader Heinrich Himmler was chronically worried about male homosexuality and did his best to track down and destroy gay men. Surén's influence may have been at work here again. Although we have no evidence that Himmler knew Surén personally, this is not unlikely given Surén's position as a major in the SS. In any case Himmler issued a police directive in 1942 that allowed individuals and groups—both same-sex and coed—to bathe nude as long as they stayed hidden from passersby. In so doing Himmler lifted all existing police regulations on bathing. Most significantly of all, although Himmler included a clause warning nude bathers not to do anything that might "injure healthy national feeling" (*gesundes Volksempfinden*), he also noted that any complaints to the police against nudists based on an "obviously unrealistic or basically antipathetic attitude" would be dismissed.[153]

Thus, the twisted path of Nazi policy toward nudism ended surprisingly—in legal protection against attacks by the conservative opponents of public nakedness. Himmler's decree, which remained in effect in both East and West Germany after the war, made nudism acceptable and no doubt helped to make it more popular in the postwar era. In the short term, the 1942 decree may have boosted membership in nudist groups. Although there are few reliable membership figures for the war years, local groups of the *Bund für Leibeszucht* in certain regions seem still to have been thriving as late as 1943. The Leipzig chapter, for instance, had some three hundred members, 40 percent of whom were female.[154] The price that nudists had been paying willingly since 1933 to win acceptance was overt support for the regime's ideology. By the time the Third Reich entered its genocidal war, the nudist utopia had become a darwinist meat market in which the body no longer had the right to "demand its rights":

All the powers of the body, that carrier of the eternal current of blood, serve the purity of the species. The naked human body becomes the means of natural selection. We celebrate the women with the best racial background and the most beautiful bodies for breeding. That which is unworthy of life (*Lebensunwertes*) has no right to breed. Only the fittest men and women will find each other through the will to have a child. No one shall be able to conceal his or her flaws and weaknesses behind clothes.[155]

Such rhetoric was repeated ad nauseam in nudist books and journals until total war denied them enough paper to print it anymore.

Conclusion

The ultimate goal of socialist nudist pedagogy was both to liberate and to regulate the body in a self-consciously "modern" way. Adolf Koch and his colleagues developed an ideal narrative of turning to a "nature" that had a double meaning as both the external, nonhuman environment and the human body. The body was the conduit of the industrial working class to the irreducible world of material nature. It was the proletariat's only concrete possession—and it was finally demanding its rights after years of being oppressed by capitalism and by the mystifying, irrational elements of religious and popular culture. To break the sense of shame about the body that everyone learned from childhood onward, the movement stripped men, women, and children of their clothes and convinced them to exercise and socialize together.

Turning to nature in the nude was intended to build both body and mind in such a way as to contribute to the larger political project of socialism. For, as Clara Bohm-Schuch told her audience at a 1929 conference given by the Berlin Koch School, "only in pure nakedness can the pure truth be seen," and truth must be the foundation of a healthy socialist community.[156] Through exposure to the nude bodies of their fellow workers, people would rise above their primitive urges, liberate themselves from bourgeois morality and the oppressiveness of urban-industrial life, and find their way toward a new and better humanity. These were the same goals that most other socialist subcultural groups in the Weimar Republic had; but the socialist nudists were the most unconventional and daring in their proposals.

To reach the ideal of the new human being in a culture that was antipathetic toward their movement, leading socialist nudists evolved a concept of freedom in which individual liberation coexisted with demands for self-discipline and self-subordination to the entire body of the proletariat. There was a precarious balance between the two that was nearly lost when the movement adopted positive eugenicist rhetoric in the late Weimar era. Refashioning their ideal narrative of turning to nature as a way to counter accusations of sexual immorality, the nudists demonized and excluded sexually deviant groups and subjected the membership to the potentially repressive "motherhood-eugenics consensus" adopted from the sex reform movement. Nevertheless, the strong focus on collective liberation and human rights never disappeared from socialist nudism. This was particularly disturbing to a Nazi dictatorship that aimed to eliminate the concept of individual freedom and human rights altogether.

The Nazis made short work of organized socialist nudism, despite Adolf Koch's efforts to appease them. Their attitudes toward the bourgeois nudist movement, however, were more ambiguous. This helped the non-socialist nudists to weather the initial phase of repression; certain ideological commonalities with Nazism enabled them to overhaul their rhetoric quickly to fit the new political conditions. By 1935 they had developed a new ideal narrative that proclaimed their moral and political purity and their will to help the "Aryan race" seize world power.

2

Social Hiking
The *Naturfreunde* Movement

IN A QUESTIONNAIRE sent in 1912 to 107 German unionized workers, sociologist Adolf Levenstein asked, "Do you often go into the woods? What do you think about when you lie on the forest floor, surrounded by deep solitude?" The written responses showed reverence toward nature. "When I lie down in the woods," wrote one textile worker, "I'm sorry that I crush plants and animals. Nature didn't create these infinitely ingenious organisms just to be annihilated like that." Another wrote more philosophically, "Someone who tends to ponder things has plenty to think about [in the woods], for the workshop of nature can only be a mystery to us, turning all of our thought and research into speechless awe."[1]

Thoughts about religion played a prominent role in many responses. Some respondents voiced a pantheistic belief in nature's divinity. One metalworker wrote, "I go as often into the forest as I can. . . . God is there, and [everyone] is a god in nature. You are right in the midst of God, in him, surrounding him." Another declared that the woods "are my church, nature my God. There I feel like rejoicing in sheer happiness and delight."[2] Other workers, however, denounced the injustice of private ownership of the forest and questioned the existence of a just God: "In the woods, I ask myself whether there's a God. What kind of God can't even grant me the little piece of earth I'm lying on as property?"[3] Some wrote that being in the forest made them bitterly aware of the contrast between rural nature and the drudgery of urban working life:

In the green woods, I lie and meditate. Every blade of grass, every flower glows with life and speaks to me in a language I can understand. The forest buzzes and hums in my ears and deludes me with visions that will never take on life and substance for me. From the heights, I look down upon the city, where haste and bustle, haggling and betrayal and a raw kind of depression make people into enemies of each other.

. . . In the woods I feel myself freer and lighter, and I admire for hours . . . the movement of organic nature. When I think of returning to the treadmill of the struggle for existence with all its untold miseries, tears of outrage fill my eyes.[4]

Some of these workers were tormented by thoughts about their own fates in industrial society. One metalworker wrote, "I go almost daily into the woods and think to myself that we're not much more than the dung beetles looking for food on the ground." For a miner, going into the woods made him think about "the way of life of the first people, about the good, natural air back then, when there were no smokestacks." Most bitter of all were the words of another miner:

Now and then I go into a little forest about ten minutes away. I lie down in a solitary place. In the rustling of the trees I hear it: You are a captive. Never will you find peace. You must sell your life and blood for a pittance. In old age, when your bones are worn down and worthless to the capitalist exploiter, you will have to find a walking stick and beg for pity, scornful and mocking pity.[5]

These responses to Levenstein's questionnaire suggest that moments of peaceful contemplation in a rural setting led some working men to think about their oppressed working-class identity under the capitalist system. To these men, nature seemed a utopian realm of escape and peace from the drudgery of daily life. The experience of nature sometimes made them feel even worse about their lives, but for most, it seems to have offered a way out of despair. For the more optimistic among them, there existed the possibility of a better world in which people would be much closer to nature as well as each other. One textile worker wrote, "When I'm in the woods and hear the leaves rustling and the birds singing, I think that here is a place where a temple to human love and peace could be built." And a metalworker imagined the following:

The treetops bend and sway, as if they wanted to call out, "Come here, everyone, to look at our magnificence." But no one comes. They are slaving away in dusty factories, halls full of haze, at noisy machines, in deadly pits. The woods fall silent, as if they could not comprehend. Patience, beautiful forest. The day will come when a happy generation walks in your shade.[6]

This evidence suggests that Marxist ideology, everyday experiences of life in an industrial society, and a quasi-religious view of nature had by 1912 become intermingled in the minds of a significant number of organized working men. We can infer from other evidence that these workers were not alone in their desire for relief from the stress of the industrial city. For example, since the nineteenth century urban workers had been well aware of the ill health effects of air and water pollution. Because they depended on industry for their livelihood, however, Germany's working people protested only occasionally in locales where pollution was especially damaging to their families' health, and such isolated protests had little if any success.[7]

Perhaps the strongest proof of the desire among many of Germany's industrial workers to experience rural nature was the existence of mass naturist movements within the Social Democratic subculture. The largest such movement was the Tourist Association "Friends of Nature" (*Tourist-enverein "Die Naturfreunde"*—TVNF), an organization that aimed to lead workers toward a more healthy, humane, and democratic society. Founded in Vienna in 1895, the organization quickly spread to other countries in Europe and North America. The *Naturfreunde* had attracted a following of some thirty thousand in Germany by 1914.[8] During the Weimar years, the German branch became more independent of the TVNF's Austrian leaders, and a national office was founded in Nuremberg.

The *Naturfreunde* dedicated themselves to proletarian hiking and everything that furthered it, including the building of a network of rural houses to serve as shelter for hikers. They erected no fewer than 230 such way stations before 1933. Their emphasis on helping workers recover from the physical stress of industrial work made the TVNF a quintessential example of "evolutionary" and reformist rather than revolutionary Marxism. They conformed to a capitalist system that forced workers to rely on their bodily health as the prerequisite of their economic survival. Nevertheless, the *Naturfreunde* cannot be justifiably accused of political apathy or "embourgeoisement."[9] TVNF leaders saw their work above all as a way to help German workers democratize the political and economic system from below. They are a classic example of the early twentieth-century attempt by the Social Democrats to transform the skilled German worker into the "new human being" who would lead the nation toward a more socially just future. The concept of the *Neuer Mensch* was the guiding principle of all organizations in the Workers' Cultural Movement (*Arbeiterkulturbewegung*), the "third column" of

Social Democracy. Central to this massive project was the belief that bettering the health of workers would increase the collective solidarity of the working class, as well as a holistic concept of health that encompassed not only physical but also psychological, moral, and political well-being.[10]

The most original contribution of the *Naturfreunde* to this ongoing project of class formation by means of culture was the notion of "social hiking." *Soziales Wandern* was the kind of hiking that would take groups of workers through their regional homeland, exposing them not only to the environment of the countryside and the industrial town, but also to the social conditions of rural and urban workers. Social hiking was intended to raise participants' consciousness of how working people lived in Germany and how capitalism was preventing them from reaching their goal of "an active mind in a strong, beautiful body."[11]

This concept of social hiking combined the experience of the rural landscape with a strong commitment to social justice. Indeed, the TVNF's practical offering of improved health, intertwined with its philosophical broadside against capitalism, held great potential to attract politically aware members of the working class. By 1923 the *Naturfreunde* had become the third-largest organization within the network of proletarian civic associations in Germany, reaching a peak membership of 116,000. Only the Workers' Exercise and Sports League and the Workers' Cycling League attracted larger numbers.

The *Naturfreunde* were also innovative in their attitude toward rural nature. The determined efforts by TVNF leaders and publicists to instill an ethic of stewardship in the working class, as well as the organization's occasional public demonstrations in favor of nature conservation, are early examples of popular environmentalism in Germany. In this the *Naturfreunde* were swimming against the main current of Marxism, an ideology that shared with capitalism a technocratic, utilitarian notion of progress through the exploitation of nature. The *Naturfreunde* saw in nature both a realm of working-class liberation and health and something that had intrinsic value and beauty.[12]

Unfortunately, this promising naturist initiative was undermined in the Weimar era by political divisions between Social Democrats and a minority cohort of Communists. Ultimately the movement fell victim to the same crises that destroyed the Weimar Republic—the Great Depression, the polarization of political culture, and the rise to power of the National Socialists. Following the Nazi takeover of power, the national leadership committee of the TVNF in Nuremberg tried to save their organization by sending assurances to the new regime of their anticommunism and their loyalty to the nation. In taking this stance, they broke with the movement's previous deployment of patriotic rhetoric, which was completely at odds with Nazi-style racial nationalism. Yet their effort to conform failed to convince the new leaders. The Nazis banned the *Naturfreunde* as a threat to the nation and did their best to track down and punish the surviving remnants of local TVNF groups throughout the 1930s. Nevertheless, through the Strength Through Joy initiative they offered organized hikes in an attempt to negotiate the consent of industrial workers to their rule. This Nazi policy was itself an ironic measure of the popularity of proletarian hiking.

The Organizational Development of the *Naturfreunde*, 1895–1928

In 1895 an announcement in a Viennese newspaper for industrial workers invited people to join a "touristic group." Behind this invitation were three members of the Marxist labor movement: Alois Rohrauer, a blacksmith; Georg Schmiedl, an elementary schoolteacher; and Karl Renner, a law student from a farming family. No fewer than eighty-five people took part in the group's first hiking excursion on Easter Sunday of that year.[13] Years later, Schmiedl reflected that the goal had been to turn "working animals" into "working human beings." "Slaves to the beer glass, playing cards, and the bowling alley" could never have struggled effectively for a new kind of humanity, he wrote. He and his cofounders wanted to initiate their fellow workers in the "mysteries of a diverse nature" and to help them understand the role of human beings in this "many-wheeled machine." The hearts of the proletariat, depressed by their monotonous work and the crowdedness of urban living, would be raised by the "powerful regularity and constancy of nature." They would get the chance "to live out their individuality" in the company of their fellow workers. All of these benefits would then be conveyed to families, friends, and comrades.[14] These ideals of rejuvenation through nature, of transcending useless activities, and of individuality within a strong political collective were to remain central to the *Naturfreunde* ethos.

The *Naturfreunde* idea quickly spread throughout the German-speaking part of the Austrian Empire and beyond. The first foreign branch was founded in Switzerland in 1900, followed by Germany in 1905. Early groups were often founded by skilled young journeymen whose itinerant training took them from town to town. These men tended to have an optimistic sense of their class identity, and they believed that political solidarity would bring real improvement to their existence. The beginnings of local groups in Germany were generally modest and dependent on the organizational skills of their journeymen founders. One successful founding occurred, for example, in the small northern town of Rüstringen in 1913. An invitation to help establish a local group appeared in the local newspaper. Fifteen people showed up at the meeting in a town pub. In his opening speech, the founder said that because of the ever-greater physical tension of industrial work, the laborer needed sport to maintain mental and spiritual power. Twelve of the visitors were convinced enough to sign a document that established the Workers' Hiking Club "*Die Naturfreunde*" of Rüstringen, and the group thrived until 1933.[15]

What was the sociological makeup of the early TVNF? As in other Wilhelmine labor movement organizations, the rank and file was largely made up of skilled male factory workers and artisans. These workers had a relatively higher standard of living and somewhat more free time than the less skilled; therefore, they also had more everyday opportunities to venture out from the city into the rural countryside. There were also regional and local differences. In towns where significant everyday social interaction took place between industrial workers and lower-middle-class people, teachers, shopkeepers, and farmers made up a significant part of the membership. It is difficult to generalize about the political results of this sociological foundation, but it would be a mistake to assume that interactions with the lower middle class depoliticized the TVNF. There was no simple one-way street of embourgeoisement, since the reformist practice of the labor movement involved adapting dominant values and traditions to the democratic socialist worldview.[16]

By 1914 the German *Naturfreunde* had 12,139 members out of an entire international membership of 31,800. Alongside the men who made up this membership were family members—wives and children—who were termed "auxiliary" but who also took part in hikes and other activities. Most local groups in Germany were small, with no more than 100 official members.[17] Nevertheless, several had members who were, or would eventually become, prominent in the labor movement leadership. For example, the Bielefeld local group included future union leader Carl Severing and

Ernst Reuter, who later became mayor in Magdeburg and West Berlin. Such articulate figures helped the movement gain respectability from the SPD and union leadership.[18]

Following the lead of the Social Democratic Party, *Naturfreunde* leaders supported war when it came in August 1914. The war drew many younger men away to the front, and women and older men became temporarily prominent in local leadership.[19] Most local groups reduced their activities drastically, some of them barely clinging to existence. War weariness was evident by 1916. For instance, in a report on a hiking trip of the Rüstringen TVNF, the author describes lying in the silent forest and thinking about hiking comrades who "had to sacrifice their young lives to the murderous world war."[20] In the four years of total war, the movement suffered heavily from the loss of its younger members to the front, where death awaited many of them. Seventy members of the local Munich group alone lost their lives.[21] As one *Naturfreund* later wrote, "Many of our best lie covered by the cool grass, and there are gaps in our rank and file that will not be closed for many years."[22]

The best years of the TVNF were yet to come, however. Under the democratic Weimar Republic, the labor movement achieved many of its political demands, including the eight-hour day and collective bargaining, the end of police repression, the liberalization of election laws, and political power in a parliament with substantial control over the government. These achievements gave workers more time and liberty to participate in the left-wing cultural movement. As we have seen, there was a consensus in early Weimar that the population of Germany had to recover, both physically and mentally, from the war experience. The political left was just as convinced of the benefits of exercise as was the right. This can be seen in a memorandum sent to the National Assembly in 1919 by the Social Democratic Central Commission for Sport and Physical Cultivation, which called for the removal of all legal hindrances to the organization of physical exercise, the introduction of work-free afternoons for young workers, and the institution of physical education courses in the schools. The memorandum also called for a law that would require the national, state, and local governments to promote physical education by creating and maintaining sporting and gymnastics areas, swimming pools, and hostels for hikers of all ages.[23] The general popularity of such ideas helped give new impetus to the *Naturfreunde* as they experienced a surge in membership and activity in early Weimar.

The early 1920s also saw the development of a national TVNF organizational network that became fully autonomous from the international leaders in Vienna. In 1923 a German leadership committee was elected and took up residence at its office in Nuremberg. It presided over a federal structure in which eighteen district branches and hundreds of local groups maintained a high degree of independence. This diversity was mirrored in the many monthly journals that began publishing throughout the country at the district and city levels. Moreover, the membership of the TVNF expanded nearly ten times from 20,753 people in 1919 to 116,124 in 1923. More nonproletarian members entered the *Naturfreunde*, most notably employees, civil servants, artists, and rural workers. The movement was unusual in that it did not immediately reproduce the early Weimar split between Social Democratic and Communist branches of the organized working class. The TVNF officially expected of its members that they simply belong to one or the other Marxist party; thus, a significant minority of functionaries and members were Communists or Independent Socialists. The most politically radical districts were Brandenburg and Thüringen, and there were also radical local groups in Berlin, Württemberg, and the Rhineland.[24]

In addition, the TVNF now allowed people under the age of twenty to become members of newly founded youth sections for a discounted annual fee, and adolescents entered the organization en masse.[25] As a result of this influx of young people, the movement apparently became more youth oriented, indeed "youthful," in its attitudes. This, combined with fears of many young people about their economic future in the crisis-ridden economy of early Weimar, probably made the ideal of the new human being attractive to the young.

The organization spent much time, energy, and money establishing collectively owned property in the form of *Naturfreunde* houses. These served members as overnight hostels and as sites of meetings and celebrations. For many local groups in the Weimar era, building a house was a project of utmost significance in which members invested time, money, skills, and emotion. From a total of 40 German houses in 1922, the number rose to 160 in 1926 and 230 by 1931.[26]

The TVNF financed these building projects through contributions from members, lotteries, and subsidies or loans from municipal and state governments. Aid from city governments sometimes came in the form of donated building sites and materials. The SPD and trade unions often lent their support to building projects by petitioning authorities in favor of local

Youths in the Upper Bavarian district of the *Naturfreunde* meet at the Rohrauer-haus in 1924. By permission of Archiv der TVNF, Ortsgruppe München.

groups and publicly singing the praises of such groups at their groundbreaking ceremonies. Still, the *Naturfreunde* had to compete for state funding with other naturist organizations. In 1926 one way they tried to solve the problem was by joining the National Federation of Youth Hostels. In return, the *Naturfreunde* houses opened their doors to all adolescents, bringing many of them into contact with socialist hikers for the first time.[27]

The *Naturfreunde* were obliged to formulate their overtures to the state in language that was as politically neutral as possible. This was not all that difficult, as the TVNF shared the Weimar state's interest in social reform in general and the welfare of young people in particular. The local group in Neustadt in the Palatinate, for instance, used typical "youth cultivation" rhetoric in arguing that working youths needed a *Naturfreund* house "to steel the body for new work, to prevent sickness, and to encourage serious weeknight activities for body and mind without the pressure to drink and smoke." Particularly during the winter, the lack of meeting places was "driving youths into the arms of pulp literature and all the other enervating, demoralizing winter activities, including the immoderate enjoyment of alcohol and tobacco." Such appeals were sometimes couched in terms of the good of the nation. The same Neustadt group reminded the Palatinate state government in 1923 that the working populace was suffering from the French occupation of the Rhineland. Due to the policy of passive resistance, many unemployed workers could be helped by participating in the building project. "This house will one day be a monument that bears witness to the fact that in a time of hardship, there were men and women here who gave their all for the good of the people and the Fatherland."[28] In no sector of Weimar political culture was this brand of defensive nationalism unusual at the time. Its use, and the use of youth cultivation rhetoric, shows the cleverness of the *Naturfreunde* in using politically consensual language in their appeals to the authorities.

How did sociological and political differences influence the organizational history of this movement? The first subject we will address is class. From the beginning the majority of the *Naturfreunde* were relatively well-educated, politically active, highly skilled male workers and their families. Large numbers of salaried employees entered the Weimar movement. A statistic from 1929 indicated that they, along with "bureaucrats," independent businessmen, and housewives, made up no less than 41 percent of some three thousand *Naturfreunde* who took a mass excursion to Switzerland.[29] The TVNF never made any serious effort to delve deeper into the proletarian milieu by appealing to poorer workers. In this they reflected the artisanal and lower-middle-class character of Weimar Social Democracy.

On the question of gender relations, the TVNF was by no means progressive from our contemporary standpoint, and this was in keeping with early twentieth-century socialism in general. An artisanal version of separate spheres ideology kept women out of leadership positions, aside from the brief hiatus of the war. Even though probably 15 to 20 percent of TVNF members were women—a typical percentage for most Weimar labor movement organizations—no woman was ever sent as a delegate to a national conference, nor did more than a handful of women hold office on the district and local levels.[30] Even female essayists in *Naturfreunde* journals wrote of domesticity as the key to the female character. The role of women was to raise children in a socialist atmosphere, wrote Mathilde Hürtgen of the Rhineland district. Boys and men should treat female members with more respect: "For the rough handling of girls leads to rough mothers who in turn pass their roughness on to the young, making them incapable of a refined sense of culture and of all beautiful thoughts and deeds." This view of women's role shaped the thinking of most people who had anything to say about gender in the Weimar era. Indeed, it was typical of the dominant ideology in most women's movements throughout the West in the early twentieth century.[31]

Political divisions also developed between Social Democratic and Communist Party members, particularly among the leaders at all levels. Although the information about political affiliation is somewhat spotty, it is clear that the majority of leaders supported the SPD. Carl Schreck of the Bielefeld local group typified the moderate Social Democratic *Naturfreund*. A carpenter who had belonged to the SPD since 1890, he was prominently involved in other cultural organizations as well. Less typical was his high political status as a member of the Weimar National Assembly, the Prussian House of Representatives, and the Reichstag.[32] Schreck's prominence allowed him to serve as an ambassador for the TVNF vis-à-vis the SPD and unions.

Over 80 percent of the delegates to national conferences between 1928 and 1932 were SPD members, and the rest were Communists or left-wing Socialists. There were, however, regional differences. Communist functionaries outnumbered Social Democrats in the Württemberg district; and 43 percent had no official party affiliation, which probably indicates resistance to the SPD. There was most likely an even lower degree of official party affiliation on the local level, although most felt themselves closer to the Social Democratic milieu, reflecting the higher numbers of Social Democrats throughout Germany as a whole. The few available memoirs claim that the rank-and-file members, whether Socialists or Communists, generally got along well in the local organizations. This seems to reflect the general lack of strict segregation between Communists and Socialists in everyday Weimar proletarian life; they often lived side by side and had various links within the neighborhoods.[33]

And yet, the political split in the Weimar labor movement can indeed be seen in microcosm in the *Naturfreunde*, and it caused serious problems for them. At two points in the Weimar era, 1924–25 and 1930–32, the organization's national Social Democratic leaders in Nuremberg chose to expel thousands of members as punishment for their attempts to push the movement in a more radical direction. One can only imagine how the battles within the TVNF leadership, which will be described in more detail later, created divisions and resentments among the general membership. Indeed, following the first open controversy in 1923–24, the membership fell sharply from its all-time high of 116,000 to 83,853 by the end of 1924. By 1926 less than one-half of the 1923 membership remained—55,479. As one delegate to the Rhineland district conference in 1925 stated, the movement had lost many people due to the period of hyperinflation, but just as many through "personal malice . . . caused by party politics."[34] After 1926 the membership stabilized and even began a phase of slow but steady growth, reaching some 61,000 people by 1929. In the late 1920s the TVNF settled into a skilled workers' and lower-middle-class movement of people who were mostly committed to moderate socialism. It might well have eventually regained its 1923 levels if the Depression, and another surge of political polarization, had not put an end to the positive trend. Membership began to fall again, albeit more gradually. There were 59,126 *Naturfreunde* in 1930, and 58,134 in 1931. Still, even as late as 1931 there remained over 800 local groups in Germany.[35]

Naturfreunde Ideology and Practice

The *Naturfreunde* movement during the Weimar era offered a particularly good example of a mutable and contested naturist narrative. We will look first at the TVNF's diagnosis of the nation's problems.

One key theme that the *Naturfreunde* developed was the lack of proletarian access to rural nature. The TVNF attacked the capitalist system for hoarding the rural landscape, making a unique contribution to the cultural formation of a collective labor movement consciousness. Co-founder Karl Renner had eloquently voiced this critique in 1896:

Not a single piece of the earth belongs to us. The house in which we live, the workshop in which we toil, the fields through which we hike—everything belongs to others. The tree under which we rest, the caves in which we seek shelter from the storm, the forest whose clean air strengthens our lungs—all of nature experiences us as strangers. We are strangers on this earth, for we have no part of it! They have left only the street to us! . . . They have divided the earth . . . among themselves and have granted us only the dust of the street.[36]

The desire to appropriate the natural world was analogous to the labor movement's ongoing attempts to appropriate both the educated-bourgeois ideal of individual *Bildung* and the high cultural capital represented by the works of Goethe, Schiller, Beethoven, and others. It also paralleled the Marxist goal of appropriating the means of industrial production for the good of workers. Moreover, the *Naturfreunde* saw access to nature as a basic human right. This aim of gaining access for the common people was even reflected in the movement's official slogan. In opposition to the powerful bourgeois German-Austrian Alpine Association, whose motto was "*Berg auf*" ("Climb the mountain"), the TVNF adopted the populist motto "*Berg frei,*" which can be loosely translated as "Free the mountain."

Another problem that the *Naturfreunde* dwelled on, particularly in the later 1920s, was a new form of capitalist exploitation—the rationalization of industry. The project of streamlining and speeding up work processes and regimenting the workforce commenced in some industries during the period of relative stabilization in the mid-1920s. Social Democratic and union leaders generally supported it as necessary if not progressive.[37] It is impossible to say with any certainty what kind of psychological effects rationalization had on workers; but the TVNF took a starkly negative view of the process, not only as a cause of structural unemployment but even more so as a threat to the worker's body and psyche. As the rationalized production process took away the individual's humanity, the worker sank "into night and horror." The process turned the flesh-and-blood worker into a docile, easily exploitable part of the machine.[38] These experiences, wrote Adolf Lau, "wear down any upward-striving powers in the human being," turning the worker into "a docile beast of burden who knows no real cultural needs and thus has no part in the lively workings of nature." Nowadays, Lau concluded bleakly, the only experience of nature left to the individual is the purely biological growth and decline of the physical body.[39] Such arguments were an extension of the Marxist critique of alienation and deskilling. For the *Naturfreunde*, the modern worker was alienated not only from the work process but from nature itself.

A third important element of the *Naturfreunde* diagnosis was the threat of urban life to workers' physical and mental health and, by extension, to the workers' political steadfastness. The city was a "stony desert" in which "millions were striving for air and light"; it distracted and weakened the working class with "its modern nonculture (*Unkultur*), its poisonous enjoyment spots, its slick streets and people, its noise and unnatural smells of factory smoke and perfume, its breeding grounds of terrible 'culture' sickness."[40] Communist and Independent Socialist *Naturfreunde* concurred in the denigration of urban culture. Like most other Weimar leftists, they despised the new and increasingly popular mass media, the movies in particular. The cinema, they announced, was a capitalist enterprise bent on exploiting the "taste of the uneducated masses," who "willingly let themselves be betrayed and deluded."[41]

This kind of forceful rhetoric against mass urban culture was a tradition among labor movement cultural activists and leaders, but there is reason to doubt that it held sway over the general membership. The debate on alcohol among *Naturfreunde* leaders shows that their attempts to "ennoble" the working class sometimes conflicted with everyday reality. The financial survival of many TVNF huts depended on the serving of alcohol, and most workers were neither drunkards nor teetotalers.[42] The rhetorical tradition of discipline and ennoblement was part of an ongoing attempt to keep workers loyal and concentrated on socialism, but people in their everyday lives took part in many different kinds of leisure pursuits, amusements, and forms of sociability including, but not limited to, organized movements. It is difficult to imagine any *Naturfreund* hiking *only* in his or her free time.

Indeed, the availability of many other ways for workers to spend their leisure hours created a problem of legitimacy for the *Naturfreunde*. Why should any worker sacrifice Saturday evening on the town and Sunday morning in bed by getting up early to go on a long hike? The need to make hiking attractive, to negotiate the consent of workers to the *Naturfreunde* project, also made it harder to develop solutions to all the problems diagnosed by the movement. All *Naturfreunde* leaders could agree on the need to restore and maintain physical and mental health. They agreed that hiking was a great way to improve circulation, to provide relief from the crowded atmosphere of the working-class apartment, and to refresh the mind through exposure to a diversity of sensory impressions.[43] But how could hiking be used to raise the political consciousness of the working class and thus help them gain access to nature, resist rationalization, and avoid the ills of mass urban culture?

The Bavarian *Naturfreund* Walter Trojan described the difficulty of appropriating hiking for political purposes in a 1925 essay. The war with its millions of dead and wounded signaled a negative turning point in world history, Trojan wrote. Would a generation come that had the energy and ability to construct a new world? Socialists had to look at present conditions clearly and pragmatically; they had to drop their utopian promise that one day would come "a magnificent empire of peace, freedom and fraternity and socialism." Many workers were reluctant to fight capitalism directly because of their lack of freedom and their obligations to family. And workers longed for enjoyment in everyday life, because they understood that at the end of the path of life stood death. The working mass did not understand why both work and free time had to involve struggle. Should their little bit of leisure also be a struggle?[44]

The TVNF's ideal narrative of turning to nature took shape within this difficult cultural context in the course of the 1920s. According to this narrative, which recurred throughout the published discourse of the *Naturfreunde*, work could provide no joy. Emotional experience had to be sought during free time, and only free time could save the worker from slavery to the machine.[45] Sport alone was not the solution, since the entire human being, not just the body, needed relief and redemption. Hiking in a group of one's peers was the best way to restore health and allow the worker to have a diversity of sensory experience and mental stimulation.

The emphasis on emotion is strong in this narrative; but the narrative also took up the Enlightenment paradigm of progress through reason. Workers needed knowledge about the natural world, because only the worker who gained access to science that had formerly been available only to the bourgeoisie could take up the class struggle successfully.[46] Hiking, then, was a form of self-education in the "book of nature, whose pages are turned by the feet."[47] In this way, political consciousness could be strengthened. "Our first duty is to give the mass of the proletariat knowledge of nature," announced the national leaders in Nuremberg. "But we will not stop at natural knowledge and hiking; both are useless if they fail to lead to the socialist deed." This deed, according to these leaders, was exemplified by the building of *Naturfreunde* houses, which were symbolic utopian acts of collective solidarity.[48]

These national leaders in Nuremberg spoke for the moderate Social Democratic majority in the TVNF. For the radical Communist and Independent Socialist minority, their narrative did not go far enough. The polarization of the *Naturfreunde* movement that took place from 1924 through 1925 was a direct result of the radicals' formulation of their own alternative narrative, at the end of which lay violent revolution.

This radical alternative narrative took shape as the moderate TVNF leadership began to clamp down on the Communist minority. At the Leipzig national conference of 1923, *Naturfreunde* delegates agreed on the programmatic separation of overtly political work and leisure activities.[49] Responding to the criticisms of a left-wing minority that such a separation would lessen the movement's political strength, Carl Schreck formulated a more specific resolution that the movement would be solely concerned with "the cultural value of hiking and the processes of nature."[50] A special conference adopted Schreck's resolution in October 1924, at the same time granting the national leadership committee the right to expel individual members as well as entire local groups. The leaders first exercised that right against the entire Brandenburg district, where local groups had been join-ing the revolutionary Communist sports movement. They also expelled local groups in Solingen, Remscheid, and Cologne for the same reason.[51] From the standpoint of organizational unity, these expulsions were prob-ably justified, since the Communist Party was definitely conspiring to destabilize the TVNF by creating Communist factions at the local and district levels.[52]

In a special issue of their district journal entitled "Against the Cur-rent," the Brandenburg leaders presented their response to the moderates. It is here that we find the radical narrative. This was much more rationalist and politically militant than the moderate narrative outlined previously. The radicals rejected the notion of a "third column" according to which the workers' cultural movement should leave economic and political issues to the parties and unions. For them there was no such thing as politically neutral cultural forms. They also rejected the moderates' emphasis on emo-tion, which they saw as emptily sentimental "gushing about nature" (*Natur-schwärmerei*). "The paths of the proletariat in the homeland of Romanticism lead not 'back to nature,' but over barricades and mountains of corpses. They are hard, stony, and shadowless." Given this emphasis on militarism, what really counted for the radicals was "the task of building, through sys-tematic physical cultivation (*Körperpflege*), a healthy, naturally developed troop of fighters to achieve and sustain a proletarian people's state."[53]

Radicals in the *Naturfreunde* were thus representing themselves by 1924 as forward-looking, energetic class warriors, in contrast to the alleged political weakness of the moderate majority. However, their actual narrative of improvement through hiking was strikingly similar to that of the mod-erates, and it was thus somewhat at odds with the radicals' hyperrationalist and militarist verbiage. As formulated by Emil Jensen, the hiking narrative began with a worker's encounter with the local natural setting of his home-land, an encounter that was simultaneously emotional and rational:

Hiking in the region of the *Heimat* reveals an unknown world to the proletarian who is eager to learn. He sees nature at work in all its restless, intermeshed, and interdependent processes; and he is seized by a great love of nature that allows him to understand it.

The narrative then moved to the healing power of nature and its ability to show the hiker how unnatural capitalism was:

[Nature] heals the worker's body and mind, [and he] comes to recognize the processes at work in human society and the unnatural state of affairs in the capitalist system.

This experience of a nature that was running according to natural laws of justice would then spark the worker's political anger and his will to fight:

He feels himself strong, in complete possession of his powers, and he dares to reproach society for its lack of morality, culture, and authenticity. But the worker does not restrict himself merely to criticism. He takes up the fight alongside his comrades to establish proletarian cultural values.[54]

The joining of reason, emotion, and political militancy in this radical rhetoric did not completely reject the moderate narrative; rather, it pushed it further toward the goal of creating an actively fighting working class. Even though the radicals were in the minority and had come under attack by the moderate TVNF leaders, their holistic notion that hiking would advance the working class physically, mentally, and politically became consensual throughout the movement once the infighting of 1923–24 died down.

Beginning in the mid-1920s the TVNF evolved a consensual narrative of turning to nature politically through a new kind of "social hiking." They used the word *social* in two senses. First, they spoke of the need for collective social solidarity among workers, which could be achieved through the group nature experience. Divisions of gender and generation could be transcended, leading to mutual respect and the sense of solidarity that was necessary for the development of new leaders.[55] Social hiking was also an opportunity to learn collectively about nature. As Mathilde Hürtgen of the Rhineland *Naturfreunde* wrote, hikers should teach themselves about "historical, regional, literary history; the study of plants, animals, geography; and human cultures and traditions." The many possibilities of collective self-education, she averred, made social hiking superior to all other kinds of proletarian sport.[56]

Second, *social* stood in this narrative for political socialism, which would arise from the collective experience both of nature and of one's fellow workers. Getting to know workers in other locales and trades was a way to achieve socialist solidarity. Hikers should study the living, working, and health conditions of other workers, their places of work and leisure, and their political attitudes and mentalities.[57] Above all, social hikers must learn about the economic backwardness and inequality that were preventing Germany's advance toward social justice. As the Rhinelander Theo Müller wrote, "A short trip in which we observe the activity of the farmer, the poor forestry worker, and the craftsman can teach us more than any heavy tome."[58]

Although *soziales Wandern* had become the dominant narrative of turning to nature in the TVNF by the late 1920s, controversy persisted between moderates and radicals over its political meaning. Whether a given *Naturfreunde* group drew attention to social inequality in its region depended on the group's political stance. Moderate groups found it easy to focus on everyday work processes in lieu of a critique of capitalist exploitation. For instance, in an exhibition entitled *"Heimat* and Hiking" held in Munich in 1928, the exhibit on social hiking contained an original weaver's room and pictures of other workplaces, as well as various examples of regional handicrafts. The presentation was merely picturesque, with no critical discussion of Bavarian workers' economic situation.[59] By contrast, more radical groups emphasized critical sociological understanding as a precondition for true social hiking. At the 1925 conference of the Württemberg district, one debate concerned whether groups should teach sociology alongside natural science. Radical delegates argued that only Marxist sociology could show workers the way to liberation. Social hiking without this knowledge was not truly social. Yet this was a minority view at the conference. One of the visiting national leaders, Xavier Steinberger, spoke against the teaching of sociology, using the tried-and-true moderate argument that the *Naturfreunde* should avoid all overtly political activity. A vote followed, and the sociology resolution failed.[60]

It appears that social hiking ideology, like the *Naturfreunde* movement itself, was dominated by the moderate Socialists. But the very idea of hiking in a more consciously political way was a contribution of the radicals. Without their critique of the moderate leadership's antipoliticism in 1924, social hiking might never have played such a prominent role in the TVNF.

What did social hiking look like in practice? The frequency of TVNF hikes is impressive. In the Baden district, for instance, a total of 10,554 hikes with 115,279 participants took place between 1928 and 1931. Of these hikes, 28 percent lasted just a few hours; 57 percent took an entire day; and 15 percent were hikes of several days' duration.[61] Anywhere from seven to seventy men, women, adolescents, and children typically participated in a *Naturfreunde* hike.

What of the solidarity-building and socialist elements of social hiking? Viola Denecke has argued that the kind of hiking in which cities were visited and political discussion took place never became popular in the TVNF.[62] In fact, there is simply not enough surviving evidence to be sure of this. Judging by the hiking announcements listed in district journals, we can determine that groups on day hikes nearly always chose to leave the town and head for the countryside. Yet longer journeys of a week or more often took hikers through towns and cities. Sometimes they even visited factories.[63]

The extent of political discussion during *Naturfreunde* activities is also difficult to gauge. Each local group held talks and discussions, but not many of them appear to have dealt directly with socialist theory or political events. In the discussion evenings and public exhibitions of the Baden district, for instance, the focus was on the natural phenomena, geography, history, and folk traditions of southwestern Germany.[64] Less formal discussions of politics may well have taken place during hikes, however. According to the memoirs of former member Fritz Bohne, the *Naturfreunde* in their everyday activities studied botany, cooked, sang, and "did silly things together" but also engaged in a great deal of political discussion.[65] Yet other evidence shows that everyday discussions dealt mainly with natural phenomena and culture. Former *Naturfreund* Georg Glaser described such occasions in another memoir:

[I remember] the weekend hiking trips and the meadows surrounding the houses where motley groups of cheerful young people would camp, interspersed with young-at-heart adult leaders, all of whom used the informal *Du* in speaking to each other. I remember the "workers' academies," where the teacher—often an older, well-known man of science—would sit naked but for a loincloth under a tree. In the grass around him would lie a crowd of tanned, naked young boys and girls. Everyone had the right to interrupt the teacher, to question and to correct him.[66]

Even if this text does not indicate overtly political consciousness raising, it does show that social hiking was taking place in the broader sense of building an egalitarian sense of community.

Although we cannot draw any definite conclusions about the extent of political discussion in everyday TVNF practice, it is clear that the *Naturfreunde* concept of nature itself was both democratic and socialist. Representations of the natural world took shape as part of the ongoing process of narrative formation that all naturist movements undertook.

Socialist movements were obliged to appeal to workers by developing nature concepts and narratives of progress that meshed well with industrial workers' everyday experiences. We have already seen that a vision of the rural landscape as a site of physical, mental, and emotional recovery emerged as an alternative to everyday living and working conditions in the industrial city. What else can we say about the *Naturfreunde* movement's representation of nature?

First, the movement fashioned a new socialist version of the *Heimat* concept. In the bourgeois conservationist movement to be discussed in Chapter 6, the concept of homeland was always infused with conservative nostalgia for preindustrial social hierarchies. In the late Weimar Republic, bourgeois conservationist rhetoric of *Heimat* became increasingly racial-nationalist in character. The Weimar *Naturfreunde* clearly distanced themselves from this conservative *Heimat* ideal, developing an alternative concept that represented the natural landscape of Germany as both rural and industrial. The journal frontispiece reproduced opposite depicts a landscape in which industry is embedded harmoniously. This is the homeland of social hiking, in which city and country, industry and agriculture were all integral parts of the modern democratic nation. No part can exist without the others, and there is a strong ideal of equality between different ways of working and living.

This holistic ideal of the *Heimat* landscape as the symbol of a socially diverse nation is also found in a 1931 speech on social hiking by a Dr. Schomburg. Addressing a meeting of *Naturfreunde* youths in northern Germany, Schomburg warned his audience not to seek only the sublime and the beautiful during a hike. Instead, the social hiker had to experience all the variety of the landscape, even those parts that seemed ugly. Thus, *Naturfreunde* needed to hike not just in the agrarian countryside but also through industrial towns. Nor should they hike only in the friendly seasons; they had also to face the storms of winter. Schomburg, in other words, was saying that there was much more to hiking than physical and aesthetic enjoyment—it was also about embracing all aspects of nature and the nation. Yet his ideal of social hiking transcended even nationalism: "We must expose the people to the diversity of life, not stopping at the political borders of the nation. . . . Whoever wants to learn to hike in a truly social way must also hike at least once into foreign lands." Doing so would save the hiker from arrogance, for only in this way could people recognize that every nation, including Germany, had both good and bad

A *Naturfreunde* depiction of the modern German landscape. Frontispiece of the journal *Rheinisches Land* (January 1926).

qualities.[67] This version of the *Heimat*, strikingly different from that of the bourgeois conservationists, demonstrates that the concept could merge with both the liberal-republican ideal of the nation and with the progressive internationalist tradition of socialism.

A second important feature of the *Naturfreunde* representation of nature was its strong current of rationalism. Hiking would give workers a chance to learn about the laws of nature firsthand. Such knowledge would show them that capitalist society was fundamentally at odds with natural evolution, which the *Naturfreunde* saw as an inevitable progression toward both a better world and a more just society. The authors who wrote along these lines were not social darwinists; they saw evolution as an orderly, egalitarian process of cooperation and symbiosis rather than a process of violent struggle.[68] The following passage in a 1930 essay by

Ludwig Ziegler constructs a parallel between nature and an ideal socialist community:

The simple observation that there is a uniform cell structure common to all plants and animals reminds us of the equality that we are striving for in society. The study of plant and animal life reveals to us the existence of mutual aid among the organisms, the kind that we desire for our highly developed human race. Concepts like the division of labor, love, freedom, and joy—they can be comprehended in the processes that take place every day along the path of the proletarian hiker.[69]

In his hiking journal another member drew similar political analogies to natural processes: "'Mountains are kings, and wind and weather are the forces that wear them down into the valley of democracy.' I read that somewhere once. So that would be progress? Leveling. Equalization."[70] It should be noted that such gradualism was not to the liking of the radical minority of *Naturfreunde*, who tended to see human evolution as a struggle between the classes. Bourgeois society, wrote one, was "condemned to death by nature, which only knows eternal advancement. . . . The dispossessed are in league with nature, and the possessing class is doomed."[71]

It seems unlikely, however, that ordinary members perceived nature in the same rationalist way as the spokespersons just quoted. We can say very little about rank-and-file attitudes toward the landscape, since the only evidence is in the form of a few handwritten hiking reports. One report from a local group in 1927, for example, describes six men and one woman taking the train to a nearby town, then hiking further.

After climbing a small hill, we stood before the cliff wall. Beneath us was an old mill with a half-decayed waterwheel covered in moss. Above us on the edge of the cliff, knotty linden trees rustled in the wind. We walked a little further and we stood before a waterfall that must present a wonderful spectacle when there is a lot of water.[72]

This rather dry language of nature appreciation is typical of such reports, in which the authors more often than not merely use prosaic words or the term "romantic" to describe the landscape. A further bit of evidence comes from the few surviving photographic collections from *Naturfreunde* local groups.[73] Without exception they show people contemplating a strictly rural landscape, with no sign of towns or factories. Often people look out over a rural landscape with their backs turned to the camera, echoing the classically Romantic landscape tradition of Caspar David Friedrich and others.

What this scanty evidence does suggest is that ordinary *Naturfreunde* encountered nature in an emotional and reverent, not strictly rationalist, way. Some of the leading members who published their thoughts in the movement's journals combined their rationalist interest in natural laws with a strong emphasis on the emotions of reverence and happiness. For Walter Trojan, "Reason and emotion go hand in hand in the hiker, and this combination alone makes the full human being."[74] And Adolf Lau of the Rhineland *Naturfreunde* offered an optimistic vision of the future in which approaching nature in both a rational and an emotional way would make nature "the wellspring (*Born*) of new life energy. . . . Every person will stand close to every other, and all these individuals' unique *internal* experiences of nature will unite, giving life to a higher community. This will be made possible by a friendship between human beings and nature that encompasses the entire world."[75] This is an extraordinary statement of solidarity among people and with nature. It demonstrates that reason and emotion, the ideal of a democratic human community across national boundaries, and protoenvironmentalist thought could indeed join together in the *Naturfreunde* concept of nature.

The *Naturfreunde* were nearly unique in the Marxist labor movement in their ongoing struggle against the abuse of nature. At the forefront of the TVNF's conservationism were the relatively moderate leaders. The few more radically left-wing spokespersons who said anything about nature protection argued that only the revolutionary destruction of capitalism itself would end the overexploitation of nature. This attitude was analogous to the dominant radical view of women's rights and human rights, and it meant putting off efforts at practical change until after the revolution. Any such efforts at the present time would be a "useless waste of proletarian energies."[76]

Perhaps out of disappointment in his quest for early German forerunners of today's social justice environmentalism, historian Ulrich Linse has criticized the *Naturfreunde* for allowing "bourgeois values" to enter the movement in the form of conservationism.[77] As we will see, German conservationism originated as an elitist and conservative project of the educated bourgeoisie. At the heart of that movement lay a strong antipathy to socialism and disdain for the "lower" classes. Thus, it seems at first glance surprising to find the *Naturfreunde* leadership in 1911 adding "the cultivation of *Heimat* and nature preservation" to the organization's national statutes.[78] However, this version of conservationism was no longer "bourgeois"; rather, it was an adaptation of the *Naturschutz* idea to an oppositional protest movement.

Conservationist ideology had much in common with the *Naturfreunde* goal of helping the common people recover from urban-industrial life. There was nothing inherently conservative, bourgeois, or German about this goal. The demand for workers' access to nature characterized many conservationist initiatives elsewhere in the late nineteenth and early twentieth centuries. John Stuart Mill and other radical British Liberals formed the Commons Preservation Society in 1865, gaining public access to open spaces around London; and the Ramblers' Association founded in Britain in 1935 agitated for access to forests and "sporting estates."[79]

What of the language of national identity that became so problematic in bourgeois conservationism? Mythical rhetoric of a "German national soul" that was organically related to the "German forest," while rare in the TVNF, did appear occasionally.[80] It would be a serious mistake, however, to interpret this as a form of protofascist nationalism, since there was none of the essentialist language of race so central to the rhetoric of the Nazis. As we have already seen, the *Heimat* concept in *Naturfreunde* ideology represented a democratic ideal of the nation. Indeed, *Naturfreunde* leaders were aware of how popular the *Heimat* concept was in Germany and believed that they could "make a much more effective and populist (*volkstümlich*) impression on people than the often unapproachable gentlemen of the bourgeois associations, who have failed to expand their very small organizations."[81]

Because conservationism was not inherently conservative, the *Naturfreunde* could incorporate it into their project of creating a socialist nation. They asserted that *Naturschutz* was a practical way to counter the harmful consequences of capitalist greed. As one essayist asserted, most human beings were driven by "the fanatical desire for property," so they looked at the landscape through the eyes of the "would-be owner." This attitude was devastating for nature, because plants and animals were helpless against the invasion of the "vastly more powerful human species." Conservationists had to take up the struggle against this "mental condition" by popularizing a sense of community (*Gemeinschaftsgedanke*) between human beings and nature.[82]

This ethos of nature protection was communicated to *Naturfreunde* members in a number of ways. For instance, it was prominent in the movement's rules of correct hiking:

Spare and safeguard nature! . . . Do not yell or make loud noise when moving through nature, especially in the woods. At resting spots, do not litter and do not break bottles and glasses. Anyone who likes to explore caves should avoid damaging their most beautiful ornaments, the stalactites and stalagmites. We ask all those who share our opinion in this matter to join us in the battle against false attitudes toward nature and to help us fight hiking abuses (*Wanderunsitten*).[83]

Naturfreunde writers called publicly for national and state conservation laws to protect relatively undisturbed natural areas; and they voiced their support for activist conservation leagues like the Nature Park Association (*Verein Naturschutzpark*). The TVNF also undertook efforts to promote conservation in the general public through local exhibits and the distribution of flyers.[84]

More daringly, the *Naturfreunde* sometimes launched or participated in local protests aimed at preserving recreation areas near the cities. For instance, local groups in the Rhineland protested against the regulation and canalization of the lower Rhenish waterways, which obliterated many of the lakes close to industrial centers. Young people seem to have been particularly active in this regard, on occasion bravely taking on the military. The *Naturfreundejugend* in Dresden held an "antiwar hike" in 1930 that culminated in their brief occupation of an army exercise field. Their purpose was to call attention to the destruction of nature by the military.[85]

Division and Destruction, 1929–1935

The period of relative ideological consensus and political stability in the *Naturfreunde* was as brief as the time of relative stability enjoyed by the Weimar Republic itself. The years 1924–28 were not adequate for a cultural-activist movement like the TVNF to put down its roots firmly in popular culture. A chasm opened between the Social Democratic majority and Communist members beginning in 1928. The sudden world economic crisis that began in late 1929, as well as the political rise of the Nazi Party in 1930–32, further weakened the movement.

Following Stalin's accession to power in the Soviet Union in 1928, the German Communist Party (KPD) underwent a phase of radicalization that put an end to any chance of cooperation with the Social

Democrats. The KPD more and more stridently criticized the SPD; and the Communist minority within the *Naturfreunde* movement worked to draw rank-and-file *Naturfreunde* away from "social fascism," their new term for Social Democracy. In 1929 a number of local groups in Saxony, Thuringia, Württemberg, Saarland, and the Rhineland joined a newly created Communist sporting federation, the Fighting League for Red Sport Unity (*Kampfgemeinschaft für rote Sporteinheit*). A new national group, the Oppositional *Naturfreunde* Committee, was formed and published its own journal, *Der proletarische Wanderer*.[86]

The Social Democratic leaders of the TVNF realized that not only the movement's political solidarity but also its property, in the form of *Naturfreunde* huts, was under threat. The national leadership committee in Nuremberg presented an ultimatum to the radical groups—either refrain from all "party-political activity" such as membership in the Fighting League, or face expulsion. By the national conference in Dresden of August 1930, the TVNF had expelled several local groups. At that meeting, a majority of delegates supported the leadership's policy of expulsion. Indeed, the central committee also managed to pass a resolution giving them power to expel local groups without the official consent of the broader organization. This put a de facto end to the federalist division of powers among the eighteen *Naturfreunde* districts; henceforth crucial powers would be in the hands of a small number of anticommunist leaders in the Nuremberg central committee. These leaders demonstrated a high degree of political hypocrisy at the conference. Xavier Steinberger announced that there was room for different political viewpoints in the organization—as long as everyone refrained from agitation in support of specific parties. Yet he went on to call on the delegates to support the SPD in the upcoming September election, earning mockery from the opposition. Although the moderate leaders in the Nuremberg central committee have been justly criticized for their behavior at the Dresden conference, it should be noted that the radical minority at this meeting contributed to the polarization by, for example, demanding that leading *Naturfreunde* functionaries leave the Christian Church.[87]

There followed many more purges of local groups—no fewer than 213 by 1932. The minority Communist factions schemed to draw local groups into the KPD fold. The "hiking section" of the Fighting League for Red Sport Unity developed directives to that effect. Communists, they wrote, should send representatives to meet with local groups during their discussion evenings. They should attempt to take over the discussion, making sure that current politics as well as advancements in the Soviet Union took up time. Should this tactic fail, they would smuggle in new members to undermine Social Democratic influence.[88] The national leaders in Nuremberg responded with their own "defensive measures," demanding that all new members undergo a background investigation to see whether they might be Communist spies.[89]

Yet the situation was more complex than it appears, suggesting that the political divisions of late Weimar were forced on the general membership from above. Despite the polarization at the level of leadership, the tradition of solidarity that came from communal hikes and house construction continued to stabilize the movement in the early 1930s. Both Communist and Social Democratic *Naturfreunde* continued to cooperate unofficially in several places. People of differing political views could still make a local group function from day to day. Also, many groups were critical of both the moderate leaders and the radicals, committing themselves only tentatively to one side or the other. The local group in Leipzig, for instance, criticized the polarizers for losing sight of "the democratic rights of the membership," and they called for a renewed commitment to party-political neutrality as the basis for reunification.[90]

The economic crisis that began in 1929 contributed to the stagnation of the TVNF's membership and caused financial difficulties. Many local groups could no longer pay their dues to the national organization.[91] Individual dues in the Leipzig group were typical of the entire movement. Monthly dues were 80 pfennig for full members, 40 pfennig for the unemployed, 50 pfennig for young persons under the age of 21, and 25 pfennig for unemployed young persons. A yearly contribution of 2.5 marks was requested from "auxiliary members," that is, family members who did not want to become full paying members but who were allowed to participate in hikes. The fact that local members had trouble paying these dues testifies to the rapid impoverishment even of better-off workers. One local group had only two employed members left, and there was a drastic decline in the numbers of young workers in the movement.[92]

The organization's property also came under threat during these years of economic crisis. Local groups were often heavily in debt because of their building projects. Before the Depression, these debts had been met in part by fees charged to nonmembers to stay overnight in the houses. But such visitors declined rapidly in number after 1929, and groups were by 1932 requesting help from the national leaders to save their houses from being reclaimed by creditors.[93] Moreover, as the Nazis' political fortunes improved in the crisis situation of late Weimar, the network of *Naturfreunde* houses became a fascist target. In 1931 the leader of the Frankfurt local group received the following letter from an anonymous Nazi:

> I warn you, honorable Herr Comrade, that we are going to spoil the attempts by you pack of proletarians to contaminate the Taunus region with your so-called *Naturfreunde* houses. . . . You dirty pack of proles belong in the factory, in prison, or at the pig trough, but not in God's free nature. Germany awake, awake, awake![94]

Nazi groups began to vandalize TVNF houses. One house near the northern town of Maschen was laid waste and smeared with swastikas in April 1932. Such thuggish attacks increased in frequency following the entry of the *Naturfreunde* into the SPD's anti-Nazi propaganda federation, the Iron Front, in early 1932.[95]

On January 30, 1933, President von Hindenburg named Adolf Hitler chancellor of Germany. The Nazis used the mysterious fire that destroyed the Reichstag on February 27 to convince Hindenburg to pass the "Decree for the Protection of Nation and State" on February 28. Using these and other police decrees, the new regime undertook to eliminate the Marxist labor movement between March and May. Underestimating the Nazis' totalitarian determination to take complete control of the state and civil society, the TVNF national leaders in Nuremberg, Xavier Steinberger and Leonhard Burger, did everything they could to save the organization. This included attempts to deny all elements of Marxist ideology and to appease the Nazis through "self-synchronization" (*Selbstgleichschaltung*). On March 16 Burger and Steinberger sent a memorandum to all local groups advising them not to do anything that might raise the suspicion of illegal activity. The TVNF had nothing to hide, they wrote, since it had always worked legally in the service of the nation. Therefore, groups must obey all state laws and decrees and must take all possible steps against attempts of the now illegal Communist Party to invade the organization.[96]

The Nazis struck first against the Baden district. In late March the police banned the TVNF there, confiscating all houses and the furniture, books, and other objects within. The National Federation of Youth Hostels now turned against the TVNF and asked the police (without success) to confiscate the *Naturfreunde* houses for the Federation's use.[97] The SA and the police began to take possession of houses elsewhere, prompting

Steinberger and Burger to complain on March 24 to Nazi Interior Minister Wilhelm Frick. They assured Frick that the TVNF had never had anything to do with political parties and that for years they had worked against Communist attempts at subversion. They reaffirmed the movement's promise to work positively toward the new regime's goal of a national community (*Volksgemeinschaft*), although they made no mention of "race" in this communiqué. On April 5 the national leaders sent a memorandum to district leaders announcing that the TVNF had been banned in Baden, Bavaria, Thuringia, and Braunschweig. They demanded that such bans be unconditionally followed and reiterated the warning not to cooperate in any way with Communists.[98]

During the spring of 1933, the Nazis exploited this kind of acquiescent behavior, which unfortunately was common throughout the Social Democratic union and cultural movement leadership. They soothed the fears of labor movement leaders before striking against them. The regime dropped its facade in early May, allowing the unions to celebrate May Day peacefully before turning on them with unexpected violence on May 2. In the wake of this event, Steinberger and Burger tried again to convince the Nazis of their will to "synchronize" the organization. On May 9 they sent Frick a long memorandum entitled "The Significance of the *Naturfreunde* Movement and the *Naturfreunde* Houses for People, State, and Nation." It was an essential characteristic of Germans, they wrote, to love nature, the *Heimat*, and hiking. The TVNF had made access to nature possible for all "estates" (*Stände*) and had improved the nation's health during the period of rapid industrialization. They had also fought for nature conservation, participated in youth welfare efforts, and promoted a spirit of camaraderie among Germany's "working peoples." They had fought an ongoing battle against Communists, who "wanted to use the organization for their own dark purposes." The movement's greatest achievement, the building of the houses, had been made possible by the workers' "boundless idealism and willingness to sacrifice." The movement as a whole had prepared Germany's workers for service to the national community:

Straightforward and unspoilt are those German laborers who gained internal values through hiking. They will easily find their way into the *Volksgemeinschaft* and the national state. The *Naturfreunde* movement, anchored in the working German people, is prepared to devote its energies to the service of the German *Volksgemeinschaft* and to work for the new formation of the German state and national life. We await our incorporation into the developing German *Volksgemeinschaft*.[99]

This kind of attempt to survive within a criminal system is never a pretty sight for historians, who wish there had been more resistance and search for the motives behind the toadying. Ulrich Linse has interpreted the May 9 memorandum as the result of bourgeois *Heimat* and conservationist ideology that had infiltrated the worldview of the national leaders. He maintains that the *Naturfreunde* leaders agreed *in principle* with the Nazis and genuinely wanted to participate, pointing to the disturbing fact that both Steinberger and Burger after 1933 found a personal niche for themselves within the Nazified *Heimat* and hiking movement.[100]

Linse's causal argument is, however, unconvincing. He ignores Steinberger and Burger's attempt to establish their anticommunist credentials, which plays at least as large a role in the document as the language of conservation and *Heimat*. And as I have shown in this chapter, the *Naturfreunde* developed a discourse of *Heimat* that, while patriotic, had none of the nationalist chauvinism of many bourgeois conservationists and *Heimat* celebrants. The memorandum simply jettisoned this democratic *Heimat* rhetoric, selecting the more folkish rhetoric of the bourgeois movement. Does that mean that the authors of the *Denkschrift* suddenly subscribed *in principle* to the conservative tenets of bourgeois conservationism? It seems more likely that they made a pragmatic rhetorical move, something that could not have been very difficult given their knowledge of the various rhetorics of *Heimat*. Supporting this thesis is the fact that one of the key points of agreement between late Weimar bourgeois conservationism and Nazism, namely racist nationalism, is nowhere to be found in the May 9 memorandum. Moreover, if we look to the rhetoric found in the national leaders' official journal just days before Hitler became chancellor, we find that it was defiantly antifascist:

The German spring of the year 1933 lies far ahead of us in the fog. Brown storm clouds obscure its entry path and keep the sunshine of spring from reaching us. The wheel of time is being inexorably turned backward; the natural process of development [*natürliche Gang der Entwicklung*] is being brought to a standstill and prevented. But let the storm blow, for the victorious young energy of natural development cannot be destroyed.[101]

Certainly the TVNF leadership's appeals to the Nazis were a betrayal of the Social Democratic emphasis on justice and democracy. But Linse's claim that the leaders were genuinely pro-Nazi in May 1933 is empirically insupportable. In my view, Steinberger and Burger were not expressing genuine support for Nazism; rather, they were opportunistically manipulating language in hopes of surviving the new regime. Given the basic simplemindedness of Nazi ideology, rhetorical tweaking cannot have been too difficult. The authors used the language of patriotism at every opportunity, especially the noun *Volk* and the adjective *deutsch*. They claimed that the *Naturfreunde* taught workers obedience to the state and love for the Fatherland. Instead of the word *worker*, they used the apolitical terms *working folk* and, better yet, *national comrade*. They demonized communism and silenced the movement's support for Social Democracy. Obviously the authors were walking a tightrope, telling the Nazis what they believed they wanted to hear while emphasizing the worth of their own tradition and experience.

It seems clear that the *Naturfreunde* leadership did not fulfill a sinister protofascist bourgeois tradition. Instead, they betrayed a progressive socialist one. We should, however, pause before condemning historical figures who were trapped, without the benefit of hindsight, in a terrifying political situation. Considering their position as Social Democratic functionaries in the days following the violent destruction of the labor movement, fear and desperation no doubt had much to do with Steinberger's and Burger's actions. Some light is shed by a comparison with another *Naturfreunde* leader's attempt to appeal to the Nazis on the local level. In late May the head of the Leipzig chapter, Werner Mohr, complained by letter to the police about their ban on the group and confiscation of its property. The Leipzig group had been neither Marxist, nor Communist, nor Social Democratic, he wrote. They had until recently been associated with the international leadership committee in Vienna, but only because they had always considered Austria to belong to the German nation. Mohr concluded his appeal by expressing the local group's desire to work for the new regime.[102] The police were not convinced and remained suspicious of Mohr. Perhaps they were aware that Mohr was a member of the SPD and that in 1930 he had written an article advising the *Naturfreunde* to learn from Marx, who had drawn "some of his best conclusions about society" during his long Sunday walks.[103]

None of this is meant to excuse leaders' betrayals of Social Democratic principles during the Nazi takeover but simply to speculate why the betrayal occurred. What the sources do make clear is the leaders' desire to save the *Naturfreunde* organization and its property. In the May 9 memorandum, Steinberger and Burger gave extensive details about the debt still owed for over two hundred houses, which amounted to nearly 2 million marks. It lay in the interest of many thousands of creditors and thus of the national economy, they wrote, "that normal activity in the houses resumes as soon as possible so that we can pay our debts." The *Naturfreunde* houses were ready to serve the new regime's "high ideal" of strengthening the German nation, but only if they were managed by an idealistic hiking movement like the TVNF. Without the *Naturfreunde* running them, the houses would be "like an organism without blood and energy." Thus, the incorporation of the movement lay in the national interest.[104]

These naive appeals fell on deaf ears. The Nazis' aim at this point was to take over civil society by destroying all competition, and their most potentially powerful competitors were the Christian churches and the Marxist labor movement. They had no intention of allowing socialists to play any important role in the new system. For state and national governments, the police, and the Gestapo, the *Naturfreunde* remained an untrustworthy, conspiratorial movement of international Marxism.[105] This suspicion abounded in internal state discussions of the movement in the spring and summer of 1933. For example, in late April the local TVNF group in Essen changed its name to Association for Nature and *Heimat* Cultivation of Greater Essen. The state prime minister in Düsseldorf refused to accept the group's repudiation of Marxism. Just because they had changed on the surface, he wrote to the Prussian Cultural Minister, did not mean that they would stop "thinking and acting in a Marxist way."[106]

It is interesting to compare such suspicions with the regime's treatment of the national leaders Xavier Steinberger and Leonhard Burger. Apparently the memorandum of May 9 convinced its readers of the leaders' anticommunist and patriotic credentials, so both were able to find a niche in the "synchronized" hiking movement. Xavier Steinberger took up a leading position in a *Heimat* celebration club in Nuremberg and managed to bring five Franconian *Naturfreunde* houses into its possession.[107] Leonhard Burger pursued a new career in the National Federation for *Heimat* Hiking and Mountain Climbing, a long-established bourgeois organization that maintained a measure of relative independence by quickly synchronizing itself following Hitler's accession to power. In the fall of that year, Burger gained permission from the Bavarian political police—apparently "due to his activity as a front soldier"—to found an official national journal for the Federation.[108] Burger published and edited *Deutsches Wandern* for several years. His writings during the Third Reich were essentially repetitions of the May 9 memorandum, to the effect that through hiking "we come to the sources of national power and national life, find our way back to the historical energies and fates of our People and our *Heimat*, and feel ourselves to be part of the national whole, which we must subordinate ourselves to and serve."[109] Burger and other writers repeated such clichés ad nauseam in *Deutsches Wandern* for the next ten years.

Thus, the national leaders managed to benefit from their activities following the Nazi takeover, even if they did not succeed in saving the TVNF as a whole. But what of the thousands of *Naturfreunde* at the district and local levels? The few surviving sources suggest that the situation was complex and varied from place to place. The state expropriated all *Naturfreunde* houses in the course of 1933 and 1934. Some of them were sold to individuals, although most were transferred to the National Federation of Youth Hostels, which itself came increasingly under the control of the Hitler Youth. Many members moved into bourgeois clubs like the German-Austrian Alpine Association and local or regional *Heimat* groups. Many apparently also managed to preserve their sense of comradeship, even taking informal hikes in small groups.[110]

"Strength Through Joy": Workers' Hiking in the Third Reich

Throughout the history of the Third Reich, Nazi leaders feared losing the support of the German people. They saw the huge industrial working class as the most significant source of potential rebellion. Founded on May 10, 1933, after the destruction of the labor movement, the German Labor Front (*Deutsche Arbeitsfront*—DAF) under Robert Ley aimed to control industrial workers through a variety of methods: for example, lengthening the work week to forty-eight hours and shortening workers' leisure time; further rationalizing factory work; and removing all avenues of complaint by punishing dissenting workers and encouraging denunciations. All of these measures were intended to decrease the sense of proletarian class solidarity, and they met with considerable success.[111]

The regime also offered bribes to win the workers' consent. The propaganda's fetishization of "German quality work" in the form of planes, cars, and armaments offered skilled workers a sense of higher status and further alienated them from the less skilled. When foreign laborers were forcibly brought into the country during the war, the state encouraged

German workers to take a place at the top of the racial hierarchy and to treat the foreigners accordingly. In this way many German workers became complicit in Nazi racism.[112]

The regime also made tangible improvements in the industrial workplace. This had long been a demand of social reformers, industrial psychologists, and unions. Apparently in an effort to counterbalance the ratcheting-up of industrial rationalization, the regime carried out practical everyday improvements within a sea of propaganda about how happy workers should be now that the Nazis were in charge. The agent of this negotiation of consent through everyday improvements was a suborganization of the DAF called Strength Through Joy (*Kraft durch Freude*—KDF). The KDF bureaucratic apparatus was immense—thirty-two districts, eighteen thousand local offices, and over seventy-eight thousand representatives in factories and other workplaces.[113]

The regime also used the KDF to gain control over workers' leisure activities. Hitler's decree of November 14, 1933, announced that leisure should be a time of "true recovery," because a "strong-nerved nation" is necessary for carrying out "grand policy."[114] This gave notice of the political instrumentalization of working-class tourism as a means of readying the nation for its future adventures. Nazi-sponsored tourism was an attempt to win the working class's acquiescence while divesting them of the means to agitate for their material interests.[115] Moreover, the regime's desire to keep workers busy even during their free time was a classic example of the totalitarian mentality. As Ley announced, boredom gave rise to criminal ideas, mental dullness, and a feeling of emptiness. "Nothing is more dangerous than that for the state."[116]

The task of controlling working-class tourism was assigned to KDF bureaucrats in the central Office for Travel, Hiking, and Vacationing (*Amt Reisen, Wandern, Urlaub*). As the name indicates, hiking played a central role in KDF propaganda and practice. In their propaganda aimed at workers, KDF spokespersons enjoyed denigrating pre-Nazi hiking, as in the following snide caricature produced by Helmut Urban in 1935:

Sunday mornings with the bowling club and with a cheese sandwich in hand, encircled by Lehmann's seven wild brats and Frau Schultze's pretty dog—Meier from the club plays the harmonica so beautifully—such a sunny little excursion, where the young folks soon disappeared into the bushes and the destination for everyone was always the "Inn at the Green Garland" or some such pub. And how lyrically beautiful was the way home in the evening! Fat Herr Meyer saw everything double and triple, which he blamed on the hike itself! Poor Frau Lehmann lost her self-crocheted purse and quarreled about it with Frau Schultz! And then at the very end, at least an hour later, came Fräulein Käthe with Herr Kurt, yammering about German hiking under the shining moon![117]

This kind of thing was not *real* hiking, Urban declared. Real hiking was "practiced according to the National Socialist leadership principle [*Führerprinzip*]! And that means order, cleanliness, and organization down to the smallest detail." With the help of district "hiking specialists" placed around Germany by the KDF, permanent hiking groups of about fifteen people would be established in apartment houses, villages, and factories. At the head of each group would be a "specially trained hiking leader" who would serve the group as a "politically and personally clean and faultless" model. Not masses of hikers but "small communities" would be able to recuperate and gain new energy for the coming work week. The ultimate purpose of KDF hiking, according to Urban and many other propagandists, was to "express the sense of the German *Volksgemeinschaft*" and "the love for *Heimat* and the soil."[118]

KDF hiking advocates often spoke of overcoming divisions between the city and the country by exposing hikers to different ways of life and work. On the surface, this seems quite similar to the notion of social hiking propagated by the *Naturfreunde* in the 1920s. Needless to say, though, the ultimate purpose of organized Nazi-era hiking was not justice and egalitarian democracy. Moreover, the small hiking communities of the KDF were intended to represent microcosms of a racially homogeneous Aryan nation.

Kraft durch Freude may well have been the most successful of the Nazis' mass organizations in terms of ideological influence. By 1939 some 30 million people—75 percent of the workforce in Germany—were members of the DAF and thus had access to KDF programs.[119] The Office for Travel, Hiking, and Vacation appealed to very real desires in the working class for inexpensive tourism. Because of the general upturn in the economy and membership dues from millions of workers in the DAF, *Kraft durch Freude* could offer very cheap fares for hiking trips and other kinds of excursions. The Franconian district, for instance, offered a six-day hiking trip in the Black Forest that included a train ticket to Stuttgart, a city tour, dinners, breakfasts, and lodgings, all for just twenty marks. Day or weekend hiking trips usually cost less than ten marks. Although there are no figures on the costs of *Naturfreunde* hikes during the Weimar era

KDF propaganda: a pure and homogeneous *Volksgemeinschaft* hikes to achieve "Strength Through Joy." From Anatol von Hübbenet, ed., *Ein Volk erobert die Freude* (Berlin, 1938).

to compare, it seems doubtful that the TVNF was ever able to offer such low-cost hikes. This affordability, as well as the fact that industrial workers were now a captive consumer public, would help explain the apparently high numbers of participants in KDF hikes during the peacetime years of the Third Reich. According to KDF propaganda, 4.1 million "national comrades" had participated in 150,000 hikes by 1938.[120]

With its balance of knowledge and passion, reason and emotion, the *Naturfreunde* naturist ideal held the potential to make the relatively democratic values of Weimar Social Democracy popular among workers who were thirsty for both knowledge and emotional experience. The movement furthermore initiated a protoenvironmentalist awareness of the need to protect the nonhuman nature from the depredations of both industrial capitalism and mass tourism. This organization really did represent one of those alternative pathways for the German people that *might* have succeeded given time. KDF hiking was in every way a betrayal of the democratic *Naturfreunde* tradition. Yet even though this aspect of the Nazi turn to nature took the form of strictly controlled hiking, the regime could count on the support of millions of workers desperate for the solace that nature could bring.

We know little about the ways in which the Nazi dictatorship observed and controlled KDF hiking; however, the state's attempts throughout the 1930s to stamp out the remnants of the *Naturfreunde* are well documented. The regime remained suspicious of former *Naturfreunde* and put them under surveillance in some places. In the Bavarian town of Holzkirchen, for example, the police spied on former members based on the suspicion that they were continuing to meet illegally.[121] Even the organizations of the National Federation for German *Heimat* Hiking and Mountain Climbing were subject to surveillance if their members included former *Naturfreunde*. The police in Hamburg reported on a meeting in late May 1935 of the North German Hiking League, noting that the meeting place was a former *Naturfreunde* house and the hosts a former TVNF local group now called the Hamburg Hiking League. Some seven hundred people attended. During a speech in which the speaker talked about the close relationship between the German people and Adolf Hitler, plainclothes police observers noted that some groups "were whispering and laughing among themselves." When the speaker ended with a "threefold hiking greeting to the Führer" and a singing of the German anthem, a large number in the audience failed to raise their arm and to sing. Some did not even stand up, nor did the band play along! The Hamburg police concluded that the majority in this organization were "Marxist elements" who opposed the state, even if their leader may well be a National Socialist. They had opportunities to associate publicly, and they were hard to observe because they knew each other and were suspicious of newcomers. Therefore, they should be kept from associating.[122]

The report, though written from the police's point of view, hints that the authorities had reason to doubt the commitment of former proletarian hikers to the Third Reich. Although we cannot determine the extent of opposition by former *Naturfreunde* and thus should not overstate it, a number of local groups clearly found ways to defy the regime. The Aschaffenburg *Naturfreunde* burned down their house rather than turn it over to the Nazis. They then rented a substitute hut and hiked there regularly until 1943. District leaders in Swabia advised people not to join bourgeois hiking groups, to work further illegally, and to maintain personal contacts with and between local groups. In the Mittelrhein/ Main district, former Social Democratic and Communist members continued to meet illegally. And in Saxony, former members of the left-wing TVNF opposition were active in the Communist resistance.[123] These examples of defiance fortified the TVNF when they refounded their movement after the Second World War. The *Naturfreunde* became active in conservation, pacifism, and the antinuclear movement in postwar West Germany.[124] And unlike "Strength Through Joy," the Friends of Nature survive in Germany to this day.

Part II   Youth Hiking

3

The Roots of Organized Youth Hiking

Wandervögel, Youth Cultivators, and Moral Panic, 1900–1915

"THERE IS HARDLY ANOTHER ASPECT of the new life of youth that has been so loved and so vilified," announced the Catholic youth movement leader Romano Guardini in 1922.[1] Guardini was referring to a seemingly innocuous activity—hiking. Why did hiking become so popular among Germany's young people? Why did adults begin to organize youth hiking as a method of socializing and disciplining adolescents? Why was hiking controversial? To answer these questions, we must begin in the late Wilhelmine era, during which ambivalent attitudes toward adolescence merged with activist projects of turning to nature.

Adolescence took on unprecedented cultural significance in early twentieth-century Germany. This trend was not peculiar to Germany; it was common throughout industrial Europe in the fin de siècle, an era in which changing family structures, class relations, and educational practices led people to see adolescence as a special period in the individual's life. Young people between the ages of twelve and twenty allegedly possessed a unique physical and psychological identity that set them apart from both children and adults. Although this was thought to be true of both boys and girls, European cultures focused primarily on the adolescent male during this era, because of both the relative privileges enjoyed by males and the service expected of them in public life.

This newly defined period of adolescence had ambiguous overtones. Adults often idealized the teenage years as a time of blooming potential when the individual began to test his capacity for action in the world. Yet teenage boys' relative freedom and desire for self-determination were also

worrisome to many. By the early twentieth century, male youths in industrializing Germany were developing their own collective styles, ethical
ideas, and notions of generational identity. Working-class boys typically
left the family household and the school around the age of fourteen, entering apprenticeships or vocational schools and eventually the industrial
workforce. In their leisure time they became adept at avoiding control
by adult institutions and were thus free to develop their own subcultural
forms. Middle-class adolescents, while remaining longer within the family
and the school system, also found ways to create informal peer groups. A
significant minority of boys from both classes founded youth movements
that encouraged their members to challenge adult authority.

Such activities sparked fears among many adults that the traditional
institutions of socialization—the family and the school in particular—
were in danger of losing their authority over the young. Public discussions
of adolescence among adults also revealed unease about changing class
relations. Cultural activists from the educated middle class, sensing their
loss of status in a society of increasingly capitalistic institutions and values,
tended to define their offspring as the vanguard of an alternative, less materialistic modernity. For them, "youthfulness" (*Jugendlichkeit*) became
"the code word for a renaissance, for the forging of a new, more healthy
world" under educated bourgeois leadership.[2] But the young generation
would serve this purpose only if its energy could be harnessed and channeled toward reform.

Complicating matters was a new discourse of "youth studies"
(*Jugendkunde*) developed by psychologists and sociologists, according to
which puberty spawned a welter of irrational, wayward drives. Under the
influence of this new human science (and no doubt also reacting to life
with their own children), adults were coming to see adolescence as a phase
in which the teenager's personality, psychology, and body were naturally
unstable. Those who aimed to turn youthful energy to the purpose of
reform thus became ever more determined to find the best way to make
adolescents into rational human beings. For even though they idealized
the quality of youthfulness, most adults had little desire to see Germany's
adolescents become a self-determining generation. Strong fears of declining authority over the young lay behind their ever more frequent warnings
of the adolescent male's alleged susceptibility to immorality, juvenile delinquency, and political demagoguery.

The paradoxical combination of idealization and fear in the cultural encounter with adolescence led to vigorous competition among adults to control the socialization of the young. Cultural activists of the educated bourgeoisie, in particular, came to believe that the success of their projects to reform the nation depended on the way in which the young generation matured. Indeed, in the language of late Wilhelmine cultural activism the young generation became rhetorically interchangeable with the nation. Competing plans for national improvement became interwoven with competing narratives of proper development from childhood to adult citizenship. For young people themselves, the new preoccupation with adolescence meant that adults other than their parents began to scrutinize their everyday lives to an unprecedented degree.[3]

This chapter concerns two organized movements that were intent on gaining an influence over young people by exposing them to rural nature during their leisure time. The first was the youth cultivation (*Jugendpflege*) movement, which aimed to inculcate norms of rationality, respectability, and patriotism in German adolescents. Leading youth cultivators were almost all educated elites, including lawyers, doctors, artists, clerics, and above all teachers and pedagogic experts.[4] The second movement comprised a group of organizations of middle-class adolescents and young adults; they were known collectively as the Ramblers (*Wandervögel*).[5] The *Wandervogel* movement contributed passionately to debates over how Germany should come to terms with industrialization, urbanization, and social change. No less a personage than the chairwoman of the League of German Women's Associations, Gertrud Bäumer, saw in the youth movement a new kind of humanism that would reform modern civilization.[6] By 1913 a number of young adult intellectuals who wished to transform the *Wandervögel* into a force for radical change had gained substantial influence within the movement. The passion and idealism of adolescents, they believed, could infuse new energy into the nation, but only if young people were able to liberate themselves from adult control. Under their influence certain segments of the bourgeois youth movement evolved for a short time into a genuinely rebellious force, eloquently criticizing Wilhelmine culture for its greedy materialism, aggressive nationalism, and hypocritical sexual conventions. This countercultural trend culminated in mid-October 1913 with the founding of a new national federation, the Free German Youth, and with an official pledge to reject adult domination.

These movements developed competing ideal narratives of maturation as well as competing concepts of nature. The more radical leaders in the *Wandervogel* movement saw adolescence optimistically as a time of extraordinary creative potential. Rationality was, in their view, overrated; freedom was everything. They therefore aimed to help young people gain a higher degree of self-determination over their lives. They conceived of rural nature as a realm of emotional, moral, and social freedom, a world beyond the reach of adult institutions. Nature was to be explored by small hiking groups under the gentle guidance of sympathetic young adults.

By contrast, the organized youth cultivators were heavily influenced by the notion of adolescence as dangerously irrational. They aspired to inculcate self-discipline, patriotism, and traditional moral values in the young generation. Searching for ways to make their project attractive to teenagers, youth cultivators attempted to appropriate the *Wandervogel* practice of youth hiking and transform it into a disciplinary method. They tended to represent rural nature as a pedagogic counterpart to the urban school, a realm in which adults could help youths progress toward adulthood as rational, productive German citizens.

This chapter investigates how competing notions of turning to nature took hold in both of these movements in the late Wilhelmine era. Three themes will be addressed. The first is the development of the youth cultivation movement and its project of socializing the young. The second is the rise of the *Wandervogel* movement and its attempt to liberate adolescents through hiking. The third theme is the moral panic over adolescent male sexuality that took place in 1913–14, an event in which the two movements clashed with fateful results for the *Wandervögel*.

The Organizations, Ideologies, and Methods of Youth Cultivation

The *Jugendpflege* movement originated around the turn of the twentieth century in response to the perceived danger of wayward proletarian youth. During the second wave of industrialization after 1880, there occurred a mass migration of young males from the countryside to the city. This significantly lowered the average age of urban dwellers. By 1900 almost 4 million mostly male adolescent workers lived in Germany's industrial cities. Among intellectual and political elites the perception grew that young urban workers' increased freedom from traditional adult institutions was a threat to the military and industrial strength of the nation. The rapid growth of the Social Democratic labor movement, with its program of organizing workers into a mass force for democratization, exacerbated this fear of the young male worker.[7]

Indeed, *Jugendpflege* was in organizational terms an offshoot of the preexisting youth welfare (*Jugendfürsorge*) movement, whose emphasis lay in saving "problem" youths from poverty, crime, and moral waywardness. However, youth cultivation took a broader approach, aiming to guide *all* young working people along the path toward respectable adult citizenship. Moreover, youth cultivators began after 1911 to extend their project even further to include not just male workers but adolescents of all classes and both sexes. The rhetoric of *Jugendpflege* also tended to be less overtly disciplinary than that of *Jugendfürsorge*. For instance, in a 1908 speech the Prussian Minister of Trade and Business called for new forms of working with youth based on an appeal to their needs and desires. Youth experts, he asserted, should allow adolescents a degree of self-administration and avoid all attempts at uniformity; they should honor "the understandable effort by young people . . . to spend their free time relaxing and being happy with their peers."[8] The commitment to winning over young people, particularly during their leisure time, was a distinct characteristic of the *Jugendpflege* movement.

Wilhelmine *Jugendpflege* was organizationally divided into sectors that paralleled the ideological divisions in Wilhelmine Germany. The most significant of these domains were bourgeois-reformist, Catholic, Social Democratic, and conservative-militarist. Bourgeois-reformist youth cultivators began to organize into a nationwide movement around 1900. At the forefront were educators, doctors, journalists, lawyers, sociologists, and city administrators. Working on the municipal level, they established an institutional framework that comprised adult-sponsored youth clubs, meeting places called "youth homes" (*Jugendheime*), and, most prominent, voluntary schools for the continuing education of working youths fourteen years of age and older (*Fortbildungsschulen*). By 1912 over 1 million boys and some 290,000 girls attended these schools.[9] Bourgeois *Jugendpfleger* treated adolescents to "character-building" activities such as games, sports, social functions, and library and museum visits. State support for this sector commenced in Prussia in 1909, when the Central Office for Social Welfare established a youth cultivation department to coordinate activities.

Bourgeois youth cultivators believed that the release of urban working teenagers from the restraints of family and school was premature. The allegedly natural irrationality of adolescents, combined with poor living and working conditions in the city, deprived them of orderliness, cleanliness, and patriotism. If these youths failed to reach a respectable and rational adulthood, a catastrophic breakdown of the social order would occur. According to a 1911 speech by the director of a youth home in Stettin, *Jugendpflege* aimed to build "a strong generation that is capable of holding its own in today's competitive workplace"; to teach a positive, accepting attitude toward life and social relations; and "to make manly courage and discipline second nature to young people in order to maintain the incomparable military power of our Fatherland."[10]

Despite the militant nationalism in this speech, the available evidence generally suggests that the majority of bourgeois youth cultivators propounded a less belligerent form of *cultural* nationalism. Typical was the statement by Hertha Siemering of the Prussian Central Welfare Office that "the highest kind of education to citizenship" entailed "delivering the treasures of German culture that we inherited from our fathers undamaged into the hands of those born after us." Behind Siemering's admonition to pass down German culture to the next generation lay an idealistic view of *Jugendpflege* as "nothing less than an awakening of the nation's conscience. . . . It is as if the nation has suddenly paused in its hasty race to compete in the world market to ask itself, 'What will become of our young people? What good will it do us to win the world if we lose our souls?'"[11] Siemering's words expressed widespread concerns among the educated middle class that the nation was becoming too oriented toward capitalist materialism.

Catholic youth cultivators shared this skepticism about industrial capitalism, and they too hoped to save young workers from its demoralizing effects. Parish priests had begun forming local youth groups as early as the 1840s. By the time the Federation of Catholic Boys' and Young Men's Associations was founded in 1896, there were already six hundred of these local groups in existence. This sector grew rapidly after 1900 and included efforts to socialize working girls as well as boys. In 1907 a central *Jugendpflege* office was established in Düsseldorf; and by 1914 there were over thirty-five hundred Catholic youth cultivation clubs with a membership of some 350,000 boys and 150,000 girls. Members came primarily from the urban working class, but some groups also served farmers' children in rural areas.[12]

The socially conservative Catholic *Jugendpfleger*, many of whom were members of the clergy, had the goal of securing the patriarchal family and preserving the Christian character of educational institutions. Their concept of maturation was based on ideals of moral self-discipline and purity. Boys were encouraged to become like Jesus in his willingness to sacrifice for the good of others. Girls were taught to follow Mary's example of chastity as teenagers and motherly love as adults. They were segregated from boys and taught the values of domesticity. Catholic youth cultivators were antisocialist and unwaveringly patriotic. Yet there was also a strong current of social justice and intellectual openness in their discussions of politics. As one Catholic *Jugendpfleger* wrote in 1914, young people on their way to citizenship should learn to see political issues from a variety of points of view so as to recognize their complexity.[13]

The Social Democratic labor movement showed little interest in youth cultivation before 1904. In that year, a grassroots movement of working youths began to draw attention to itself. The genesis of this self-mobilization was the suicide by hanging of a Berlin apprentice following harsh maltreatment by his master. In response, an Association of Apprentices and Young Workers of Berlin was formed. In the same year another protest movement of young workers was founded in southern Germany.[14] Soon these youths moved beyond their demand for legal protection of apprentices and attacked militarism as the cause of Germany's political backwardness. Most leaders of the Free Trade Unions and the Social Democratic Party were hostile to these initiatives from the beginning, declaring that they threatened labor movement solidarity. Most likely they simply did not take the opinions of working youths very seriously. The Social Democrats would not be lectured to by teenagers, declared the unionist Robert Schmidt, and instead of wasting their money on the youth movement's "bad magazines," young workers should buy "good sausages."[15]

In 1908 the Reichstag passed the Association Law, which forbade anyone under eighteen to join a political organization. For once, Social Democratic leaders welcomed a repressive law, for it put an end to the grassroots youth movement and enabled the SPD to regain control over some 10,500 young workers. The party and the unions henceforth took up the tasks of youth work in tandem. The unions undertook to enforce the rights of apprenticeship and offer continued professional training; and a new cadre of youth cultivators within the SPD began to found "youth educational clubs" (*Jugendbildungsvereine*) to expose adolescents to high culture and teach them about socialism. In 1909 the party founded a central office to coordinate youth cultivation under the direction of Friedrich

Ebert. As the Social Democrats gained more political power in the state and national parliaments, their *Jugendpflege* network spread rapidly. By October 1913 there were 655 youth educational clubs with approximately 90,000 members, most of whom were male adolescents in the manufacturing industries.[16]

Like all Wilhelmine youth cultivators, the socialists aimed to guide youths along the path toward good citizenship. They too emphasized helping young workers mature into morally upright human beings, but concepts of personal liberty played a stronger role in their rhetoric than in that of bourgeois and Catholic *Jugendpflege*. Working citizens, they argued, should be capable of arriving at their own judgments; they should work to improve their own education through the study of the natural and social sciences; and they should learn to help in the general improvement of humanity.[17] Club life in the evenings and on weekends included discussions of literature, art, and science as well as physical exercise and artistic activities. Due to the Association Law, discussion of current politics was forbidden. (This may have been something of a relief for working youths; as one participant in a club recalled years later, "Our idealism was deadened by sheer exhaustion."[18]) Nevertheless, hostile state authorities used the law as an excuse to intimidate club members, placing them under police surveillance and carrying out periodic raids. Yet the authorities had difficulty finding legal grounds to ban socialist *Jugendpflege* because they were unable to demonstrate the clubs' political nature.[19]

The fourth branch of Wilhelmine *Jugendpflege* took shape in 1911 as a reaction against socialism. This conservative-militarist sector aimed to teach young people of all class backgrounds to value hierarchical authority, absolute obedience, and self-sacrifice for the nation. There were two important conservative organizations. The first was the German League of Boy Scouts, which was founded in 1911 and rapidly gained a membership of 80,000 youths by 1912. The Scouts soon showed an interest in reaching girls as well. In 1912 a group of conservative women founded the German Scouting League for Young Girls, whose purpose was to "protect young girls from the dangers of the big city" and to prepare them for motherhood. By 1914 there were thirty-one groups for girls with approximately 3,000 members.[20]

The leaders of the German Boy Scouts were military men who saw the world as a collection of aggressive nations. The model of good citizenship that they presented to young people was Germany's own Kaiser

Wilhelm II, whom they portrayed as "the premier Scout of our time and a shining example, not only for youth and their leaders but also for all classes of the German People." Their historic ideal for the German nation as a whole was Sparta, the Greek nation that "was most militarily skilled and had the strongest character." They refused all relations with their Scouting counterparts in other countries and admonished their members not to use any foreign words. Their activities emphasized quasi-military training by means of orientation exercises, drills, and marching.[21]

The second conservative group, the Young Germany League (*Jungdeutschlandbund*) of Prussia, was a federation of male *Jugendpflege* organizations founded in 1911. Its goal was the "necessary self-discipline of the entire nation" through "the hardening of the body, the sharpening of the senses, and the raising of practical intelligence and masculine virtue in general."[22] These characteristics were to be impressed upon adolescents through team sports and "terrain games" (*Geländespiele*). Exercises based on the principle of uniformity, such as group marching, would help the young transcend class, religious, and political differences.

Bourgeois *Jugendpflege* organizations and vocational schools contributed a large membership to the Young Germany League. This was due less to a commitment to the League's goals and methods than to the fact that it enjoyed strong financial support from the Prussian state. The League channeled some of the state's funds for youth welfare to its member organizations; therefore, it made financial sense to join. But many bourgeois youth cultivators disagreed adamantly with the League's militaristic training methods, and consequently their organizations' everyday participation was limited. Catholic youth cultivators were even more critical, decrying what they saw as the League's overemphasis on physical activity at the expense of moral education. They refused to associate with the League until 1913, when a special agreement allowed them to join officially while remaining autonomous in practice. Thus, although the *Jungdeutschlandbund* claimed a membership of 750,000 members by 1914, only some 69,000 youths really participated in the day-to-day activities of the League's local branches.[23] Membership in the conservative-militarist sector was probably not more than 90,000, placing it on a par with the socialist sector but far below the bourgeois and Catholic sectors in terms of popularity.

Most early youth cultivation efforts enjoyed little financial support from the Wilhelmine state. The turning point came in 1911, when the

Prussian Minister of Religious, Educational, and Medical Affairs, August von Trott zu Solz, presented a new decree to the state parliament: "The task of youth cultivation is to help build a young generation that is happy, physically strong, morally fit, God-fearing, public-spirited, and filled with love for the Fatherland."[24] The minister proposed a state-supported system of regional, district, and municipal *Jugendpflege* committees throughout Prussia. His speech on this occasion clearly revealed the project's conservative, antisocialist character. Trott zu Solz characterized *Jugendpflege* as a battle against political seducers of youth, "those false friends of the young who poison every heart with hatred, who destroy respect for authority, who smother cheerfulness in envy and wrath," and who "make a travesty of the Savior's command to 'Let the children come to me' by offering to young people the leadership of Fräulein Rosa Luxemburg."[25] Clearly aiming to cripple the socialist youth education clubs, the decree promised financial support only to those organizations deemed loyal to the state.

With the encouragement of Kaiser Wilhelm himself, the parliament voted to finance *Jugendpflege*. The result was a new bureaucracy that coordinated activities among the various nonsocialist organizations, maintained contact with relevant government ministries, and distributed state subsidies to member clubs. The Prussian state allocated 1 million marks to *Jugendpflege* in 1911, and by 1914 that amount had risen to 4 million marks. The other states—with the exception of Württemberg, Baden, and Hesse—soon followed Prussia's lead by establishing similar bureaucracies. Socialist clubs were always excluded, and measures to repress them through police surveillance were now openly discussed in the state parliaments.[26]

As a result of this trend toward state-supported, antisocialist bureaucratization, the influence of bourgeois, Catholic, and conservative youth cultivators grew rapidly throughout Germany after 1911. In 1913 over 26,000 adults participated in state-sponsored training courses for youth cultivators in Prussia alone. That year, some 1 million people between the ages of twelve and twenty-one belonged to adult-directed youth organizations, including roughly one-fifth of all working-class male adolescents.[27]

Yet, as their influence increased, youth cultivators grew more nervous about their attempts to guide young people along the proper path toward maturity. Some began to voice their disappointment that only a minority of working youths had been integrated into their institutions.[28] This loss of confidence was due in part to the failure to shut down Social Democratic youth cultivation. A deeper source of their crisis of confidence, however, was the discourse of youth studies, which increasingly drew youth cultivators' attention to adolescent sexuality.

As advanced by sociologists, psychologists, doctors, and sexologists, *Jugendkunde* asserted that each child "progressed through all the previous stages of civilization in the child's education toward self-understanding."[29] Youth studies was also intertwined with the imperialist "civilizing mission" narrative of development from irrational barbarism to enlightenment and reason. (Indeed, the German Institute for Youth Research was founded in 1913 as a branch of the Hamburg Colonial Institute.) Spokespersons for *Jugendkunde* defined adolescence as a period of impulsive, irrational natural energies. The physician Rudolf Schneider, for example, spoke of "a period of swelling energy in which the vital energy of the turbulently evolving mind and body is under the utmost stress."[30] In a culture obsessed with controlling human energy,[31] such a characterization of adolescence was bound to cause great concern. Thus, youth cultivators increasingly feared that their attempts to socialize youths into rational adults would be undermined by teenagers' fundamentally *ir*rational character. In addition, *Jugendkunde* implied that the problem was not so much social as natural, that is, irrationality was not just a problem of working-class youths but of *all* young people.

The chief culprit, according to the alleged experts on youth, was the adolescent sex drive. This is not surprising in the context of early twentieth-century Europe with its intense public discussions of the characteristics and implications of sexuality. Such discussions stemmed in part from the new science of sexology, which had a positivist tendency to research, define, and categorize "normal" and "abnormal" sexuality. But the preoccupation with sexuality was also essentially political, for it expressed in a metaphorical way deep unease about social conflict and imperialist competition. Deviant, nonreproductive sexuality came to represent one aspect of the "emergency" faced by the industrial nation from both within and without.

In Germany the years 1907 through 1914 constituted a watershed in the cultural association of deviant sexuality with internal and international conflict. One of the primary objects of public attention was male homosexuality. The Eulenburg scandal that began in 1907, in which prominent members of Kaiser Wilhelm II's entourage were accused of homosexuality, drew negative public attention to the allegedly traitorous characteristics of sexually deviant men. The controversy also deepened existing concerns about homoerotic bonding within a civil society in which predominantly male groups were the norm.[32] This helps to explain why the figure of the gay man became a principal demon for conservatives. In a 1908 speech by a prominent physician and moral apostle, Dr. Max Gruber, we learn that just as the Greeks and the Romans ran aground on sexual license, "so must every nation fall into ruin that sees the sexual only as a source of enjoyment, rather than honoring it as a means for the breeding of fit offspring." Sexual libertarians, "foolish female advocates of free love," and "the disgusting breed of perverts and homosexuals" were "criminals against the life of the German nation." Homosexual men should all be shut away, crushed, beaten to death, or otherwise silenced: "Do not let yourself be stopped by false compassion. You may happen to kill the occasional genuine freak or even some mentally ill persons, but they all have to die, for they are infectious! There are supposedly fifty thousand homosexuals in Berlin alone, and I would not be surprised if tomorrow there are one hundred thousand!"[33] Gruber, like most homophobes at the time, accused gay men of pedophilia. Many equally hysterical tirades of the era held up for public contempt the stereotype of the pedophile who was out to "convert" adolescent boys, making them unfit for citizenship and military service. This accusation was one of the chief hindrances to the fledgling gay rights movement in its struggle against the criminalization of homosexuality.[34]

Another source of the preoccupation with sexuality in Wilhelmine culture was the polarizing debate over women's rights. By 1913 the bourgeois women's movement had attained a membership of over 330,000; in the same year antifeminists organized themselves into the German League for the Struggle Against Women's Liberation. Antifeminists were at the forefront of the influential Christian morality leagues as well. They were obsessed with their own demons of uncontrolled female sexuality, above all the prostitute, whom they accused of having an overwhelming desire to seduce and infect male adolescents. Leading sex reform organizations, such as the German Society to Battle Venereal Disease and the League for the Protection of Mothers, shared this view of prostitution. Much of their rhetorical energy was spent scaring adolescent males away from prostitutes by raising the specter of disease.[35]

These seductive demons of male homosexuality and female prostitution together sharpened fears that Germany was in danger of losing its youth and its future. The discourse of seduction intensified youth cultivators' unease about adolescent sexuality. Many were convinced that adolescents, already subject to their naturally irrational drives, could not stave off sexual risks on their own, and the threat was even greater given the presence of deviant adults. Indeed, the sexual nature of the adolescent seemed to be the largest hindrance on the path toward adulthood. This preoccupation with adolescent sexuality was the primary reason why youth cultivators began after 1910 to extend their focus beyond working male youths to all adolescents. Youth cultivators now took it upon themselves to win over youths from all social backgrounds and shouldered the task of directing youthful drives into nonsexual channels.

This expanding perception of the problem to be solved by *Jugend-pflege* intensified the debate over methods. Beginning in 1911 representatives from the bourgeois, Catholic, and conservative sectors were obliged to work together within the new, state-supported *Jugendpflege* bureaucracy. Finding consensual methods became necessary to maintaining support from the state, the churches, the schools, parents, and the young people themselves. Moreover, youth cultivators were determined to compete against the Social Democrats by offering a solid alternative to socialist practice. Consensus was not always easy for such an ideologically diverse movement, as can be seen in the ongoing debates between the conservative advocates of military discipline and those who preferred more emphasis on character-building activities. Nor did a consensus emerge on the issue of sex education. Sex reform organizations called for lectures by school doctors on the risks of masturbation and prostitutes. While some bourgeois youth cultivators supported this idea, conservatives and Catholics were adamantly opposed. The Catholic Bishops' Conference denounced sex education lectures, coeducational exercise, and any other activities that did not teach a sense of shame and an admiration of chastity. "What we need today," they wrote, "is not more discussion of these matters, but silence."[36] Moreover, parents' associations and the states' educational authorities rejected sex education as an intrusion into the family's privacy. The school board in Munich, for instance, demonstratively sent a pamphlet to parents entitled "Sexual Pedagogy in the Home."[37] Given such resistance, sex education in vocational schools or *Jugendpflege* clubs remained taboo.

Nevertheless, three methods had become broadly accepted among nonsocialist youth cultivators by 1914. The first involved a concerted attack on "trash and smut" in the mass media. Youth cultivators vilified pulp fiction with a violent or erotic content. In this they had the support of state authorities, who believed that reading such publications made adolescents "lazy, scatter-brained, crude, and violent."[38] Interestingly, Social

Democrats concurred in this attack; the difference was that they cast smut in explicitly political terms as bourgeois. The leading SPD *Jugendpflege* journal tended to describe the effects of escapist bourgeois literature in terms of disease and death:

Creeping poison! What would you say to a person who imbibed, day after day, stuff that slowly but surely undermined his health? Such a person is nothing more or less than a suicide. But is not also he who poisons his spirit—a person's most magnificent possession—a suicide? These books poison their young readers by giving them a basically wrong view of the world and of life.[39]

Youth cultivators in all sectors banned pulp fiction within their organizations while providing their charges with lists of edifying books and visits to libraries. The emphasis on exposing youths to ennobling works of high culture was prominent throughout the *Jugendpflege* movement.[40]

The second consensual method of late Wilhelmine *Jugendpflege* was the separation of the sexes. Only Social Democratic youth cultivators saw coeducation as a way to counterbalance the erotic temptations that adolescents faced. Their youth educational clubs, they hoped, would reduce adolescent sexual drives by "ennobling" everyday social interactions between the sexes.[41] Nonsocialist *Jugendpfleger* explicitly rejected such notions as dangerous, remaining committed to the dominant cultural view whereby the sexes should be kept within separate spheres.

This gender segregation was in accord with the states' view of *Jugendpflege*. The aforementioned 1911 Prussian *Jugendpflege* decree had excluded girls' organizations from its bureaucracy. As the Social Democrats pointed out at the time, girls were excluded largely because the state had little interest in people who could neither fight nor vote.[42] By 1913, however, youth cultivators had begun to convince the states to support female *Jugendpflege* by claiming that the deficient health of working-class girls was hurting the nation demographically. Here again the focus was on adolescent sexuality: girls were susceptible to the immoral temptations of the city, and their sex drive robbed them of the ability to resist. Their seduction was leading to thousands of miscarriages, premature births, and out-of-wedlock births.[43] This pronatalist argument influenced the Prussian state's decision to fund female *Jugendpflege*, as is evident in its decree of April 30, 1913:

Whoever desires to build a physically and morally strong, God-fearing, and loyal generation must see to it that the young female is healthy in mind and body. She must be internally sound and armed with the knowledge and abilities that are indispensable for her future profession as helpmate of the man, educator of children, cultivator of family happiness, and custodian of good morals.[44]

The decree made it clear that girls were to remain mostly segregated from boys in their everyday activities. Increased state support for separate female *Jugendpflege* activities in Prussia and other states after 1913 opened up a new field of welfare activity for upper-class women. The states began to include women in their youth cultivation training courses; and women's entry into the *Jugendpflege* bureaucracy gave them considerable decision-making power on the local and regional levels.[45]

Most significant for the purposes of this study was the third consensual method of youth cultivation—group hiking. In Germany the notion that physical training could be used to teach self-discipline and patriotism had its origins in the early nineteenth-century exercise clubs (*Turnvereine*). Such clubs became some of the most popular civic associations in Imperial Germany.[46] The focus on hiking originated with the Romantic movement of the late eighteenth and early nineteenth centuries, when such cultural dignitaries as Goethe, Alexander Humboldt, and Caspar David Friedrich sang its praises as a form of communion between the reverent individual and the natural world.

This Romantic hiking tradition was central to the *Wandervogel* youth movement, as will be discussed later in this chapter. For now it is important to point out that the Wilhelmine youth cultivators viewed hiking not in Romantic terms as a form of nature worship, but as a practical method for improving young people's physical, mental, and moral health simultaneously. *Jugendpflege* rhetoric particularly stressed hiking's alleged ability to reduce the pesky sexual drive of adolescents. For instance, one Dr. Touton of the Society to Battle Venereal Disease advised middle-class boys: "If your studies and subsequent occupation allow time for other pursuits, then climb out of the lowlands up to the heights, where you will see and feel the transcendent workings of nature in all their glory. . . . There you will be lifted above the stifling lower realm of physical drives."[47] There were several other reasons why youth cultivators considered hiking beneficial for young people. Boys and girls of all classes could take part in hikes, and the health benefits, especially for working adolescents suffering from the crowded, dirty conditions of city life, were considered superior to those produced by more strenuous forms of sport. Hiking supposedly made young people more rational in their thinking, created a sense of well-being and contentment, and taught them to love their local and national *Heimat*.

Conservative-militarist youth cultivators also thought that hiking could help them teach adolescents how to orient themselves in the landscape, estimate distances, and endure physical challenges.[48]

Youth cultivators saw the activity of hiking as intrinsically nonpolitical, as a neutral ground upon which youths from different classes could meet and get to know each other. For the author Anton Fendrich, hiking into the rural countryside temporarily freed people from the political ideologies and social divisions that distorted everyday life. He admonished hiking leaders, "Do not drill a political and social dogma into the youthful soul that does not of its own free will swear to it, but abstain from such mischief! . . . Anything else is an accursed misuse of that part of creation—nature—that humanity has not yet dishonored with its torment and hatred."[49] Such attacks on the politicization of the nature experience were no doubt aimed squarely at socialist *Jugendpfleger*, who viewed hiking as an excellent way to promote subcultural solidarity among young workers.[50]

Late Wilhelmine youth cultivators guided thousands of young people on excursions into the rural countryside. Local *Jugendpflege* committees in Prussia, for example, held some twenty-nine hundred hikes of male youths in 1913 alone. The hiking consensus also led to the founding of a variety of local federations, such as the Berlin Central Committee for Exercise and Youth Cultivation (1911) and the Munich Local Committee for Youth Alpine Hiking (1913). Not only bourgeois, Catholic, and conservative youth cultivators joined such umbrella organizations; so did prominent local educators and sporting groups.[51]

The organization that was eventually to become the foremost popularizer of youth hiking, however, was the National Federation for German Youth Hiking and Youth Hostels (*Reichsverband für deutsches Jugendwandern und Jugendherberge*). Richard Schirrmann, a schoolteacher in the Ruhr industrial region, was the founder of the German youth hostel network. According to Wilhelm Münker, an early colleague who later wrote a history of the hostels, Schirrmann was a reformist pedagogue who was never content simply to impart knowledge inside the classroom. He shared with his students, most of whom lived in crowded working-class areas, an "urge to be in the free outdoors" and wanted to use hiking as a means of education. But Schirrmann was hindered from taking his students on longer forays due to a scarcity of overnight shelters. In 1911 he became involved with a regional *Jugendpflege* organization, the Central Committee for Folk and Youth Games, which supported his plan for a network of hostels that would give hikers a clean, inexpensive place to spend the night.[52]

Schirrmann appears to have been extremely talented at sparking enthusiasm for the hostel concept. He typically couched his appeals for funding in terms of national decline, which youth hiking could help reverse:

German national power is in the process of disappearing. No one doubts this today. Things are worst in our large cities and industrial districts. The municipalities, public service organizations, and noble friends of mankind sacrifice millions and millions in an attempt to restore nervous human beings to health and strength. If the situation is to improve, we must begin with the young. If we create a healthy young generation, we will have a healthy, strong nation.[53]

This argument held great appeal for conservative youth cultivators, the state, and the military. By 1913, eighty-three youth hostels had been built with state support, and the army had opened nearly three hundred of its barracks to organized hiking groups. Schirrmann's speech to the Young Germany League at its annual meeting in 1914 resulted in a commitment to contribute between twenty thousand and thirty thousand marks annually. There was also considerable support from bourgeois and Catholic *Jugendpflege* organizations, many of whom had joined the National Federation of Youth Hostels by the time the war broke out and halted its building projects.[54]

Above all, the apparent popularity of hiking among young people made it seem an ideal method of socializing youth. Participation in *Jugendpflege* groups was voluntary, and youth cultivators were obliged to win over young people by making their leisure activities seem fun. They saw hiking as a way to teach young people the proper values while providing them with an experience of relative freedom from overt adult authority. With striking frequency, hiking advocates told the adult leaders of group hikes not to push their charges too hard and to remember that "hiking is not the same thing as classroom teaching. Learning will simply occur as you go along."[55]

The *Wandervogel* Movement and Its Ideal of Youthful Freedom

The concept of the group hike as an experience of youthful freedom was not original to youth cultivators. They appropriated it from the relatively independent middle-class youth movement known as the *Wandervögel*. The *Wandervogel* movement had its roots in the small Stenographic Club of adolescent male students and young male teachers formed in 1897 at the humanistic secondary school (*Gymnasium*) in Berlin-Steglitz. The purpose was to organize small group hikes into the rural environs. Apparently the school's directors saw nothing wrong with the club taking two-week trips during their school holidays, such as the one to the Bohemian Forest in 1899. In 1901 Karl Fischer, a former student at the Steglitz *Gymnasium* who had taken a teaching job there, moved to make the club more official. He called a meeting of nine other young male acquaintances, including four writers, a doctor, three students, and an apprentice, to found a committee for student hiking. In searching for a name, some of them recalled seeing an epitaph on a tombstone in a Berlin graveyard that read, "Who gave you wandering birds (*Wandervögeln*) the knowledge never to go astray?" They adopted the name, and the director of the Steglitz *Gymnasium* lent his support by helping to advertise the club to students and their parents.[56]

Over the following decade the *Wandervogel* idea spread quickly to those schools whose teachers and directors saw a need for pedagogic innovation. Moreover, the movement gradually took on a semi-independent status vis-à-vis the school system. By 1911 three main national *Wandervogel* organizations had emerged with a total (unofficial) membership of some 18,000 adolescents between the ages of twelve and twenty. In addition, young adults who were former members of *Wandervögel* groups began to form their own university student organizations, such as the German Academic Volunteer Corps (*Deutsche akademische Freischar*). This added some 6,000 more members, so that by 1913 the organizations affiliated with the independent youth movement numbered approximately 24,000 people. Most of them came from middle-class Protestant families, and around 90 percent were males—not surprising since less than 10 percent of students in the secondary school and university system were female.[57]

The early success of the movement was due to its effective popularization by young male adult teachers and reformist school authorities. Indeed, the movement depended heavily on adult support. Each *Wandervogel* group had an adult oversight committee, a Council of Parents and Friends made up of parents and teachers as well as local notables, including writers, artists, and pedagogic experts. And because some states had regulations that restricted youths' participation in clubs to keep them from aping college fraternities, the *Wandervögel* counted as official members only the parents and other adult supporters of the rank-and-file members.[58]

Given the importance of adults and the school in the *Wandervogel*

The first *Wandervögel*: the Stenographic Club Steglitz on a hike in Berlin-Grunewald in 1897. By permission of Archiv der deutschen Jugendbewegung.

organizational structure, the youth movement can only be called independent in a relative sense. How did this movement differ from the bourgeois-reformist branch of the youth cultivation movement discussed earlier? Like the youth cultivators, adult supporters of the *Wandervögel* as members of the educated middle class no doubt saw the socialization of adolescents as a way to maintain their leadership in the cultural realm. The key difference seems to lie in a somewhat more positive attitude toward adolescence among the adult supporters of the *Wandervögel*. The friends of the *Wandervögel* were more willing to grant their children a relatively autonomous realm for self-discovery and self-determination—that is, small hiking groups and their guides, who were either older adolescents or, more commonly, young adult teachers. Why? The evidence is scarce, but we can reasonably infer that the *Wandervögel*'s adult supporters valued youthful creativity and emotion more than did the youth cultivators, who prized rationality and discipline above all. Possibly they were influenced by the nostalgia for youthful adventure found in classics of Romantic literature like Eichendorff's *The Life of a Good-for-Nothing* with its good-hearted, rambling young protagonist.[59]

In any case, what began as a simple leisure movement was increasingly cast by its supporters as a "rebellion of the learned" in which youth would be the "source of our rescue."[60] Many young participants and guides came to see their movement in this way as well. They experimented in a kind of "rebellious primitivism" that included elements of *Lebensreform*, including "reformed" clothing, abstinence from alcohol, and occasional nudism in some groups.[61] And they developed a neo-Romantic conception of the pastoral landscape as a realm of freedom and ennoblement. Writers for *Wandervogel* journals represented the simple act of venturing into that emancipatory nature as ennobling, an act of discovering a more genuine alternative to Wilhelmine society. As one anonymous author wrote, "From the first hike on the first day, I was there, and that was my world. An honest world, not the world of illusions that was called 'society.'"[62] This vision of nature can already be seen in one of the earliest texts of the Steglitz Stenographic Club, an 1898 article by Hermann Hoffmann. "Go out into the wide, open world with a light heart," he wrote, "free yourselves from the anxieties and pressures of the school, from worries about the future, from the supervision of your every step. Be your own man and find your own way." Moreover, hiking "would benefit some of our young gentlemen who pass their leisure time in the city clad in gloves and elegant clothes, instead of refreshing and steeling the body and mind in free nature." Hoffmann continued:

Through hiking, the city boy breaks the habit of perceiving every gust of wind, every rain shower, every wet boot as another nail in his coffin. Instead he . . . ventures out, laughing, into the wind and the rain. So go out into forest and field, German boys, and open your eyes to the life and activity of nature. Long live hiking, which sharpens the senses and keeps the spirit pure and fresh![63]

Independent hiking was also a natural way for young people to become patriotic. "The more you see its beauties with your own eyes, [and] the more familiar you become with its inhabitants . . . the more you will learn to truly love our magnificent Fatherland!"[64] Thus, in *Wandervogel* ideology, hiking exposed young people to freedom in nature. Yet that freedom was to be used not merely for personal enjoyment but for self-education in toughness, self-discipline, and patriotism. The motto "Work on yourselves; make your hikes more and more exemplary" became central to the movement's ideology.[65] The sense of elite mission and commitment to the more honest world of nature was more evident than ever by 1913, when we find the youth movement representing its origins mythically: "Who knows, whence the *Wandervögel* came? No one. A great impulse shot through the people; the individual felt stirred and attracted but knew not by what."[66]

As a movement proudly representing a young generation that had never had much of a public voice before, the *Wandervögel* were bound eventually to draw the attention of outsiders. Unfortunately for the movement, when that attention finally came, it was mostly negative. Three developments in 1913 led to an intense moral panic regarding the *Wandervogel* movement among politicians, moral apostles, and youth cultivators that lasted until the outbreak of war in August 1914. In each case, the initiators of controversy were individuals and groups affiliated with the youth movement who had radical ideas about youthful autonomy and adolescent sexuality. They believed that the youth movement had the potential to become a truly effective force for reform—if only the natural impulses of adolescence, including its sexual energies, were given room to thrive.[67]

The first of these developments stemmed from the most radical of the three national *Wandervogel* organizations, the *Jung-Wandervögel*. The degree to which the three groups took a consciously oppositional stance to Wilhelmine society varied in 1913. The published rhetoric of both the *Alt-Wandervogel* organization and the *Wandervogel, eingetragener Verein* (WVEV) was respectful of the family, the school, and the military. The small *Jung-Wandervogel* group was another matter, claiming to be the only organization that truly lived up to the ideal of youthful autonomy. This defiant tone resulted in part from its controversial founding. In 1910 some directors of the *Alt-Wandervogel* group had denounced their colleague Wilhelm Jansen, a popular and charismatic leader, for his alleged homosexuality. Jansen had seceded and taken supporters with him to found the *Jung-Wandervögel*.[68] This remained the smallest of the three organizations, with only 2,300 members in 1913. But in their published rhetoric the *Jung-Wandervögel* gleefully attacked "mentally constricting" adult institutions, including the youth cultivation movement in general and the Young Germany League with its "superficial soldierly game playing" in particular. As the *Jung-Wandervogel* Willie Jahn argued in a speech in October 1913, the purpose of the *Wandervogel* movement was to let young people be among their peers. Together they should be allowed to "discuss all of their wishes and values" without interference from adult authorities. The leader of the group should be himself a peer, "never a superior, always a friend with the same rights and the same duties as everyone else." The influx of youth cultivators into the other *Wandervogel* organizations, Jahn concluded, had divested them of all elements of youthful freedom.[69]

It was therefore no coincidence that the first publication to raise controversial sexual issues was written by a supporter of the *Jung-Wandervögel*. At the end of 1912, the young psychologist Hans Blüher published a book entitled *The German Wandervogel Movement as an Erotic Phenomenon*, which celebrated the movement's potential to become a truly reformist, morally heroic league of males (*Männerbund*). Its most shocking feature, however, was Blüher's theory of homoerotic psychological ties between adolescent *Wandervögel* and their adult male leaders. According to Blüher, charismatic leaders like Wilhelm Jansen were not "the so-called normal men," men who had "no creative or organizational talent," but hypermasculine homosexuals or "inverts." They were the "calm center of every youth movement, the actual commanders-in-chief of youth. [They are] often revolutionary figures. Passionately they devote their entire lives to helping youth. [They are] usually contemptuous of the teaching professionals who do it for money. There are no youth groups without them."[70] Blüher maintained, without offering any concrete evidence, that many adolescents in the movement developed passionate feelings for their inverted leaders. This was to be expected given their "romantic, wild, and often unrestrained" activities. And because the *Wandervögel* emphasized hiking, the kinds of martial drills that could "prevent feelings of love from boiling over" through a rhythmic dispersal of libidinal energy were not available to the boys. Thus, Blüher provocatively quoted one unnamed leader's statement, "Every successful hike is a love story."[71]

Yet Blüher went on to assure his readers that such attractions were not harmful, since neither the boys nor their leaders acted upon them in a sexual way. In fact, homoeroticism was beneficial, for the inverted leaders were able to channel their sexual energy into the noble task of guiding the young toward adulthood. The boys themselves were going through a necessary stage of development in which homoerotic feelings were common and, for most, temporary. Indeed, not only would the majority of *Wandervogel* youths conclude their adolescence as "normal" heterosexual men but the influence of inverts would improve their adult relations with women. Homoerotic adolescent friendships, Blüher asserted, taught boys a "style of love" devoid of the "false tenderness" and psychological sadism that characterized heterosexual relationships.[72]

Blüher was no progressive. He was vehemently antifeminist and socially conservative, and he harped on the racial superiority of the *Wandervögel*. However, in casting "inverts" as beneficial for the nation and in calling for an end to their persecution, his book was subversive for its time. His assertions sharply contradicted the aforementioned dominant conceptions of male homosexuality as unnatural, effeminate, and traitorous. His assertions, combined with general knowledge of the sex-segregated character of most *Wandervogel* organizations, were bound to spark adult fears of homosexual seduction.[73]

Leaders in the largest group, the WVEV, responded to Blüher's book by swearing to anyone who would listen that his thesis was utterly ridiculous. They sent an open letter to hundreds of school directors in February 1913 assuring them that the WVEV would purge anyone suspected of homosexual tendencies.[74] Edmund Neuendorff, a youth cultivator who took over as national leader of the WVEV in September, called the book "offensive to the highest degree" and guaranteed his audience that homoeroticism was insignificant in the movement.[75] Outside the youth movement, though, Blüher's thesis drew little attention initially. Public concerns swelled later within the context of the moral panic that was directly ignited by two other radical developments in 1913—the founding of a new organization of youths known as the *Anfang* Circle, and the national conference of the *Wandervogel* movement at a mountain called the Hoher Meissner.

The Beginning (*Der Anfang*), a monthly journal that began publishing in May 1913, was the mouthpiece of a group of some three thousand secondary school pupils and university students in Berlin and Vienna. Since their affiliation to the youth movement was rather loose—some belonged to *Wandervogel* or student organizations; others did not—this group became known simply as the *Anfang* Circle. One-third of the membership was Jewish, including some who later became quite well-known intellectuals, notably the psychologist Siegfried Bernfeld and the philosopher Walter Benjamin, who in 1913 was a student at Freiburg University. *Der Anfang* was a conscious effort on the part of some articulate young people to create a new countercultural arena of critical discussion. As contributor Georges Barbizon announced in one article, "Now the young generation wants to take matters into their own hands. It will attempt [reform] according to the motto 'By the young, for the young!' A sphere of youthful public opinion must take shape."[76]

Opposed to all forms of adult authority, including youth cultivation, *Der Anfang* was the first students' journal in German history to reach the public legally and without the approval of school authorities. In order to exist legally, however, any publication written by minors had to have an official adult editor. The reformist pedagogic theorist and teacher Gustav Wyneken agreed to take the title of responsible editor of *Der Anfang*, but he left the young writers' contributions untouched. This hands-off policy was in keeping with Wyneken's idealistic goal of founding schools that would offer adolescents a "higher style of youthful community." These Free School Communities (*Freie Schulgemeinden*) would be assemblies of self-educating youths of both sexes, independent of state control and under the mentorship of sympathetic adults. He counterposed this ideal of self-determining youth to the goals of youth cultivation by adults, writing that in the Free School Community, "No one is cultivated, but rather each person will cultivate himself." Individuals would learn on their own the self-discipline necessary to reach a higher level of cultural and social advancement, becoming "better, more beautiful, purer, and more honest." Wyneken's ideas about sexuality were particularly radical. Like Blüher, Wyneken believed that the education of adolescents could "benefit from eros, from the drives and passions," although he remained vague on just how this would proceed in practice.[77]

Gustav Wyneken's ideal of an autonomous, self-educating generation became the guiding principle of the young writers for *Der Anfang*. Beginning with the first issue in May 1913, they published their own unabashedly critical articles as well as essays sent in by other young people. They also arranged "salons" (*Sprechsäle*) for adolescents in Vienna, Munich, Berlin, Heidelberg, Göttingen, and other cities. Within these venues the *Anfang* Circle criticized the school, the church, and the family for failing to produce individuals who could contribute fully to society. *Der Anfang* represented adolescence as a unique time of freedom. As Walter Benjamin dramatically intoned, "We are seized by the feeling that youth lasts only one brief night, so fill it with ecstasy!" Another contributor wrote, "Youth lives like the lilies of the field; never again is the individual so free as in his youth. His existence is not yet determined by economic objectives, the struggle to survive, or the 'seriousness of life.'" Because young people had not yet lost their idealism, they had the potential to improve society through the "world-historical work" of radical criticism. Adolescents "measure all things against their highest ideals, and all things become problematic."[78]

One of the things that these young people criticized specifically was the militarism that was so pronounced in Imperial Germany. The way to serve the nation was not with "patriotic hollering" but through "positive work for a better life for the nation's youth and for a deeper understanding of youth's needs."[79] The most daring aspect of the *Anfang* Circle's rhetoric, however, was the dramatic emphasis on sexuality. They accused adults of damaging adolescents by either ignoring or trying to suppress their sexual drives:

Your moral rules and opinions, your social prejudices, your superficiality and lack of conscience, and your greedy capitalism are raping the young, [and] their bodies rebel in wild pain as they are confronted again and again with some new physical mystery. You think I am exaggerating, but you know nothing of the sleepless nights when your children have to fight all alone and abandoned.[80]

Some of the *Anfang* writers offered radical, concrete alternatives to this sexual crisis. Boys and girls should educate themselves sexually within coed groups: "We have a duty to mold our own drives." Such groups should also practice nudism as the best way to return to an innocent and pure nature.[81] Other authors were more vague but just as provocative. Herbert Blumenthal, for instance, announced, "We celebrate in winters and summers our festivals, which are *by* us and only *for* us. We make our dances unmistakably erotic; we flirt and love wherever we can. We are creating new chances for youthful erotic sociability."[82]

Such opinions were bound to draw public attention. No doubt because *Der Anfang* had only around eight hundred subscribers, it maintained a fairly low profile until late 1913, when the third radical development finally sparked a vehement public reaction against the entire independent youth movement. The festival on October 11 and 12, 1913, at the Hoher Meissner, a mountain near Kassel, finally brought radical tendencies in the bourgeois youth movement to the attention of the German public. Over two thousand representatives of fourteen different youth and university student groups, accompanied by their most prominent adult champions, met there to found a new nationwide confederation, the Free German Youth (*Freideutsche Jugend*—FDJ). In a succession of flyers and speeches and in an essay collection published for the meeting, prominent cultural-reformist figures from the realms of literature, pedagogy, and philosophy voiced their hopes that the youth movement would be a rejuvenating force for the nation.[83]

The rhetoric of the Meissner Festival signaled the temporary triumph of radicalism within the *Wandervogel* movement. Speakers and essay authors strongly criticized many aspects of Wilhelmine society, some going so far as to express contempt for the "moral stupor, superficiality, thoughtlessness, and hypocrisy" of social conventions such as marriage.[84] One of the most remarkable contributions, an essay written for the festival by the neo-Romantic philosopher Ludwig Klages, passionately assailed the capitalist exploitation of the natural world. This "orgy of destruction" was leading to the annihilation of the "natural peoples" (*Naturvölker*) and of folk culture, as well as to a drastic reduction of the diversity of biological species. For Klages, its roots were to be found in Christianity, according to which "all life is worthless except insofar as it serves humankind." But the modern rationalistic, darwinist view of nature was also to blame, for it depicted nature in humankind's image in order to legitimate human greed and brutality: "Since the human being sees the world as a reflection of his own condition, he thinks he sees in nature a wild power struggle and can believe himself justified when he alone survives the 'struggle for existence.'" This, despite the fact that there could be no comparison between natural selection and the growing human desire for mass destruction. That desire to destroy stemmed not from the irrational natural instinct to survive but from a rationalistic, utilitarian worldview: "We must realize that it is part of the essence of rational will to rip [nature] to shreds and that a humanity that gives in to that will must inevitably lay waste to its own mother, the earth, in blind fury—until all life, including human life, is consigned to the void."[85]

There was also a critical discussion of nationalism that was unusual for its time. The organizers of the Meissner Festival had set the date to coincide with nationwide anniversary celebrations of the 1813 Battle of Leipzig in order to offer an alternative to the inevitable wave of "cheap patriotism."[86] And the philosophers Gertrud Prellwitz and Paul Natorp wrote essays for the occasion that eloquently opposed jingoistic racial nationalism. Prellwitz declared that the love of the nation was a "healthy, strong force of nature. It is a positive, not negative force: not a limitation on the love for humanity but a broadening of the love of the self." But patriotism in Germany had degenerated into "vainglorious boasting, superficial, jingoistic, dumb, and cowardly."[87] For Natorp, it was a good sign that the youth movement was commemorating the liberation from Napoleon not with attacks on the French but with a quiet determination to lay the groundwork for a new Germany based on "a life of naturalness, truthfulness, genuineness, and straightforwardness." Far from being unpatriotic, the youth movement would stand up for its country "without blinking." But now the danger to Germany was not international but internal—it was "the loss of ourselves." What the country needed was a return to the idealistic, unifying national spirit of the Wars of Liberation that would be directed toward internal rejuvenation.[88]

The authors and speakers rejected youth cultivation in general and the conservative-militarist branch in particular. The Young Germany League came in for particular criticism. In an implicit attack on the League during his speech at the festival, Gustav Wyneken warned his young audience of the growing "mechanization of enthusiasm": "Should every importunate chatterer earn the prize of your enthusiasm because he has the right phrases? And do you, who have with this bright and varied festival shown how little you are concerned with the superficiality of all uniforms, want to let your very souls be made uniform?"[89] Wyneken, too, upheld an alternative kind of cosmopolitan cultural nationalism, praising such intellectual heroes of the Wars of Liberation as Johann Fichte for remaining "citizens of the world" who put the whole of humanity above their own people. There was no greater gift to humankind in moments of world crisis than a young generation "that through the turmoil of parties and the dust of the daily struggle ceaselessly directs its sight and its will to the Highest." And if youth eventually chose to fight for the nation, they would only be justified in "fighting the great, general battle of light against darkness."

Ask if the war you are leading is a holy war. And this is the sign: whether your war is a war for the spirit, whether it leads all of humanity out of the darkness into the light. It behooves youth more than anyone else to think beyond the limits of the state's interests and the impulse of national self-preservation. . . . Youth's special privilege of freedom obligates it to uphold freedom.[90]

Wyneken never discussed concretely what he meant by "light" in this speech. But the choice that the Meissner authors and speakers constructed between the "dark" status quo and a "light" future was evident throughout their rhetoric. The choice was between utilitarianism, rationalism, social uniformity, militant nationalism, and war on the one hand and spirituality, emotion, beauty, healthy national pride, and peaceful progress on the other. Wyneken expressed this ideological opposition by posing a choice between

Radical pedagogic reformer Gustav Wyneken (left middle ground) speaks to delegates from the bourgeois youth movement at the Meissner Festival, October 12,
1913. By permission of Archiv der deutschen Jugendbewegung.

the *Wandervogel* tradition of self-liberation and the youth cultivators' aim
to inculcate adult norms of proper citizenship:

Should we make youth reasonable, mature, and practical—that is, old? Or should we
not instead celebrate and take advantage of the right of youth to believe . . . in that
which *should* be, for its own sake? Youth desires the unconditional. . . . This birth-
right of youth prevents us from selling ourselves for the murky gruel of bourgeois
utilitarianism.[91]

He thus equated a liberated young generation with the promise of a more
peaceful and more democratic Germany. To succeed, the members of the
youth movement would have to trust their instincts in the face of adult
attempts to transform them into obedient, rational citizens.

Toward the end of the Meissner Festival, Gustav Wyneken proposed that the new national confederation of *Wandervogel* and student
groups, the *Freideutsche Jugend*, should be conceived as a fully autonomous
Jugendkultur. With the support of delegates from the *Jung-Wandervogel*
and several student groups, Wyneken was able to imbed this *Jugendkultur*

concept in the official "Meissner Proclamation" composed at the meeting. Henceforth, according to the proclamation, the *Freideutsche Jugend* would "shape their lives according to their own rules, responsible only to themselves, and guided by inner truthfulness. They will stand in unconditional solidarity for inner freedom."[92]

What role did nature play in the turn toward a critical counterculture? The advocates of youth autonomy implicitly contrasted the status quo of Wilhelmine society with a *Wandervogel* movement that was inspired by nature. Nature had two coexisting meanings—the pure, free nature of a rural landscape to be explored with reverence, and the basically noble human nature essential to the adolescent. This positive vision of nature was truly in the Romantic tradition. Indeed, the conceptual structure of this rhetoric can be depicted as a set of oppositions between the corrupt status quo and a turn to nature that promised salvation for Germany (see Table 3.1).

The radical turn of 1913 put the bourgeois youth movement on a collision course with the adult youth cultivation movement. A comparative look at the concepts of hiking in the two movements attests to the philosophical depth of this generational conflict. In the *Wandervogel* subculture, hiking brought small groups into a nature that liberated them, albeit temporarily, from adult surveillance. They approached nature with reverence and strong emotion. Their discussions of sexuality in 1913 also implied that nature could become the setting for erotic exploration. Youth cultivators, on the other hand, were still in the process of developing their own methods of adult-supervised hiking as the best way to guide the young into rational and self-disciplined adulthood. Recognizing the popularity of both hiking and the *Wandervögel* among adolescents, they

TABLE 3.1   Oppositions within countercultural *Wandervogel* rhetoric

The status quo	The turn to nature
utilitarian rationalism	idealism, emotion
capitalist exploitation of nature	reverence for nature
arrogant militant nationalism	cosmopolitan cultural nationalism
outward-looking aggression	inward-looking improvement
social convention	social innovation
repression of sexuality	celebration of sexuality and/or eroticism
cultivation of youth	liberation of youth
adult socializing institutions	*Jugendkultur*

imposed somewhat more control and direction on hiking groups while still endeavoring to maintain the aura of youthful freedom. But youth cultivators considered the innate *human* nature of the adolescent to be unruly, irrational, and vulnerable to the temptations of sexuality. Hiking was meant to pacify and subjugate this chaotic inner nature.

When the youth movement began to call on young people to develop their own *Jugendkultur*, bourgeois, Catholic, and conservative youth cultivators apparently felt the need to distance their own practices from those of the bourgeois youth movement, just as they were trying to do the same vis-à-vis the socialist youth cultivators. Radically emancipatory currents in the bourgeois youth movement thus set the stage for an attempt by youth cultivators and other worried adults to discredit the *Wandervögel*. The Meissner Proclamation and the founding of the *Freideutsche Jugend* were fragile victories for the ideal of youthful autonomy. Many members in the youth movement—probably the majority—understood little about the meaning and aim of *Jugendkultur*. Indeed, the rhetoric of a youthful counterculture was very obscure when it came to the question of practice. Just how would a youth counterculture rejuvenate the nation? *Jugendkultur* became the catchword of the independent youth movement for a short time, but the vagueness of the notion enabled critics of the *Wandervögel* to fill the conceptual vacuum with their own fears.

Moral Panic and Its Consequences for the *Wandervögel*, 1913–1915

Public controversy erupted in mid-October 1913 in direct response to the Meissner Festival. The reaction of the German press was mixed. All agreed that the *Freideutsche Jugend* "stands consciously opposed to youth cultivation commanded from on high; its principle instead is that a youth movement exists for youths and their needs alone."[93] At issue was whether the notion of *Jugendkultur* was superior to that of youth cultivation. The promise of strong, independent youth activism struck a chord among those on the left who were suspicious of state-sponsored *Jugendpflege*. Commentators in the Social Democratic and Progressive Party press upheld the concept of youth as a valuable and creative period too often dominated by adults. Franz Pfemfert, editor of the Expressionist weekly *Die Aktion*, wrote, "For the first time youth is speaking of its desire, its need, its longing, without worrying whether anyone wants to hear. If this is the youth we hope it is, then it will make itself heard. Youth, the future, is speaking." Youths should fight for "the right to be young against a narrow-minded and ossified world!"[94]

Commentators in Center, National Liberal, and Conservative Party newspapers, however, saw *Jugendkultur* only as a menace; and they deployed the specter of evil adult seducers. The Meissner Festival had been "a defiant action planned and instrumented by democrats who cleverly hide in the shadows, sending forth holy fools to do their work, most of whom have no idea that they are being manipulated."[95] For another conservative commentator, "Youth has no right to 'free individuality,' which can only degenerate into willfulness and license. Youth needs . . . to become used to firm, strict, moral order, without which no true freedom can exist." He went on to attack the *Freideutsche Jugend* as both Social Democratic and "liberal-Jewish" in character.[96] Conservatives and Catholics intensified their attacks in early 1914, turning their attention to the *Anfang* Circle. In mid-January, an anonymous "Bavarian school man" published a sensational pamphlet in Munich that cobbled together quotations from *Anfang* articles, misrepresented the journal as the official mouthpiece of the *Freideutsche Jugend*, and accused the youth movement of subversion.[97] Immediately the Bavarian government banned *Der Anfang*.

But it was the series of speeches in the Bavarian parliament in late January that finally brought broad public attention to radicalism in the bourgeois youth movement. The man who launched this parliamentary offensive, Sebastian Schlittenbauer, was a schoolteacher in Munich and a member of the Catholic Center Party. It was he who had put together the anonymous pamphlet against *Der Anfang*. During a debate on the budget for cultural matters on January 29, Schlittenbauer gave a long speech deploring the invasion of "irresponsible elements" onto the terrain of education. He singled out Gustav Wyneken, noting that the latter's attempts to establish Free Schooling Communities had run aground on the authorities' suspicions. Wyneken was one of many modern subversives aiming to destroy the "moral foundations of our national life." Schlittenbauer then extended his attack to the *Anfang* Circle and the *Freideutsche Jugend*, who were encouraging youths to seek "the freedom to live according to their own nature."

What are the goals of this Free German *Jugendkultur*? Battle against the parents, battle against the school, battle against all positive religion, battle against Christian morality, battle against healthy patriotism. . . . In other words, the goal is the anarchic dissolution of indispensable, irreplaceable values.[98]

Schlittenbauer held his trump card, eroticism, for last. He approvingly quoted an earlier attack on Wyneken and *Der Anfang* by one Richard Nordhausen:

With pitiless tenacity we must exterminate or banish to a dark cave the eroticism that is emerging furtively among our pupils. It reflects nothing but disgusting, poisonous, precocious depravity. Counselors of the young who remain silent about youthful aberrations are sinners against the marrow of the young generation and of the entire nation. Just as sinful are those who gleefully fill youths' heads with their own fantasies, who make them and their thoughts more precocious than they should naturally be. . . . The nation has only one young generation to lose: when this one is ruined, so will the entire nation be ruined!⁹⁹

Schlittenbauer concluded his speech by calling on the state Minister of Religious and Educational Affairs to adopt a hard, unyielding policy against the youth movement as a whole.[100] Since the government had already banned *Der Anfang* the week before, Schlittenbauer apparently desired both the expulsion of Wyneken from his residence in Munich and a ban on the *Freideutsche Jugend* in Bavaria. Over the next few weeks, the Catholic press kept up his offensive, attributing the radicalism of the *Anfang* Circle to the entire youth movement and warning, "This movement is infiltrating silently and secretly, like creeping poison." One immediate result was an official warning about the youth movement sent out to parents by the headmasters of several Munich secondary schools.[101]

How did moderates and progressives in Munich respond to this tirade? Parliamentarians from the Bavarian Liberal Union attempted both to salvage their ongoing critique of the school system and to distance themselves from the youth movement. The Liberal representative Buttmann called *Der Anfang* an "open wound" that was caused by authoritarianism in the schools. Suffering under heavy pressure, young people were resorting to an "exorbitant and offensive" form of self-expression. Indeed, it was natural for them to "go beyond the appropriate limits, boil over emotionally, and throw out the good with the bad."[102] Other Liberals in the parliament distanced themselves unequivocally from *Der Anfang*. Dr. Sigmund Günther, for one, announced, "Liberalism is not libertinism. This *Jugendkultur* will not produce men with character but puffed-up frogs."[103] The only defenders of the youth movement were Social Democrats and a few progressive intellectuals. Writers for the socialist *Münchener Post* called for all "friends of liberal progress" to support the *Freideutsche Jugend* because it stood for "independence and frankness of expression, a spirit of toleration, and a love for the Fatherland that is free of reactionary political hatefulness."[104]

On February 9, 1914, the *Freideutsche Jugend* themselves went on the offensive, convening a public forum in Munich to discuss the controversy. Over one thousand people attended, and the atmosphere was charged. The head of the Munich Parents' Association, Dr. Albert Rehm, stood up to accuse Gustav Wyneken of "arrogance and lovelessness" and fumed that wherever Wyneken went, he brought disaster. According to one parent known to Rehm, Wyneken had "stolen the soul of his child." Yet several speakers staunchly defended the youth movement. The prominent economist Alfred Weber, brother of Max Weber, assured the audience that the movement never attacked any "well-founded" adult institutions. The goal of educators should be "to influence the young so that they may of their own free will avail themselves of the worthwhile things in life." Wyneken seized the opportunity to defend himself and *Der Anfang*. He noted that members of the *Anfang* Circle were "educating themselves in self-criticism and a higher sense of responsibility." By no means were they sexually licentious; rather, they abhorred the precocious sexual behavior common among urban youths, longing instead for "a higher, purer, and more natural relationship between the sexes." Wyneken ended by denying that he had deprived any youths of their love of country.[105]

Nevertheless, attacks on Wyneken and *Der Anfang* continued in Bavaria. In an address to the People's Alliance for Catholic Germany on March 11, Sebastian Schlittenbauer criticized the Meissner Proclamation, the author of which he assumed to be Wyneken alone: "Just what does 'self-determination' mean? Wyneken overlooks the dual nature of the soul—its striving for transcendence, but also its attraction to lower, animalistic things." Without good adult examples, young people would always be immoral. Resorting to a Jewish conspiracy theory, Schlittenbauer informed his audience that "most of Wyneken's followers belong to the Israelite tribe" and declared that the German nation had "absolutely no need for reform by the Semitic nation."[106]

The moral panic in Bavaria had immediate consequences for Wyneken, the *Anfang* Circle, and the bourgeois youth movement as a whole. Wyneken fell under the surveillance of the Munich police.[107] The police in Vienna clamped down on the branch of the *Anfang* Circle there, forbidding a planned archive for *Jugendkultur* and intimidating them into dissolving their "salon."[108] The most important consequence for the entire youth movement was the intimidation of the *Freideutsche Jugend*. During an FDJ congress at Marburg in March, speakers called on the leaders to abandon the goal of *Jugendkultur*. The leadership gave in to these demands, pressuring Wyneken into withdrawing his own small organization, the League for Free Schooling Communities, from the FDJ. The ostensible reason was that an "autonomous" youth movement had to free itself from all adults who were trying to impose their own agendas. In fact, the FDJ leaders were jettisoning the radical goal of a more independent and critical countercultural project. Thus, the meeting at Marburg ended with the replacement of the Meissner Proclamation, with its call for youths to "shape their lives according to their own rules," by a new "Marburg Proclamation":

The youth groups in the *Freideutsche Jugend* have been founded by young people themselves, and they intend their federation to be borne by the young. The *Freideutsche Jugend* wants to impart the values that the older generations have acquired and handed down, but we will also develop our own powers guided by inner truthfulness and a sense of our own responsibility. We reject economic, religious, and political affiliations as restraints on our self-instruction.[109]

This new mission statement was an attempt to backtrack by striking a balance between youthful autonomy and socialization by adult institutions. The emphasis on traditional values signified a compromise with the youth cultivation project of guiding the young along the path toward a disciplined and uncritical adulthood. As some observers from the *Anfang* Circle surmised, the Marburg Proclamation meant that the youth movement had "again submitted to the schoolmaster, willingly taking up the yoke of authoritative education and claiming for themselves only a little 'supplemental' freedom."[110]

Despite the repudiation of *Jugendkultur* at the Marburg conference, the moral panic against the youth movement continued for several more weeks, spreading beyond Bavaria. In April the subject of *Der Anfang* arose in the parliament of Baden, where the Minister of Education called the journal "one of the most distressing phenomena of our times."[111] His Prussian counterpart, Trott zu Solz, the founder of the state-sponsored youth cultivation bureaucracy, deployed the theme of seduction in attacking adults like Wyneken who "took advantage of adolescents' natural volatility . . . by calling on them to resist authority, by inveighing against human and religious powers, and by leading youths into a battle against the school, the mother, and the father." Other Prussian parliamentarians accused the *Jugendkultur* advocates of promoting a "descent into wildness" and "crimes against morality." Here, too, only left-liberals and Social Democrats defended the youth movement.[112]

The moral panic of 1914 led to a decreased tolerance for the entire youth movement throughout Germany and a corresponding increase in support for adult-led youth cultivation efforts. Ministers of Education in Bavaria and Saxony requested school authorities to undertake the surveillance of local youth groups, to punish students found reading "dangerous" texts, and to develop their own hiking organizations as an alternative to the *Wandervögel*.[113] Commentators also began to cast aspersions on *Wandervogel* hiking practices. The Catholic youth cultivator Hans Bormann claimed that there was growing public antipathy to the *Wandervögel* and their allegedly disruptive, violent hiking groups. He cited newspaper reports that "hyenas of nature" were stomping down entire sections of meadowland, that "scantily clad men and women" were bathing together in a creek and "singing the commonest kinds of songs," and that the hikers were threatening defiant landowners with a beating. Offering no proof that such groups were affiliated with the organized youth movement, Bormann asserted that the youth movement had degenerated to the point where its members "carried on like gypsies" and pursued a "Jewish agenda." Catholic youth cultivators should promote the more rational tradition of chaperoned hiking in order to protect itself from the influence of the *Wandervögel*, "whose time is past and whose path is coming to an end."[114]

In the context of the moral panic, commentators also finally began to take more notice of Hans Blüher's theory of homoeroticism in the youth movement. Youth cultivators began to debate the extent to which homosexuals had taken over the *Wandervogel* clubs. Although some asserted that Blüher had exaggerated "inversion" in the movement, others attacked the supposed tolerance of homosexuals as indicative of the generally "degraded" character of the *Wandervögel*. It was easy for these critics to move from the sex-segregated character of *Wandervogel* hikes, which they in fact approved of, to a suspicion that male hiking groups might succumb to "very serious lapses."[115]

In the mid-summer of 1914, however, the public attack on the youth movement ended abruptly, giving way to more pressing discussions about the international political crisis. Yet the events of 1913–14 had tragic results for adolescent males in the *Wandervogel* movement. Occurring shortly before the outbreak of the First World War, the moral panic appears to have heightened the desire of the movement's leadership and its rank-and-file members to prove themselves to the nation in its hour of need. In the wake of attacks, the movement attempted to demonstrate that it was worthy of public respect.

During the First World War, between ten thousand and fifteen thousand members age seventeen and older who belonged to *Wandervogel* organizations volunteered or were inducted into the army. They died in disproportionately high numbers. In the army as a whole one out of every eight soldiers was killed. But one out of every four soldiers from the WVEV met this fate. This was in part due to both the willingness of many in the youth movement to volunteer for the infantry early in the war and to the desire of younger boys to participate. Many of them joined the war effort as errand boys or medical aids at the age of sixteen or seventeen.[116]

Why did the bourgeois youth movement prove willing to devote itself so enthusiastically to the war effort? Some historians see this as the logical outgrowth of militaristic tendencies present in prewar *Wandervogel* organizations. But this monocausal explanation is not convincing. Although groups sometimes played "terrain games," these did not dominate everyday ideology and practice, nor were they as militaristic as similar activities in the Young Germany League and Scouts.[117] Nor is the argument persuasive that the movement attempted to escape the general complexities of modernity by rushing into war.[118] Based on a reading of evidence from early wartime journals of the WVEV, I contend that the reason behind the youth movement's early and ardent support of the war effort can be found in its rhetorical attempts to give meaning to the carnage in the wake of the moral panic.[119]

The rhetoric of the WVEV in 1914 and 1915 had much in common with the many other calls to arms throughout Europe. Youth movement spokesmen described the war as a glorious defense of the nation and a way to unify society. But their particularly strong emphasis on one apparently commonplace idea—that war would help immature young males become heroic men—was directly influenced by the moral panic. Fresh memories of the attacks on the movement's morality and patriotism led writers to reiterate the notion of self-improvement again and again. As the author of an early wartime flyer announced, the movement must begin the process of "conquering ourselves! Our superficial, common, mistaken . . . and un-German characteristics!"[120] The insistence on triumphing over internal flaws was the unique feature in an otherwise archetypal discourse of becoming a man through battle.

This concept of self-transcendence through war shaped the WVEV's discussions of both the youth movement and the individual adolescent. Essay writers played down the emotional, individualistic, and antiauthoritarian elements in the prewar *Wandervögel*. They redefined hiking solely as a nationalist and self-disciplinary method of preparing the young for warfare. The head of the organization, Edmund Neuendorff, wrote in September 1914, "The days of cheerful hiking, of dreaming and singing are past. But they have not been for naught. Wherever the good old *Wandervogel* spirit has reigned, we have made our will hard and strong through physical work and sacrifice. This shall guide us to victory." In another article Willi Maschke defended the movement against a critic who thought it to be "addicted to enjoyment" (*vergnügungssüchtig*), "swimming against the current," and inferior to conservative-militarist *Jugendpflege* organizations. Maschke reassured his readers that the *Wandervögel* had long been preparing themselves to bear "the wind and weather and the simple food" of the battlefield. Truly, the movement was proving itself "German to the core."[121] This was the rhetoric of damage control, asserting that the *Wandervögel* had always done their part to cultivate adolescents into obedient servants of the nation.

Such texts were also sending the reassuring message that the *Wandervögel* had no reason to hide from their detractors, since they were engaged in a process of self-discipline that was transporting them "from subjection to freedom, from the stifling prison of impulse to conscious action." But there was a challenge involved, for this process of improvement required individuals to relinquish themselves to a collective "struggle to maintain internal order." They asserted that "[we must] free ourselves from the external slag. Our enemies are hammering the truth into us: the individual exists only within the whole." According to another essayist, "alongside the battle against our foreign enemies, there is another battle that each individual must fight with himself. It is the battle to cast aside all that is humane. All memories and hopes must be sacrificed to the one, great thing that we must all serve unto death." Yet another writer entreated youths on the home front to resist "the powers of temptation within yourselves."[122]

With these admonitions to "grow up," authors in national and regional *Wandervogel* journals were telling young members that the individualistic, emotional, and idealist elements of the prewar movement had become a hindrance to the heroic masculinity demanded by the war effort. In light of the moral panic immediately preceding the war, it is significant that those elements of the prewar tradition to be jettisoned were represented in wartime youth movement discourse as fundamentally immature because they lacked self-discipline, rationality, and masculine toughness. And this rhetoric negatively associated the desires of the individual *Wandervogel* youth with the prewar notion of radical youthful autonomy from adult control. Gender and sexuality formed a powerful subtext here, for in sacrificing one's individuality to the collective war effort, one had also to suppress one's own sexual desires and any suspicion of emotional, "feminine" qualities.

In defining the war as the way for every individual *Wandervogel* to achieve adulthood in Wilhelm II's Germany, the youth movement was calling on male youths to sacrifice their minds and bodies to the nation. Although sexuality was never mentioned directly, the constant devaluation of individual impulses, dreams, hopes, and temptations must be seen as a legacy of the moral panic. This development marked the utter rejection of the radical possibilities that had been contemplated in the youth movement just one year earlier.

Both the moral panic and the subsequent rhetoric of the youth movement may well have had a deadly influence on young male soldiers psychologically. Although we have too little direct evidence about the attitudes of most members to build a conclusive argument, there is enough to suggest that the moral panic led to a wave of self-doubt among *Wandervogel* members about their sexuality. In particular, Hans Blüher's widely read *Wandervogel Movement as an Erotic Phenomenon* appears to have caused many to question their close relationships with male friends and distanced ones with girls.[123] They were no doubt less influenced by Blüher's minority view of "inversion" as heroically male than by the prevailing contempt for male homosexuals as allegedly stunted, traitorous, and unnaturally feminine. This sexual self-doubt among sexually inexperienced and searching adolescents probably contributed to *Wandervogel* soldiers' willingness to obey their commanders beyond the call of duty. Thus, some of their letters home praise the army as an institution in which to learn self-mastery and obedience, "a simply wonderful organization in which each person's realm of work has exact boundaries. . . . I need something like this to master, bind, and hold me fast."[124] And the desire to prove their male honor in battle was promoted by the commanders' rhetoric, which always couched the demand for young soldiers to sacrifice themselves in terms of heroic masculinity. Before the battle of Langemarck near Ypern on November 17, 1914, for instance, General von Deimling spoke as follows to the infantry regiments, which included a number of volunteer *Wandervogel* soldiers:

Your task is easy. The enemy is worn down and shaken. They are just Scotsmen, with naked legs and short little skirts and nothing on underneath. They are just waiting for you to storm them; then they will throw up their hands and give themselves up without resisting. . . . You have nothing to fear. You need only take them by storm as a mass, and behind you the regiment's musicians will accompany the attack.[125]

The valiant attempt by these young soldiers to break through the lines at Langemarck failed miserably. One *Wandervogel* soldier later described the experience as a "mass murder of the volunteers."[126] Yet this event came to symbolize for war supporters back home the will to self-sacrifice in Germany's male youth. According to the "myth of Langemarck" spawned by this debacle, the youths had attacked voluntarily with the "Song of Germany" on their lips.[127]

The language of the youth movement and its members during the first year of the war attempted to impose some kind of meaning on the carnage. One of the most prevalent motives for joining the war effort seems to have been a desire to prove the manly courage and self-discipline of the young bourgeois generation. Tragically, in constructing battle as a method for every individual *Wandervogel* to achieve manhood, the youth movement identified that goal with the willingness to sacrifice oneself for the nation.

4

Between Authority and Freedom
Youth Cultivation Through Hiking, 1916–1928

HOW DID *Jugendpflege* concepts and practices of youth hiking change during the war and the Weimar era? We will focus primarily on the bourgeois-reformist and Social Democratic sectors, although other branches of youth cultivation will also be addressed when relevant. The independent middle-class youth movement plays a central role as well, albeit more in terms of ideology than organization.[1] The first section of this chapter deals with the perceived crisis of generational authority during the period 1916–23, when youth cultivators depicted the risks of out-of-control sexuality in ever more vivid language. The second section traces how *Jugendpflege* and the independent bourgeois youth movement began to cooperate institutionally and influence each other ideologically. This began during the war, when both youth cultivators and the youth movement undertook resistance against a state program of premilitary training for boys. In the liberalizing atmosphere of early Weimar, youth cultivators from all ideological sectors were obliged to cooperate with each other as well as with the leaders of independent youth organizations. In terms of ideology, a consensus developed around a notion of youthful freedom that combined the *Wandervogel* ideal of generational autonomy and the *Jugendpflege* principle of discipline and control over individual drives. This ethos of liberation through self-discipline and ennoblement transformed both *Jugendpflege* and the youth movement.

The third section of the chapter shows that within this new context, a renewed consensus about the benefits of hiking emerged among youth cultivators early in the 1920s. Seeking ways to reestablish adult authority while at the same time winning the consent of young people, the youth cultivators promoted hiking as a liberating form of exercise. In so doing they walked a thin line between youthful freedom and adult authority.

The Youth Emergency: Apprehensions of Generational Crisis from the War to the Early Republic

During the period 1914–23, youth cultivators came to see the war and political upheaval as extreme threats to the orderly maturation of adolescents into adult citizenship. As argued in the 1918 book *How Germany's Youths Are Experiencing the War*, war always brought social disorder. For adults this disorder was counterbalanced by the imperative that soldiers and wives fulfill their duties to the nation. But for adolescents, war brought "seductive prospects without binding them more tightly to their duties."[2]

Such rhetoric exaggerated the degree of youthful rebellion. Yet there is no doubt that a significant decline in institutionalized adult authority occurred during these years. In the educational system, for instance, apprenticeships and vocational schools were casualties of war. The state school system suffered disruptions as well; and into the 1920s youth cultivators argued that the loss of so many male teachers to the battlefront had made "the street" into the "most significant educational institution."[3] Organized *Jugendpflege* fell into a state of relative stagnation and, in some places, decline during the war. This was due partly to losses of personnel as thousands of male teachers and club directors left for the battlefield and partly to a sharp drop in state funding.[4] The degree to which organizations suffered varied from place to place depending on their numbers and financial strength. Youth cultivators in large cities were better off because of the availability of personnel replacements. The Berlin Committee for Exercise and Youth Cultivation, for instance, held biweekly "patriotic evenings" in an effort to indoctrinate youths in the mind-set of total war.[5]

A special case was Social Democratic *Jugendpflege*, which gained state support for the first time during the war. Under the direction of Friedrich Ebert, socialist youth cultivators joined the rest of the labor movement in supporting the war effort. After overcoming some residual suspicion, the wartime state began in 1915 to reward the socialist *Jugendpfleger* for their loyalty. For example, in May 1916 Ebert sent a request to the Prussian Minister of Railways for the same ticket discounts that were granted to nonsocialist groups on their way to hikes in the countryside. Ebert couched his letter in terms of the need to maintain the health of young workers for the war effort:

These hikes have a high pedagogic and health value for all participating adolescents. The health value is even higher because it involves young male and female workers who are exposed every day to physical damage in their workplaces. Recovery in the fresh air is even more essential now, since the war is making strong economic demands on young workers.

Although Ebert had to wait four months, a positive answer finally came from the Minister of Public Works. The minister wrote that since the request indicated a purely educational rather than political aim, socialist youth clubs would receive the discount.[6]

In any case, the expansion and professionalization of *Jugendpflege* generally came to a halt during the war years. The number of young people who belonged to youth cultivation organizations also seriously declined. The membership of the SPD clubs, for instance, fell from one hundred thousand in 1914 to thirty-one thousand in 1919.[7] Youth cultivators everywhere saw their organizations as endangered, a perception that deepened their more basic concerns about adolescents. Their chief worries were the decline of patriarchal authority in the proletarian family and the rise in juvenile delinquency, the emergence of politically radical currents among working-class and middle-class youths, and an alleged increase in adolescent sexual activity.

The wartime decline of patriarchy within the working-class family was real and caused youth cultivators great concern. As many fathers went off to the front and mothers went to work in the war economy, male and female adolescents took on grown-up responsibilities, at the same time enjoying a relative decline of parental discipline over their lives. Young workers did not often use this newfound autonomy in ways that pleased youth cultivators and state authorities determined to win the total war of attrition. The military commanders in charge of keeping order on the home front took over some *Jugendpflege*-oriented attempts to regulate youths' behavior. They enacted curfews; forbade the purchase of alcoholic drinks and cigarettes by minors; and banned visits by young people to movie theaters, dance halls, ice-cream parlors, and any public addresses "not governed by the higher interests of art and science." Loitering and "aimless walking back and forth" were prohibited as well.[8] The military commanders' propaganda spoke in terms that were typical of total warfare, demanding that adolescents sacrifice voluntarily for the nation:

Germany expects sacrifices from you all. You should renounce your diversions and crude enjoyments, renounce unsuitable books that your parents would never give to you, and renounce all those unclean activities that you would have to hide from their eyes. Instead, you should learn and work so that your mothers will have support and your younger siblings will have a good example to follow on their way to becoming valuable citizens of the Fatherland.[9]

We must doubt the overall success of such decrees in controlling young people's actions. The small amount of statistical evidence that has survived indicates a worsening of juvenile delinquency, particularly vandalism and theft. The Berlin Youth Court, for instance, reported that new cases of juvenile crime rose from 1,702 in 1914 to 5,967 in 1917.[10]

Even more shocking to youth cultivators was a growth in political radicalism among a significant number of adolescents. Politically subversive ideas began to emerge in 1916 among young people in both the socialist labor movement and the independent bourgeois youth movement. Youth cultivators interpreted these strains of antiwar, anarchist, and youth-liberationist sentiment as the beginning of a massive generational rebellion. The truth was more mundane. For their part, rebellious working-class adolescents were in fact reacting against the conditions of total war, which subjected them to deprivation, chronic undernourishment, and economic exploitation of a kind not seen since the earliest stage of industrialization. Many had to give up their apprentice training and contribute to the upkeep of the family by taking jobs that had formerly belonged to adults. Male youths under sixteen were second only to women as replacement labor in heavy industry; and the required unskilled labor meant long hours at dangerous heavy industrial work and low wages.[11]

As a result, some working-class youths began to criticize the socialist *Jugendpflege* movement, which they saw as not adequately representing their interests. Indeed, as head of the movement, Friedrich Ebert showed little respect for the views of the rank and file. Ebert declared in 1915 that young people were not suited to discuss "the infinitely difficult and complex questions" of the SPD's support for the war.[12] Factions of young workers within the socialist youth cultivation networks begged to differ. Members of youth education clubs in Berlin wrote letters to the Social Democratic Party demanding that it speak in the Reichstag for the eight-hour workday and other social benefits. Some groups in Berlin and Hamburg attempted to exclude adults older than their midtwenties from all participation in the youth clubs. This was an attack on the very idea of *Jugendpflege*.[13]

These criticisms were only the beginning. Working-class youths became one of the key antiwar forces on the home front after 1915. Ever more youths gravitated toward the antiwar wing of the SPD, which seceded in 1916 to form the Independent Social Democratic Party (USPD) and, even further to the left, toward the Spartacus League under Rosa Luxemburg and Karl Liebknecht. The latter faction inaugurated an antiwar youth protest movement with a meeting of some thirteen thousand young people in April 1916. Male adolescents were also at the forefront in food riots alongside working women.[14] The state governments called on the military commanders and police to "control the particularly dangerous mass of women and adolescents" by arresting youth leaders, banning radical clubs, and closing the pubs where they gathered.[15] Yet the influence of the USPD and the Spartacus League was too strong to break, and many radical youths participated in the revolution that finally brought down the Kaiser and ended the German war effort in November 1918.[16]

Politically radical factions also came to the fore in the independent bourgeois youth movement. The first emerged in 1915 around a new journal called *The Awakening* (*Der Aufbruch*), whose contributors included the very intellectuals who had sparked the prewar moral panic—Hans Blüher, Gustav Wyneken, and the *Anfang* Circle. *Der Aufbruch* propagated the same antiestablishment values that had led to the moral panic of 1913–14; but its rhetoric was now augmented by hefty doses of socialism and anarchism. Needless to say, the journal was not able to survive the censor for very long, but its producers were able to continue publishing their ideas in less pacifist language. In a 1916 book entitled *The Class Struggle of Youth*, for instance, the anarchist Friedrich Bauermeister called for a generational struggle against youth cultivation. Adapting the language of the *Communist Manifesto*, Bauermeister concluded his text with the words, "May the ruling classes tremble before a revolution of the young! The spirit has nothing to lose but its chains. Youth of all classes, unite!"[17]

This anarchist current no doubt encouraged an anti-*Jugendpflege* faction that emerged in early 1918 among the leaders of the bourgeois youth movement's federation, the *Freideutsche Jugend*. Reacting against the rapprochement between the *Freideutsche Jugend* and bourgeois youth cultivators that had begun in 1916 (discussed later), this faction wrote an open letter in spring 1918 that called for a return to the "genuinely youthful spirit" of the early *Wandervögel*. Adults would have to be expelled: "Away with all unyouthful older people who claim to serve us while they in truth secretly practice youth cultivation. An end must come to all arrangements with those parents' advisory committees and school authorities whose goal is to tame and control the old rebellious *Wandervogel* spirit."[18] In fall 1918, as the war effort collapsed and revolution began in German cities, members of this faction rejected capitalism in favor of a democratic, socialist "national community." And *Freideutsche Jugend* leaders in Berlin formed a group that demanded freedom of expression, equal voting rights, a national assembly, economic socialization, the right of all nations to self-determination, a League of Nations, and an end to militarism. They pledged to offer their services to the new provisional government and to make alliances with adolescent workers.[19]

This democratic strain in the *Freideutsche Jugend* led to some limited, temporary contacts with both the socialist youth movement and the USPD in 1919 and 1920. But it also spawned a right-wing counterfaction that was conservative and promilitarist in its politics and racist in its nationalism.[20] The ideological division into left-wing, right-wing, and moderate factions that occurred late in the war soon led to an organizational disintegration of the entire bourgeois youth movement into myriad small groupings. The independent youth associations, which became known collectively in the 1920s as the "league youth" (*bündische Jugend*), were weakened by this splintering.[21] Yet as we will see, the notion of youthful independence remained common to all of the movement's organizations and considerably influenced Weimar *Jugendpflege*. At this point I would stress that the existence of antiwar, anti-*Jugendpflege*, and politically radical groups within the wartime youth movement contributed to the youth cultivators' sense of declining authority over both working- and middle-class youths.

The third reason for youth cultivators' sense of an emergency was the supposed increase in adolescent sexual activity. This perception, which was strongest among liberal-reformist, Catholic, and conservative youth cultivators, stemmed in part from the prewar discourses of the irrational nature of adolescents and of moral panic. However, fears of adolescent irrationality intensified in the wartime context of family breakdown and growing youth radicalism. Another factor also contributed to this development. As historian Elizabeth Domansky has shown, the war-making German state intervened to an unprecedented degree in private life in an attempt to control adult sexuality. The military state meddled in the realm of reproduction with the aim of increasing both the quantity and quality of the German people. According to Domansky, the wartime tightening of ideological connections between militant nationalism, the emerging welfare state, and biological reproduction brought long-lasting upheavals in gender and family relations.[22] This argument should be extended in two ways. First, the attempt to control sexuality was directed toward both adults and adolescents. Second, it was undertaken by both the state and many civic associations.

Many organized cultural activists turned their attention to population policy in light of mass bloodshed and the sharp wartime decline in the birth rate. The German Society for Population Policy, for example, was composed of some of the most prominent reformist luminaries of the time, including the women's movement leader Gertrud Bäumer, the industrialist Walther Rathenau, the socialist doctor Alfred Grotjahn, the future chancellor Wilhelm Cuno, and many other leading intellectuals and politicians. Such associations warned about "the hopeless running wild (*Verwilderung*) and exhaustion of sexual life," which they believed was being furthered by a wartime upsurge in mass irrationality.[23] Sexuality and criminality were often intertwined in this rhetoric, especially when the focus was on adolescents. Organizations like the League for the Protection of Mothers and the Society for the Battle Against Venereal Disease claimed that although adolescents had always been vulnerable to prostitutes, venereal disease, and "abnormal sexual debauchery and indecent assault," the breakdown of the family had led to a strong increase in venereal sicknesses as well as youth criminality.[24]

Heavily influenced by this panic-stricken rhetoric and by questionable "facts" about sex and VD among adolescents, youth cultivators in the early Weimar years made the notion of rampaging wartime sexuality a key element in their diagnosis of the "youth emergency."[25] In this postwar rhetoric, homosexuality and mass culture came increasingly to the fore as alleged threats to male adolescents.

In a 1921 book advocating sex education in the schools, Dr. Martin Chotzen informed his readers (without offering evidence) that the war had led to a drastic increase in "the tendency toward same-sex intercourse" not only in cities and harbor towns but also in the smallest rural villages.[26]

This growing emphasis on homosexuality was partly due to the identification of normal adult citizenship with heterosexuality, but it was also no doubt a reaction against the increasingly visible urban gay subculture and rights movement.[27] In Weimar *Jugendpflege* rhetoric, the emphasis on gay men as predators was also a legacy of the prewar moral panic, especially in reference to Hans Blüher's thesis about pedophilic attachments among the *Wandervögel*. Blüher himself continued to propagate his ideas throughout the 1920s, arguing that erotic bonds between men were the foundation of society and could be found in all "male leagues" (*Männerbünde*) in the military, the government, and so on.[28] Thus, in the writings of many Weimar sexual reformers, youth psychologists, and youth cultivators, Blüher became a paradigm of the sexual renegade, one of the leaders of a widespread conspiracy to seduce Germany's adolescent boys into becoming gay. For instance, a memorandum written by prominent members of the Munich Medical Association and sent to the Educational Minister in early 1920 warned of the "homosexual infection of our youths" by the likes of Blüher and the *Wandervogel* movement. The doctors rejected Blüher's positive definition of "inverts" as having a beneficial influence on the young, arguing on the contrary that gay men were pedophilic psychopaths.[29] Over the course of the 1920s, the opinion that gay men posed an extreme threat because of their inevitable desire for young boys became widespread among scientists, politicians, teachers, and youth cultivators. A federation of school directors in Hannover, for instance, wrote:

A formerly unknown realm, homosexuality has become a common topic of conversation among school pupils even in the smaller provincial cities. The increasing number of disciplinary cases involving homosexuality casts a harsh light on the destructive effects of homosexual propaganda among young people. They are the bitter consequences of the lax response to the flooding of our people with perverse literature. The warnings of our school authorities to be vigilant against growing efforts by homosexuals to recruit youths are only too appropriate. But it is even more essential that we grasp the homosexual abomination by the roots and stop up its dirty wellsprings without mercy.[30]

Mass culture was also closely associated with these fears of sexual seduction. Weimar youth cultivators took up the battle against mass culture and its alleged effects on adolescents with renewed strength, casting the producer of "trash and smut" as another adult seducer of the young. Weimar culture is renowned for its avant-garde innovations, but the development of mass cultural forms, particularly pulp literature and the movies, was at least as significant in these years. Thus, the critique of mass culture that had been part of *Jugendpflege* ideology from the beginning now expanded to include "junk film." The Munich city council's 1921 regulations for movie theater admission indicated the primary concerns of adults, from all political standpoints, regarding the content of mass media:

The program must both educate and entertain. Forbidden to youth are all films that could have a damaging effect on moral, mental, or health-related development or that may overstimulate the youthful imagination. Educational film mainly depicts natural and earth sciences, history, religion, social studies, technology, exercise, and sport. Love stories and horror stories are not permitted; adapted novels and comedies, fairy tales, and sagas can be allowed, although not indiscriminately. . . . Young people who appear without a chaperone must sit separately according to their sex.

Despite these restrictions, eight months later the Munich police were still discovering adolescents in shows where they did not belong. They punished the theater's owner by closing the cinema for two weeks.[31]

Schund und Schmutz became a matter of public concern in large part because of the youth cultivators' diagnosis of a youth emergency. The Weimar constitution declared that young people must be protected against "moral, mental, and physical degeneration"; and a general consensus developed among cultural and political elites over the need to regulate the mass media. Chancellor Cuno, for instance, argued that immoral forms of entertainment had to be fought; and the best way to do so was to combine censorship with the inculcation of a "better concept of morality" in the young. A number of national laws to protect youth from mass culture were passed, culminating in the 1926 Law Against Trash and Smut.[32]

Much more could be said about the youth cultivators' sense of crisis in the years 1914 through 1923. For my purposes it suffices to show that their rhetoric of "youth emergency" stemmed from the perception that the disruptions of war and revolution were making adolescent irrationality far more problematic than it had been before. The supposed manifestations of this emergency included everything from loitering to petty crime to political radicalism and increased sexual activity. The fact that the war was lost and the nation forced to embark on a new and unknown path, of course, deepened the sense of national crisis; and the trauma of a lost war and political revolution was an enormous hindrance to a calmer, more reasonable discussion of adolescents and their problems in the 1920s. Nevertheless, it is to their credit that youth cultivators in the Weimar Republic attempted to win back control over the young not by using authoritarian methods but by offering them a certain measure of freedom. We turn now to the *Jugendpflege* concept of freedom and the ways in which it became intertwined with the turn to nature in the 1920s.

Refounding a Social Contract Between the Generations: The Synthesis of the *Jugendpflege* and *Wandervogel* Traditions, 1919–1923

The Weimar social welfare state strongly emphasized social harmony and the common good, and it demonstrated a willingness for the state to take over some of the child-rearing duties of family. According to the National Youth Welfare Law of 1922, for example, "Every German child enjoys the right to education in bodily, moral, and social fitness. . . . When this right is not fulfilled by the family, . . . public youth aid takes its place."[33] In emphasizing the betterment not just of poor, delinquent youths but of the entire young generation, this law reflected the growing influence of *Jugendpflege* in the postwar welfare system.

Following its relative decline during the war, *Jugendpflege* was officially refounded as part of the Weimar welfare state and became more professionalized in the process. Before 1918 the government had not generally paid those who worked within the state-sponsored youth cultivation committees; such people were almost always part-time volunteers. With the payment of salaries, the number of full-time youth cultivators at all administrative levels grew rapidly. This increase led to an expansion of the scope and purview of the *Jugendpflege* movement. A larger number of women became involved in directing youth cultivation for girls. Municipal, district, and state *Jugendpflege* committees laid claim to a broader field of activity, including the establishment of youth libraries, a more organized battle against mass cultural trash and smut, and the promotion of exercise. City governments also established new municipal youth offices (*Jugendämter*) that combined welfare for poor youths with *Jugendpflege* for everyone.[34]

During this era, youth cultivators presented their project as the best way to build health and character given the breakdown of the family and the collapse of youth discipline during the war. As in the prewar years, their goal was to help youth along the pathway to disciplined, rational adult citizenship. Now this project took on the new aims of overcoming military defeat and the upheaval of revolution by creating a politically and socially unified nation. In a decree of November 22, 1919, Prussian Welfare Minister Adam Stegerwald presented this goal as follows:

Jugendpflege should contribute to a situation in which every German youth, regardless of whether his crib stood in a hut or a castle, cherishes the German character and preserves his love and loyalty to the Fatherland in its deep unhappiness. In the ranks of youth, a fraternal spirit must reign that, without being detrimental to a general love of humanity, teaches respect and love for every fellow German. Youths should become willing and able to fulfill their obligations to the nation conscientiously and with a sense of self-sacrifice to the community.[35]

What role did the freedom of the individual youth play in the Weimar *Jugendpflege* ideology of improvement? Youth cultivators across the ideological spectrum defined youthful freedom as the individual's self-liberation from his or her irrational impulses. Exemplifying this version of freedom was the Prussian Education Minister's decree of November 1919. The decree announced that the new liberties granted by the Weimar constitution could be enjoyed only if Germans embarked on "the serious striving for *moral* freedom, the struggle to liberate the inner human being from the lower drives and to strengthen the will toward the good, true, and beautiful."[36] This concept of individual liberation as a process of ennoblement and commitment to the general community was certainly not unique to early Weimar Germany. In fact, it is strongly reminiscent of Jean-Jacques Rousseau's concept of the social contract as morally elevating:

The passage from the state of nature to the civil state produces a very remarkable change in man, by substituting justice for instinct in his conduct, and giving his actions the morality they had formerly lacked. Then only, when the voice of duty takes the place of physical impulses and right of appetite, does man . . . consult his reason before listening to his inclinations.[37]

For Rousseau, entry into the social contract meant rising above one's selfish impulses, gaining a sense of reason and social justice, and committing oneself to a community of one's equals. It also meant gaining political sovereignty as a citizen. Given that Germans were embarking on a refounding of the political system along the lines of liberal democracy, it is not at all surprising that they would turn to this Rousseauist tradition of the ennobling, "rationalizing" social contract. Furthermore, this definition of freedom was in accordance with what had been the youth cultivators' purpose from the beginning: the guidance of young people beyond their own inner desires toward rational, disciplined adult citizenship.

Youth cultivators agreed that in order to help adolescents transcend their own natural irrationality, their leisure time needed to be occupied with adult-supervised pursuits. Controversy arose over the best ways to occupy young people, however. At issue was how authoritarian *Jugendpflege* methods should be. To trace this debate, we must return briefly to the beginning of the war, when the Prussian state launched a new program for the premilitary training of boys.

This project commenced in mid-August 1914, when the Prussian Ministers of War, the Interior, and Education jointly decreed, "Adolescents aged sixteen and above shall be called into the military aid and work service according to their physical strength. For this, and for their coming service in the army and navy, they will need special military preparation."[38] The ministers called upon the military to form special "youth contingents" (*Jugendkompagnien*) to which schools, youth cultivation groups, and exercise clubs would send their adolescent members. Training sessions were to occur on weekday afternoons under the direction of veteran army officers, who would provide participating youths with certificates that would ease their later entry into the army or navy.[39] The decree also gave the Young Germany League a privileged leadership position in the program, a proviso that signaled the Prussian state's scheme of gracing the entire young generation with conservative-militarist *Jugendpflege*. The head of the Young Germany League reacted by trumpeting the apparent victory of militaristic methods, which he promised would finally unify the nation: "After the war there will be no more parties, no more divisions within the maturing young generation. . . . Young Germany will truly envelop all of Germany's youth, just as we have planned from the beginning."[40]

The military pretraining directions that accompanied this decree were over thirty pages long and were a compendium of the Young Germany League's methods. Thirty-three activities were listed, including "quick, noiseless falling into formations"; teaching about the terrain (*Gelände*) and its importance for the battle; and carrying out marching drills. Marching was said to be particularly important since it both improved health and awakened "love for nature, cheerfulness, and appreciation of comradeship." All of this practical training was to be accompanied by indoctrination: "In the evening hours youths should be regaled with stories of their ancestors' great deeds, and their wrath against the enemy should be kindled by news from the battlefront."[41]

Unfortunately for the *Jungdeutschlandbund*, however, the state's militarist version of *Jugendpflege* faced strong resistance from socialist, bourgeois-reformist, and Catholic youth cultivators. The Social Democrats had always rejected premilitary training and continued to do so. Although many nonsocialist youth cultivators supported the state's program, they wanted to maintain boundaries between premilitary training and "true" *Jugendpflege*, which they saw primarily as training in character and morality. They publicly admonished the state not to let the military take over the latter kind of youth work.[42] Premilitary training even caused controversy within the conservative-militarist *Jugendpflege* sector. The youth contingents alienated the Boy Scouts, who feared losing their organizational autonomy. Scouting leaders argued that young people did indeed need preparation for the military but not strictly through military training. The youth companies were threatening the "beautiful educational concepts of our system" with its diverse possibilities for "independent, individualistic development," instead subjecting adolescents to deadening monotony.[43]

There was also considerable debate over whether membership in the youth contingents should be compulsory. For instance, in the fall of 1914 Richard Nordhausen of the *Jungdeutschlandbund* insisted that "iron necessity" was needed, not some "nicely thought-out, well-intentioned right to self-determination." As this went against the grain of bourgeois-reformist *Jugendpflege*, Nordhausen did not have to wait long for a reaction. Dr. Otto Braun retorted that compulsion would be a major mistake, for "the terrible earnestness of war will come soon enough—let us therefore keep our youths free of compulsion as long as we can!" Surprisingly in view of the recent moral panic, Braun represented the *Wandervogel* movement as a superior alternative. "The secret of the independent youth movement's great success lies in the voluntary character of its activities," he wrote. "It is only too easy to spoil young people's enthusiasm by applying force."[44] This heated exchange between Nordhausen and Braun encapsulated the debate over the rights of the individual youth versus the authority of militaristic *Jugendpflege* early in the war.

The wartime program of premilitary training met with some early success—six hundred thousand had joined the youth contingents by the end of 1914. Yet the initial surge reversed itself in 1915. The program apparently never attracted significant numbers of nonorganized adolescents, partly in consequence of the breakdown of industrial continuation schools and the opportunities for recruitment that they would have offered. One also has to wonder how enticing premilitary exercise would have been for teenage boys after the initial excitement wore off.[45] Moreover, there is evidence that parents feared the influence of the training on their children. Some parents in Munich, for example, took their sons out of the program in 1916 when they heard a rumor that members of a youth contingent in Berlin had been used by the state to put down a food riot and had gunned down their own mothers.[46]

In response to the program's failure to attract youths, the military dictatorship under Hindenburg and Ludendorff in 1916 drew up the Reich Youth Defense Law (*Reichsjugendwehrgesetz*), which made premilitary training compulsory and even extended it into peacetime. Youth cultivators and leaders of the independent *Freideutsche Jugend* concurred in their resistance to such a law. This led to a gradual rapprochement in 1916–17 between bourgeois-reformist youth cultivators and the independent youth movement. There was a growing consensus in the reformist *Jugendpflege* sector that the *Wandervogel* model of youthful autonomy was preferable to the authoritarianism of the conservative militarists.

This reconciliation was evident, for instance, in the argument by leading youth cultivator Hertha Siemering that all nonmilitary *Jugendpflege* was part of the youth movement. Siemering wrote that youth cultivators like herself were enthusiastic about the *Wandervögel* because that organization had over the years developed hiking practices that could serve as a model. Moreover, *Wandervogel* volunteers had proven themselves through their self-sacrificial war service, in the process managing to overcome their "soft" phase of "merely gushing about nature" (*Naturschwärmen*).[47] Siemering was suggesting that the youth movement was now available as a source of promising *Jugendpflege* methods, having gotten past the controversial period of radicalism that had led to the moral panic of 1913–14. By the time a national conference of youth cultivators convened in November 1916, the rapprochement with the youth movement was well under way, as indicated in the conference's formal declaration: "All our *Jugendpflege* must educate youths to independence and self-determination. In this sense, *Jugendpflege* must be in harmony with the youth movement."[48] Thus, even though the concepts of self-discipline and sacrifice to the nation remained central to the wartime ideology of the *Jugendpfleger*, the bourgeois-reformists rejected the state's militarization of youths in favor of the *Wandervogel*-oriented concept of self-education. This wartime shift in ideology, combined with the collapse of the conservative state and the establishment of democracy, led in early Weimar to a new synthesis of *Jugendpflege* and the *Wandervogel* tradition. Ironically, the acceptance of the *Wandervögel* became possible only because many young members of the youth movement had sacrificed themselves during the war, proving their commitment to the nation.

Youth cultivation, as it reestablished itself during the early years of the Weimar Republic, underwent three important developments that had further bearing on the theme of adult authority versus youthful freedom. These trends involved a breakdown of barriers between various sectors of the *Jugendpflege* movement, as well as between organized *Jugendpflege* and independent youth movements.

First, there developed a democratic ethos of compromise and cooperation across ideological boundaries. For the first time, Social Democrats worked alongside church-affiliated and bourgeois youth cultivators on all institutional levels. The state admonished all participants in *Jugendpflege* not to seek direct political influence over young people. The Bavarian government, for example, decreed that *Jugendpflege* clubs had to obey only two conditions: (1) they could not operate in connection with a club for adults; and (2) their leaders had to direct students to "lawful behavior and to respect for state authority."[49] There was a basic consensus that *Jugendpflege* should support the new democratic system. State welfare ministries refused to subsidize and sometimes banned youth groups considered to be politically antipathetic to the republic—notably communist and far right-wing nationalist groups.[50] Furthermore, state-supported *Jugendpflege* committees included representatives from the independent youth organizations descended from the *Wandervögel* and *Freideutsche Jugend*, which suddenly gave the latter a great deal of positive influence over the youth cultivation project. These delegates were now able to promote the *Wandervogel* tradition at the very heart of institutional youth cultivation. The committees served as a direct conduit between youth cultivators, the youth movement, and the state.

The most significant example of this cooperation across ideological and generational lines was the National Committee of German Youth Federations (*Reichsausschuß der Deutschen Jugendverbände*), an umbrella organization for both *Jugendpflege* and *bündische* groups that was founded in 1919. The *Reichsausschuß* undertook a broad field of endeavor. It regularly held national conferences; gave professional advice to young workers and apprentices; produced educational materials (for example, pamphlets on tuberculosis, alcohol, and venereal disease); carried out statistical studies of Germany's adolescents; and advised the Reichstag on ways to improve the situation of the young. The *Reichsausschuß* was subsidized by the state and thus served an important gatekeeper function for individual youth organizations, which had to belong to the organization in order to receive state subsidies, train discounts, and other such benefits.[51]

By 1926 the *Reichsausschuß* contained representatives from almost one hundred organizations, to which nearly 40 percent, some 3.5 million young people between the ages of fourteen and twenty-one, belonged. One-third of this number were girls and young women, signaling a far higher degree of female organization than had been the case before the war.[52] We can infer from these numbers that both *Jugendpflege* and youth movement organizations rapidly gained a strong foothold in the pluralistic civil society that was Weimar Germany.

The second important development in the early Weimar years saw the *Wandervogel* tradition, with its call to liberate the young generation, gaining unprecedented influence in the youth cultivation movement. This was true throughout all four *Jugendpflege* sectors but was particularly obvious among conservative-militarist and Social Democratic youth cultivators. Having discredited itself with the failed effort at premilitary training, the conservative sector waned in influence. The Young Germany League disappeared, and all military training of youth was banned by the Treaty of Versailles. True believers in such training tried to promote their ideas to the state governments and the public throughout the 1920s, but their pleas came to nothing, at least before 1930.[53] The majority of the Boy Scouts' leaders moved away from authoritarian militarism, instead merging the *Jugendpflege* element of guidance by adults with the *Wandervogel* ideal of self-determination. Typical of their early Weimar rhetoric was an optimistic vision of a strong, independent yet self-controlled young generation: "May the young tree, freed from its wilder sprigs, bloom and grow strong! May it put an end to our twisted, forced, untruthful, apathetic, narrow-minded culture!" Those leaders who still clung to militarism formed small right-wing splinter groups in the early 1920s, while the majority of Scouting leaders became more committed to youthful freedom, abandoning their earlier commitment to authoritarianism.[54]

There was a similar influx of *Wandervogel* ideas of youthful autonomy into the Social Democratic sector. The Social Democratic Party founded a new *Jugendpflege* organization in 1919—the Federation of Worker Youth Associations, which soon changed its name to the Socialist Worker Youth (*Sozialistische Arbeiterjugend*—SAJ). The party intended the SAJ to serve as an ideological training ground for future party members. To this end, the party made certain that the national SAJ leadership remained firmly in the hands of adult Social Democrats. The first president of the SAJ, from 1919 to 1921, was one of the prewar founders of socialist *Jugendpflege*, Heinrich Schulz. Nonetheless, the SPD also decided to grant young members leadership positions at the local level, giving working youths unprecedented influence in shaping the SAJ's practices.[55]

Furthermore, beginning in 1919 some liberal members of the surviving bourgeois youth movement began to forge alliances with local SAJ leaders. Those SAJ groups that were so influenced became outspoken in their *Wandervogel*-style rebelliousness, announcing that they were now free of all adult authority. One W. Dahrendorf of the Hamburg SAJ, for instance, declared, "We are not beholden to the Social Democratic Party. The party gives us money and meeting space; but it can buy neither the youth organization nor the individual young soul. Both go their own ways free from the influence of party politics."[56]

Swayed by this ideal of autonomy, the SAJ leaders soon served notice that organized working youth would not submit to a reestablishment of adult-dominated youth cultivation. The youth rally of some two thousand youths and SAJ leaders at Weimar on August 27–29, 1920, was strongly reminiscent of the *Wandervögel*'s rebellious Meissner Festival of 1913, for it too announced the creation of a subcultural realm in which young people could guide themselves independent of adult authority. And like the Meissner Festival, the Weimar rally defined the young generation as a vanguard with a mission of reforming society. This youthful reformation of society would also require the rejuvenation of socialism itself. Organized working youths, proclaimed SAJ spokesman Johannes Schult in a speech to the assembly, were the "vanguard of a new cultural movement" that must "set new goals for the labor movement":

In the closely knit life of a community of both sexes, we will develop our nobility in order to help build a socialist future. We will replace hate, envy, and pettiness with the love of human beings for one another within a victorious community of our nation and of *all* nations. We pledge to help renew socialism through the exemplary activities of our youth movement.

This new socialism would strive for a republican "national community" that would combat capitalism based on the humanistic principles of trust, compassion, and love.[57]

As speakers at the rally were announcing this project of *Wandervogel*-inspired rejuvenation, young people were enjoying activities that were themselves derived from the bourgeois youth movement. The program of the Weimar Festival included traditional folk songs and dances as well as group hikes into the surrounding countryside. In their own way these goings-on gave notice of a strong affinity with the *Wandervogel* tradition. Taken as a whole, the ideology of the *Sozialistische Arbeiterjugend* signified that the rebellious, liberationist, and democratic current in the prewar *Wandervögel* was taking on new life after the revolution. In its new socialist guise of the "spirit of Weimar," this ideology appears to have solidified early support for the republic among young workers. National membership in the SAJ rose from 31,000 in 1919 to 105,000 in 1922.[58]

Leaders of Social Democratic *Jugendpflege* also supported the SAJ's striving for independence. Heinrich Schulz, who had attended the Weimar rally, wrote the following in the pedagogic journal *Arbeiter-Bildung*: "New life is stirring in our youth movement. Earlier youth activity was more or less devoted to youth cultivation. But youth cultivation can be nothing more than a last resort; it should represent above all the beginnings of a youth movement. . . . We pledge to help our children and young friends to make brisk progress down the path they have chosen."[59] Given the prewar history of socialist *Jugendpflege* as a repression of independent proletarian youth initiatives, it seems surprising that the SPD would allow this degree of youthful independence. The party's acquiescence to the "spirit of Weimar" made good political sense within the context of early Weimar, however. The Social Democratic leadership apparently realized the need to negotiate the consent of a young working-class generation that had become deeply politicized during the war and revolution. They needed enthusiastic young supporters in this time of unrest, particularly in light of the widening chasm within the organized working class between Communists and Socialists.

This made the SPD more accepting of youthful self-mobilization, particularly as the SAJ's claims to autonomy did not seriously go against the grain of Social Democratic ideology. Indeed, the notion of a rational, self-disciplined, and socialist "new human being" announced by the SAJ was fully in keeping with the optimistic Social Democratic ideology of progress in early Weimar. And, as we have seen, that notion of self-discipline on the way to adulthood was shared by youth cultivators. In the political situation of early Weimar, then, SPD leaders simply recognized the SAJ for what it was—a synthesis between the *Jugendpflege* commitment to a disciplined community and the ideal of youthful autonomy derived from the *Wandervögel*.

In the second important development in early Weimar, not only did notions of youthful autonomy from the independent bourgeois youth movement begin to influence organized youth cultivation, but the youth movement was, in turn, heavily influenced by *Jugendpflege*. As the youth movement refashioned itself following the war, its leaders revived the *Wandervogel* ideal of generational autonomy and national rejuvenation by the young middle-class generation. There must occur a reformation of the soul, they announced, a forward-looking moral renewal that would lead Germany out of the old, desolate civilization with its "unnaturalness, empty phrases, lies, and selfishness."[60] The youth movement would henceforth strive to develop a type of noble, self-disciplined, and free "new human being." We are the fighters for a "new moral order," they typically proclaimed—self-conscious, strong individuals "who live truthfully and in so doing become leaders."[61]

However, along with these proclamations of the youth movement's purpose came a direct critique of the prewar *Wandervogel* tradition. The movement's new leaders castigated the prewar *Wandervögel* for overemphasizing emotion and personal liberation. There was, they claimed, a legacy of ineffectuality and solipsism that had to be overcome if the movement were to live up to its purpose. As one Scouting leader wrote in a critique of the *Wandervogel* tradition,

I do not believe that one becomes a human being merely by ignoring one's surroundings and listening to one's own inner being. . . . All human affection, all the greatness and magnanimity of the soul becomes constrained by self-satisfaction. The very things that separate people from one another are strengthened. Disintegration into tiny, insignificant groups is inevitable; for the more one considers one's own uniqueness to be the only valuable thing, the less one is able to live with others. The final result of individual self-development is merely a hermit who destroys himself in megalomania and romantic emotional breakdown.[62]

This rejection of "romanticism," emotionality, and individual desires was the foundation upon which the independent bourgeois youth movement began to cooperate closely with the *Jugendpflege* movement. The youth movement's rhetoric began to mirror the youth cultivators' emphasis on helping the individual youth progress toward adult citizenship by rising above internal emotions and drives. The *Jugendpflege* ideal of freedom as self-discipline led to attacks against any "weaknesses" that might be considered detrimental to the individual's steady development toward rational and respectable adulthood.

This can be seen in the example of sexuality in the *bündische Jugend*. The organizational form that became dominant in the movement was a tight league (*Bund*) of individuals under a democratically elected and answerable leader. However, the guiding principle of the *Bund* was not democratic pluralism but self-subordination to the group. Leaders were nearly always chosen from older members in their early twenties who allegedly demonstrated a natural ability to guide younger members. By far the majority of *bündische* youth organizations were dominated by males; any females were generally segregated into separate group in keeping with the alleged differences in gender roles. However, as we have seen, the supposed threat of homosexuality was thought to be one source of the youth emergency in the aftermath of the war. This fear of homosexual seduction perpetuated memories of the prewar controversy over Blüher's interpretation of the *Wandervögel*, making the *bündische* movement vulnerable to outsiders' accusations of deviant sexuality.[63] In an effort to guard against such attacks (and perhaps to overcome any lingering self-doubts they might have experienced after the moral panic), the movement's leaders took pains to eradicate any sign of homoeroticism and effeminacy, indeed of any kind of active sexuality. As one spokesman for the leading Scouting organization put it, eroticism led to "exhaustion and decline"; it precluded progress by undermining the "ethic of striding forward and fighting."[64] The eros that took shape was, as Marion de Ras states, "powerful, energetic, manly, and creative—also loving—but [it] was to be understood as unequivocally nonsexual [and] never blurring the boundaries between the masculine in the masculine body and the feminine in the feminine body."[65] This new version of youth movement (a)sexuality imposed standards of masculinity and femininity that encouraged the individual to repress his or her individual sexual drives. In other words, the *bündische* movement was jettisoning the prewar movement's aspirations to sexual autonomy, teaching its members the self-disciplinary principles of *Jugendpflege*.

The *bündische Jugend* represented in a photograph taken at the national meeting of the *Wandervogel e.V.* in Coburg in 1919. By permission of Archiv der deutschen Jugendbewegung.

Taken together, these three developments brought a rapprochement among youth cultivators and the independent youth movement. There developed an ideological synthesis between *Jugendpflege* and the youth movement that was based on a forward-looking, self-disciplinary, rationalist understanding of freedom strongly reminiscent of Rousseau's political theory. The refounding of both organized *Jugendpflege* and the independent youth movement can be seen in hindsight as a kind of generational social contract, in which there was a fine line between individual youthful liberty and the demands of adult society. We can see elements of personal liberation, but also of personal repression, in the changes that came about when the *Wandervogel* ideal of generational autonomy merged with the *Jugendpflege* ideology of progress toward adulthood. This was the cultural context in which organized youth hiking became the dominant form of youth cultivation and one of the most popular activities among Weimar Germany's young people.

The Youth Cultivators' Version of Hiking

At this point we can trace the beginnings of an ideal narrative of turning to nature in the Weimar youth cultivation movement. All such ideal narratives began with a diagnosis of the problem to be solved. As we have seen, the question of how much independence young people should have vis-à-vis adult authority, when combined with growing fears of adolescent irrationality and sexuality, led youth cultivators in the late Wilhelmine and early Weimar years to identify a serious "youth emergency." Young people were under threat from unscrupulous, seductive adult renegades; their very nature as adolescents made them susceptible to temptations that were sexual and immoral, as well as politically dangerous. The moral panic that began in 1913 was perpetuated by the breakdown of the family and of organized *Jugendpflege* itself during the war. During the revolutionary phase, many young people exerted unruly political power, further threatening adult control. Thus, in the early Weimar years, youth cultivators' worries about the loss of control over the young were at their height. This sense of crisis galvanized youth cultivators as they carved an institutional niche for themselves within the new welfare state.

The second step in the ideal narrative described the actual turn to nature—that is, the methods of experiencing nature in an organized way. Weimar youth cultivators were quick to arrive at the notion that nature could be turned to their goal of socializing the young. They felt urgently that their role in restoring the postwar nation was to overcome the generational crisis and restore adult leadership over the young. Yet they realized that *Jugendpflege* offerings had to remain voluntary and that they would thus always have to compete with all the other leisure possibilities available to young Germans. Youth cultivators would have to win over young people by appealing to at least some of their everyday desires. They would have to deal with the obvious reality that there were myriad characters, wills, and desires among Germany's adolescents. They would also have to find methods that could achieve consensus within the new institutional and ideological context of Weimar.

Exercise soon became the practical method that youth cultivators favored. In this they were in complete agreement with teachers, parents, state ministers, and independent youth clubs. There was a strong current of nationalism in the consensus surrounding exercise. Federations of exercise clubs began to take shape on the municipal, state, and national levels.

They were often sites of everyday cooperation that transcended political differences. The benefactors of one such federation included a wide range of prominent political and cultural figures, such as the founder of the Deutsches Museum in Munich, the director of the Rosenthal porcelain works, and several mayors of large cities, including Konrad Adenauer, then the Catholic Center Party mayor of Cologne.[66] Such organizations were held together by a strong belief that national strength and social unity depended on physical rejuvenation. No less important a figure than the new president of the republic, Friedrich Ebert, announced, "If we want to work our way upward to new national strength, then we must also become physically healthy and strong."[67] Nationalism was a focal point in the consensus surrounding youth exercise.

The *Jugendpflege* concept of exercise was also holistic. Exercise seemed to offer the best way to restore simultaneously the health of the adolescent's body, mind, and morality. It would keep down the young person's unruly sexual drives as well.[68] The "making fit" (*Ertüchtigung*) of the *entire* individual became central to remaking the German nation in youth cultivation discourse. There was, however, some disagreement among youth cultivators over which exercises were most suitable for the young. Social Democrats, for instance, were suspicious of gymnastics (*Turnen*) because of its traditionally strong currents of conservative nationalism. They generally rejected competitive sports, which they believed promoted a bourgeois desire for prizes instead of collective solidarity.[69] There were also sharp differences among youth cultivators concerning the effects of exercise on girls. The more antifeminist proponents of exercise sought to exclude girls from participation in the strenuous sports, which they thought were at odds with "natural" norms of feminine behavior. As Dr. August Bier wrote,

We should neither underestimate nor overestimate [the significance of exercise for the female sex]. Throughout the animal kingdom, contest and battle are the preserves of the male; and among all peoples of the world . . . the same rule has always applied. The reasons for this behavior must lie in the differing natures of the sexes. It should be stressed that light exercise—which promotes gracefulness—is better suited to the female sex. . . . That more strenuous exercise is bad for the female can be seen in the fact that women, when they undertake hard work that would not do damage to men, quickly become old and ugly.[70]

Furthermore, most youth cultivators continued to reject the conservative-militarist concept of premilitary training. *Jugendpflege* would fail, they argued, if it deployed methods of discipline that were too regimented and superficial.

Given these self-imposed limits, youth cultivators sought the kind of exercise that was politically innocuous, that served the goals of youth cultivation, and that promised to appeal to adolescents and their adult guardians. The solution they arrived at was hiking. The turn to hiking was very much in accord with the cross-fertilization between *Jugendpflege* and the independent *Wandervogel* tradition described previously. Youth hiking had been made famous before the war by the *Wandervögel*. They had depicted nature as a realm of freedom that could be reached only through a hike with one's generational peers. Turning to nature in this way could help liberate those youthful energies that were so crucial to reforming culture and society.

As we saw in Chapter 3, there had been precedents in the immediate prewar years for turning *Wandervogel*-style hiking to the purposes of *Jugendpflege*. In particular, the National Federation of Youth Hostels, founded in 1911, had continued throughout the war to sing the praises of hiking. Even though no new hostels were built during the war, these men had persisted in their efforts to popularize youth hiking. Julius Schult, for instance, wrote seventy-eight essays between 1917 and 1918 on the benefits of hiking and managed to have them published in over five hundred newspapers and magazines![71]

Such diligent propagandizing paid off in the 1920s, when the Federation came to enjoy generous state funding and broad support across class, generational, and political lines.[72] In their appeals to the state for support, the Federation's spokespersons developed an ideal narrative of hiking. They portrayed it as a healthy alternative to urban living conditions, a method of guiding youths toward maturity, and a way to unify the nation. Its benefits would thus be simultaneously physical, psychological, moral, and political.

According to the Federation, the growth of the metropolis with its demographic shift from country to city, its crowded apartments, and its high infant mortality had been a negative development for Germany. The war had only made urban living conditions worse, as could be seen in comparative statistics on infant mortality by 1925: each year 68 out of 1,000 infants under one year old died in Norway, 87 in France, 95 in England, and 151 in Germany. This was one result of the "much-lauded progress toward an ever-higher culture. We have had to pay for it with the

most valuable things on earth—with human energy and human lives! . . .
Of all the sins committed during the past decades, the turning away from
nature by ever-larger numbers of people was the most serious."[73] Although
this rhetoric was clearly critical of urban-industrial modernity, the National Federation of Youth Hostels had no pretensions of reversing urbanization in any permanent way. Instead, spokespersons for the Federation
saw hiking as a way to regain control over modern developments. They
depicted hiking as the simplest and least expensive way to compensate
urban boys and girls for the stress of the city. It would ultimately give rise
to a grassroots movement of urban reform; for once the desire for light and
air, cleanliness, and dwelling space was awakened in millions of young
people, the desire to change their living conditions through self-help and
through the vote would grow.

According to this ideal narrative, exposure to nature through hiking would also help distract adolescents from their own desires and thus
protect them from "invaders" such as alcohol and venereal disease. Nature was the best guide for girls, since it led them away from "fashion
slavery, primness (*Zimperlichkeit*), and superficiality to self-sufficiency,
health, and natural grace." Hiking from hostel to hostel also gave adolescents of all classes the opportunity to explore their regional and national *Heimat* and to learn to love it.[74] Finally, in bringing young people
of all social and cultural backgrounds together, hiking would "wear
down all kinds of prejudice" and "serve to bond the People."[75] The ideal
narrative of turning to nature developed by the National Federation of
Youth Hostels thus combined the goals of a healthier young generation,
a unified national community, and a better urban modernity in which
people could regain control over their environment.

These were advantages that all youth cultivators could agree upon.
For the same reasons, the state and national governments passed favor-
able laws and distributed funds to promote youth hiking throughout the
1920s. Education Ministers in Prussia, Bavaria, Saxony, and Baden decreed monthly hiking days in the schools (a measure that was never consistently enforced). They also sponsored courses for adult hike leaders and
arranged discounted train tickets for organized youth groups. However,
the most support from national, state, and municipal governments went
to enhancing the youth hostel network.[76]

Yet at the same time that hiking was becoming a consensual and
state-supported method of *Jugendpflege*, youth cultivators were engaged

in an ongoing process of suppressing certain troublesome elements within the youth hiking tradition. The controversy surrounding the prewar *Wandervögel*, as well as the ongoing sense that young people acting autonomously were a threat to adult authority, had led many adults to look upon youth hiking with suspicion. During the war, the same mentality that prompted military authorities to attempt to control young people's movements was present among youth cultivators. There emerged a discourse of "wild hiking" (*wildes Wandern*), through which proponents of *Jugendpflege* attacked unsupervised, unorganized hiking, For example, in 1916 a Catholic youth cultivator attacked the "packs of false *Wandervögel*" who were "raising a stench on our outdoor footpaths and hiking trails with their loud, vulgar activities and their bellowing of dirty songs." He continued:

Instead of taking joy in nature, they are contaminating it with the grime of the metropolis; and they are confusing harmless gaiety with a rude lack of consideration. This low-class behavior is unpleasant enough in peacetime. But it becomes downright abominable at a time when thousands of national comrades, each of whom is more valuable than a whole pack of these excursionists, are risking life and limb for the Fatherland.

"A thorough whipping would be the mildest punishment, but we do not want to encourage lynch justice," continued the author. Instead, he recommended that the police intervene and that the courts "harshly punish these drunken 'heroes.'"[77] Catholic youth cultivators were not the only ones who were appalled by this kind of unsupervised behavior. As a Social Democrat wrote in early 1918, all too many young people were disporting themselves in "wild clubs" instead of joining the SPD *Jugendpflege* groups. Therefore, socialist youth cultivators should spread enlightenment about their movement, civilizing the masses of nonorganized young people just as Christian missionaries dealt with "wild peoples in faraway lands."[78]

The rhetoric of *wildes Wandern* continued to represent unsupervised hiking as a symptom of the youth emergency into the early 1920s. It can be found, for instance, in the discussions among state authorities about whether to fund *Jugendpflege* hiking projects. They almost always made such support conditional on hiking leaders maintaining strict control over their adolescent charges.[79] This official rhetoric against *wildes Wandern* reached a high point during the hyperinflation of 1923–24, when state authorities were preoccupied with groups of unemployed young vagabonds entering foreign countries in search of work or food. Even the diplomatic corps grew annoyed by what they called "*Wandervogel*" groups in Italy. The German consulate in Naples reported:

Typically, the body is clothed only in a shirt and short pants; on the feet are sandals, the head is bare, and the hair is unkempt . . . and occasionally plastered down by dust and sweat. . . . Since the numbers of these bedraggled figures have increased rapidly, they have become a nuisance to the Italian people, who have little tolerance for this kind of romanticism. Furthermore, by practicing a kind of begging poorly disguised as street music, these bands of vagrants have stirred up unflattering views of the German character and German honor.[80]

Such attacks cast the real economic problems of young Germans as yet another version of adolescent "waywardness." State authorities thus continued to see unsupervised movement by youth groups as a potential threat to social order and even to national pride. Their qualms about hiking posed a real challenge to *Jugendpflege* organizations as they lobbied for state support.

In response to these doubts about the more liberating elements of youth hiking, Weimar youth cultivators undertook to "tame" hiking by divesting it of its allegedly wayward characteristics. At the same time, youth cultivators perpetuated important individualistic and emancipatory connotations that came out of the *Wandervogel* hiking tradition. They walked this tightrope because of the need both to win the support of adults and the state *and* to popularize hiking among the adolescent generation.

First, youth cultivators attempted to rein in youthful hikers who had in one way or another escaped adult surveillance. The National Federation of Youth Hostels launched a tirade against *wildes Wandern* and its perpetrators—that is, "cheeky young rascals; silly, spoiled city girls; sissies; boors; hangers-on; pickpockets; and slobs." The Federation set rules for hiking that ranged from "Don't litter," to "No drinking," to "Don't make fun of the locals." The "Ten Commandments for Hikers" told young people that they would be sharply observed by other young people and by adults. "So watch your attitude, your speech, and your actions! Be clean and neatly dressed but not like a fashion plate [*Stutzer*]! Be cheerful but not rash! Be friendly but not annoying and sassy!"[81] Such calls to self-discipline always revolved around the notion that individual freedom meant responsibility, the responsibility to rise above one's own selfish urges and set a good example for others. This rhetoric was clearly attempting to inculcate in the hiker a specifically rational, mature identity in opposition to that of the "wild" hiker.

Second, proponents of *Jugendpflege* hiking banished all party politics from hiking clubs. In the place of "politicism" there developed an official worldview based on the utopia of a socially harmonious "national community." The best pedagogy, according to the Federation, took place within a microcosmic community of hikers that taught a sense of social equality, self-subordination, and dedication to the nation:

In the hostel the young worker spends the night alongside the student. The factory owner's son cooks at the fire next to the proletarian. Catholics and Protestants, middle-class and working youths practice folk dances and songs together with mutual respect. Where can there be a more obvious and promising way for heretofore alienated classes to learn mutual understanding and for the unification of the rising generation? . . . On the path to nature there is no right and no left.[82]

In addition to overcoming political and religious differences, youth cultivators claimed that hiking could help bring together the children of urban and rural families.[83]

Third, youth cultivators and their governmental supporters imposed a specific pedagogic practice on hiking to turn it into a lesson in patriotism and social harmony. This pedagogy was *Heimatkunde*, the study of the homeland.[84] The notion of hiking as a way to become acquainted with the *Heimat* had long played a role in *Wandervogel* hiking ideology, but it was not nearly as central there as it became under the aegis of Weimar youth cultivators. Moreover, as we will see in the case of the conservationist movement, the *Heimat* concept was fundamentally ambiguous and sometimes divisive along regional lines. Overcoming regional and class divisions among young people was a paramount goal of both youth cultivators and the state authorities; thus, both groups imposed a defensively *nationalist* meaning on *Heimat* in their discussions of hiking. The national and state governments gave special subsidies to the National Federation of Youth Hostels and to hiking groups who were active in the "border marches" (*Grenzmarken*) and in the occupied territories of the Rhineland. They depicted hiking in such regions as a national bulwark against insidious attempts at "cultural infiltration" by the Czechs, the French, and the Poles. Nationalist associations such as the Association for a German Rhine appealed successfully to the state along these lines, arguing that youth hiking groups were helping to "reoccupy" the Rhineland and fighting separatism there.[85] The 1928 dedications in the guest book of a Rhenish youth hostel following the French departure reveal that leading conservative and socialist politicians also ascribed to youth hiking an important role in national defense:

> President Paul von Hindenburg: May the love of the *Heimat*, loyalty to the Fatherland, and the spirit of true national community accompany the youth of the occupied territory . . . on their travels and along their path through life.

> Emil Hartwig [member of the German National People's Party]: The youth hostels, promoted by the Reich and built at the most beautiful points of the homeland, are places for youths of all social rank to muster national strength and for youths to assemble to attain readiness for times of national decision.

> Dr. Phil. Dilthey [Social Democratic government minister]: May this youth hostel . . . serve not only as a fountain of youth for German strength but also as a memorial to Germany's gravest hour of need, reminding our youth always that the unanimous cooperation of all social groups in the Rhineland and the Ruhr was crucial to preserving the German Fatherland.

Only Germany's chancellor, the Social Democrat Hermann Müller, used this opportunity to move beyond defensive nationalism, writing, "The duty of youth in a Rhineland free of foreign occupiers must be to build sturdy bridges of understanding to other peoples."[86]

The fourth key method of reshaping hiking along *Jugendpflege* lines involved the attempt to control youthful sexuality by keeping the sexes separate. Surprisingly, given the aforementioned concerns about homosexuality among male youths, there was virtually no discussion of that particular risk among same-sex hiking groups. Apparently the fears of *female* influence on male sexuality and the breakdown of "natural" gender roles outweighed concerns about same-sex groups. For instance, the hiking proponent Fritz Müller-Marquardt wrote of the dangers to sexual identities that inevitably resulted from mixed hiking:

Girls who are boyish and boys who are effeminate in hairstyle and clothing, in speech and bearing, are for *genuine* girls and boys an outrage and a laughingstock. One of the misfortunes of today's overrefined culture is that it tries to blur the divinely willed and natural differences between man and woman. But this attempt will not succeed. For as long as our youth is given a healthy education in the ways of our fathers, Schiller's words will triumph: "The boy proudly breaks loose from the maiden and rushes wildly into life." Mentally healthy boys and young men do not wish to hike in the society of girls, and the same thing applies conversely to girls.[87]

Segregated hiking became the norm, although Social Democratic groups were a significant exception here. Most nonsocialist youth cultivators saw to it that hiking groups were separated by sex on the grounds that this was "normal" and desired by the young people themselves.[88]

These rhetorical and organizational changes were intended by both youth cultivators and state authorities to standardize hiking. The purpose was to make it a safe, uncontroversial method for cultivating adolescents. At the same time, the *Jugendpflege* version of youth hiking, as a synthesis of youth cultivation ideology with the *Wandervogel* tradition, retained strong elements of antirationalism, antiauthoritarianism, and individualism. Such elements no doubt helped youth cultivators to attract young people to their hiking groups, but they may also have undermined the basic project of making young people self-disciplined and respectable.

The neo-Romantic and liberationist legacy of the *Wandervögel* resurfaced in a number of youth cultivation texts from the early 1920s. These works, written to promote youth hiking in the schools, offered everyday practical guidelines for the adult leaders of male hiking groups. The authors represented hiking in the terms of social harmony and patriotism described previously; yet they clearly rejected hierarchical and authoritarian forms of adult guidance. On the contrary, they argued that hiking was a way to bridge the gap in everyday relations between adults and youths. Schoolteachers were encouraged to abandon their didactic tones while leading group hikes, adopting instead a relaxed persona more suited to a fun experience. "Hiking and schoolmasterly behavior," announced Fritz Müller-Marquardt, "are as antithetical as water and fire"; and Fritz Brather asserted that the only kind of teaching that would ever be successful during a hike was the Socratic method of a questioning discussion. Ernst Enzensperger wrote that teachers should serve as models of leadership on didactic hikes but should also allow "free hikes without a strong emphasis on education." Even those "patriotic hikes" devoted to teaching about the national *Heimat* should be guided in "a conversational, nondidactic tone."[89]

These authors also criticized authoritarianism in their discussions of militarism. This rhetoric could be oddly contradictory, as in Walter Schönbrunn's passages on the war experience in his 1927 book *Youth Hiking as Maturation Toward Culture*. At one point Schönbrunn wrote of "that delicious primitiveness" of the battlefront that made the soldiers appreciate all the simple needs in life—eating, drinking, sleep, and movement. Soldiers at the front had experienced "that feeling of a carefree existence far from the confusion of modern bustle" only motivated by "a few constant moods, feelings, and a very few thoughts":

And then we were filled suddenly with a heartening realization: that we were only human, only a part of nature. As we lay day and night in the trenches, we were compensated by a feeling of closeness to the earth, by the warm, enlivening breath that rose from the ground. Like a purification, a rejuvenation, it soaked into our urban bodies. We became like peasants.[90]

In sharp contrast to this idealization of the masculine trench community, Schönbrunn at a later point in his book admonished adults to teach naive boys about the extreme horrors of mechanized mass slaughter. When talking about the war experience, the teacher had to make the "death, great tragedy, and oppressive senselessness appear to come alive" in order to quell the "thoughtless desire for adventure" that made all boys curious and desirous of war. Schönbrunn wrote:

One dare not prettify it. Above all, one must talk of the destruction of morality that the war perfected and that every war will bring. The picture of battle must be illuminated from all sides. . . . The annihilation of all heroism through the incredible pressure of the heavy bombardment. . . . The wetness, the filth, the cold, the hunger and thirst, the bleak tiresomeness of eternal monotony, all this should be described to the boys. Above all, the legend, propagated by Moltke, that the main activity of the soldier was fighting, needs to be destroyed. We should depict the crushing feeling that all resistance was useless: the feeling of inevitability and abandonment in the face of the grenades coming from an enemy who could be neither seen nor heard. The enormous roar of exploding grenades, the howl and whistle of shots overhead; the smashing of bravery under huge fountains of smoke . . . and the immeasurably gruesome tearing apart of the human body—all this must be used to conjure up the reality of the past.[91]

Absurdly contradictory in its discussion of the war, Schönbrunn's book at least implied that militarism had outlived its usefulness for Germany's young generation. Other authors specifically advised hiking leaders not to use any militarist methods of discipline. For example, Ernst Kemmer developed a critique of such methods around the theme of soulless rationalism. Germany's wartime military leaders, he wrote, had created "the greatest masterwork of modern technology and had our million-strong army working together like a precise machine." But they had failed to include "the power of ideas and the human soul" in their calculations. Thus, they had lost the war, proving that national pride was not an adequate foundation for national unity, for "the love of the Fatherland must be founded in religion and morality. This should be a warning to all those who see the sole cure for our ills in a restoration of external strength (*äusseren Machtmitteln*), civic order, and strict organization." Hiking must also avoid this kind of soul-destroying discipline, for "we do not make people happier when we arrogantly teach them to conform and submit. . . . [Exercise] should not be allowed to suffocate the nobler emotions and brutalize the individual; it must help the person's better self to unfold." Hiking must be kept free of drilling and marching. Only then could it "touch the very center of the human being."[92]

According to these texts, the vitality particular to young people could come fully to light only in a collective youth community relatively free of overt adult authority and militaristic methods. But even within that community, each individual should be allowed to maintain proudly his own unique identity. Schönbrunn wrote that "awakening every single boy to true individuality [and] educating him to individual daring and cheek (*Frechheit*) [is] the final goal of all modern education. . . . That is the basis of freedom." Within the correctly guided hiking group, a community of unique individuals would form in which each individual would become part of a spontaneous and diverse social order according to his own natural abilities: "The feeling should gradually prevail of just how valuable the complementary mix of very different characters, talents, and attitudes is."[93]

Projects of social discipline, of which youth cultivation was a classic example, do not have to be overtly authoritarian or anti-individualistic as long as they succeed in getting individuals to regulate their own behavior according to prescribed norms. However, in order for the disciplinary project to be effective, it must have a firm foundation in a clear and homogeneous conceptual system.[94] The chief goal of *Jugendpflege* hiking was to bring young people into contact with nature in order to turn them into self-disciplined individuals according to particular norms of moral and physical health. Thus, the conceptual foundation of *Jugendpflege* hiking was a rationalistic and health-centered view of rural nature. Bringing German youths into contact with rural nature was supposed to both cure the ills caused by urban life and suppress the irrational urges of the young. *Jugendpflege* rhetoric such as that produced by the National Federation of Youth Hostels, in turning nature into a tool for human improvement, often tended implicitly to deny it any intrinsic value.

However, even this basic anthropocentric concept of nature was undermined by the pedagogical texts on hiking. These works were obviously influenced by the *Wandervögel*'s neo-Romantic, reverent vision of nature. In this discourse, nature resurged in relatively *non*anthropocentric terms—that is, as an infinitely diverse, awesome, and powerful entity with its own existence apart from human concerns. Schönbrunn lamented, "We are all lacking a sense of wild nature, the genuine and untouched!" and declared, "We go on hikes to take part in the oscillations of the cosmos."[95] According to Fritz Müller-Marquardt in one of the most popular hiking texts of the 1920s, the separation from nature had resulted in the alienation from work, the atrophy of the senses, and "too much comfort":

Woe betide the People that "hikes" using only the auto and train and that goes up to its mountains and glaciers in a comfortable gondola! Pathetic and poor in soul is the nation, the young generation, that desecrates in this way the deep mysteries of nature. . . . We need fewer scribblers and servants to the machine, more searchers for God and servants to eternity! Those whose relationship to nature has degenerated must . . . become complete through intimate contact with nature. Hiking must not be allowed to be only an activity of clubs; it must become a popular activity, a subject that is important to the collective, a necessity for life.[96]

Müller-Marquardt also demanded that hiking leaders teach admiration for all of life:

It cannot be stressed often enough to young hikers that nature was not created as an object upon which to try out one's raw strength senselessly. May the leader make clear to his charges that nature is a shrine that we must enter with reverence. Whoever . . . wanders through the beautiful garden of nature with feeling and sensitivity sees himself related to her and bound by fate to joy and sorrow. He knows that he is only a particle, like a plant or animal, in the mighty creation of the highest being.

For a person who could achieve this sense of transience and humility, death would lose its horrifying aspect.[97]

A reverent view of nature also characterized the hiking discourse of the *Sozialistische Arbeiterjugend*. Reverence for natural beauty and the sense that humankind is merely one tiny part of an all-encompassing universe abounded in journal essays and books by spokespersons for the SAJ.

Johannes Schult, for instance, saw nature as that which "teaches the hu-man being to be silent and astounded."[98] Another author, Hermann Sendel-bach, declared that socialist youth hiking was "hiking in the present, life from our life, an urge that is ancient and immortal," and all of nature sang "a brotherly song, the song of the great oneness of the world."[99] One local chapter of the SAJ offered the following advice to young hikers:

When you venture into all-encompassing nature, remember that . . . life in all its thousands of forms, in all its powers and miracles, is talking to you. So leave be-hind all thoughtlessness, vulgarities, and dull, everyday moods; and bring with you cheerfulness and a reverent, open soul. And avoid any misdeeds against flower, leaf, branch, or bark, or busily striving animals, or *any* of the beautiful forms with which living nature surrounds you.[100]

These sources reveal that the antiauthoritarianism and reverent vision of nature in the *Wandervogel* hiking tradition remained a powerful strain in *Jugendpflege* hiking ideology. Taken together, these individualistic and neo-Romantic elements appear to have been at odds with the youth cultivators' project of subjugating the individual, with all his or her wayward desires and emotions, to the group and to a rational adult leader. Because the ad-vocates of youth hiking in Weimar were turning over some of the power to young people themselves, they had to take it on faith that hiking would be of ultimate benefit to the nation. This was the youth cultivator's compro-mise with the reality of Germany's young, who were not willing to go along quietly with adult attempts to teach them reason and self-discipline.

Youth hiking became ever more popular during the Weimar era. Table 4.1 indicates that as the number of youth hostels increased in the Weimar era, so did the number of overnight visitors.

The hostels were open to all hikers under the age of twenty-one, whether single or in groups. Older hikers could stay in a hostel if it had not filled up by 7 P.M. Between 1919 and 1932 an average of 30 percent of the guests were elementary school students, 31 percent were second-ary students, and 33 percent were no longer in school; 70 percent were male and 30 percent, female. The number of overnight stays, of course, cannot be equated with single individuals, since there were repeat users. The National Federation of Youth Hostels estimated that each hostel user averaged five overnight stays per year, which if accurate would mean that the hostel network was serving some 650,000 individuals annually by 1928 and that the number continued to increase until 1932.[101] Considering that

TABLE 4.1   Use of youth hostels run by the *Reichsverband für Deutsche Jugendherbergen*, 1911–1932

Year	No. of hostels	No. of overnight stays	Avg. overnights per house
1911	17	3,000	177
1913	83	20,000	240
1920	700	186,200	266
1921	1,300	506,000	384
1925	2,100	1,400,000	667
1926	2,319	2,107,000	908
1927	2,383	2,560,000	1,074
1928	2,486	3,276,000	1,318
1929	2,668	3,783,300	1,418
1930	—	4,233,400	—
1931	—	4,322,000	—
1932	2,760	4,278,600	1,550

SOURCES: Compiled from Anon., "Das Jugendherbergswerk im Jahre 1931," *Jugend-Führer* (1932), 45; Mewes, *Jugend*, 180; Münker, *Jugendherbergswerk*, 29.

many more people took day hikes or stayed in places other than hostels, this figure is probably just the tip of the iceberg.

Other evidence suggests that hiking became one of the most popular activities among youths. When answering questionnaires for surveys carried out by youth cultivators, adolescents often called group hiking the most enjoyable leisure activity.[102] A detailed 1932 survey of leisure activities among five thousand of Berlin's working-class youths revealed that 84 percent of the boys and 74 percent of the girls took part regularly in various sports. Table 4.2 lists the most popular activities.[103]

"Outings" (*Ausflüge*) were day trips to parks and beaches or hikes undertaken individually, with friends, or with family. Hiking came under the auspices of a hiking club or youth organization. The gender differences in the popularity of these two activities probably reflect the greater degree to which boys were organized in independent youth groups and youth cultivation organizations.

The evidence shows that turning to nature in the form of hiking, either informally or in an organized way, became during the 1920s one of the most popular ways for young people to fill their free time. The few sources that shed some light on young people's attitudes in the Weimar

TABLE 4.2   Participation of Berlin youths in sports in 1932
(in percentage of those youths who reported any
sporting activity)

	Boys	Girls	Average
Wrestling	6	0	3
Handball	12	4	8
Other	8	9	9
Winter sports	9	11	10
Rowing/sailing	7	14	11
Soccer	24	1	13
Biking	23	18	21
Track/gymnastics	20	29	25
Swimming	20	35	28
Outings	21	36	29
Hiking	41	31	36

SOURCE: Adapted from the table in Robert Dinse, *Das Freizeitleben der Großstadtjugend* (Eberswalde, 1932), 87.

years suggest that they were attracted to hiking for the emotional satisfaction it brought, and certainly not because the socializing project of youth cultivation was in any way enticing. Indeed, some young people had their own romantic, reverent concept of nature. They seem positively awestruck in the face of nature's magnificence, and their thoughts turn rather often to the metaphysical:

When storm clouds, thunder, and lightning pass over us, there must be someone calling to us: "I rule over you all—you belong to me."[104]

How beautiful, when you see God's world waking up. Then you realize how small and insignificant we are in the face of nature.[105]

I feel so small, so meaningless in the face of God's greatness, but I also have a sense of safety and protection that I have never felt under the care of people. Just as God keeps alive so many tiny creatures, so will he protect me from ruin.[106]

There were also those who, while rejecting organized religion, combined a natural-scientific viewpoint with pantheistic religious feeling:

My mother and grandmother still believe in God and go to church. That's not for me. If I want to pray, I can do it when I take a hike. There I see nature, and that is my God.[107]

Religion is a far-reaching idea. Many people think that it is pious to go continually to church. . . . I find that repulsive; for I and my colleagues have discovered that of fifty people who go to church, only five are truly pious. The rest go only to be admired in their new clothes or to have a rendezvous. My religion is nature with its many wonders. Here I feel divinity; here God's omnipotence reveals itself; here one sees that there must be a higher power.[108]

Such musings had very little to do with youth cultivation and a lot to do with youthful individuality and emotion.

The Weimar youth cultivation movement, in its synthesis with the *Wandervogel* tradition of hiking, appears to have successfully won over many German adolescents of both sexes. But in order to do so, the *Jugendpfleger* had to give up some of their authority to young people. After 1928, however, the youth cultivators were confronted by a new crisis and the rise of a political movement that laid claim to the right to guide young people toward adulthood. Their fragile compromise between adult authority and youthful liberation was about to end.

5

The Assault on Youth Hiking, 1929–1940

DURING THE LATE WEIMAR REPUBLIC, young people between the ages of fourteen and twenty-five lived in a society that offered them little hope of an economically stable future. They made up what historian Detlev Peukert called "an expendable generation" suffering from "deep existential uncertainty and a fear of the future."[1] Mass unemployment affected young workers harshly during the Depression. No fewer than 1 million young people were unemployed by 1930 and 1.5 million by 1933.[2] Even in the decade before the Depression began, the labor market had become severely overpopulated with fourteen- to twenty-five-year-olds, giving rise to a new generational underclass that earned 30 to 50 percent less than older workers. Industrial rationalization in the 1920s had further destabilized young laborers' economic situations, especially among the unskilled and semiskilled. Intent on protecting the working-class family, the trade unions generally agreed to lay off young single workers first during phases of unemployment.[3]

This dire existential crisis was not limited to young industrial workers. The Depression struck young white-collar workers especially hard; and middle-class students suffered poor health, an acute lack of adequate housing, and a drastic worsening of their professional opportunities. A pervasive fear of pauperization accompanied the social decline of many middle-class young people.[4]

Given the failure of the Weimar welfare system to fulfill its promises of better living, working, and educational conditions, it is no wonder that many, perhaps most, young people lost faith in the republic. The early 1930s brought a renewed crisis in generational relations and in the legitimacy of adult institutions within the republican system. This was reflected in political culture. Most political parties were unable to appeal to young people and were failing to incorporate those under eighteen into their organizational structures. The conspicuous aging of the leadership and rank and file of the moderate republican parties made them less and less attractive to the young generation. By 1929, for instance, the Social Democrats had become a party of middle-aged men and women; over half of the members were older than forty, and the percentage over the age of sixty exceeded that under the age of twenty-five. In fact, the SPD had 2.5 times fewer people under twenty-five than did the German populace.[5] The drastic decline of the moderate middle-class parties stemmed in part from a similar loss of young supporters. The consequences for democracy in Germany were dire. As Larry E. Jones explains, "When the younger generation began to lend its voice to the cacophony of protest against the way in which the existing political system had consistently frustrated the formation of a genuine national consensus, this represented a dramatic intensification of the legitimacy crisis that had plagued the Weimar party system since the middle of the 1920s."[6]

The graying of the moderate political establishment became an effective propaganda weapon in the hands of radical antirepublican parties. Nazi and Communist propagandists alike revived the cult of youthfulness as a weapon to attack the "republic of old men."[7] In the state and national elections of the early 1930s, young adults cast their votes in disproportionate numbers for Communists and Nazis. Electoral statistics from the early 1930s show that many of the protest voters who helped the antirepublican forces to their mass success were newly enfranchised voters in their early twenties.[8]

The late Weimar youth cultivation movement responded to this double crisis of the economy and political culture by reverting to the panic-stricken rhetoric of emergency. Youth cultivators' suggested solutions tended increasingly toward authoritarianism. Although a disciplinary project like *Jugendpflege* always carried the potential for such a development, the movement had generally progressed to methods of negotiating young people's consent by offering them a considerable degree of everyday liberty. As discussed in the previous chapter, this progress resulted from a synthesis of the *Jugendpflege* disciplinary project with the liberationist *Wandervogel* tradition. Facing the crises of late Weimar, youth cultivators began to jettison antiauthoritarian and individualistic elements.[9] They entered into a coalition with the national government and the military for the purpose of "youth training" (*Jugendertüchtigung*), which in this case meant premilitary training. In 1932 a new state-sponsored organization, the National Advisory Board for Youth Training, was founded under the leadership of military officers. Its purpose was to teach youth cultivators how to carry out military-style drills and terrain games, which it privileged over hiking. In militarizing youth activity, the youth cultivators were reverting to the conservative-militarist precepts of the war era.

The militarization of youth exercise involved a rhetorical process by which the concepts of both youth and nature were simplified and standardized. It is here that we find a continuity between Weimar youth cultivation and the youth policies of the National Socialists. The Nazis further militarized and standardized youth exercise after their seizure of power—with the acquiescence of many leading youth cultivators. Starting in 1933 the Hitler Youth undertook to eradicate the liberationist *Wandervogel* hiking tradition, replacing it with military drill and marching in order to train Germany's young generation for the next war.

Youth Cultivation, Hiking, and Militarization in the Great Depression, 1929–1932

Beginning in 1930 structural difficulties created a pervasive sense of frustration and decline among the leaders of the youth cultivation movement. The scaling back of the welfare system under the presidential dictatorship of Hindenburg and Brüning was a blow to *Jugendpflege*, heavily dependent as it was on state support. Local *Jugendpflege* committees and youth welfare offices experienced massive financial cuts of up to 90 percent in Leipzig, Hannover, and other cities due to the crisis in municipal budgets. Subsidies for organized youth hiking were ended or substantially reduced, and even the previously well-supported National Federation of Youth Hostels received much less than it asked for from state and municipal governments.[10]

Equally worrisome to youth cultivators was a seeming increase in adolescent waywardness. As we have seen, the alleged threat of adolescent irrationality had never been far from their minds; during the mid-1920s, however, the rhetoric of out-of-control sexuality, wild hiking, and so on had died down somewhat. In the early 1930s youth cultivators reverted to the rhetoric of youth emergency because adolescents appeared to be acting increasingly in ways that directly challenged the disciplinary project of *Jugendpflege*.

There was, for instance, a striking decrease in adolescent participation in *Jugendpflege* organizations. In 1926 some 40 percent of the 9.1 million fourteen- to twenty-one-year-old Germans had belonged to a group affiliated with the National Committee of German Youth Associations; but by 1932 this percentage had fallen ten points to 30 percent.[11] Furthermore, a sense of fatalism about mass culture took hold among youth cultivators in the face of evidence that youths were indulging in mass-produced "trash and smut" more than ever before. Of nearly ten thousand Berlin adolescents questioned in a 1932 survey, some two-thirds went to the movies either weekly or occasionally.[12] Although a handful of youth cultivators responded to such information by calling for the incorporation of mass cultural forms into their everyday practice, the vast majority simply continued their rhetoric of moral endangerment. For instance, despite evidence that girls went to the movies less often than boys, Heinrich Hirtsiefer wrote that a large percentage of those girls who were not in a *Jugendpflege* organization could be found at the movies. Their minds were "stunted by work and made vacuous by the Americanized entertainment industry." The "general mass of youths," under the influence of "a foregrounding of the sexual things in life," showed a "shocking lack of responsibility . . . and moral strength."[13]

More specifically in regard to *Jugendpflege* hiking, the prevalence of autonomous youth "outings" without adult supervision was known to youth cultivators and showed clearly that many youths were still taking "wild hikes."[14] Moreover, even though the Reich Federation of Youth Hostels had grown into a very substantial organization, the working population began to use the hostels in ways that the movement's leaders had never intended. Evidence on the sociology of hostel use after 1929 showed a sharp rise in semiemployed and unemployed young people who were taking advantage of the cheap youth hostels for room and board. They were trying to survive by saving money on housing and food as they moved about searching for work. At the same time the number of middle-class youths who used the hostels sharply declined.[15]

This trend toward proletarianization sparked a debate within the Federation's leadership between those who worried about an increase in wild hiking and those who thought the influence of the hostel movement would benefit the unemployed. The representatives of the latter position, including the founder and president Richard Schirrmann, announced, "We must make a virtue out of necessity. Just as the horse without work must nonetheless be exercised daily, so should we encourage the unemployed worker to hike daily."[16] They apparently prevailed in this debate for the time being; yet concerns about wild hiking grew. The youth welfare office in Hannover, for instance, complained about groups of unemployed, unsupervised youths who during their outings were "making an unpleasant impression with their lack of discipline and ugly behavior" and called on local youth cultivators to establish more hiking groups.[17] Given the evident class bias behind such descriptions of *wildes Wandern*, we cannot judge their accuracy. Judging by what we know of the psychological consequences of unemployment, however, it would certainly not be surprising to find frustrated, hungry, and embittered youths engaging in undisciplined behavior.

The structural weakening of organized *Jugendpflege* and the perceived failure to cure the problem of adolescent waywardness led to a loss of confidence among late Weimar youth cultivators. For the Prussian Minister of Welfare Hirtsiefer, "The soul of our People has sickened. Suffering and misery are at the very heart of the nation. The destructive powers today are not outside; rather they are within us."[18] In search of an effective therapy for the nation's youth, many youth cultivators threw in their lot with a new state initiative that commenced in 1932.

In a presidential decree on September 13, 1932, President von Hindenburg announced, "The steeling of the body and the training of youth in discipline, the love of order and camaraderie, and the spirit of self-sacrifice for the general good are tasks that the state has a duty to undertake."[19] This decree signaled the determination of the authoritarian state to take over the task of socializing youth, as well as a reversion to the conservative-militarist strain of *Jugendpflege*. Hindenburg authorized the establishment of a new exercise federation, the National Advisory Board for Youth Training (*Reichskuratorium für Jugendertüchtigung*—RKJ). General of the Infantry Erwin von Stülpnagel was appointed managing director. The RKJ leadership consisted of representatives of the state and national governments and of various youth exercise organizations. The government's plan was to establish some twenty "terrain sport schools" (*Geländesportschulen*) on the sites of former army training camps. Each school would offer three-week courses to one to two hundred adult representatives from youth cultivation and exercise clubs. These men would then be expected to use their new methods in training their organizations' adolescent members. The teachers were to be veteran army officers, who would be assisted by civilian exercise instructors and police. The *Reichskuratorium* was an obvious attempt by the government and high-ranking military officers to circumvent the Versailles Treaty's ban on any form of military training. Indeed, the training camps were to be closed to the press "so as not to cause problems for the government's foreign policy," as the Reich Interior Minister explained.[20]

As one critical observer astutely noted, a key aim of this new organization was to gather the many youth and exercise organizations and place them under lasting state control.[21] The focus was exclusively on males, and the desire to standardize young male identity and behavior along militaristic lines is obvious in the stated goals and methods of the *Reichskuratorium*. Youths had to learn to conform to strict discipline. "Habituating the young man to meticulous order, to punctuality, bodily hygiene, and a simple way of life that eschews comfort will train him to be hard on himself—a trait that he needs in life." The end result would be "bodily and mental courage and self-sacrifice in the interests of the whole." The RKJ's proposed methods were aimed at teaching youths how to traverse the rural "terrain" (*Gelände*). Cross-country marching and orientation exercises would be used to this purpose. The key method, however, would be "terrain games" (*Geländespiele*), a collective term for such activities as hiding and seeking, escaping and pursuing, and ambushing.[22]

The use of terrain games was no doubt based on the realization that, for all the emphasis on strict discipline, youth training would still be voluntary and young people's consent still had to be negotiated. Terrain games had long been a common form of play in youth organizations. The Scouts, for instance, liked to playact medieval dragon slaying, the Thirty Years' War, and "cowboys and Indians." The following was typical of their discussions of *Geländespiele*: "There is between the Lech and the Danube rivers a hilly, sparsely forested terrain. It is a real battlefield, has clear views, good fortifications, and rich villages to burn and pillage."[23] Although some historians have overinterpreted such games as signs of grassroots militarism in the independent youth movement, they were little more than typical adolescent playacting. In the case of the Weimar Social Democratic youth movement, *Geländespiele* could coexist with consciously pacifist ideologies and rituals. Not even the Weimar police in

Bavaria worried about the mock battles of youth; they announced that they were in no way "military events."[24]

On the other hand, conservative youth cultivators could rather easily turn such games into premilitary training exercises. *Geländespiele* had been a common activity within the Young Germany League; and the wartime state's attempt to create a mandatory training program for teenage boys had put such games at center stage. Some more conservative youth cultivators in the late 1920s came to favor war games over all other forms of exercise, describing them as particularly suited to "awaken personal strengths; promote chivalric battle; strengthen courage, dexterity, energy and endurance; [and] teach constant readiness to put oneself in the service of the community."[25] The methods of the *Reichskuratorium* were firmly in this tradition of militarized terrain games.

The foregrounding of the popular terrain games also enabled the RKJ to jettison another form of exercise that was, from a militaristic point of view, troublesome—that is, youth hiking. There was no place for *Wandervogel*-style sauntering in the new regime of youth training. The requisite weekly "hike" was to be a quick-tempo march, in orderly formation, of at least twenty-five kilometers with heavy backpacks![26] Moreover, the rhetoric of youth hiking had always represented nature as a realm of youthful freedom. But the *Reichskuratorium*'s rhetoric reduced nature to mere "terrain" to be explored, mapped, and conquered. *Gelände* in German is a purely anthropocentric and utilitarian concept; it is "a piece of land seen in terms of its usability for definite purposes."[27] Of course, one could argue that proponents of the *Wandervogel* tradition also instrumentalized nature; but their purposes had above all to do with liberation, and their nature was to be approached with reverence.

The first training facilities that the *Reichskuratorium* set up in the late fall of 1932 were moderately successful. They attracted representatives from a wide assortment of organizations—youth cultivation and exercise associations, youth organizations of occupational groups, youth cells of political parties, and paramilitary groups ranging from the Social Democratic *Reichsbanner* to the Nazi SA. Communist youth groups were explicitly excluded, and the Socialist Worker Youth movement, suspicious of the government's motives, refused to take part. So did the Hitler Youth (*Hitler Jugend—HJ*).[28] Following the Nazi takeover of power in late January 1933, the RKJ project was not actively pursued; and the regime absorbed it into the SA in October of that year. The real significance of the *Reichskuratorium* lies in what it reveals about late Weimar *Jugendpflege*—exhaustion, frustration, and a willingness to turn to statist, authoritarian, and premilitary methods. Indeed, there was considerable agreement among all sectors of *Jugendpflege* that youth had to be taken control of again in this time of crisis, even if this meant dispensing with the principles of individualism and youth liberation. In the process the language of working with youth shifted—from "cultivating youth" (*Jugendpflege*) to the more social darwinist "making fit" (*Jugendertüchtigung*), and from "nature" as a realm of health and liberation to "terrain" as a platform for premilitary training. The undermining of the *Wandervogel* hiking tradition began in late Weimar, even before the Nazi regime set about destroying it.

The Nazi *Gleichschaltung* of Youth

The Nazis were determined to take total control of the hearts, minds, and bodies of Germany's young people. In the well-chosen words of historian Eric Michaud, their youth policy was aimed at "subjugating and infantilizing an entire people."[29] In the course of the *Gleichschaltung* of civil society in 1933 and 1934, the Nazis undertook to crush all possible sites of resistance in both the established youth cultivation sector and the independent youth movement.

The regime used a "carrot-and-stick" approach. On the one hand, they appealed to the tendency toward authoritarianism among late Weimar youth cultivators, inviting them to participate in yet another "renewal" of youth under the leadership of the Hitler state. Many youth cultivators chose to do so, and those who came under political suspicion or simply refused to go along were quickly purged from the state *Jugendpflege* bureaucracy. On the other hand, during the spring and summer of 1933 the Nazis forcibly shut down the National Committee of German Youth Associations, took over the National Federation of Youth Hostels, and banned nearly all associations within the independent youth movement. By the fall, only the Catholic youth organizations remained, for the Concordat of July 20, 1933, between the Catholic Church hierarchy and Hitler had preserved them—for the time being. This varied approach to existing *Jugendpflege* and youth movement institutions was typical of the methods by which the Nazis consolidated their power. By the end of the *Gleichschaltung* phase, the Hitler Youth had begun to take over the tasks of "youth training," and its attack on the *Wandervogel* tradition was in full swing.

Baldur von Schirach, whom Hitler appointed Reich Youth Leader on March 17, 1933, directed the *Gleichschaltung* of organized youth cultivation. One of his first moves was to declare himself chair of the National Committee of German Youth Associations after members of the Hitler Youth raided its offices on April 5, 1933. Schirach soon dissolved the Committee, putting a sudden end to an institution that had promoted compromise and cooperation across the generations and among many diverse organizations. Schirach retained the established network of municipal, district, and state *Jugendpflege* committees; but he directed the authorities to purge them of socialists, Jews, and anyone else who did not fit the new regime's ideological profile. In November 1933 the regime issued a twofold command to the youth cultivation committees. They were to develop methods of indoctrination through the "deliberate and thorough physical building of the young into a healthy, truly German generation" and "a mental and spiritual appropriation and re-formation (*geistig-seelische Erfassung und Umgestaltung*) of youth through the ideology of National Socialism." These tasks were to be carried out in close collaboration with the Hitler Youth.[30]

Many, if not most, moderate and conservative youth cultivators acquiesced to their incorporation into the Nazi system. The reasons for this are not difficult to fathom if we consider the middle class's rejection of the failed Weimar system and their desire for something radically different. The Nazi promise of economic recovery, restored national power, and a *Volksgemeinschaft* that transcended social divisions was too attractive to turn down. After all, the goals of national recovery and social harmony were at the heart of the Weimar *Jugendpflege* project, and those hopes were intensified by the renewed perception of a youth emergency that prevailed in the early 1930s. Youth cultivators now placed their hopes in the totalitarian aim of incorporating young people from all classes and age groups into one organization, something that had been impossible in the pluralistic society of Weimar.[31] As historian Hermann Giesecke puts it, "Resistance could only mean that one desired to hinder the work of unifying the people and to hold fast to one's own particularistic strivings."[32]

The synchronized *Jugendpflege* committees took up their work energetically. In the Lower Saxon town of Clausthal-Zellerfeld, for instance, the committee established voluntary, sex-segregated educational evenings and brought in Nazi Party speakers to teach the students about "racial questions." Yet local Nazi leaders who directed these schooling efforts complained about a lack of discipline among the students and antipathy of their parents toward the regime.[33] Indeed, despite the efforts of the committees to carry out the regime's directives, Nazi leaders had by 1935 apparently concluded that the established *Jugendpflege* network was doing more harm than good. This paralleled the growing organizational strength of the Hitler Youth. In May 1935 the network of *Jugendpflege* committees in existence since 1911 was completely taken over by the Nazi paramilitary and youth organizations, and their new purpose became simply to persuade the entire young generation to enter the HJ and its female branch, the League of German Maidens (*Bund deutscher Mädel*—BDM).[34]

In hindsight we can see that the regime's use of voluntary *Jugendpflege* between 1933 and 1935 was no more than a temporary step on the path toward totalitarian compulsion, the real instrument of which became the Hitler Youth. Nevertheless, it is interesting to note that the professed aim of the Hitler Youth at their most basic echoed that of Weimar *Jugendpflege*—that is, the holistic "education of the youth's body, mind, and character."[35] This basic ideology of progress toward adulthood was the common denominator between *Jugendpflege* and Hitler Youth discourse, even if the methods and final goals were, in fact, quite divergent.

The one part of the youth cultivation movement that survived for some years after 1933 was the Catholic sector. The regime's treatment of organized Catholic youth was another example of provisional tactics. During the spring of 1933, the new regime attempted to repress the large Catholic youth organizations with bans on public meetings, confiscations of documents, raids on youth centers, and direct physical attacks on club members. The HJ and Baldur von Schirach undertook a propaganda campaign demanding that youths turn their backs on the "particularistic religious-confessional clubs" since the young generation was "neither Catholic nor Protestant, but GERMAN!"[36] Powerful organizations such as the four hundred thousand–strong Catholic Young Men's Federation (*Katholischer Jungmännerverband*—KJMV) joined other mass organizations to warn publicly against the regime's efforts. One such announcement in February 1933 stated that the Nazis were sinning against German unity by "conjuring up thoughts of hatred and revenge and by declaring dissenters to be outlaws. This is ravaging Germany's youth and destroying the bases of a healthy state."[37]

Nevertheless, Catholic leaders soon demonstrated their willingness to make their peace with the regime. The Catholic Center Party had already begun this process in March by voting in parliament for the Enabling Law that destroyed democracy. Soon thereafter, the Catholic bishops withdrew their previous official warnings against Nazism, declaring on June 8 that the two worldviews had important commonalities. The way was open for the signing of the Concordat between the Vatican and Hitler on July 20, 1933, according to which organized Catholics in Germany were to abandon all political activity in return for the regime's toleration of cultural activities.

This agreement preserved Catholic *Jugendpflege*. Following the Concordat, Ludwig Wolker, head of the KJMV, sent the following message to youth leaders in the dioceses: "We require from all a steadfast bearing and a realistic judgment of things as they are. We have no use for youth leaders who are cowardly defeatists or for those who cannot recognize the positive aspects of the new [state]."[38] Other leaders went beyond such calls to stoicism, admonishing young Catholics to contribute their spiritual energies in order to help Christianize the Third Reich. Cardinal Eugenio Pacelli (after 1938, Pope Pius XII), who was a representative of Pius XI in Berlin at the time and a key orchestrator of concordats with both Mussolini and Hitler, addressed Catholic youth directly in one of the leading *Jugendpflege* journals. "You would not be Catholic young people," Pacelli told them, "if an apostolic urge did not burn within you, an urge to activate, unselfishly and happily, the indispensable energies (*Kraftquellen*) of Christian thought and Christian will as your Fatherland is newly shaped."[39]

Within this situation of limited autonomy, the Catholic youth movement represented the only legal organized alternative to the Hitler Youth, and it was popular. Mass periodicals such as *Junge Front* and *Die Wacht* outpublished those of the Hitler Youth in 1934, a clear sign of the movement's popularity. Indeed, by 1935 there were locales in which participants in the still voluntary Hitler Youth switched over to a Catholic organization. This was an act of civic courage, especially since the regime did its utmost to hinder organized young Catholics from finding and keeping a job. Furthermore, there were increasingly common instances after 1934 of censorship and police repression, attacks from the Nazi press, and acts of everyday violence and vandalism against Catholic youth groups by the HJ, the SA, and the SS.[40]

The Nazis were concerned not only about their ideological differences with the Catholics, but also about the religious subculture's ability to mobilize adolescents and devise an everyday alternative to the Hitler

Youth. The years 1935 through 1938 brought intensified persecution of Catholic youth cultivation. Feeling that they had consolidated their power well enough to violate the Concordat, the Nazi leadership began to clamp down on their last remaining organized competitors for the hearts and minds of the young. Himmler's directive to the police forces of July 23, 1935, made continued state toleration of the Catholic youth sector conditional on the latter giving up uniforms and insignias; group marching, hiking, camping, and music making in public; and all sport and "military training." These activities were now redefined as political and thus in violation of the Concordat.[41] Many groups refused to acquiesce to the new restrictions. One former member of a youth club in Wetzlar later reminisced about the early Third Reich:

Despite oppression by the state, we regularly held social meetings, hikes, and camps. Beginning in 1934, public demonstrations were impossible; however, church events for youths were widely attended (and, by the authorities, suspiciously observed) avowals of Catholic activism. Discussions of the character of National Socialism . . . arose naturally out of the Christian consciousness of morality and history but also out of general political traditions. Close contacts existed with those persons . . . who were known to oppose National Socialism.[42]

The Gestapo felt compelled to observe Catholic *Jugendpflege* groups who were suspected of "terrain sports" such as hiking and camping.[43] In February 1936 the Gestapo arrested fifty-seven youth leaders on the grounds that they were planning a "unified Catholic-Communist front." Although most of the prisoners were released within weeks due to a lack of evidence, the People's Court held, tried, and condemned seven of them to prison sentences and official "loss of honor" in April 1937. "Communist leanings" was one of the reasons the Gestapo gave for its total ban on all Catholic youth organizations on January 25, 1938. The Gestapo stated further that the movement had continued to disobey the ban on sport, uniforms, and insignias and had continued to hike, camp, and carry out premilitary training through terrain games and small-caliber rifle shooting.[44]

Hitler's regime tried to quickly neutralize the network of independent middle-class youth organizations known collectively as the "league youth" (*bündische Jugend*). By early 1933 the *bündische* movement had a membership of approximately sixty thousand males and seven thousand females between the ages of fourteen and twenty-five.[45] A minority conglomeration of far-right-wing, racist groups quickly synchronized themselves by flocking en masse into the Hitler Youth. Yet the majority of *bündische* groups were not fascist but conservative in their ideology. As such they followed the general pattern of conservative elites after the Nazi takeover—that is, they tried to preserve their organizational and ideological autonomy within the new state of affairs.

The *bündische Jugend* tried to carve out an organizational niche for themselves. In early April 1933, a coalition of *bündische* groups containing some fifty thousand members formed a new umbrella association, the Greater Germany League (*Großdeutscher Bund*—GDB).[46] The League's leader was Adolf von Trotha, retired vice admiral of the navy and member of the German Nationalist Party. Trotha hoped that his close professional relationship with Reich President von Hindenburg would ensure the survival of the independent youth movement; but like most traditional conservatives at this moment in German history, he seriously overestimated Hindenburg's power over Hitler. The Greater Germany League quickly announced its commitment to National Socialism and offered to enter the Hitler Youth as a suborganization. Echoing the elitism of the *Wandervogel* tradition, the GDB was claiming for itself a position of autonomy from

Members of the *Großdeutscher Bund* at their national meeting on the Lüneburg Heath, June 1933. By permission of Archiv der deutschen Jugendbewegung.

which it could help to ennoble the Nazi youth movement from within. And Trotha's statement of purpose upheld the *Wandervögel's* balancing act of "helping members develop into self-sufficient personalities" while teaching them a sense of community.[47] Yet these aims were at total cross-purposes with the new regime's totalitarian approach to youth, as the League was soon to discover.

Over the next two months, the League sought without success to import the *bündische* youth into the new system intact. Its leadership continually stressed the organization's commitment to help the Nazis renew the German nation. They also apparently believed that the Nazi youth movement would favor the independent youth movement tradition over state-sponsored *Jugendpflege*. "We want to keep the creative energies of the young nation from turning cold (*erstarren*) in organized youth cultivation, in order that they may work independently to perfect the Reich," wrote Erich Küsel to Schirach. Trotha complained to Hitler in at least two letters about the League's "persecution" by Schirach. He asked the Führer for advice on how the GDB could be put to work and suggested an "organic merger" with the Hitler Youth.[48] Meanwhile, the press began to attack the League, calling it the "sad remnant of a dying era." Trotha was decried as someone who wanted to divide Germany's young generation, someone who failed to recognize the "law of the stronger." The Hitler Youth organ *Junge Nation* blasted the "nauseating impertinence" with which the League was trying to pervert the new youth movement: "In the name of our fallen comrades, destroy the youth leagues!"[49]

After at least two letters of complaint from Admiral von Trotha to Adolf Hitler, Hitler finally answered on June 1. He probably made this move only because he was aware of the admiral's close relationship to President von Hindenburg. Indeed, the latter had in the meantime called upon Hitler to force Schirach into a meeting with the admiral. Hitler now informed Trotha that if the League's members wanted to enter the Hitler Youth, they could only do so as individuals. In any case, he currently had no plans to dissolve the League.[50] This letter appears to have been a stalling maneuver, for Hitler soon began to exert his own influence to turn the old president against the GDB. Hitler wrote to Hindenburg on June 15: "In Germany's young generation there is such a great longing for unity that the overwhelming mass can no longer tolerate the splintering of the youth movement." "Fatal particularism and strife" had to be overcome, and the youth movement was a good place to start.[51]

This was Hitler's standard justification for *Gleichschaltung*—that is, the main problem to be overcome was that the Germans tended toward too much diversity, and that the pluralism and tolerance of the Weimar "system" had drastically worsened that tendency. Such arguments apparently had a strong impact on Hindenburg. After Schirach announced on June 17 a total ban against the *Großdeutscher Bund*, Trotha complained bitterly to Hindenburg, to no avail.[52]

Most of the *Bund*'s constituent groups chose at that point to dissolve themselves, and they urged their members to join the Hitler Youth in the hopes of bringing *bündische* ideas of national renewal to bear within the Nazi system. *Bündische* leaders convinced themselves that the HJ signified recognition of the right of young people to govern themselves. After all, Schirach in these early years constantly trumpeted the principle of self-leadership by the young, and he seemed to live up to that principle by instituting a system whereby older adolescents were appointed to prominent positions in the leadership hierarchy.[53] Once they entered the HJ, these former youth movement leaders were either corrupted or silenced by the Nazi system. Apparently many former youth movement leaders found a comfortable niche in the Third Reich; some, like former Scouting leader Karl Erdmann, even joined the SS.[54] This was not, however, due to a strong protofascist ideological affinity in the *bündische* youth movement. Rather, those former youth movement leaders who joined the Nazis did so *in spite of* their earlier *bündische* identity.

The leaders of the Nazi youth organization did their best throughout the 1930s to demonize their biggest competitor for the young—the *Wandervögel bündische Jugend* tradition. This had begun even before Hitler had come to power, when the Hitler Youth had been a small fringe organization, one of many "youth sections" of the Weimar political parties. Such rhetoric was part of the process of self-definition that the Hitler Youth underwent throughout its entire history. This project of gaining total control over the young generation was determined to eradicate the "other," both within the HJ and without. Yet before 1939, when membership of ten- to eighteen-year-olds of both sexes became compulsory, the HJ still was obliged to win over the young. One key way they did so was to give lip service to a *Wandervogel*-influenced ethic of "youthful self-education" (*Selbsterziehung der Jugend*). Their faith that the HJ meant this seriously may well have been an important reason why many former members of the *bündische Jugend* joined. Furthermore, the huge increase in the Hitler Youth's membership between 1932 and 1935—from about 108,000 to over 8 million—seemed to require the presence of experienced *bündische* leaders.

This influx of *bündische* leaders and youths only made the HJ, with its oft-repeated claim to utter originality and newness, feel more pressed to denigrate the pre-1933 youth movement. Moreover, the Nazi youth leadership was serious in its belief that the *bündische* influence posed a threat to the total takeover of Germany's adolescents. How could an organization determined to indoctrinate, infantilize, and send to war the nation's young generation tolerate the ideal of youthful self-liberation? As Jürgen Zarusky has written, the *bündische* tradition held the "latent but potentially explosive power of the youthful desire for autonomy."[55] Indeed, there were some very real schemes by certain former *bündische* leaders to subvert the HJ from within.[56] Thus, it is not surprising that as the Catholic *Jugendpflege* organizations came under increased pressure from the HJ, they also became more defiantly *bündisch* in their rhetoric, visual symbolism, and activities.[57]

For all of these reasons, *Wandervogel/bündische* "tendencies" within Germany's young generation became one of the Hitler Youth's primary targets for eradication beginning in 1933. The HJ's aim was political in the sense that they wanted to intimidate former *bündische* youth leaders and members into conforming. Thus, they began a campaign to redefine the pre-Nazi youth movement as a misguided and dangerous failure. The movement came under particular attack for having been backwardly "romantic," both in its view of modern technology and in its politics.

The HJ attacked the youth movement's "yammering about nature" (*Naturschwärmerei*) and its alleged backwardness in regard to technology. For instance, one 1928 article blasted the *Wandervögel*'s "raving" about the Middle Ages, which blinded it to the marvels of modern, "genuinely German" technology: "Has [the German soul] become so weak in the German youth movement that it cannot see the truth about the supposed soullessness of technology? . . . How philistine and blind you are, narrow-minded and cowardly, sometimes even hateful, when it comes to any manifestations of technology."[58] According to Schirach in 1934, the movement's dismissal of modern technology was part and parcel of its bourgeois elitism, for it meant that *bündische* leaders had no interest in the working-class boy:

This little clique of megalomaniacal romantics stands for the eternal spirit of negativity [*Verneinung*] among the young. . . . The vague ideals of the *bündischen* have faded.

In place of the "hiking experience," the "youth league" and similar pretty things, we now have an ideal that belongs not to a mere thirty pupils but to the entire nation: the ideal of work.[59]

For the HJ, the earlier youth movement had also been deficient in its romantic politics. Depending on who was writing the polemic, the movement was blasted as reactionary, liberal, or apolitical. According to Shirach, the *bündische Jugend* had been something of an improvement over the *Wandervögel*, because they had learned the duty of self-sacrifice in the trenches of the "Great War." But political reality and their own weaknesses had made them obsolete, and "these times do not demand yet another version of the campfire romanticism of bourgeois pupils."[60]

Others attacked the *bündische Jugend* for "submitting to the dishonorable democracy of Weimar" rather than fighting it. According to a 1935 essay by Friedrich Hymmen, it was quite wrong to see the HJ as the final stage in the evolution of the bourgeois youth movement. The latter had merely "taken flight into a peaceful illusionary empire (*Scheinreich*) based on a bond with nature" so as to avoid taking up the challenges of reality. The "wandering birds inevitably left firm ground and lost themselves in the clouds of 'humanity'" rather than commit themselves to helping the German nation in its time of need. The youth movement had grown "stubborn" when the time came for the HJ in 1933, "but without success; for whoever was not with us was against us and had to give way!"[61]

Elitism; disorderly individualism and emotionalism; "romanticism" in the sense of naiveté, softness, and backwardness; and treason against the nation—all these alleged characteristics were used to discredit the *bündische* youth movement. An intensification of the attacks occurred in 1935, with the HJ accusing remnants of the *bündische Jugend* of being politically and sexually dangerous. This coincided with a determined effort to finally rid the HJ of all clandestine *bündische* groups. Such groups were "plague bacilli of communism" made up of "pathetic figures with long ponytails, pale faces, mostly effeminate, and wearing all too short pants." These "seducers of youth" were scheming to win over young people in the HJ to communism.[62] In April 1936 the Gestapo banned all *bündische* insignia, clothing, and literature. It also specifically banned unsupervised "friendly meetings" of male adolescents. Such meetings exhibited the "*bündische* principle of friendship among *individuals*" and were therefore completely at odds with the HJ's anti-individualistic obsession with community.[63]

This rhetoric signified that the Hitler Youth leadership had not forgotten about the moral panic of 1913–14 and the lingering suspicions of deviant sexuality in the independent youth movement. Indeed, the Nazis' preoccupation with male homosexuality played a prominent role in the repression of *bündische* youth. Heinrich Himmler in particular was convinced that there was a gay conspiracy to seduce youths, and his reading of Blüher's theories of the homoerotic *Männerbund* evidently made him uncertain of exclusively male groupings like his own SS.[64] Thus, although Paragraph 175 of the national law code had criminalized male homosexuality since 1871, the new regime made practical use of this law to an unprecedented extent. In 1934 the Gestapo set up a department to collect information on "homosexual offenses," taking the first step toward the goal of total registration. Local police and Gestapo officers began the surveillance and interrogation of hundreds of men, many of whom had been denounced by their neighbors and acquaintances. In 1935 the regime revised Paragraph 175 to include not just men caught in the act of sex but "any indecency" among men, including looking at each other for too long and swimming nude together. The number of convictions immediately jumped from 948 in 1934 to 2,106 in 1935.[65] In 1936 Himmler established the Office for Combating Homosexuality and Abortion in Berlin, which soon set up a card index of Germans accused of homosexuality. In 1938 the Office of Racial Policy announced that Germany faced an "epidemic of some 2 million homosexuals, representing 10 percent of the entire adult male population."[66]

At the core of this project was the tried-and-true specter of the adult gay male seducer of youth. The Office for Combating Homosexuality played on fears of pedophilia, announcing that homosexuals constituted "a serious threat to young people."[67] Given the Nazis' project of eradicating homosexuality, the general stereotype of the gay male as pedophile, and the memory of earlier scandal surrounding *Wandervogel* sexuality, it is no surprise that the regime began to accuse former leaders of the *bündische Jugend* of homosexuality. We still have no figures on the number of men who were arrested and incarcerated, but a Reich Youth Office report of 1941 provides indirect evidence that this was the final blow to the leadership of the *bündische* movement: "In the political struggle against the *bündische Jugend*, the destruction of the youth leagues usually proceeded by means of Paragraph 175."[68]

Common to all of the Nazi regime's attacks on the independent youth movement tradition was the accusation of treason against the nation's young generation. That treason was cultural, political, and sexual, and it stemmed from a uselessly emotional and naive, effeminate romanticism. In view of this anti-romantic rhetoric, we must challenge the notion that the Hitler Youth was committed to an antimodern, antitechnological, and neo-Romantic worldview. In the following section, we will look at how the Nazi youth organization dealt with the *Wandervogel* tradition of youth hiking.

The Hitler Youth and Hiking

By 1936 the Hitler Youth had become the largest youth organization in German history.[69] Young people from all classes belonged, and the membership gap between boys and girls was gradually closing. The Hitler Youth's rapid growth in membership encouraged the Nazi leaders' belief that the state would one day be able to control *every* German youth. Statistics produced by the HJ showed drastic jumps in membership between 1932 and 1934 and again in 1936. Table 5.1 shows membership trends between 1932 and 1939.

These figures must be interpreted with caution. There was increasing state and social pressure to join; and the sudden jumps in membership resulted from a number of factors, primarily the mass, nonvoluntary incorporation of youths who had formerly belonged to other organizations. For instance, a 1933 agreement between Schirach and the Protestant leader Ludwig Müller led to the incorporation of eight hundred thousand Protestant youths.[70] Thus, the numbers alone can tell us little of how popular the Hitler Youth movement actually was among the young.

TABLE 5.1   Hitler Youth membership, 1932–1939

	10–18-year-olds	% in HJ	HJ members	Male:female ratio
End of 1932	c. 7,400,000	c. 1.4	107,956	78:22
End of 1933	7,529,000	31	2,300,000	74:26
End of 1934	7,682,000	47	3,577,000	63:37
End of 1935	8,172,000	48	3,900,000	59:41
End of 1936	8,656,000	62	5,400,000	54:46
End of 1937	9,060,000	64	5,800,000	52:48
September 1939	8,870,000	98	8,700,000	61:39

SOURCE: Adapted from Hellfeld and Klönne, *Generation*, 35.

If we consider, however, that these were the only figures available to Hitler, they help explain his increasing confidence in the HJ as a means of total indoctrination. In the Hitler Youth Law of December 1936, Hitler declared, "In the household, the school, and the Hitler Youth, the whole of Germany's youth is to be educated physically, mentally, and morally in the spirit of National Socialism to serve the People and the *Volksgemeinschaft*."[71] This further increased the pressure on those young people who had not yet joined; and follow-up decrees in 1939 made HJ membership compulsory. By 1939, about 98 percent of the Third Reich's youth between the ages of ten and eighteen officially belonged to the Nazi youth organization.

The Hitler Youth was neither a *Jugendpflege* organization nor a genuine youth movement. Rather, it was a dependent subsidiary of a political party. Its goal, therefore, was not to socialize young people into being good, rational citizens in a general sense, but to transform nonpolitical young people into avid supporters of the Nazi Party in everything it did. The HJ was at best a sham youth movement based on a mythical facade of popular sovereignty. The Nazis had made clever political use of the "cult of youthfulness" in order to gain popular support from the young before 1933. Soon after taking power, however, we find the HJ trying to do away with generational identities, declaring the oppositional youth movement dead, and trumpeting the unity of the generations within the *Volksgemeinschaft*. They still tried to attract youths with the promise that "the young should lead the young"; and indeed, many HJ units had young adult leaders who were only a few years older than their adolescent charges. Yet as Arno Klönne has shown, this was a sham, for older functionaries determined everything in strict hierarchical fashion from above, and these leaders were imposed from above rather than chosen by the rank and file. Youths were ordered into groups, which prevented spontaneous groupings from forming based on choice or sympathy. Methods of self-education through the discussion of particular themes that had taken shape before 1933 gave way to authoritarian "listen and learn" teaching methods. And, as Klönne writes, the HJ tried to disguise its inflexibility by constant group projects and competition, "simultaneously forcing and taming the youthful urge to activity." The HJ became a realm of education in which there was no spontaneity or free will but only "unconditional identification" and submission.[72]

The ultimate aim of the Hitler Youth, in fact, was to indoctrinate adolescents in a specific ideological outlook that combined social darwinist militarism, racial nationalism, and the demonization of those people who were defined as threats to the race. Only so would the regime be able to send them to war. "The crowning achievement of all pedagogical work of the folkish state," proclaimed Hitler, "must be to inculcate in youths the understanding of and feel for race, both instinctually in the heart and rationally in the brain."[73] Racist ideology played a huge role in the schooling of HJ leaders and in every HJ publication. Boys were informed that they carried a "genetic consciousness" of discipline, soldierliness (*Soldatentum*), and submission to the national community. Girls were the "racial conscience" (*Rassegewissen*) of the nation and should be "strong, proud, and heroic protectors of the purity of the blood."[74]

In truth the Hitler Youth was fundamentally at odds with the *Jugendpflege/Wandervogel* synthesis described previously, for it completely dispensed with any notions of individual rights and freedoms. The processes by which Hitler Youth leaders edged out organized *Jugendpflege* and demonized the *bündische* movement made clear their utter rejection of the notion of youthful autonomy. Youth exercise in the HJ made manifest the Nazis' authoritarian intentions in everyday practice.

Despite the HJ's lip service to holistic training of both the intellect and the body, the Nazis had no intention of creating a young generation that could think for itself. As Hitler himself announced, "The training of mental abilities takes second place"; and Schirach stated that two-thirds of all schooling of both sexes should be dedicated to "making the body fit" (*körperliche Ertüchtigung*).[75] This emphasis was no doubt an effective way to gain support from many young people early in the regime. Exercise, after all, had proven tremendously popular during the 1920s; and youths living in the countryside were no doubt particularly attracted to local HJ groups that offered many of them guided forms of exercise for the first time.[76]

Any youth hoping for individualistic forms of exercise soon discovered that self-realization was not on the HJ's agenda. The unwavering goals of Nazi youth exercise were officially formulated as follows:

1. It should promote in the present generation the best possible (genetically inherited) abilities of bodily movement, form, posture, and strength and should thereby make [young people] co-responsible for preserving the species.

2. It should educate in the idea of the *Volksgemeinschaft* by offering the opportunity to participate in a community.

3. It should raise people's consciousness of their warlike destiny and of a heroic, dynamic way of life.[77]

For the Nazis, both male and female adolescents had to be disciplined through exercise in order to inculcate the regime's racial-nationalist values and to divest the individual of independent judgment. The goal was a perfectly obedient warrior for the nation, either on the home front of reproduction or in battle.

The Hitler Youth had no tolerance for the kind of youth hiking that the *Wandervögel* and youth cultivation movements had practiced. We can trace the destruction of that liberating hiking tradition, first, in the takeover of the youth hostels; second, in the renewed demonization of wild hiking; third, in the replacement of hiking by marching in the Hitler Youth; and fourth, in the HJ's concept of nature.

On April 10, 1933, representatives of Schirach showed up at the National Federation of Youth Hostels' central office at Burg Altena near Bremen. They demanded that founder and president Richard Schirrmann resign; otherwise, all hostels would be closed and all twenty-five regional offices would be occupied. Schirrmann refused, stating that all the youth hostels' affairs were in order and that Schirach had nothing against them. This was a brave but fruitless attempt to avoid *Gleichschaltung*, for on that very day, the press announced that the Federation had been incorporated into the Hitler Youth.[78] Also on the same day, the regional HJ leader Lauterbacher proclaimed the reason for the synchronization. The hostel network was one of the greatest inventions of Germany's young generation, stated Lauterbacher. The HJ did not intend to destroy it but to save it from "criminal elements" that were trying to poison youth by promoting "international fraternization of a pacifist kind." No doubt referring to the influx of unemployed workers and to the small number of foreign tourists who visited the hostels, Lauterbacher concluded as follows: "When German youth hostels become strongholds of Marxist contamination, when their administrators think that they can waste them on sheltering Negroes and Chinese, then the hostels are obviously failing to serve German youth!"[79]

The HJ quickly took over the Federation, replacing most of the leading functionaries or relegating them to mere ceremonial roles.[80] Some of these former leaders, such as the regional Bavarian chairman Ernst Enzensperger, voiced their support for the HJ despite their loss of power. Enzensperger offered his "most ardent wish that prosperity and growth accompany the youth hostels under their new leadership." In June 1933 he proudly announced the building of a new hostel in Berchtesgaden named after the Führer.[81] However, many if not most of the former leaders were eventually hounded out, including Richard Schirrmann. The HJ had no use for representatives of the old hostel movement; and between 1933 and 1934 the Nazi press launched a series of attacks on the hostel movement's former leaders for allowing the hostels to become "Jewish and Marxist contaminated," mere places to spend the night rather than the cultural centers they should have been.[82]

In fact, the hostels *had* been cultural centers. As peaceful overnight lodgings for individual and group hikers, they had been lively places of sociability. They had sponsored courses to teach parents, teachers, and youth cultivators how to lead groups of young hikers. The *Gleichschaltung* of the Federation was the beginning of a process that put an end to all that, reducing the hostels by 1937 to ideological schools for the Hitler Youth alone.[83] One step in this process involved the HJ convincing the Reich Minister of Education that school hiking trips were overcrowding the youth hostels. The Minister proceeded to limit schools to just four "teaching trips" per year, and they were only to visit urban sites like museums and factories. These limitations put an end to overnight group hiking trips by school pupils.[84]

Another step in the reduction in the number of youth hostels was the turn to surveillance of all hikers. In May 1936 the Surveillance Department of the Reich Youth Leader's office put the Hitler Youth Patrol Service (*Streifendienst*) in charge of observing the youth hostels. They had the right to enter any hostel and demand that the hostel administrator give them information on all the youths who were staying there. The official directives to the patrols indicated the Nazis' intention of drawing a very clear line between politically correct HJ behavior and non-HJ, "wild" hiking, particularly that practiced illegally by Catholic and *bündische* youths. The patrols were taught to recognize telltale signs of "*bündische* activity," such as "casual, disorderly, unclean behavior" and unkempt hair and clothes. Overtly "religious-confessional" clothes or insignia were signs of Catholic activity. If any illegal hikers were discovered, either singly or in groups, they were to be reported to the police.[85]

The final step was a ban on all those youths who did not belong to the HJ. According to a decree by Schirach in November 1937, the official ID card allowing repeated overnight stays in the youth hostel network was available for free only to HJ and BDM members. Others had to pay each time they spent the night, even if they had a membership. This was also intended to supervise HJ members, as the decree forced them to wear a uniform to the hostels, and hostel administrators were now required to report anyone who failed to do so.[86] The segregation of wild hikers was accompanied by an ever more thorough regimentation of the HJ membership.

Wildes Wandern once again became a demonized activity; but it now fell into the category of nonconformity to the regime's principles. Like most instances of nonconformity in the Third Reich, it was redefined as both a political and a *racial* threat—as a sign of "hereditary criminal tendencies."[87] This is how the regime diagnosed the "sickness" of those youths who persisted in forming renegade groups. A new generation of working-class youths began in the late 1930s to form such unsupervised and rebellious groups. The Edelweiss Pirates and the "Packs" (*Meuten*) all engaged in nonconforming behavior by wearing their own uniforms, singing songs from the *bündische* youth movement, and taking illegal, coed hikes. Only some saw themselves as a political alternative to the HJ, but all were against the Nazi youth movement and sometimes fought groups of Hitler Youths. The authorities asserted not only that they were political enemies but also that they were sexually precocious and/or homosexual.[88] This rhetoric against rebellious groups combined a resuscitated *Jugendpflege* rhetoric of moral panic, with its emphasis on the threat of adolescent sexuality, and a specifically Nazi emphasis on racial inferiority. Beginning in 1938 the regime launched a concerted but only partially successful effort to capture and imprison renegade youth leaders.[89]

Another type of *wildes Wandern* persisted after 1938, carried out by small underground Catholic youth groups. The following reminiscence by a member of the Catholic youth organization in the town of Wetzlar suggests that for those Catholic young people who refused to acquiesce, there were opportunities to meet with like-minded groups even into the war years:

Lively groups of Catholic youths existed all over Germany. Right up to the outbreak of the war, such groups visited us in Wetzlar almost daily; usually they would catch our attention in front of the youth hostel. . . . Even during the war, these people met and recognized each other. In the barracks, on the military training grounds, and in fighting units there were everywhere living cells of Catholic youth.[90]

That such subterranean cells existed even on the battlefront in World War II reminds us that the Catholic youth underground did not amount to truly effective political resistance. As the author of the above reminiscence

admits, the actions of himself and his comrades—even if they, too, drew
the wrath of the Nazis—could not be considered true resistance:

Of course, real insight into the diabolical and inhumane character of National Socialism was not possible for [us] at the time. This was no great organized opposition
that could have liberated the Fatherland from its tyrants. But we wanted our own
rights and freedom—also the freedom of religion. And we had, despite our fears, a
kind of boyish enthusiasm for our independent and adventurous group life. . . . Not
even the weapons of state oppression could crush the desire for our *own* way of life.
Police interrogations were an everyday event for us—mostly regarding forbidden
"demonstrations" in forbidden uniforms with forbidden banners or pennants.[91]

Although the wild hiking and other activities of these rebellious youths
posed no real political threat to the regime, the Nazis viewed any gathering
outside the Hitler Youth with great suspicion and undertook to stamp out
all forms of youthful sociability. The effort reflects the regime's totalitarian
intent, and the regime's ultimate lack of success demonstrates that total
state domination was impossible in Nazi Germany. There were interstices
in which nonconforming behavior could survive. Renegade youth hiking
groups apparently still existed as late as 1943, when a Gestapo directive noted
an increase in reports of non-HJ hiking. We know little of what these wartime groups were doing. But the courage of these unnamed young people
was remarkable, for under the Nazi regime, any form of youthful resistance
to adult authority carried the risk of arrest, internment, and death.[92]

The Nazification of youth exercise left no room for the emancipatory
elements of hiking. In everyday practice this meant the end of hiking as
an officially sanctioned activity. The turning point was 1936–37, simultaneously with the final HJ takeover of the youth hostels and the clampdown on *bündische* and Catholic youth. In 1937 the Nazi youth leadership
went so far as to purge its own discourse of the last remnant of the hiking
tradition—they banned the use of the word *Wandern*.[93]

We have already seen that the Nazis viewed unauthorized hiking as
a threat and that the emancipatory traditions of *Wandervogel* hiking were
antipathetic to the regime's totalitarian aims. But there were other connotations of the concept of *Wandern*, in its broader sense of "wandering,"
that the Nazis hated. First, the concept of "wandering" implies individuality, aimlessness, and a lack of authority. This may well be what the HJ leaders had in mind when they cast small hiking groups as too individualistic.
Youths in the HJ, they announced, should voluntarily reject individual or

small-group hikes, "for they do nothing to build community."[94] Wandering groups, moreover, seemed to the HJ too egalitarian in their decision making, resulting in aimlessness. "The strict, merciless commando [is] the foundation of *our* community. Only when weaklings are in charge is anything *decided*. It makes a real guy happy to carry out the commands of his leader. It fills him with pride when those commands require work and struggle!"[95]

Second, the alternative subcultural community that a wandering group might represent clashed with the Nazis' social darwinism. Despite the constant references to community in HJ rhetoric, the emphasis on struggle and competition in the Nazi youth organization reveals a contradictory aim of alienating young people from each other. Competition is by its very nature socially disunifying. In fact, if the HJ had truly been devoted to creating a strong sense of community, they would have leapt at the opportunity to instrumentalize hiking rather than denigrate it.

Third, *Wandern* has connotations of rootlessness, a characteristic that was unwelcome in the Third Reich. Here we can recognize a bourgeois, socially conservative characteristic of Nazism—the idea that social respectability derives in part from "staying put." The Nazi's "blood and soil" concept, for example, was deeply traditionalist in its glorification of rootedness. This norm of stability and a corresponding contempt for itinerant outsiders goes far back in German history; but the Depression drastically increased the number of uprooted, unemployed people wandering around the country in search of work and food. One of the best-known descriptions of these wandering groups in early 1933 even compared them to the *Wandervögel*: "The only people who shouted and waved at me and ran along beside my automobile hoping for a ride during their journey were the newcomers, the youngsters. They were recognizable at once. They still had shoes on their feet and carried knapsacks, like the *Wandervögel*."[96] Wandering groups of the unemployed after 1933 would remind people that the Nazi promise of complete employment might be slow in coming. This surely also accounts for the intensity and viciousness with which the regime attacked the "work shy." The imagery of itinerant unemployment and begging merged easily into attack on "asocials" and probably contributed to the HJ leaders' efforts to disassociate themselves from *Wandern*. For example, a 1938 Reich Youth Leadership decree declared that every HJ trip must be financially secure and every trip must have a specific aim and a clear destination.[97]

Finally, the Nazis associated *Wandern* with dangerous and inferior races. They held "gypsies" in contempt as itinerant hereditary criminals. Filmed pseudo-documentaries and scholarly books identified Jews with plague-carrying rats spreading across the globe.[98] Some HJ writers directly connected this "wandering Jew" with the *wildes Wandern* of pre-Nazi youth: "Liberalism and Judaism had imported into German life a nomadic principle, and the trips of adolescents degenerated into loitering."[99] This conflation of Jews and aimless wandering may well be the key to understanding why the Nazi regime allowed Jewish youth groups alone to continue hiking in the old way. Excluded from both the German school system and the Hitler Youth, they were allowed to maintain their own youth hostels, to be called "Jewish overnight houses." Organized youth activities were also allowed as long as they did not disturb nearby residents and could be easily observed by the police. Formal restrictions pointedly forbade Jewish youth groups from appearing similar to the HJ. There were to be no large tent camps, no hikes in groups of more than twenty, and no uniforms and "orderly formations."[100] Thus, the regime associated the HJ with uniformity, discipline, and purpose and freestyle hiking with the Other.

Wandern was banned both from the Hitler Youth's vocabulary and from its everyday practice. In its stead the Hitler Youth introduced the regimented "trip" (*Fahrt*) of large groups, all in uniform, marching in lock step. Furthermore, the tent camp (*Zeltlager*) became the center of HJ trips that took place during school breaks and that lasted for several days at a time. The HJ leaders seemed to have tried everything they could to overcome any notion that the camps might be there for fun. "Everyone must know why he goes to the camps and on trips. This is not a nice vacation (*Erholungsreise*). Even these freest days of the year mean the same thing as all other days—service."[101]

The Hitler Youth used marching in lock step as a form of physical and mental "steeling," as a way to cultivate the submissive, nonthinking, self-subordinating "new human being" that was the goal of Nazism. "Trips" were praised for their ability to eradicate all particularism, whether of individual, class, religious, or regional identity.[102] We read in one BDM text, for instance, that, "Whenever we are marching together in a city on the hard pavement, the sharp rhythm of our echoing steps lets us feel most clearly that we are one. Our little 'I' is merely one member of the whole." Marching "shoulder to shoulder with other German tribes," according to the Nazi director of the Federation, Karl Rodatz, allowed the young person to "quickly comprehend that the supposed differences between the tribes do not really exist, that we all belong together because we are of one blood."[103] HJ propaganda also presented marching as a metaphor for the stoic endurance of the German nation and for the nation's determined movement through history toward a paradise on earth.

We have only very limited evidence on how many youths in the HJ found its exercise activities attractive and fun. Some youths chafed at the lack of opportunity for individuals or small groups to do anything spontaneously outside of strictly regimented movement. Others enjoyed the HJ for a number of reasons, including comradeship and the opportunity to enjoy some freedom from parental control. Some adolescents probably liked the nearly complete regimentation of daily life. Many older youths were no doubt proud of their physical achievements in the HJ, which were rewarded with certificates of achievement. The BDM certificate, for instance, was awarded to those girls who could march twenty-five kilometers (fifteen miles) in three hours.[104]

What was the Hitler Youth's concept of nature? In the HJ rhetoric on marching, nature is conspicuously absent. There is little landscape description and no "yammering about nature" but lots of forced hilarity about how hungry everyone is and what they get to eat. The rhetoric of gaining happiness by giving up one's individuality and merging into the national community seems to have left no room for admiring nature for its own sake. "Knowing the *Heimat*" no longer meant experiencing the nonhuman landscape. In HJ propaganda Germany was no longer "merely" a land of "forests, lakes, and mountains, a land of culture, spirit, and feeling; it has now become a land of work and struggle."[105] Indeed, marching became an instrument of exploring the German people rather than nature. To this purpose the HJ leadership assigned to each district group specific destinations that changed from year to year.[106] Thus, HJ publications related ad nauseam the marching youths' encounters with city folk and farmers, all of whom clap them on the back and cheer them on.[107] Indeed, the German landscape, when it was discussed at all, was reduced to a reflection of German national identity. In the landscape one saw "strength, will, joy, loneliness, freedom, stubbornness and truth and struggle, struggle against all that is impure, low, and alien! The depths and heights of the landscape are the depths and heights of the national soul; its abysses are our abysses. Not the artist but rather every working German should see the landscape not as a 'romantic' place of enjoyment, but as the German soul."[108]

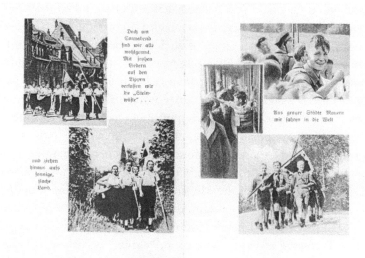

The joys of marching in the Hitler Youth. From Reichsverband für deutsche Jugendherbergen, *Schafft uns Jugendherbergen* (Berlin, 1934).

HJ rhetoric reduced nature in two other ways as well. First, nature became the "terrain" for tent camps and the increasingly common activity of war games. Second, nature was conceived as the organic foundation for social darwinist theories of racial difference. The HJ vision of "natural laws" was bleak indeed and anything but reverent in a romantic sense:

Everywhere in nature we can observe this struggle: the plants wrestle each other for light, the animals for the best feeding spot. Only the strong and able can win this struggle; the sick and weak are exterminated without mercy. A young bird that is too weak to learn to fly is matter-of-factly nudged out of the nest by its parents to die. In this way only the healthy and strong can reproduce.[109]

If the German people were to remain strong and healthy, they would have to carry out their own "rational selection," thereby returning to the natural laws that had been stifled by liberalism and Christianity.[110]

Conclusion

The history of naturism in the form of youth hiking was complex and ever changing in early twentieth-century Germany. In the years preceding the First World War, competing definitions of the relationship between youth and nature heavily influenced generational conflict. For the *Wander-vogel* movement, rural nature was a realm beyond the reach of direct adult supervision. Hiking in a group of one's peers became a way to embrace nature in an emotional and liberating way. By 1913 a number of leaders in the youth movement had become convinced that this closeness to nature gave youth a better insight into Germany's problems that would ultimately help them find solutions. A new youth movement narrative of turning to nature emerged, calling upon young people to take up a more natural way of life in order to build a more humane society. This neo-Romantic, countercultural vision gave rise to the ideal of an erotically liberated *Jugendkultur*, to the social critiques of the Meissner Festival, and to the founding of the *Freideutsche Jugend* with its claim to absolute youthful independence.

However, for Wilhelmine youth cultivators determined to guide boys and girls toward rational citizenship, "nature" was above all the irrational, unpredictable, chaotic *human* nature that lurked in every adolescent. Young males in particular could achieve their potential as the vanguard of a strong and morally healthy society only if their surging, irrational drives and passions were quelled. According to the ideal narrative of turning to nature that was just beginning to take shape in prewar *Jugendpflege* discourse, hiking under the gentle stewardship of older adults would tame the adolescent. When scandalous "revelations" of precocious and/or "inverted" sexuality in the youth movement emerged in conjunction with the concept of *Jugendkultur*, adult observers began to associate the generational challenge of the movement with out-of-control sexuality.

The moral panic of 1913–14 was a negative response to the sudden emergence of previously ignored voices—the voices of intelligent, critical middle-class adolescents and their supporters. Indeed, the *Wandervogel* challenge to the conventions and power structures of late Wilhelmine Germany paralleled growing challenges from other, less economically privileged groups. The fact that Social Democrats were competing for influence over youths and voiced support for the *Jugendkultur* idea made nonsocialist teachers, politicians, and government ministers even more determined to combat radicals in the *Wandervogel* movement. With great vehemence, the youth cultivators and their supporters redefined the concept of *Jugendkultur* as a threat to the moral safety of the young. Even the *Freideutsche Jugend*'s attempt to escape these attacks by backing away from their claim to generational autonomy (the Marburg Proclamation of 1914) failed to rehabilitate the movement. The effects of the moral panic on the bourgeois youth movement continued after the war began, making its members particularly susceptible to the demand that they prove themselves to the nation. Just as they were encountering the realities of industrial warfare firsthand, *Wandervogel* soldiers came under a barrage of rhetoric from the military, the state, the churches, the schools, and their own leaders demanding that they make the ultimate sacrifice.

During the war and the early years of the Weimar Republic, the specter of an alleged youth emergency took on sharper contours in the view of youth cultivators. The deepening fear of an out-of-control young generation was in part a legacy of the moral panic; but it also stemmed from uncertainty in the face of total war, revolution, and the refounding of the social contract. This uncertainty was existential, in the sense that many adults perceived a breakdown of their authority over the young and with it a breakdown of their identity as the *guiding* generation. During the war the youth cultivators perceived that the working-class family was suffering a collapse of patriarchal authority as millions of fathers departed for the battlefield and mothers took up work in the war economy. This, they believed, was creating a power vacuum that allowed teenagers dangerous freedoms of movement and association. At the same time, the fledgling network of official *Jugendpflege* committees was barely clinging to existence as the state diverted personnel and funds to the war effort. The loss of adult authority became even more obvious in 1917 and 1918 as working male adolescents joined political rebels on the left in carrying out food riots, antiwar demonstrations, and finally the November Revolution itself.

With the founding of the Weimar welfare system, however, youth cultivators gained unprecedented support from the national, state, and local governments. They used their new position of high influence during the 1920s to draw public attention to what they saw as a lingering emergency of youth. According to youth cultivators, in the wake of a lost war the young generation had to be guided back onto the path of discipline, reason, and loyalty to the nation. Germany's youth had to be trained to "integrate itself smoothly into the entire body of the people and obey the generally binding laws and needs of the state."[111] Throughout the 1920s the project of overcoming the youth emergency remained the youth cultivators' reason for being. But in the newly democratic and pluralistic society of Weimar, they were obliged to find ways of winning over young people to this project of discipline. Employing a Rousseauist notion of self-liberation by overcoming one's own primitive urges and desires, youth cultivators did their best to coopt the *Wandervogel* tradition of youth hiking. Yet they retained the liberationist, individualistic, and antiauthoritarian tenets of that tradition, at least until the new turn toward authoritarianism during the crisis of the early 1930s.

The Hitler Youth was directly at odds with the independent youth movement tradition. It was much closer to the most authoritarian, anti-sexual, and conservative-militaristic forms of youth cultivation that had risen during the late Wilhelmine era. Yet the HJ's project of taking control over the young generation was the most ruthless to date, and any voices of opposition were quickly silenced. Indeed, the Hitler Youth was the most brutal setback for youthful independence that Germany had ever seen. Its attack on the romantic, emancipatory youth hiking tradition reached its nadir in the ban on hiking in both word and deed. In the end, only wild hiking groups remained, demonized and persecuted. These were the last and bravest children of the *Wandervögel*.

Part III Conservation

6

From Preserving to Planning Nature
The Bourgeois Conservationists

IN THE EARLY 1930S, Dr. Konrad Guenther, a longtime advocate of nature conservation (*Naturschutz*), was exhorting the German people to return to "the soil of the homeland." In the past, according to Guenther, whenever the German people had been forced to respond vigorously to the pressure of hard times, they had returned to their "natural" roots. He called on the population to learn about the *Heimat* and its natural environment, "not only through reason alone but with the entire soul and personality; for the chords of the German soul are tuned to nature. Let us allow nature to speak, and let us be happy to be German!" The stakes were high, for if the German people failed in this way to unite into a strong, "natural" community, they would become "fertilizer for other nations."[1] During the Nazi takeover of state and social institutions, Guenther became one of the most vocal exponents of the notion that conserving nature would aid in the cultural unification and "racial cleansing" of Germany.[2] Indeed, Guenther and his fellow conservationists saw their long-standing dream of a nationwide conservation law at last fulfilled under the Third Reich. The 1935 Reich Conservation Law guaranteed state protection of "the nature of the *Heimat* in all its manifestations."

If *Naturschutz* had the support of Nazis, and conservationists themselves approved of Hitler's regime, what does that tell us about the ethics of "green" thinking? This is a troubling question for present-day supporters of environmentalism, and one that has prompted more research on conservation than on any other naturist movement in Germany. Some historians have argued that this nature protection movement, founded by

educated middle-class professionals at the turn of the century, was a clear
forerunner of Nazism. For them, the movement was from the beginning
backward looking, antiurban, irrationally romantic, and radically nationalist. In a passage that typifies this view of German conservationism, Klaus
Bergmann, author of a book on antiurbanism and agrarian romanticism,
quotes Kurt Tucholsky: "It started out green and ended bloody red."[3]
Polemicists, most infamously Anna Bramwell, have used such arguments
to attack present-day environmentalist movements in Germany and elsewhere. Bramwell alleges that there was a strong current of "green" thought
within the Nazi Party and that ecology is a uniquely German "disease."[4]

The argument that environmentalist thinking was uniquely German
is easy to refute, as there were many conservationists throughout the West
by the early twentieth century. Nature protection in the United States
predated German efforts. John Muir, who was instrumental in the founding of Yosemite National Park in 1890, wrote, "Thousands of tired, nerve-
shaken, over-civilized people are beginning to find out that going to the
mountains is going home; that wildness is a necessity; and that mountain
parks and reservations are useful not only as fountains of timber and ir-
rigating rivers, but as fountains of life."[5] Moreover, the conflation of the
rural landscape with national identity is less unique to Germany than has
sometimes been claimed, even if the Nazi "blood and soil" version of it
was uniquely vicious. Thomas Dunlap and others have shown that the
appropriation of landscape, animals, and climate to communicate a sense
of national identity has been a common cultural phenomenon throughout
the West over the last two centuries.[6] To take another American example,
Stephen Mather, the first director of the U.S. Park Service, wrote in 1921
that national parks "are not only show places and vacation lands but also
vast schoolrooms of Americanism where people are studying, enjoying,
and learning to love more deeply this land in which they live."[7]

The question of ideological continuity before and after 1933 is more
difficult to answer, but several historians have begun to try. Their close
reading of organizational and ideological evidence has revealed the complexity of early twentieth-century conservation. My approach here is in
accord with the emerging view that organized conservation traveled a
twisted path from its Wilhelmine beginnings to its self-incorporation into
the Nazi system.[8]

German conservationism had its roots in a late nineteenth-century
reaction to the rapid growth of cities and the accompanying destruction

of much of the rural landscape. Wilhelmine conservationists were at the center-right of the ideological spectrum, fearing social change and the influence of socialism on the urban working class. They were driven by a desire to combat the damages to the rural landscape caused by industrialization and urban growth, but they chose to work with the capitalist economic system in order to reform it from within. This choice made sense at the time for two reasons. First, the early conservationists in their social conservatism were simply not prepared to appeal in any concrete way to "the masses" in order to lead a populist movement critical of capitalism. As a consequence, their popular support was negligible compared to that of many other reformist movements of the time. Second, given that the rural German landscape was not an unspoiled wilderness but rather the lived-in rural environment of fields, forests, and mountains, it made practical sense to work within the existing economic system rather than attempt somehow to turn back the clock on capitalist modernity. Within these confines the movement managed to develop a strong neo-Romantic critique of the damage to the landscape caused by industry and the city. This Wilhelmine-era critique, however, was almost exclusively aesthetic, and no real harbingers of present-day ecological thinking or social justice environmentalism can be found in the sources.

The conservationists were embedded in their times, and their views were shaped by a growing sense of social crisis. Following the period of war and revolution, the movement attempted to conceptualize new relationships between the individual, nature, and the nation as a way to help the German people overcome their national trauma. The most drastic ideological transformation of conservationism came between the middle years of the Weimar Republic and the early years of the Third Reich. During this phase leading spokesmen for *Naturschutz* redefined their project as a battle against what they called the "homeland emergency" (*Heimatnot*). This sense of crisis derived from fears, typical of the educated Weimar middle class, of a powerful working class and an unruly young generation. Late Weimar conservationists formulated a new ideal narrative of returning to nature that conflated nature, the nation, and the region into a single *Heimat*. That narrative offered an alternative to the uncertainties of Weimar—a socially unified, morally healthy, racially and culturally homogeneous homeland in which nature and the nation were identical. There was at the same time a significant shift in the movement's rhetoric toward racial and social darwinist concepts of national identity. Although it is possible to find isolated examples of such language in preservationist sources even before the war, this biologistic strain of nationalism had hitherto been in the minority—it had been subordinated to a culturally based understanding of national identity and to strong currents of regional particularism. Now a view of the nation that had much in common with Nazism began to dominate.

This ideological shift of the late 1920s / early 1930s heavily affected conservationists' relationship to urban-industrial modernity. While some late Weimar conservationists nursed a certain nostalgia for the rural-agrarian past, the movement as a whole jettisoned its long-standing critique of industrialization, dismissing it as outmoded and too romantic. Many turned instead to a self-consciously modernist project of "landscape cultivation" (*Landschaftspflege*) that aimed to integrate industrial technology into the landscape in rational, yet aesthetically pleasing and environmentally acceptable ways.[9] Far from rejecting modernity, then, many leading conservationists envisioned a forward-looking nation in which nature itself would be well ordered and in harmony with the work of human beings. This tendency toward landscape cultivation coexisted with ongoing, more traditionalist efforts to establish nature preserves and protect singular natural monuments. These two currents were both supported by the 1935 Reich Conservation Law, which gave unprecedented legal powers to the advocates of nature protection.

By the 1930s conservationist ideology was a complex and in some ways contradictory mix of persistent class elitism, antiurbanism, technocratic visions of the future, and racial nationalism. The greatest commonality between late Weimar conservationism and Nazism was that both harnessed concepts of a more or less orderly nature and an undivided society to their agenda for restoring the nation. Many conservationists were thus able to adopt the racist language of Nazism quite easily in the process of carving out a niche for their activities within the new dictatorial system. Ironically, then, the "golden age" of state-sponsored conservation—at least up to that time—occurred under what was arguably the most criminal dictatorship in modern European history. Yet this should not lead us to suppose that the Nazi leadership was firmly committed to protecting nature. For them, conservation was a low priority compared to a program of economic autarky and war preparation that inevitably brought damage to the environment. Nonetheless, the enthusiastic response of the conservationist movement to the Third Reich continued into the early 1940s; and some leaders of the movement gave their support to the regime's wartime plans for "landscape cultivation" in the occupied East at the expense of the subject population.

The Origins of Conservation in the Wilhelmine Era

Naturschutz emerged as an organized project around the turn of the twentieth century out of a much larger movement of the educated middle class for "homeland preservation" (*Heimatschutz*). The term *Heimat* is an old one in Germany, but it was apparently first combined with the word *Schutz* (preservation) in Ernst Rudorff's 1897 book *Heimatschutz*. In this influential work, Rudorff, a wealthy musician and writer, argued that the millions of "average people" should be taught to respect the traditional aesthetics, the strictly defined social order, and the pastoral landscape. This was the only way to combat the materialistic and egalitarian "threat" of the urban masses, for "where the soul speaks, the baser drives are silenced; in the enjoyment of nature lies a morally cleansing power." If the rural landscape were to work its harmonizing magic, it would have to remain "unviolated and unadulterated."[10]

Such conservative fears about the democratizing potential of mass society were typical of an educated middle class that felt increasingly challenged in its position of cultural leadership by both the working class and capitalist industrialists.[11] The rhetoric about social harmony was part of an attempt to guarantee educated-bourgeois leadership over a developing mass society. Yet Rudorff did not reject modernity out of hand; rather, he combined a conservative and nationalist glorification of the pastoral landscape with a fundamentally modern project of mass pedagogy.

Rudorff had enormous influence within the increasingly organized central preservationist movement and its offshoot, conservationism. The German League for Homeland Preservation (*Deutscher Bund Heimatschutz*—DBH) was founded by Rudorff in Dresden in 1904 as a national umbrella organization for hundreds of *Heimat* organizations throughout Germany. Under its guidance, the preservationist movement developed a regionalist and holistic concept of the *Heimat* as a realm that included specific cultural traditions (including dialect, folklore, and architecture) and landscapes.[12] At first glance the League's bylaws appear to be a fine example of reactionary antimodernism. Germany's folk culture, traditional architecture, and natural features all needed protection from the "intrusion of modern life with its brutally one-sided pursuit of practical goals."[13] The DBH's president, architect Paul Schultze-Naumburg, railed in his opening address against "the international world pattern, which has in its rational nakedness spread across our country." He continued:

In old books and travel descriptions, it is often written that Germany is an endlessly beautiful land in whose cities, villages, and forests it is a pleasure to wander. Such words will one day be only a dream from forgotten times for our children. We are confronted with the fact that Germany is losing its character as our beloved homeland, becoming an abode for the dullest kind of sobriety. If this continues unchecked, city and country will soon be transformed into uniform proletarian suburbs whose buildings are in the style of the penitentiary. All remnants of the fine culture we inherited from our ancestors will be either destroyed or falsely restored; in place of our beechwood and oak forests, there will be straight rows of skinny pine trees for commercial timber. There will be no more delightful gardens, no churches, and no bridges to round out the landscape into a harmonious picture. The former beauty of our land will be ruined forever.[14]

This attack on urbanization and rationalism reeks of bourgeois "cultural despair." Yet the bylaws made clear that the DBH would attempt to come to terms with modern technological and economic developments. The DBH did not have "the foolish intention of turning back the clock on the extraordinary practical achievements of the present." They pledged instead to "work to balance the heartless exploitation of the soil of the homeland with the demands of the spirit, the roots of which will find no more nourishment if we continue to destroy the beauties of Germany. If we do not find this balance, we will lose the best and most meaningful part of our culture."[15] Thus, the League's founders cast themselves as leaders who were capable of guiding the German people toward a future in which their cultural distinctiveness would survive and the nation would remain strong.

The *Heimatschutz* movement developed a "greener vision of home" that hearkened back to the pastoral aesthetic of the pre-industrial Romantics.[16] This ideal of the German landscape depicted a society living in harmony with rural nature. Towns and cities nestled "organically" into nature, and people cared for the natural diversity of mixed forests, hedgerows, and unregulated streams. The *Deutscher Bund Heimatschutz* thus pledged to protect both unique natural features and something much broader, the "uniqueness (*Eigenart*) of the cultural landscape."[17] Although this ideal of a "cultured" landscape differed markedly from the wilderness aesthetic of early American conservationists, it was typical of early conservationism throughout Western Europe and certainly was closer to the reality of the German landscape. It was also socially paternalistic and conservative in idealizing the traditional hierarchies of German society.[18]

How successful were early preservationists in actually protecting the landscape? Despite the explicit acceptance in the DBH of "the extraordinary practical achievements of the present," that organization's first project was an effort to halt an electrical project on the Rhine. The dam threatened to destroy a series of picturesque rapids near the town of Laufenberg. The DBH attempted to convince the citizens of Laufenberg that the aesthetic experience of the rapids, not electricity, was the true *Rheingold*. This argument failed to triumph over the ideology of economic progress touted by the government of Baden and private capitalists. The lack of popular support forced the conservationists to give up their demand for a complete end to the project in favor of an alternative compromise that would have preserved the rapids. Even that plan ultimately failed, and the rapids were submerged.[19]

Other preservationist initiatives failed elsewhere for similar reasons. The Isar Valley Society (*Isartalverein*) in Munich, for instance, protested the canalization of the Isar River along aesthetic lines similar to those of the Laufenberg protest. But they, too, ultimately had to submit to governmental and public opinion that favored mastery over the flood-prone waterway. The organization succeeded only in convincing the municipal authorities to build the canals to conform to the natural curves of the river.[20] These early conflicts revealed the practical difficulties of advocating conservation along purely aesthetic lines in the face of antipathetic public opinion and organized capitalism. Moreover, the failed attempts at popularization no doubt encouraged elitist tendencies within this largely male, highly educated, and upper-middle-class movement.[21] As a result, the conservation sector that emerged around 1904 within the *Heimatschutz* movement was statist in its orientation and compromising in its view of the relationship between nature and industrial capitalism.

Ironically, the capitalist state itself took the initiative in practical conservation. Given the timing of governmental conservation initiatives throughout Germany, we can infer that at least one aim was to co-opt the increasingly loud protests of the *Heimatschutz* movement. For instance, following a protest against billboards in the Prussian Diet, the Prussian state in 1902 passed the Law Against the Disfigurement of Outstanding Areas of the Landscape, which banned outdoor advertising in certain places.[22] More significantly, the Prussian Minister of Culture in 1904 called upon the DBH to suggest goals and an organizational framework for *Naturschutz*. The DBH member Hugo Conwentz thereupon wrote a detailed memorandum that set the pattern for state-sponsored conservation for the next twenty-five years. Moving away from the focus on the landscape, Conwentz rejected the idea of national parks like Yellowstone and Yosemite because there were almost no similarly "untouched" areas in Prussia, and the ones that did exist were under private ownership. He called instead for the preservation of unique natural monuments (*Naturdenkmäler*). Worthy monuments were by definition specific and small—"here a lake, there a meadow, dune, or sunny hill; here a boulder or cliff, there a small moor, a heath, or forested area." Showing a willingness to compromise with capitalism, Conwentz blamed not industry but agriculture and "the lack of education" for the destruction of nature. It would be the task of the conservationist movement to work closely with architects and engineers in planning industrial development.[23]

In response to this essay, the Prussian state authorized Conwentz to found the State Agency for the Care of Natural Monuments (*Staatliche Stelle für Naturdenkmalpflege*—SSNDP) under the supervision of the Cultural Ministry. The Agency was to identify, research, and watch over natural monuments in Prussia; discuss measures to preserve them; and give advice to property owners and state officials. Funding would not be provided to the SSNDP, nor were any policies announced for the popularization of *Naturschutz*.[24]

This general model of civic protest leading to state-sponsored but underfunded conservation recurred in several other German states between 1904 and 1910. In Bavaria, a coalition of groups petitioned the state in 1904 to begin expropriating valuable natural monuments such as ancient trees from private landowners, "by force if necessary." The Interior Minister promptly invited these groups into the new State Committee for Nature Cultivation (*Landesausschuß für Naturpflege*). Yet the government declared that only those trees, waterways, and forests whose preservation would be in the general interest (that is, in the interests of science and aesthetics) deserved recognition as natural monuments. Furthermore, "By no means will economic interests be sacrificed for these endeavors." Expropriation of private property was out of the question, and the committee received neither financial nor legal support.[25]

Conservationists who came under state tutelage were almost always obliged to relinquish their early neo-Romantic celebration of the entire landscape in favor of the piecemeal protection of "beautiful and interesting natural details (*Einzelheiten*), such as cliffs, boulders, sites with rare plants, and so on."[26] Given all of the limits imposed by the state, conservationists saw little choice but to make a virtue out of their merely advisory role. By 1912 their publications were repeatedly exhorting all those concerned with protecting nature to find compromises with economic interests and governments.[27] The state *Naturschutz* committees' willingness to compromise drew fire, however, from a minority of outspoken conservationists who had never fully abandoned their general protest against industrialization and urbanization. The popular north German *Heimat* writer Hermann Löns, for example, railed in 1911 against "merely" preserving natural monuments:

It is all very nice when a few little natural details are protected; but this work has no general significance. The conservationism we have at present is mere pussyfooting. The plundering of nature, on the other hand, is proceeding with great generosity [*Großzügigkeit*] and in a general way, while conservationism is losing itself in details. I am gnashing my teeth in fury as I witness the terrible disfiguration of the German landscape.

Soon all that would remain would be a Germany that looked like any other modern industrial country: "a boring, treeless and bushless steppe, blotched with stinking factories, disgusting brick structures, ostentatious weekend houses, and pernicious church steeples."[28]

Löns and other critics of state-sponsored conservation favored the more encompassing, protoecological solution of protecting large areas of natural habitat and the interconnected biotopes that they contained. A number of private organizations began propagating the concept of "natural parks," chief among them the League for Bird Protection (*Bund für Vogelschutz*) and the Association for Nature Conservation Parks (*Verein Naturschutzpark*). The latter was able to raise money with the endorsement of Wilhelm II and the Prussian legislature, which authorized a series of lotteries between 1911 and 1914. Indeed, by 1914 these associations had relatively large memberships of around forty-one thousand and twelve thousand, respectively, and had gained the support of such luminaries as Thomas Mann and Hermann Hesse. The *Naturschutzpark* movement's success remained limited, however, in the face of resistance from industrial and agricultural interests and even from state-sponsored conservationists. Thus, these relatively radical conservationists had to scale back their hopes, turning instead to establishing smaller nature preserves (*Naturschutzgebiete*) through private land purchases. By 1920 the *Verein Naturschutzpark* had purchased enough moorland in Lower Saxony to establish Germany's first nature preserve, the Lüneburg Heath.[29]

The concept of nature preserves that were larger than natural monuments but smaller than national parks found some success in Bavaria as well. The Bavarian State Committee for Conservation founded a private co-organization in 1913, the Bavarian Conservation League (*Bund Naturschutz in Bayern*), which was legally allowed to raise money through membership dues and contributions. Together, the two organizations, one state sponsored and the other private, had the strength to halt the Bavarian government's plan to carve a huge Bavarian lion into the cliff walls above Lake Königsee. After the war the conservationists convinced the new Bavarian government to approve a nature preserve that would protect the lake for posterity. Yet Bavarian conservationists were much less successful when they confronted projects of economic development. Their longstanding attempts between 1910 and 1920 to halt the building of a power plant on Lake Walchensee, for example, came to nought.[30]

During the First World War, conservationist efforts, both state sponsored and private, more or less stalled as the state directed all of its energies toward winning the total war of attrition. Efforts by the Prussian SSNDP to preserve moors slated for agricultural development, for instance, failed in light of the state's need to fight the enemy blockade of food shipments.[31] The broader *Heimatschutz* movement, however, seems to have thrived in this atmosphere of aggressive racial nationalism. *Heimat* associations throughout the country jumped at the opportunity to cooperate with the state's propaganda efforts to sustain popular support for the war. The preservationists also took up several new war-related activities, the most significant of which were efforts to help reconstruct battle-damaged areas of East Prussia. *Heimat* organizations in the Rhineland became particularly fervent in their self-appointed role as protectors of the nation's "border marches" against the French.[32]

As a result of its participation on the home front during the "Great War," *Heimatschutz* rhetoric developed a homogenizing tendency in which the pastoral German landscape was conflated with the embattled nation. This integral-nationalist vision of the *Heimat* was to play an important part in the evolution of conservationism. In the wake of the revolution in the late fall of 1918, Hugo Conwentz formulated what was to become the dominant ideal narrative of turning to nature in the Weimar conservation movement—the protection of nature as a way to restore the unity and strength of the German nation. "We too want to work to help the coming generations who will continue to suffer from our breakdown," Conwentz announced. "We already stand burdened enough in their eyes; thus we dare not leave them a decimated *Heimat* in addition to all the other wreckage."[33]

Standardizing the *Heimat*: Conservationist Ideology in the Weimar Republic

German conservationists had reason to take heart from the postwar republic's apparent interest in their project. The increased prestige of *Heimatschutz* in the wake of the "Great War" was evident in Article 150 of the new constitution, which placed "monuments of art, history, and nature, as well as the landscape" under state protection. This pledge encouraged conservationist leaders as they re-formed their movement in the early 1920s. A new desire for centralization led to a series of national conferences sponsored by the Prussian State Commission for the Care of Natural Monuments. Such efforts established contacts between the regional movements and helped set the stage for the founding of a new national umbrella organization in 1922, the People's Conservation League (*Volksbund Naturschutz*), which was centered in Berlin under the chairmanship of the school director Hans Klose.[34]

The *Volksbund* was in part an attempt to find private funding for conservation. By 1922 it had become apparent that the state's commitment to conservation was not living up to the promise of Article 150. State-sponsored conservation committees still had only an advisory capacity and used it to urge governments to "keep in mind not only the economic but also the cultural (*geistige*) interests of the nation" and preserve *Naturdenkmäler* such as moors.[35] But the state had neither the will nor the financial wherewithal to confiscate private property. As the Bavarian Interior Minister bluntly explained, "An effective conservationist policy would have to provide for the compensation of private property owners, and the means to do so are not available."[36] Most natural monuments deemed worthy of protection had to be purchased, and the funds had to be raised by private conservation organizations.

Indeed, Weimar conservationists had little room to maneuver given the lack of substantial support from the state. Even though the number of natural monuments slowly grew in the mid-1920s with help from private donations, they were usually very small—rarely more than 250 acres. The governments appear to have rejected more proposals for larger nature preserves than they supported.[37] A growing number of conservationists, inspired by the preservationists' concept of landscape protection, were increasingly frustrated with the limited principle of "natural monuments," agitating instead for the broader protection of "cultural landscapes." Yet Prussia was the only state government that showed any interest in this; and even there, the 1927 proposal for a wide-ranging conservation law failed to win sufficient political support in the Diet.[38] The most basic hindrance for conservationists was the fact that once the economy regained its footing in the mid-1920s, the ideology of industrial progress regained its dominance in German popular culture.

How did the conservationist ideology of turning to nature take shape in this difficult situation? Like the other movements treated in this study, the *Naturschutz* movement underwent a process of refounding in the aftermath of war and revolution. Part of this process involved identifying and describing the new problems to be overcome by turning to nature. In the early 1920s, conservationists asserted that Germany's key internal weakness was rebelliousness among both the industrial working class and the young generation.

That middle-class conservationists took this view is hardly surprising. Fear of the leveling implications of labor movements and urban mass society had long been an integral part of the educated bourgeoisie's sense of class identity. The experience of a revolution in which young working men and women were at the forefront greatly increased this anxiety. Germany had suddenly become a mass democracy in which Marxist parties and unions had unprecedented power. Moreover, the bourgeoisie underwent a severe economic decline in the early 1920s that culminated in the disastrous hyperinflation of 1923. As Bernd Weisbrod has shown, when the economic uncertainty of the working class came to be shared by the Weimar middle classes, the sense of security—"the very essence of 'bourgeois' existence"—was lost. Far from encouraging solidarity with workers, this decline seems only to have made the bourgeoisie insist more vigorously on its moral and cultural superiority.[39]

As we have seen, concerns about the young generation grew among the educated bourgeoisie during the early Weimar years. In Weimar a rising mass culture offered young people even more opportunities for autonomy during their leisure hours. Chronic youth unemployment and the economically uncertain future of their children also fueled bourgeois adults' worries about the next generation.

Early Weimar conservationist rhetoric expressed these social anxieties through images of nature suffering under the onslaught of the urban masses. For example, the Bavarian State Advisory Committee for the Care of Nature warned in 1919 that the "social aftereffects" of the Munich Soviet Republic—code language for the revolutionary working class—were contaminating Lake Königsee, "irrevocably destroying the idyllic peace of the lake and the surrounding mountains." Furthermore, Bavarian game had come under threat from unrestrained poaching since the revolution: "Animals are suffering under the greed, ignorance, and superstition of a segment of the populace and under the brutality and thoughtlessness of youth."[40] Although this kind of rhetoric became less panic-stricken after 1920, Weimar conservationists never tired of castigating the unruly masses for tramping loudly through the rural environment, littering the landscape, and mistreating wild animals and plants. Such opprobrium was a specialty of Walther Schoenichen, who after Conwentz's death in 1922 became the director of the Prussian State Conservation Agency.[41]

A leading goal of the movement, therefore, was to strengthen the commitment of workers and young people to nature as a way to restore national health and stability. But how would this appreciation for nature be taught? The conservationists did not develop a coherent answer to that question in the early 1920s. Instead, they revived an ideal narrative of turning to nature that had originated in the rhetoric of the Wilhelmine movement. In the 1919 reprint of Konrad Guenther's 1912 book *Conservation*, the author described a worker walking home from the factory through woods and fields. Guenther wrote hopefully that the worker would naturally experience a sense of contentment and freedom in the countryside, "For only in nature is there no difference between poor and rich, high and low; only there does it cost nothing to gain a wealth of knowledge and happiness."[42] The appreciation of nature served a pacifying, class-transcendent function in this narrative. Yet early Weimar conservationists remained vague as to how that mentality could be induced among workers to whom it might not come naturally.

This began to change in the mid-1920s when the conservationist movement finally realized the need to develop concrete ways of winning a popular following. As an article in the conservationist journal *Naturschutz* announced, "These days, you must go before the public. Not just once, but as often as possible. . . . Today here, tomorrow there, and always with the participation of the press."[43] But how were socially elitist conservationists to appeal effectively to the mass public that they had long bypassed? They quickly arrived at a consensus that popular pedagogy was the answer.

This shift in the conservationists' methods led to a stronger emphasis on the "homeland" concept in their rhetoric. Indeed, conservationists turned their attention to a specific project of teaching the love of the *Heimat* to Germany's workers and the young generation. The language of *Heimat* must have seemed well suited to the new aim of popularization. There appeared to be no limit to the readership for such celebrants of the regional homeland as Hermann Löns and the *Plattdeutsch* writers. The many *Heimatschutz* organizations bent on preserving local and regional traditions enjoyed the patronage of state interior and cultural ministries. In the wake of the Treaty of Versailles and the Ruhr invasion, *Heimat* associations in the areas bordering France, Poland, and Czechoslovakia had gained the support of the state governments to an unprecedented degree. Such organizations as the Bavarian Forest Association and the Rhineland *Heimat* League received funds from both state and national governments to help them protect the traditional heritage of areas considered under threat from Germany's enemies.[44]

In these years there was also a growing tendency on the part of both the state and educators to promote "homeland studies" (*Heimatkunde*) in primary and secondary schools, universities, and public exhibitions. The 1920 guidelines on "School and Homeland" drafted by the Reich School Conference declared, "For cultural, pedagogic, and social reasons, *Heimatkunde* within and outside the school must be afforded the greatest attention and cultivation." Subsequent national guidelines in 1922 built upon this principle, requiring "homeland schooling techniques" such as hiking, field trips, teaching outdoors, gardening, and stays in the country.[45] The main purpose of *Heimatkunde* in the primary and secondary schools, as the pedagogue Eduard Spranger wrote in an influential 1923 article, was to overcome social divisions by teaching children a collective sense of place. Spranger and other educational reformers assisted the governments of Bavaria, Baden, Prussia, Württemberg, Thuringia, and Saxony in developing guidelines for the teaching of homeland studies.[46]

The conservationists thus began in various ways to advocate popular *Heimatkunde* in the hopes of strengthening their influence. State advisory committees drew up homeland studies courses. The *Volksbund Naturschutz* began to lobby the state for *Heimatkunde* in the schools, at the same time launching an appeal to the public to take part in organized Sunday hikes, field trips to nature preserves, lectures, study courses, public exhibitions, and museum tours. And new organizations that combined conservation with *Heimatkunde* sprang up throughout Germany.[47] We can see in hindsight, however, that when Weimar conservationists shifted their focus to *Heimatkunde*, they unwittingly created a conceptual problem for themselves. For *Heimat* was an extraordinarily slippery concept containing an abundance of potentially conflicting meanings, for several reasons.

First, the concept had strong connotations of regional particularism that were potentially at odds with a project of *national* unity. In a country as culturally diverse as Germany, and in a federalist political system in which the national government suffered from an ongoing crisis of legitimacy, the individual's strongest emotional affiliation tended to be with a locale or region. Indeed, *Heimat* language in the 1920s often boosted centrifugal political forces. Some county governments in Bavaria, for instance, cultivated local identity as a means of resisting what they saw as "exaggerated centralism in the state and in the Reich."[48] Such rhetoric had an influence in many regional preservationist movements as well. Even though many *Heimatschutz* activists viewed regional identity as a component of national identity, there was no guarantee that the love of the region would commit a young person or worker to greater national unity.

Second, each individual's relationship to the *Heimat* was shaped by unique personal experiences and memories. As pedagogic experts pointed out, teachers of homeland studies had to take into account that *Heimatkunde* was a relativistic science; by definition it had to include the perspective of every individual who felt a bond with his or her native surroundings. Unlike most students of science, the "knower" (*Erkennende*) of the homeland did *not* attempt to transcend his or her unique vantage point in space and time. The student of *Heimatkunde* thus always *created* the subject based upon his or her unique existential position. Every person's local environment was "individually appropriated through experience, shot through with spirituality, and thoroughly colored by personal perspective."[49] Indeed, a 1922 survey that asked adolescent students to define the term *Heimat* resulted in answers such as the following:

> I understand my homeland above all as the area in which I was born and where I spent my youth. But my homeland is also that part of my Fatherland whose dialect I speak and whose customs and traditions I practice.

> My homeland is the woods where we played cops and robbers, and the pond where we swam in the summertime and skated in the winter.[50]

This subjective understanding of the homeland by each individual could also undermine a collective commitment to national unity.

Finally, the *Heimat* concept was ideologically vague enough to be appropriated by groups with divergent political aims. As we have seen, the Social Democratic *Naturfreunde* developed an alternative concept of *Heimat* that was both regionalist and socialist. Gaining knowledge about one's homeland for them meant comprehending the depredations of capitalism on the common people. Such political appropriations of the *Heimat* concept were clearly at odds with the bourgeois conservationists' goal of social pacification.

Given this variety of possible homelands, *Heimat* was something of a conceptual Trojan horse for the Weimar conservationist movement. It would not be a simple task to deploy *Heimatkunde* as a means of marshaling support for conservation, pacifying the masses, and inculcating the desire for national unity. Leading conservationists apparently began to realize this problem in the late 1920s, for they undertook a rhetorical effort to clarify and standardize the *Heimat* concept. As the fragile political and economic stability of the mid-1920s broke down, a growing sense of dread further galvanized that effort. By 1930 the middle class faced a political resurgence of the Marxist left, an economic depression of unprecedented magnitude, and an upsurge of social conflict. The standardization of *Heimat* was therefore an attempt by conservationists to simplify their chief conceptual category. But it was also intertwined with the urgent effort to justify the movement anew in a period of national uncertainty.

Leading conservationists made two important standardizing changes in their representation of *Heimat*. First, they conflated the homeland with nature itself. Nature was recast as the root of the homeland, the stable physical foundation of the social order. In this fully anthropocentric conception of the "natural homeland," nature's significance derived almost exclusively from its meaning for society.

Second, they identified this natural homeland with the totality of the German nation rather than the region. In this they committed themselves fully to the integral nationalist rhetoric of *Heimatschutz* that had emerged in the war and early Weimar period. Conservationist leaders depicted the crisis of late Weimar in images of an endangered *national* homeland. As their solution to this "homeland emergency," they developed a new ideal narrative of turning to nature in which conservation would help save the nation. The result would be a strengthened natural/national homeland protected from both social conflict and environmental degradation.

The late Weimar movement for *Heimatschutz* and conservation offered this narrative over and over again to the public. In a 1929 speech, for instance, Heinrich Hassinger of the Rhineland *Heimat* League warned of worsening social conflict. During the French occupation in the early 1920s, he explained, Rhinelanders had united behind the *Heimat*, and their appreciation for the nation had grown. Unfortunately, Germans as a whole were not yet a united people, because "the antipathy of one against another has hindered the final, great, national unity that would bring us together under one flag of common ideas and convictions." This disunity was "one of the great emergencies of our time, ranking with unemployment, the housing shortage, and the disintegration of the family under the burden of poverty." Hassinger acknowledged that *Heimat* meant many things to people, but he urged that the concept be standardized along nationalist lines. Teaching about and celebrating the regional homeland must bind young Germans to the entire nation:

The world is complicated, and the homeland is always simple. The longing for home that is alive within us is the most natural, the most deep-seated, and the most elementary of longings. . . . He who has found a *Heimat* in his people has dropped an anchor; never again will he be tossed about by the wind and waves of life. Secure in his locality, love will grow in him, and energy will be set free so that he can serve the nation.[51]

Concluding with a metaphor of homogeneity, Hassinger announced that the hearts of those who share a feeling for the *Heimat* beat in the same rhythm: "We feel ourselves understood, and we understand."[52] Probably the most representative text of late Weimar conservationism, however, was an anthology entitled *Der deutsche Heimatschutz* published in 1930 by the newly founded Society of the Friends of German Homeland Preservation (*Gesellschaft der Freunde des Deutschen Heimatschutzes*—GFDHS).

Composed of an impressive roster of political, cultural, and economic elites, the GFDHS aimed to communicate the vision of a "truly national culture" to the people "so that it will become self-evident for everyone."[53]

The Society's ultimate goal was a national community that would transcend regional, class, and political divisions. In propagating this goal, the essayists in *Der deutsche Heimatschutz* consciously distanced themselves from their forerunners. They explicitly called for a rejection of bourgeois elitism in favor of a class-transcendent *Volksgemeinschaft*. The authors shifted the blame for the problem of social division from industrial workers to "cosmopolitanism" and "foreign elements." Karl Wagenfeld, leader of the *Heimatschutz* movement in Westphalia, wrote:

> The lack of connection with *Heimat* and with traditional worldviews weakens the sense of morality and trivializes feeling; and it is reflected in action that is unmoored, impulsive, and ruthless. And so the proletariat has grown . . . racially, culturally, and socially inferior, into cultureless and dissatisfied masses who complain, "We have become strangers, and the machines are idols of cold iron upon which gray priests sacrifice our youth and spill our blood."[54]

Although Wagenfeld's depiction of the enemy is quite vague in this essay, knowledge of his other writings leads to the conclusion that his "gray priests" stood for Jewish capitalists.[55]

The obsessive harping about "German blood" in this anthology exemplified the kind of racial nationalism that had become dominant on the moderate and far right since the war. Racist pseudoscience ran rampant throughout the collection. The prominent racial hygienist Dr. Eugen Fischer contributed an essay entitled "Homeland and Family." Fischer wrote that a German's feeling of connectedness to the national *Heimat* was the product of thousands of years of heredity: "As the people themselves say, it is in the blood." A healthy racial nation could absorb a modicum of blood from another race, so long as that influence was kept within reasonable bounds. But the family—"the location at which two [generational] links in the hereditary chain meet and intertwine to bring into existence a new chain reaching into the future"—was being destroyed by the pernicious influence of the metropolis with all its cosmopolitan influences.[56]

For other essayists in the collection, regional identity was just as dangerous a threat, for it denied the basic biological unity of the German nation. Karl Hahm claimed "a deeper *scientific* knowledge of the foundations of the German national character" and rhetorically subordinated

both the individual and the region to a racially homogeneous natural/
national homeland.[57] Karl Giannoni rejected the traditional regionalism
of the *Heimat* concept by defining the region as a mere building block of
national identity:

Heimat does not signify simple exceptionalism; rather it is the partial expression of
a larger national geographic space (*Volksraum*). Furthermore, the individual in the
homeland is the partial expression of a singular national identity (*Volkstum*). Both
the national space and the national character are truly to be experienced and understood on the level of the homeland. We receive our national character from the hand
of the *Heimat*.[58]

Anton Helbok directly attacked regional pride, using Bavaria as his negative example. The peculiarities of Bavarian physiognomy, psychology, and
culture, he wrote, had only originated since the tribal settlement of that
area. Therefore, they were determined not by tribal Bavarian blood but
by geography and climate. *German* blood was primary even in the Bavar-
ians. "Culturally blinkered" celebrants of particular regions fostered "a
philistine local patriotism, . . . degrading the figure of the inward-looking
German into a dwarf who looks ridiculous next to the modern, active
individual," Helbok asserted.[59]

   Der deutsche Heimatschutz was a seminal text in the formulation of a
new ideal narrative of turning to nature. It set the tone of conservationist
rhetoric into the mid-1930s, at least among the movement's national leaders.[60] The narrative began with the problem of internal and external dangers that together signaled a crisis of the racial nation. Conservation was
then presented as the solution. By popularizing conservation, the movement would be doing its part to help the German people overcome the
threats to its well-being. The result would be an ideal natural/national *Heimat* that was healthy, unified, and strong. The structure of this narrative,
with all its normative oppositions, can be outlined as shown in Table 6.1.

   What effects did this new narrative have on the conservationists'
view of nature itself? Two important changes occurred. First, there was a
tendency among many to cast natural diversity in a negative light and to
treat a more homogeneous natural order as preferable. Soon a "cleaner"
and simpler nature took precedence over visual and biological diversity.
Many late Weimar conservationists seem to have transferred their fear of
social complexity and the hopeful vision of a united national community
onto the metaphorical field of nature.[61]

TABLE 6.1   Narrative structure of conservationist rhetoric in the early 1930s

Heimat *emergency* →	*Conservation* →	*Strengthened* Heimat
class and generational conflict		national community
rebellious workers and youths		contented workers and youths
masses ruin the environment		masses respect the environment
lack of rootedness in the nation		commitment to the nation
regional particularism		homogeneous national identity
foreign influences		racial purity
national weakness		national power
decline		progress

This trend can be illustrated by juxtaposing three texts from 1912, 1926, and 1932 by the prominent conservationist Konrad Guenther. Guenther wrote in 1912 that although the "friend of nature" had nothing against the "moderate and rational exploitation of nature," the "inexhaustible diversity" of the earth was rapidly fading and there was a dire need to preserve what remained of the natural habitat. In a 1926 article, he reformulated this protoecological viewpoint using the mechanistic metaphor of a clock. Nature was an "organic work of art" whose plant and animal species hung together by invisible threads. If one species were exterminated, the damage would become apparent at some other place in the system.[62] Yet by 1932 Guenther saw nature solely in terms of the natural/ national *Heimat*. The forest was the "primal *Heimat*" of the Germans, "a living landscape for the Germans' health and spirit." Because the flora and fauna on German territory had coexisted with Germans for thousands of years, they were now strictly German animals and plants. Guenther took a further step away from natural diversity in the following passage:

The forest promotes individual life. Its animals are mostly loners, forming herds much more rarely than the animals of the steppes. The Germanic tribes lived like this as well, affirming only to a limited degree the equality of their blood. The former influence of the separating trees and impassable wilderness is still alive in the [Germans'] addiction to segregating themselves into parties and associations.[63]

Guenther thus transformed a description of natural diversity into a negative metaphor for the chaotically divided political culture of the late Weimar Republic.

This inclination to cast diversity in negative terms was intertwined with, and reinforced by, a second change in the conservationists' view of nature. As the movement's leaders took up their forward-looking goals, many of them harnessed nature to a modernist vision of national economic progress. In the early 1930s they began to consider their movement's earlier reverence for the traditional agrarian landscape to be outdated and overly romantic. Karl Giannoni, for instance, proclaimed in *Der deutsche Heimatschutz* that the current movement's forward-looking goals were superior to the antimodern critique of industrial modernity that had characterized the prewar movement:

Protection of the homeland is not a form of romantic longing for the "good old days" but the vigorous pursuit of good *new* days. We desire not things that are similar in form to the past but things that are equivalent in value. The *Heimatschutz* movement stands in the middle of contemporary life; it takes the view that a merely material civilization must be reshaped into a culture based on the soul and on morality.[64]

Along the same lines, many conservationists and preservationists now argued that the ideal German landscape must embody a synthesis between the old and the new. Indeed, human beings had a right to impose order on nature. This shift to a modernist ideology of technological progress led many prominent conservationists in the early 1930s to acquiesce to the encroachment of industrial capitalism into the rural landscape.

These tendencies in the conservationists' conception of nature had practical consequences, for they promoted a policy of *Landschaftspflege*.[65] The word can be translated as either "landscape care" or "landscape cultivation." The conceptual difference between the two translations parallels the emergence of the relatively more rationalist, modernist view found in late Weimar conservationism. Wilhelmine conservationists had aimed for "landscape care" in their efforts to preserve the rural landscape from industry and mass society. A good example is the 1909 book *The Disfigurement of Our Land*, in which preservationist Paul Schultze-Naumburg railed against "the majority of people [who] seem to believe that our country will become ever more beautiful and magnificent through an industrious program of construction and increasing economic prosperity." They see "the ugliness of modern times as a necessity."[66] This attack on the modernist ideology of industrial-technological progress fit squarely within the landscape care tradition. But "landscape cultivation," which entailed the active shaping of nature, expresses better the trend in the late Weimar movement's discussion of policy. Walther Schoenichen, head of the Prussian State Conservation Agency and the most prolific publicist for *Naturschutz*, wrote that the German landscape was "a genuinely life-or-death matter for the entire nation" that could only be solved by the conservationists' "active influence in the configuration [*Ausgestaltung*] of the landscape."[67]

Thus, the aim of many conservationists after 1930 extended beyond the protection of natural monuments and limited areas to a wider-ranging method of landscape planning that included afforestation and the regulation of agricultural land use. As we have seen, this had been typical of the preservationist movement from the beginning, but state-sponsored conservationists had had to settle for the piecemeal protection of small natural monuments. Now, under the influence of a newly energized vision of the natural/national *Heimat*, even the conservationists began to call for the orderly and harmonious integration of new industrial and transportation facilities into the landscape. This synthesis of nature and industrial technology was to be achieved by a coalition of industrialists, scientists, engineers, architects, and conservationists—what one conservationist called a "spontaneous alliance between technicians and all who were hitherto opposed to technology."[68]

Proponents of landscape cultivation took pains to convince the public and the state that they took an optimistic and forward-looking view of technological change. It should be absolutely clear, wrote Hans Schwenkel of the Württemberg state conservation commission, that when conservationists battled gas stations and billboards, they did so not because they were opposed to economic progress, but "because of the harsh ugliness with which these things disfigure the landscape." Writing in *Der deutsche Heimatschutz*, Friedrich Hassler advised Weimar conservationists not to stand in the way of economic and technological developments, which were "absolutely necessary in a land as economically damaged as Germany" after the Treaty of Versailles. "Without falling back into false romanticism," he concluded, technicians, industrial planners, and engineers would see to it that the "character of the landscape" was harmed as little as possible. The conservationists' self-appointed task within the *Landschaftspflege* project was to act as midwives in the blending of nature and technology. According to Carl Fuchs, conservationists would henceforth try to influence industrialists and the state to (1) "destroy as few of the beauties of the *Heimat* as possible or as is absolutely necessary"; (2) guarantee that technical facilities in the rural landscape serve the national economy, not just private enterprise; and (3) see to it that "these new enterprises . . . create new beauties where they destroy old ones."[69]

It is important to recognize that this policy shift was closely related to the conservationists' pedagogic project of indoctrinating the masses in a commitment to the natural/national homeland. Given the acceptance of industrial workers into the new ideal narrative of progress toward the harmonious national community, there was both a practical and a symbolic logic to the incorporation of the modern nation's industrial workplaces into the rural landscape.

By 1933 conservationist ideology was neither simply antimodern nor romantic in its understanding of the nation and its concept of the relationship between nature and technology. Its primary component was not "the fateful fetish of agrarian romanticism,"[70] but the utopian vision of a peaceful, racially homogeneous national community, a vision that rhetorically brought together an allegedly more harmonious past and a bright new technological future in order to help the German nation overcome its crisis in the present. Thus, the bourgeois conservationists' response to the crises of late Weimar brought them into close ideological proximity to another project of overcoming the supposed emergency of the *Heimat*—National Socialism.

The Fate of Conservation Under the Nazi Dictatorship

Following Hitler's accession to power in January 1933, the *Gleichschaltung* of organized conservationism proceeded rapidly and for the most part voluntarily. The German League for Homeland Protection and the People's Conservation League chose to join the new Reich League for Nationhood and *Heimat* (*Reichsbund für Volkstum und Heimat*—RVH); and leading conservationists such as Walther Schoenichen and Hans Klose moved easily into high offices in the *Reichsbund*.[71] Many smaller regional and local *Heimat* groups also joined the RVH, although *Gleichschaltung* was slower at this level, and some regional organizations maintained a degree of ideological independence even within the Third Reich.[72] Linguistic self-synchronization took place quickly in conservationist journals, which busily relocated the love of nature within the Nazi rhetoric of "blood and soil."

The unique German character originated out of the German forest, and out of that forest flow new energies into our blood. . . . Lakes, swamps, waterfalls, characteristic rock formations, and other geological curiosities—all of these belong to the face of the German landscape. Honor and love that face as the face of our great mother! Protect and preserve it![73]

Why did so many bourgeois conservationists accept Nazism so easily? The answer lies in a combination of ideological affinities and simple opportunism.

Conservative and educated middle-class elites such as the conservationists shared several ideological positions with the Nazis by 1933. Both the Nazis and conservationists defined the national emergency in part as a problem of social division; and both groups believed that only authoritarian measures such as the destruction of organized socialism could overcome those divisions. Moreover, the rise of Nazism gave the more reactionary members of the conservation movement a blank check to voice their disdain for liberalism, materialism, "intellectualism," and feminism, disdain that had hitherto been muted in their publications. Schoenichen railed against the "overdone, un-German intellectualism that has brought our nation almost to the edge of the abyss" and the "proponents of liberal ideology" who were trying to "extinguish our uniqueness (*Eigenart*) with insidious poison."[74] Whereas the movement had had nothing to say about gender relations before 1933, there was now a wave of antifeminist rhetoric in *Naturschutz* publications. Konrad Guenther wrote that women were closer to the earth, as demonstrated by the fact that the female body's "center of gravity," the womb, was lower than that of the man. The German woman's calling was to mediate between nature and the national community by preserving folk traditions and raising children.[75] Others denigrated the increase in women's rights since the war, combining antifeminism with the older critique of mass tourism.

Other ideological affinities with Nazism related more directly to nature. Overt support for conservation was absent from the writings of Nazi leaders and ideologues before 1933, yet conservationists had reason to believe that with a little consciousness raising, the new leaders could be brought on board. Hitler's propaganda occasionally glorified a pastoral, idealized Aryan landscape: "The German landscape must under all conditions be preserved, for it is and always has been the source of the nation's power and strength."[76] Conservationists repeatedly quoted this statement as if to reassure themselves that the Nazi leader was genuinely committed to *Naturschutz*. Even more promising from the conservationist point of view was the prevalent notion of "blood and soil" (*Blut und Boden*) in

Einstmals zu Fuß unter seiner Führung

Heute in der Cabriolimousine und sie am Steuerrad

Lamenting the development of motorized mass tourism through misogynistic images: "They used to go by foot under his guidance. Today they go by convertible, and she is in the driver's seat." A cartoon by W. Schultz in *Naturschutz* (April 1935), 168.

Nazi propaganda. As formulated by the Nazi Agricultural Minister Richard Walther Darré, *Blut und Boden* was a deterministic theory of the relationship between the natural environment and German national identity. In essence it was a metaphor for rootedness in an idealized German agrarian landscape, a landscape that the German "race" itself had controlled and shaped for thousands of years. The rhetoric of *Blut und Boden* gave conservationists many opportunities to express their support for the regime. We must be careful, however, to distinguish between the Nazi idea of *Blut und Boden* and the conservationists' appropriation of it during the Third Reich. Although *Blut und Boden* rhetoric contained no truly environmentalist ideas, it could be deployed by those who hoped to influence the new regime to take conservation seriously. Walther Schoenichen, for instance, told his readers that under the influence of *Blut und Boden*, the Nazis viewed nature "not as a machine that is controlled by man but as an essence (*Wesenheit*) that has rights equal to those of mankind." In adapting *Blut und Boden* language, Schoenichen reversed the causal determinism at its core. For him, the land had determined the race, not vice versa: "The nature of our *Heimat*, combined with heredity [and] with the chain of historical events, has formed and engraved (*geprägt*) the identity of the German."[77] Furthermore, not even the Nazis' ideal of a homogeneous German identity was safe once conservationists began to adapt *Blut und Boden* language. Some conservationists on the regional level deployed the rhetoric to glorify the regional *Heimat* landscape rather than the nation, which was directly at odds with the Nazis' propagandistic intentions and with the national conservationist leaders.[78]

Creative deployments of rhetoric aside, the *Blut und Boden* concept was instrumental in winning the movement over to the new regime. Most important, it helped to overcome any contradictions between the two dominant strains of conservationism, for its vision of a harmonious natural *Heimat* appealed both to those who still clung to the neo-Romantic ethos of "landscape care" and to the more technocratic advocates of "landscape cultivation." Indeed, as leading conservationists committed themselves to the rhetoric of *Blut und Boden*, they apparently relinquished most of their remaining qualms about "integrating" modern industrial technology into the landscape. "The determined protection of German uniqueness in the landscape of our *Heimat*" could be rather easily reconciled with industrial technology.[79] It was only necessary to assert that factories and other technological projects were "installed in harmony with the landscape" and/or absolutely necessary for the survival of the nation in its "struggle for existence" (*Kampf ums Dasein*). Conservationists were not "unrealistic fanatics who dream of 'the good old days,'" wrote Schoenichen; rather, they knew that the German people had to "make the highest demands on their *heimatlichen* soil" in order to "overcome the insanity of Marxist dictatorship" and to compete with other nations. Thus, the conservationist movement would be at the forefront of technological developments:

There is indeed beautiful technology, and many of its creations valuably enrich the landscape. . . . Who can deny the impressive force of the mighty power plants that tower over the landscape, or of the enormous factories of heavy industry with their gigantic smokestacks pouring out picturesque clouds of smoke?

In the future the movement would have to abandon its "resistant position" and agree to cooperate "in the new formation of the *Heimat*. . . . In this the caretakers of national monuments (*Vertreter der Naturdenkmalpflege*) will have to go hand in hand with the landscape planners (*Landschaftsgestalter*)."[80] In passages such as these, Schoenichen undermined his own professed commitment to the equal rights of nature.

Schoenichen's decision to support the regime reflects the other key reason why conservationists cast their lot with the Nazis—sheer opportunism. Very few leading conservationists joined the Nazi Party before 1933.[81] But the statist orientation that had characterized their movement from the beginning, combined with the ideological affinities outlined earlier, allowed conservationists to support a new dictatorship that had potentially unlimited power over nature in Germany. As Schoenichen hopefully announced in 1934, the movement expected the government to fulfill "many significant demands and wishes of our People for whom sympathy has heretofore been lacking."[82]

One area in which conservationists requested the regime's support was popularization. The Weimar conservationists had been determined to win popular support from workers and young people, in part because they saw this as a way to pacify the unruly masses. There is no evidence that would indicate any great success in this endeavor, however. Recognizing that the new regime was determined to regain control over both the working class and the young generation, conservationists now began to ask the government to distribute their writings to the schools, Hitler Youth groups, and Reich Work Service contingents. In this way the masses might finally be indoctrinated into respecting nature.[83] Moreover, wrote Schoenichen, the state should construct more recreation areas and hiking paths in order to give "a deeper meaning" to the workers' free time and to help the national community overcome the disunified mass society. The rural landscape, too, should be observed by the state in order to quell the "hiking abuses" (*Wanderunsitten*) and "lack of culture" (*Kulturlosigkeit*) that took the form of littering, picking wild plants, carving graffiti on tree trunks, playing radios, using vending machines, and erecting billboards for outdoor advertising. The fact that Schoenichen was still writing exactly the same kind of thing in 1939 suggests that his appeals to the dictatorship to popularize conservation may have been falling on deaf ears.[84]

The other great hope that conservationists placed in the regime was fulfilled. Within the first two years of the Nazi regime, it became apparent that the new leadership was interested in passing the nationwide conservation law that conservationists had been longing for. The Reich Conservation Law (*Reichsnaturschutzgesetz*—RNSG) of June 26, 1935, grew out of a situation in which conservationists and Nazi leaders took advantage of each other's opportunism. On the one hand were leading conservationists like Hans Klose and Walther Schoenichen, who had been intensely disappointed with the Weimar government's failure to pass a national law. They were willing to do almost anything to achieve this goal. On the other was the Prussian Prime Minister and "Reich Forestry and Hunting Master" Hermann Göring. After the Prussian Cultural and Justice Ministers had spent months wrangling over who would take charge of conservation, Göring intervened in the spring of 1935, took control, and solicited leading conservationist Hans Klose and the lawyer Adolf Vollbach to compose the law.[85] By late June, the RNSG was complete, and Göring issued it without bothering to ask for the Nazi Reichstag's approval. The law was cosigned by Adolf Hitler, Minister of Justice Gürtner, Minister of Agriculture Darré, Interior Minister Frick, and Minister of Science and Education Rust.

In all likelihood Göring's principal interest lay not in conservation for its own sake but in his desire to increase his power in the Nazi Party and to protect specific areas where he wanted to indulge his love of hunting. He apparently had little to do with the writing; and the RNSG was based almost entirely on a number of pre-1933 Prussian conservation decrees and blueprints.[86] Indeed, the law should be seen as a culmination of pre-Nazi *Naturschutz*, for it brought together the strands of saving unique natural monuments and certain plant and animal species, designating small to medium-sized nature preserves, and protecting the rural landscape from massive transformation:

Conservation will apply to (a) plants and nongame animals; (b) natural monuments and their immediate surroundings; (c) nature reserves; (d) other parts of the natural landscape, to be protected on account of their rarity, beauty, distinctiveness, or because their scientific, cultural, forestry, or hunting significance lies in the general interest.[87]

The law also announced three major changes in the organization and enforcement of conservation. First, the Prussian State Conservation Agency was transformed into the National Agency (*Reichstelle*) in charge of the entire state-sponsored *Naturschutz* bureaucracy. It was placed under the tutelage of Reich Forestry Master Göring rather than that of the Cultural Minister as in previous years. This change exemplified both the Nazis' antifederalist, centralizing urge and Göring's lust for power. Second, the law allowed the state to designate private property for protection without compensating the property owner financially. This indemnity clause was a direct violation of the Weimar constitution's protection of property. The promulgators justified it through the Nazi Law for Ending the Emergency of the Nation (*Notstandsgesetz*) of March 24, 1933, according to which "the needs of the entire society trump individual needs" (*Gemeinnutz geht vor Eigennutz*).[88] Third, Paragraph 20 strengthened the everyday practical influence of conservationists by obligating all governing authorities to solicit their input in any technological planning that could lead to "significant changes in the landscape."

This law combined pre-1933 conservationism and Nazism. The confiscation clause both reflected Nazi totalitarianism and satisfied the conservationists' quest for power against capitalists. Paragraph 20 opened the way for "landscape cultivators" to influence decisions about industrial technology. And the preamble to the RNSG paid homage to the racial nationalism of the Nazi dictatorship: "Only a political system that recognizes the relationships between blood and soil, between national identity and the *Heimat*, a state that values the general good over individual self-interest, can grant nature and *Heimat* preservation its rights and proper place in the state."[89] Not surprisingly, conservationists throughout Germany praised the government for finally setting nature protection above private property rights and for "offering a means of maintaining the entire landscape in a *heimatlichen* condition so that Germans with their German sensibilities can feel themselves permanently at home there."[90]

The effects of the RNSG, however, were ambiguous, and there remains uncertainty among historians on this subject. The most thoroughly researched study of Nazi-era conservation, Frank Uekötter's *The Green and the Brown*, argues that conservation boomed in the years 1936 to 1941, as seen in the fact that more nature preserves were established within this brief span than at any other time in German history.[91] Although he acknowledges that such gains were ultimately outweighed by the regime's environmental depredations, Uekötter writes convincingly that conservationists were full of activist energy, "euphoria, and hope. . . . The late 1930s were probably not a 'high time' for conservation, but this was a time when conservationists were 'high.'"[92] This is a convincing argument that tells us much about the movement's bargain with the Nazis. Yet evidence exists to suggest that conservationists may not have gained as much power as it appears. The RNSG provided neither adequate funding nor enough personnel to enforce its impressive-sounding aims. Unpaid conservationists were still faced with the long, arduous task of identifying, researching, and promoting the preservation of specific natural monuments and areas.[93] Also, conservationists complained that Paragraph 20, which seemed to give them more advisory power in planning technological installations that would affect the *Heimat* landscape, was rarely put into everyday practice.[94] Indeed, it is hard to imagine that industrialists and planners involved in planning and carrying out the Nazis' war of conquest would have paid much attention to the demands for nature protection.[95]

There also remains considerable uncertainty over the extent to which the "indemnity clause" was put to everyday use. Frank Uekötter infers from the rapid increase in the number of nature preserves between 1936 and 1941 that the clause must have been used often as "a perfect instrument to pressure property owners into concessions."[96] This is a reasonable circumstantial argument. Yet some conservationists at the time pointed out that decrees that followed in the wake of the RNSG toned down the right to confiscate without compensation. According to Ilse Waldenburg, the Enforcement Order (*Durchführungsverordnung*) of October 31, 1935, "removed all hardships against the owners of nature preserves and monuments by allowing them to intervene in the form of written statements, the right to appeal, and so on. Individual rights have thus been preserved."[97] This ability of individuals to fight back may be a reason why Uekötter finds little evidence in his sources that the indemnity clause was applied directly during negotiations—though conservationists certainly could have wielded it more subtly.

It seems to me that the RNSG was only a relative and partial victory for conservationists. For it simultaneously gave state sponsorship to *Naturschutz* and set strict boundaries. The great caveat was a clause announcing that conservation was "not allowed to set restrictions on areas in use by the army, important public roads, shipping, or essential economic endeavors."[98] Every subsequent state conservation decree in the late 1930s and early 1940s that I have found contained a similar caveat, which protected the interests of hunters and farmers as well.[99] This gives us a different perspective on the apparent success in protecting natural monuments and establishing nature preserves. One has to wonder whether a nature preserve where economic exploitation and hunting were allowed was, in fact, a preserve.

What does seem clear is that state authorities were much more willing to protect nature when they also saw some kind of economic or political benefit. For example, the Bavarian state's motive for preventing the building of more gondolas in the Alps lay only in part in preventing more "hectic metropolitan crowds" from invading the mountains. Just as important was the fact that there were already enough gondolas, and increased competition would hurt them economically.[100] By the same token, if a request to protect nature appeared unusually ambitious or seemed to imperil economic health, Bavarian authorities would invariably turn it down. In 1936 two conservationists sent a request to Reich Forestry Master Göring for the establishment of a huge "national nature preserve" in the Bavarian Forest. The Bavarian director of forestry urged Göring not to do so, since much of the forest was already protected, and further enlargement of those areas would demand untenable economic sacrifices "far out of proportion to any purely emotional advantages." Apparently Göring was slow to decide, as we find Bavarian authorities still discussing the proposal in negative terms in 1939. The forestry department wrote to the state *Naturschutz* office that because the German *Lebensraum* has been so restricted in recent years, any further restrictions had to be avoided.[101]

Such insinuations that *Naturschutz* requests were antipathetic to the nation's health were increasingly common in the Nazi state's post-RNSG rhetoric. Veiled accusations of treason surely made conservationists think twice about voicing their opinions. Thus, some of the leading conservationists and lesser-known figures on the regional level deserve credit for persistently complaining about the Reich Work Service's project of "recovering wastelands." Even though their critiques expressed a growing ecological understanding of the interconnectedness of climate, water, plants, and animals, they had no effect on the Nazi state.[102] In truth the regime's commitment to *Naturschutz* turned out to be mostly a sham. The regime had no interest in enforcing any measures that would limit the country's economic recovery or its plans for military buildup. Indeed, if we survey the history of the Third Reich after 1935, we find agricultural development, public works projects, and the extraction of natural resources always taking precedence over nature protection. The primary reason was war preparation.

Very soon after the RNSG was announced, the same Hermann Göring who had authorized it began to oversee the destruction of the German landscape on an unprecedented scale. In his new capacity as plenipotentiary of the Four Year Plan, Göring was determined to achieve complete economic autarky for Germany. He presided over intensified exploitation of the forests, directing state forests in 1934 and private forests in 1936 to increase their harvest by 50 percent per year. In 1937 he sacked General Forestry Minister von Keudell, who was dedicated to forest conservation; and the new ministry subsequently declared, "The purpose and goal of forest development is not a natural forest but a naturally *economic* forest."[103] The Reich Work Service undertook river "correction" and the draining of wetlands for agricultural development. With rearmament came a massive buildup of heavy industrial factories. Air and water pollution worsened to unprecedented extremes throughout the 1930s; and Germany's first initiative to develop an "air hygiene law" was nipped in the bud in 1936 when its enemies proclaimed that it would make industry "fail in its duty to the People and the state."[104]

Ironically, war preparation gave something of a boost to the type of conservationist who was committed to "harmonizing" industry and nature through landscape cultivation. Beginning in 1936 any state-affiliated conservationist who spoke out publicly for conserving nature against the "general interest" was sacked. Attacks on the "romanticizing feeling" of early *Naturschutz* as ill suited to the modern technological world abounded.[105] By about 1940 only those advocates of conservation were thriving who had pledged themselves to technocratic Nazi projects of "landscape planning" along racial-biological lines.

While some conservationists took this step either opportunistically or out of conviction, many others did not. The new planning avant-garde in the massive *Landschaftspflege* projects of the late 1930s and early 1940s was composed of a few older conservationists alongside a growing number of landscape architects and geographers.[106] In a development that has to disturb present-day environmentalists, this technocratic cadre subscribed fully to the *Blut und Boden* concept of an organic bond between race and the landscape, but they also added a protoecological component. The healthier parts of the German landscape, they argued, had developed organically over hundreds of years, and any large-scale human intervention would have wide-ranging consequences. The destruction of a forest, for example, would affect the water table and the animal population, and the destruction of hedges would increase erosion, turn the area into a steppe, and eradicate the birds that controlled insects.[107]

These "landscape cultivators" enthusiastically participated in the construction of the new highway system, inspired by the government's professed commitment to careful, "organic" landscape planning. Moreover, their acceptance of the regime's basically *anti*environmentalist goal of motorizing Germany was eased by state propaganda glorifying the Autobahn as a symbol of "national unification through struggle." The architects of the Autobahn claimed to conform the road to the natural features of the landscape, a practice that they deemed superior to other countries' coldly utilitarian "rape" of the landscape through the use of straight lines. Thus, the discourse about the new highways combined *Landschaftspflege*-oriented conservationism, technocratic modernism, and *Blut und Boden* nationalism. Yet most of the protoecological elements in the planning of the highway system were based not only on a false and racist understanding of "plant sociology" but also on the myth that the landscape could escape damage merely through the conforming of roads to its topography. Despite the trumpeting enthusiasm of state propaganda, historians have uncovered a considerable amount of criticism of the Autobahn from conservationists who were less committed to *Landschaftspflege* and who could not help noticing that the new highway system was a severe blow to the traditional *Heimat* landscape.[108]

The most destructive war in history rendered the forward-looking, technocratic vision of *Landschaftspflege* thoroughly utopian. In hindsight we can see that the rhetoric of landscape cultivation was in the Third Reich little more than a mythical cover for the Nazi exploitation of nature.

Ironically, leading conservationists had already sown the seeds of a technocratic version of *Landschaftspflege* in the late Weimar years. Those conservationists in the Third Reich who used *Landschaftspflege* rhetoric to justify their acquiescence to the Nazi state's rapacious policies ultimately became handmaidens to environmental destruction.

Naturschutz and Racism

Considering the extent to which bourgeois conservationists placed their hopes in the Nazi regime, subscribed to the racist ideology of *Blut und Boden* and deployed racist terminology, and lent practical support to the regime, they made themselves complicit in the criminality of the Third Reich. Konrad Guenther, for instance, became one of the loudest exponents of the notion that people with blond hair and blue eyes had a much stronger feeling for nature than others, and that the conservation of nature would aid in the "racial cleansing" of Germany. And in an article entitled "'The German People Must Be Cleansed'—and the German Landscape?" Walter Schoenichen declared that the hereditary makeup of a nation directly determined its relationship to nature. "In the past the German soul always drew strength from German nature and the German landscape when it became necessary to overcome foreign influences and help Germanness break through again." He then reverted to his tried-and-true attack on mass culture as manifested in billboards, kitsch, and "foreign ways of building." But now the blame lay with the "merchant's spirit," Schoenichen's code term for the influence of "Jewish" capitalism. Schoenichen made such statements again and again throughout the Nazi era, and his writings became ever more explicitly anti-Semitic.[109] Such rhetoric buttressed the Nazis' deployment of the racially homogeneous natural/national *Heimat* concept as a justification for persecuting Jews and other minorities.

The ideological connection between this vision of nature and a "cleansed" national community was particularly obvious in Nazi discussions of the relationship of Jews to the landscape. For example, some Nazis and their followers on the local level attempted to eradicate "Jewish influence" from nature itself. In the spring of 1933, complaints from the small Franconian town of Streitberg began to arrive at the Bavarian State Chancellery. Some townsfolk were annoyed by the Jewish ownership of local caves called the Bing-Höhle. According to the editor of the

Nürnberger Zeitung, the local people, who were "the oldest and most dependable National Socialists in the area," were tired of being deprived of this source of tourist income. As a result, their anger toward the Jewish owners of the caves was "growing markedly." Meanwhile, the Nazis were destroying the family Benario, who owned the caves. They removed the head of the family from his professorship at a Nuremberg business school, and they imprisoned the son in the new concentration camp at Dachau. He was shot "while trying to escape."[110]

Even though this murderous persecution enabled the de facto "Aryanization" of the caves, more letters arrived from the Streitberg townspeople complaining that this natural monument was still "disfigured simply by having to bear a Jewish name." As one anonymous writer declared, "[O]ur Lord God did not create these caves in order that Jews could make money off them; rather he placed them on German soil so that the German people could enjoy them." In February 1934 the Bavarian government directed the district authorities to turn the caves over to the town. The Bing-Höhle were henceforth to have a different name, and the caves' rightful owners were to be notified that "any further exploitation by non-Aryans of this natural monument for private profit is under the present circumstances undesirable."[111] This incident exemplifies the way in which the rhetoric of cleansing the natural/national *Heimat* could easily be used to justify Aryanization.

We must also consider the participation of some conservationists and the role of *Landschaftspflege* ideas in the regime's radical wartime plans for the occupied East. We find certain conservationists drooling over the possibilities that seemed to open up with the Nazi invasion of Poland and the Soviet Union. Showing a stunning disregard for the rights of the conquered peoples, Walther Schoenichen took this opportunity to call on the state to establish a national park in annexed western Poland (the *Warthegau*) as well as thousands of new nature preserves in the other occupied areas.[112]

Even worse, certain leading conservationists of the "landscape cultivation" type were complicit in the regime's plan to replace Slavic peoples in the occupied East with "pure-blooded Germans." Beginning in late 1939, SS chief Heinrich Himmler as head of the Reich Commission for the Strengthening of Germandom (*Reichskommissariat für die Festigung deutschen Volkstums*—RKFDV) established a staff to develop plans for "reordering the expanded living space" in the annexed territories of

Poland. Viewing the Slavic "race" as inferior, the Nazi leaders thought that this region had been sadly neglected. The present population would have to be "cleansed" in order to make room for German settlers, through deportation, murder, and starvation. And once the colonists had "regained" control of land that rightly belonged to Germans, they would need direction in how to "re-Germanize" the area.[113]

Himmler put the agronomist Konrad Meyer in charge of formulating the *Generalplan Ost*; and in May 1942 the RKFDV made an agreement with the Reich Forestry Office soliciting the participation of conservationists who were committed to *Landschaftspflege*. The office planned district agencies for *Landschaftspflege* for the occupied territories, which would incorporate the principles of landscape cultivation into the planning process. The venerable director of state conservation in Württemberg, Hans Schwenkel, was put in charge of this new *Landschaftspflege* bureaucracy alongside Heinrich Wiepking-Jürgensmann, Himmler's colleague in the SS. The two worked with the geographer Erhard Mäding to formulate a blueprint for one part of the larger *Generalplan Ost*. The RKFDV approved this document as the General Directive on the Shaping of the Landscape in the Annexed Eastern Territories of December 21, 1942.[114]

This directive was a series of detailed suggestions on how the landscape of the occupied East could be transformed into a standardized version of the natural/national German *Heimat*. The landscape should be pastoral, yet modern, with a new Autobahn and railway lines and new towns and villages nestled carefully into the topography. Ecological measures should be taken to prevent erosion, build hedgerows, and keep air and water clean.[115] In his introduction to the directive, Mäding wrote in the tortuous logic of *Blut und Boden*: "It is not enough to settle our national race in these territories and eliminate foreign races. The spaces must be made to correspond to our specific natural character (*Wesensart*) in order that the Germanic human being will feel himself at home, will become settled there, and will be prepared to love and defend his new *Heimat*."[116]

Franz-Josef Brüggemeier has argued that the *Generalplan Ost* was a "singular alliance between belligerent expansion, racism, conservation and preservation, and ecological arguments." The "green" suggestions in the 1942 directive "took up traditions of *Heimatschutz* and *Naturschutz* and can be seen as a particularly radical and uncompromising attempt to reconcile society and nature."[117] But is it really fair to associate the debacle of conservationists' participation in this project of racist imperialism so generally with the entire history of the conservation movement? We need to recognize that German conservationism at its worst was bad due to its relatively recent infection by virulently racist nationalism. This is not to excuse any of the actions of leading conservationists in the Third Reich. They, like all other "Aryan" Germans, had choices.

Is there something suspect about conservationist ideology in general? In a provocative 2003 essay entitled "Conservation and National Socialism: What's the Problem?" historian Joachim Radkau argued that during the Enlightenment, the concept of human rights was in harmony with the love of nature; this was manifested in the notion of natural rights. But a "fatal process" of differentiation between love for human beings and love for nonhuman nature began in the late nineteenth century; one example was the worldwide conservation movement. Radkau posed the question whether the fascination with wild nature and its preservation might "inevitably lead to disinterest in or even contempt for human rights." In other words, does the *German* conservationists' acquiescence to the murderous Nazi regime indicate something potentially genocidal in the entire movement to protect nature, and even in a reverent attitude toward the natural world?[118]

The answer in this case is no. Neither the conservationists nor the Nazis were firmly committed to protecting *wilderness* during the 1930s. As we have seen, a technocratic form of landscape cultivation triumphed over the older, neo-Romantic current of landscape care. Despite its occasional mystifying rhetoric of unspoiled nature, the Nazi regime had little interest in "wildness," either in human nature or in nature itself. The Nazis were fundamentally modern in their efforts to control, cultivate, and "cull" both nature and society.[119]

Indeed, despite the apparent idealization of the landscape in *Blut und Boden* rhetoric, the Nazis' concept of nature was utilitarian. Nature served an ideological and a practical purpose for them. It was the source of the alleged natural laws that would, they thought, justify their attempts to cleanse the world of human imperfections. In a practical sense, nature was the source of the material resources needed to reach the economic autarky necessary for fighting an imperialist war. This instrumentalist, purely anthropocentric view of nature was anything but reverent, and it was perfectly compatible with raping the environment. Even if the Nazis had won the war, they would have proceeded to tame their own version of the Wild West in Eastern Europe.[120] There is no reason to think they would have valued the rights of nature any more than they respected the rights of human beings.

Even if we reject the myth that the Nazis themselves were "green," however, we still have to wonder how conservationists could lose sight of the rights of their fellow human beings. The answer lies in part in the long-standing social elitism and contempt for the masses that had marked conservationism since its beginnings and that intensified during the 1920s. The growing racial nationalism of the late 1920s and the 1930s helps to explain the blunting of conservationists' moral faculties as well. Finally, the Nazi dictatorship's legal support for *Naturschutz* encouraged delusions of grandeur that morally compromised those conservationists who participated in planning for a better world for the German people at the expense of non-Germans. It would be wrong to suggest that the very idea of conservation is somehow suspect. Nevertheless, we can learn from the German case that preserving nature is only a moral endeavor if it goes hand in hand with a commitment to social justice and human rights.[121]

Conclusion
The Cultural Appropriation of Nature
from the Kaiserreich to the Third Reich

"OF ALL THE SINS OF THE PAST DECADES, the worst was the turn away from nature by more and more people."[1] This announcement by the National Federation of Youth Hostels in 1925 embodies the passionate call of Germany's naturists for a closer connection to nature. The temptation when reading such exhortations is to interpret naturism as a reactionary, antimodern phenomenon. Yet a closer look reveals that organized conservation, hiking, and nudist movements, although they worried intensively about the consequences of industrialization and urbanization, were anything but antipathetic to the modern world. In calling for a turn to nature, they were not calling for Germany to turn back the clock but for the nation to find a way to navigate the treacherous waters of contemporary life and strive toward a brighter future.

The chief matters of concern to German naturists were the consequences of rapid industrialization and urbanization; social conflict between the classes, genders, and generations; and the health of the populace. In diagnosing the ills of modernity and developing ideal narratives of progress, naturist movements were creating the kind of reformist discourses that have powerfully influenced Western culture since the Enlightenment. Even though they criticized urban-industrial society, organized naturists were an altogether modernist force within German popular culture. Absorbed as they were with diagnosing and improving modern life, naturist organizations no doubt had a powerful influence over how their thousands of members perceived contemporary society.

For conservationist, hiking, and nudist movements, "turning to nature" involved appropriating the nonhuman environment for the purpose of improving society. Nature became a metaphor for a better future world in which the German people would live together in greater harmony. Although most of these movements directed their attention to specific class and generational groups, all naturists ultimately wanted to forge a passage that the entire German people could embark upon together. The socialist goal of the new human being, the *Wandervogel* striving for an autonomous young generation, and the youth cultivators' attempt to shape adolescents into rational adult citizens all aimed for a harmonious national community. Of course, their notions of the crises to be overcome, their methods of doing so, and even their visions of the future nation diverged. For naturists were involved in what Jarausch and Geyer call the "struggle over German identities among different groups that tried to shape the emergent nation in their own image. . . . The process of constructing a national identity was . . . a struggle over who would define the nation and which of the competing visions would control the state."[2]

We should not allow the Nazis' murderous utopia of the "racial-national community" to cast its shadow over other German projects of community building on a national level. For as the examples of socialist naturism and even of the *Wandervögel* show, such projects of nation building were just as likely to be liberal or Social Democratic as conservative or fascist. The desire to build community was palpable across the ideological spectrum; and it is surely understandable given the social dislocations and divisions of the era. Nor is it surprising that cultural activists appropriated Germany's rural landscape as a symbol for a future, better national community. As David Arnold has pointed out, "[I]magined communities" use "certain images and symbols, drawn from the environment" as an "emotional rallying point and a focus for an emerging sense of national identity."[3]

At the core of the turn to nature was a desire for better health. Naturists pointed to real physical problems of urban overcrowding, pollution, and public health, as well as to psychological damage stemming from social alienation and the stress of working life. Moreover, the early twentieth century brought transformations in gender, generational, and class relationships that naturists often addressed indirectly through metaphors of health. The expansion of "health" as a metaphor for a better future further politicized projects of turning to nature, simply because it raised the stakes.

The ideal narratives of turning to nature that naturist leaders fashioned and elaborated followed a common pattern. First, the narrative defined and described a social problem that was threatening the collective. Second, the narrative proposed specific ways to overcome the problem by turning to nature. Third, the narrative promised a future in which human beings would live in harmony with nature and with each other. This book has analyzed how conservationist, hiking, and nudist movements constructed each part of this narrative differently and how the changing, everyday historical context influenced the elaboration of the narratives. We have seen that narrative paradigms often changed in the face of pressures beyond the control of the movement. One example was the rhetorical backtracking of the *Wandervögel* in defense against the moral panic of 1913–14; another was the shift toward stronger sex reform and eugenicist language in the late Weimar socialist nudism movement in response to moralists' attacks. We have also seen that conceptual instabilities within naturist rhetoric sometimes undermined a narrative and sparked a process of rethinking and rhetorical standardization. One example in Weimar conservationism was the increased focus on the controversial and multifaceted concept of *Heimat*, which led to efforts to redefine the *Heimat* along simply nationalist lines. A second example was the ideological struggle between Social Democrats and Communists within the *Naturfreunde* movement, which led to a stronger focus on "social hiking." Yet another example was the incorporation of *Wandervogel* principles into youth cultivation hiking ideology in the 1920s, which undermined the latter movement's project of creating disciplined and conformist young citizens.

Furthermore, we have seen how concepts of nature itself took shape within naturist narratives. One general concept of nature represented it as the realm of the nonhuman environment outside society that promised freedom. Particularly for the *Wandervogel* movement and the Social Democratic naturist groups, this version of nature offered liberation from the institutions of social and political authority, an intimate sense of community with one's peers, a sense of emotional and physical wholeness, and simply a time to relax and recover from the pressures of everyday life. Hikers especially ventured into the rural landscape with a reverence for its beauty, as well as for what it could teach them about freedom and a better future. This vision of nature was a remnant of the Romantic worldview, but it also manifested an understandable desire for a temporary escape from the pressures of everyday urban life in the company of like-minded comrades.

We know that the socialists in particular decried the effects of industrial rationalization on the worker's body and mind. Was this reverent vision of nature, indebted as it was to Romanticism, also an attempt to resist modern rationalism in a broader sense? Max Weber wrote that modernity in the West had brought with it the demystification of nature. Through secularization and the rise of modern science, nature had been redefined as rational instead of mystical. With this "disenchantment of the world," he wrote, "the ultimate and most sublime values have retreated from public life, either into the transcendental realm of mystic life or into the brotherliness of direct and personal human relations."[4] The view of nature that predominated in some naturist movements appears to have been in part an attempt to idealize nature again in an emotional way; yet this did not mean that they "remystified" the natural world in a religious way. Socialist naturist writings were determinedly secular even as they wrote with great emotion about turning to nature. The socialist nudists and hikers sought to uncover the rational natural laws that they believed could be found in the nonhuman environment. They saw these laws primarily as darwinist, referring often to the "struggle for existence" (*Kampf ums dasein*); and they believed that society followed similar lines. It would be easy to interpret them as social darwinist if they had used natural laws to justify inequality, but this was not the case. They were interested in achieving greater *equality*, democracy, and social justice. Thus, we find in their combination of rationalistic notions of natural law, a neo-Romantic attitude toward nature, and a quest for freedom and justice a project of turning to nature that had almost nothing in common with the cynical ideology of social darwinism. Theirs was a far more complex and promising response to modernity than that of the bourgeois conservationists, many of whom by the late 1920s had rejected the Romantic critique of industrialization in favor of a technocratic kind of racial nationalism.

Indeed, the versions of nationalism found among the *Wandervögel* in their radical phase (1912 to early 1914) and in socialist naturism were far removed from the social darwinist, racialist nationalism that was becoming more and more prevalent in European culture. The rhetoric of the 1913 Meissner Festival consciously rejected such jingoism in favor of an older, more humanistic and Romantic version of cultural nationalism. And the Weimar *Naturfreunde* evoked a vision of the *Heimat* that emphasized the struggle for social justice and democratic equality within Germany, not competition with other nations. Nationalism is almost entirely absent from socialist nudism except as a target of criticism. This is not to say that the nation was not important for these movements; but their concerns revolved around improving the situation of class and generational countercultures that, they believed, held the keys to a better future for everyone in Germany. And there were occasional, striking examples in their discourse of efforts to transcend nationalism and think about the good of all humanity. In hindsight these three movements appear as promising reformist alternatives, the attempts at "self-synchronization" by their leaders in 1933 notwithstanding. These ignominious efforts stemmed not so much from the movements' ideologies as from their vulnerability as the Nazis tightened their grip.

On the other hand, the concept of a primitive, irrational *human* nature also pervaded the organized turn to nature. This was a more problematic element in naturism than any remnant of Romanticism. It reflected a much broader tendency in Western civilization to categorize, demonize, and punish groups of people for their allegedly threatening irrationality. In naturist rhetoric this negative concept of human nature quickly came to dominate diagnoses of social problems. It was particularly salient in discussions of childhood and adolescence, urban mass culture, and sexuality. Among youth cultivators and bourgeois conservationists, the concept of natural human irrationality heightened fears of social disorder. Socialist movements, too, saw the "instinctual drives" of a working class dazzled by capitalist mass media as a severe challenge to their goal of creating the new human being.

Such fears expressed an ongoing sense of crisis. They peaked in the immediate pre–World War I years of mounting class, gender, and generational tensions (1910–14); in late wartime and the revolutionary era (1917–23); and during the Depression and the rapid decline of Weimar democracy (1929–33). *Natural* human instability became a readily available metaphor for *social* instability. We encounter here a dark side of German naturism that was both modern—in the sense of rationalistic—and authoritarian. Frustration at the apparent irrationality of the human object of their concern—young people and workers—led naturists in times of crisis to resort to the panic-stricken rhetoric of moral panic and demonization. However, in times of relative calm, particularly during the more stable years of the 1920s (1924–28), even the more socially conservative movements of youth cultivation and conservationism settled into quieter efforts to come to terms with the less-than-rational desires of their constituents. Youth cultivators in those years were able to compromise with the emotional ethos of *Wandervogel* hiking, and conservationists tried to adapt the nonrational concept of *Heimat* as a way to pacify workers and young people.

It seems probable that at least the youth cultivators would have maintained their conciliatory relationship to "the masses" if the Depression had not occurred. But that event was a disaster for all attempts to develop a peaceful solution to Germany's social divisions. It opened the door for a political movement that was bent on eradicating all the diversity of German society. If we look at the Nazis from the perspective of the history of naturism, we find that their version of turning to nature was far from Romantic. They sneered at emotional "yammering about nature" (*Naturschwärmerei*) as sentimental, effeminate, and weak. For the leaders of the Hitler Youth, youth hiking was polluted by the emancipatory legacy of the *Wandervögel*; and they ultimately purged both the practice of *Wandern* and the word itself from their vocabulary. The Romantic ethos of nature as a realm of personal or group liberation barely survived among renegade youth hiking groups during the Third Reich—under a regime in which any quest for personal freedom became a matter of risking one's life.

Instead, the Nazis appropriated the more rationalistic strain of naturism and perverted this into a project of turning to a nature that they conceived in purely social darwinist terms. From this version of nature, in which the cold eradication of useless variations was a necessary part of the striving toward perfection, the Nazis dredged up such "natural laws" as the principle that "every action of the human being rests upon inalienable and nonacquirable hereditary characteristics."[5] Nazi scientists and doctors produced sociobiological explanations for any differences from the acceptable norm. Socially deviant "community aliens" (*Gemeinschaftsfremde*)—such as alcoholics, juvenile delinquents, and "idlers"; those who were considered to have no economic utility; those who deviated from "natural" gender and sexual roles; and "racial" groups defined as "non-Aryans"—all were categorized along hereditary and biological lines as threats to the health of the "national body" (*Volkskörper*). This was a pathological form of rationalism that saw individual freedom and human diversity as mortal enemies. As Hitler predicted in *Mein Kampf*, "[T]he state must . . . in the light of reason, regard its highest task as the preservation and intensification of the race, this fundamental condition of all human cultural development. . . . Its end lies in the preservation and advancement of a community of physically and mentally homogeneous creatures."[6]

Even though the Nazis appropriated nature as the ultimate source of their genocidal social policies, they had little respect for the rural environment, the Reich Conservation Law of 1935 notwithstanding. There was in the Third Reich, in fact, an integral connection between controlling society and controlling nature. Both processes were part of an all-encompassing project of reshaping the world. This was a great difference between the National Socialists and the naturist movements that predated them. Most German naturists before 1933 tried to improve their world by finding a *peaceful* way of turning to nature. Naturists at their best sought a way to master industrial modernity by preserving the rights of human beings and of nature itself. "Every person will stand close to every other, and all these individuals' unique *internal* experiences of nature will unite, giving life to a higher community. This will be made possible by a friendship between human beings and nature that encompasses the entire world."[7] Reclaiming such a hopeful vision of the future may be the only way for humanity to face the dangers of the new century.

Abbreviations

AdJb   Archiv der deutschen Jugendbewegung, Burg Ludwigstein

BA   Bezirksamt

BArch   Bundesarchiv, Berlin-Lichterfelde

BayHStAM   Bayerisches Hauptstaatsarchiv, Munich

BDM   Bund deutscher Mädel

DAF   Deutsche Arbeitsfront

DBH   Deutscher Bund Heimatschutz

DNVP   Deutschnationale Volkspartei

eco-Archiv   eco-Archiv im Archiv der Sozialen Demokratie der Friedrich-Ebert
    Stiftung, Bad Godesberg

FDJ   Freideutsche Jugend

GDB   Grossdeutscher Bund

GFDHS   Gesellschaft der Freunde des Deutschen Heimatschutzes

HJ   Hitler Jugend

HKB   Historische Kommission zu Berlin

IfZ   Institut für Zeitgeschichte, Munich

KDF   Kraft durch Freude

KJMV   Katholischer Jungmännerverband

KPD   Kommunistische Partei Deutschlands

MA   Ministerium des Äussern

MInn   Ministerium des Innern

MJu   Ministerium der Justiz

MK   Ministerium für Unterricht und Kultus

MWi   Ministerium für Wirtschaft

JADJB   Jahrbuch des Archivs der deutschen Jugendbewegung

LAB   Landesarchiv Berlin

LRA   Landratsamt

NSDAP   Nationalsozialistische Deutsche Arbeiterpartei

NSHStAH   Niedersächsisches Hauptstaatsarchiv, Hannover

PDM   Polizeidirektion Munich

PPL   Polizeipräsidium Leipzig

RKFDV   Reichskommissariat für die Festigung deutschen Volkstums

RKJ   Reichskuratorium für Jugendertüchtigung

RNSG   Reichsnaturschutzgesetz

RVH   Reichsbund für Volkstum und Heimat

SA   Sturmabteilung

SAJ   Sozialistische Arbeiterjugend

SAPMO-BArch   Bundesarchiv Berlin-Lichterfelde, Stiftung Archiv der Parteien und Massenorganisationen der DDR

SPD   Sozialdemokratische Partei Deutschlands

SS   Schutzstaffel

SSNDP   Staatliche Stelle für Naturdenkmalpflege

STA   Stadtarchiv Augsburg

STAA   Staatsarchiv Augsburg

STAH   Staatsarchiv Hamburg

STAL   Staatsarchiv Leipzig

STAM   Staatsarchiv Munich

StK   Staatskanzlei

STL   Stadtarchiv Leipzig

STM   Stadtarchiv Munich

TVNF   Touristenverein "Die Naturfreunde"

USPD   Unabhängige Sozialdemokratische Partei Deutschlands

WVEV   Wandervogel, eingetragener Verein

Notes

Introduction

1. Adolf Koch, "Die Wahrheit über die Berliner Gruppen für freie Körperkultur," *Junge Menschen* (August 1924), 2.

2. My use of this term is not to be confused with the occasional tendency to call *nudism* "naturism," e.g., Karl Dreßen, *Geschichte des Naturismus: Von der Nacktheit über die Nacktkultur zum Naturismus* (Antwerp, 1995).

3. Quoted in Adolf Levenstein, *Die Arbeiterfrage: Mit besonderer Berücksichtigung der sozialpsychologischen Seite des modernen Großstadtbetriebes und der psychophysischen Einwirkungen auf die Arbeiter* (Munich, 1912), 377.

4. The best example of this is the socialist hiking organization, the *Naturfreunde* (see Chapter 2).

5. See, for example, T. J. Jackson Lears, *No Place of Grace: Anti-Modernism and the Transformation of American Culture, 1880–1920* (New York, 1981); Jan Marsh, *Back to the Land: The Pastoral Impulse in England from 1800 to 1914* (London, 1982); Kenneth Olwig, *Landscape, Nature, and the Body Politic: From Britain's Renaissance to America's New World* (Madison, 2002). There is not enough space in this book for comparative discussion of non-German naturist organizations, but references will be provided throughout.

6. Konrad Jarausch and Michael Geyer, *Shattered Past: Reconstructing German Histories* (Princeton, 2003), 12.

7. George Mosse, *Nationalism and Sexuality: Middle-Class Morality and Sexual Norms in Modern Europe* (Madison, 1985), 112, 137. Other examples include Hans Kohn, *The Mind of Germany* (New York, 1960); Fritz Stern, *The Politics of Cultural Despair: A Study in the Rise of the Germanic Ideology* (Berkeley, 1961); Hermann Glaser, *The Cultural Roots of National Socialism* (Austin, 1978, orig. 1964); George Mosse, *The Crisis of German Ideology* (New York, 1964), *The Nationalization of the Masses: Political Symbolism and Mass Movements in Germany from the Napoleonic Wars Through the Third Reich* (New York, 1975), and *Masses and Man: Nationalist and Fascist Perceptions of Reality* (New York, 1980);

Peter Gay, *Weimar Culture: The Outside as Insider* (London, 1969); Klaus Bergmann, *Agrarromantik und Großstadtfeindschaft* (Meisenheim, 1970); Roderick Stackelberg, *Idealism Debased: From Völkisch Ideology to National Socialism* (Kent, Ohio, 1981); Rolf-Peter Sieferle, *Fortschrittsfeinde? Opposition gegen Technik und Industrie von der Romantik bis zur Gegenwart* (Munich, 1984); Robert Pois, *National Socialism and the Religion of Nature* (London, 1986). Somewhat more nuanced interpretations began to emerge in the 1980s, notably Christoph Conti, *Abschied vom Bürgertum: Alternative Bewegungen in Deutschland von 1890 bis heute* (Reinbek, 1984); Ortwin Renn, "Die alternative Bewegung: Eine historisch-soziologische Analyse des Protestes gegen die Industriegesellschaft," *Zeitschrift für Politik* (1985), 153–94.

8. Thomas Mann, "Rede, gehalten zur Feier des 80. Geburtstages Friedrich Nietzsches am 15. Oktober 1924," in Thomas Mann, *Essays* (Frankfurt, 1994), 2:240.

9. This conflation of "Romantic irrationality" with Nazism persists in some of the recent historical literature, e.g., Paul Rose, *Wagner: Race and Revolution* (New Haven, Conn., 1992); Anton Kaes et al., eds., *The Weimar Republic Sourcebook* (Berkeley, 1994); Albrecht Lehmann and Klaus Schriewer, eds., *Der Wald: Ein deutscher Mythos? Perspektiven eines Kulturthemas* (Berlin, 2000); Hans-Ulrich Wehler, *Deutsche Gesellschaftsgeschichte, Band III: Von der "deutschen Doppelrevolution" bis zum Beginn des Ersten Weltkrieges* (Munich, 1995), and *Band IV: Vom Beginn des Ersten Weltkrieges bis zur Gründung der beiden deutschen Staaten, 1914–1949* (Munich, 2003). The conflation remains influential in present-day German culture as well. Any reader of historical articles in *Die Zeit* or *Der Spiegel* will often encounter it, e.g., Johannes Salzwedel, "Jauchzen der Zukunft," *Der Spiegel* (July 12, 1999), 102; Michael Naumann, "Bildung—eine deutsche Utopie," *Die Zeit* (December 4, 2003), 45. Philosopher Jürgen Habermas's ongoing battle against postmodern critiques of rationalism has reinforced the denigration of "romanticism" in Germany. See Jürgen Habermas, *The Habermas Reader* (New York, 1989). Beyond the historiography of modern Germany, the general thesis that fascism was simply an irrationally antimodern movement remains prevalent in popular works ranging from college textbooks, e.g., Marvin Perry et al., eds., *Sources of Twentieth-Century Europe* (Boston, 1999); Roy Matthews and F. Dewitt Platt, *The Western Humanities*, 4th ed. (New York, 2004), to studies of literature and art, e.g., Robert Harrison, *Forests: The Shadow of Civilization* (Chicago, 1992); Simon Schama, *Landscape and Memory* (London, 1995). It has recently appeared in post–September 11 theories of "Islamo-Fascism" and "Occidentalism." See Petra Steinberger, "In der Mitte ein Wort: Ist die Vorstellung vom Islamofaschismus absurd?" *Süddeutsche Zeitung* (March 24, 2004); Gustav Seibt, "Religionskriege können nicht gewonnen werden," ibid. (April 10–12, 2004); Ian Buruma and Avishai Margalit, *Occidentalism: The West in the Eyes of Its Enemies* (London, 2004). For useful scholarship on the Romantic movement, cf. Roy Porter and Mikulás Teich, eds., *Romanticism in National Context* (Cambridge, 1988); Gerald Izenberg, *Impossible Individuality: Romanticism, Revolution, and the Origins of Modern Selfhood, 1787–1802* (Princeton, 1992); Isaiah Berlin, *The Roots of Romanticism* (Princeton, 2001). On neo-Romanticism in the early twentieth century, see Steven Aschheim, *The Nietzsche Legacy in Germany, 1890–1990* (Berkeley, 1992); Gerald Izenberg, *Modernism and Masculinity: Mann, Wedekind, Kandinsky Through World War I* (Chicago, 2000).

10. Historians continue to debate the relationship between Nazism and moderniza-tion. Cf. Joachim Radkau, "Nationalsozialismus und Modernisierung," in Hans-Ulrich Wehler, ed., *Scheidewege der deutschen Geschichte* (Munich, 1995); Mark Roseman, "Na-tional Socialism and Modernization," in Richard Bessel, ed., *Fascist Italy and Nazi Ger-many* (Cambridge, 1996), 197–229; Robert Gellately and Nathan Stoltzfus, eds., *Social Outsiders in Nazi Germany* (Princeton, 2001); Young-Sun Hong, "Neither Singular nor Alternative: Narratives of Modernity and Welfare in Germany, 1870–1945," *Social His-tory* (May 2005), 133–53. Scholars have also challenged the thesis that pre-1933 conserva-tives and the folkish right were simply antimodern, e.g., Jost Hermand, *Old Dreams of a New Reich: Volkish Utopias and National Socialism* (Bloomington, 1992); Larry E. Jones and James Retallack, eds., *Between Reform, Reaction and Resistance: Studies in the History of German Conservatism from 1789 to 1945* (Oxford, 1993); Uwe Puschner et al., eds., *Handbuch zur "Völkischen Bewegung," 1871–1918* (Munich, 1996). Some historians in the 1980s attempted to reconcile the right's alleged antimodernism with the fact that Germany was by 1900 one of the most advanced nations in the natural sciences, medi-cine, and industrial and military technology. The technocratic bent of German culture, asserts Jeffrey Herf, combined with antirationalism to yield a synthesis of "reactionary modernism." Jeffrey Herf, *Reactionary Modernism: Technology, Culture, and Politics in Weimar and the Third Reich* (Cambridge, 1984). For Modris Eckstreins, the First World War offered Germans a paradoxical escape forward from rationalism into an ever-deeper obsession with "speed, newness, transience, and inwardness." Modris Eckstreins, *Rites of Spring: The Great War and the Birth of the Modern Age* (New York, 1989). Although these scholars recognize the strongly modernist element in German culture, both cling to a reductive focus on "irrationality" as the central continuity to Nazism. There is a striking difference between this argument and that found in Thomas Rohkrämer, *Eine andere Moderne? Zivilisationskritik, Natur, und Technik in Deutschland, 1880–1933* (Paderborn, 1999). Rohkrämer breaks completely with the irrationality thesis by arguing that intel-lectuals who criticized industrial technology or attempted to reconcile it with nature were quite rational in their critical response to industrial modernity.

11. See, e.g., Franz Walter, Viola Denecke, and Cornelia Regin, *Sozialistische Gesund-heits-und Lebensreformverbände* (Bonn, 1991); John A. Williams, "'The Chords of the German Soul Are Tuned to Nature': The Movement to Preserve the Natural *Heimat* from the Kaiserreich to the Third Reich," *Central European History* (1996), 339–84, "Steeling the Young Body: Official Attempts to Control Youth Hiking in Germany, 1913–1938," *Occasional Papers in German Studies* 12 (July 1997), "Ecstasies of the Young: Sexuality, the Youth Movement, and Moral Panic in Germany on the Eve of the First World War," *Central European History* (2001), 162–89, and "Protecting Nature Between Democracy and Dictatorship: The Changing Ideology of the Bourgeois Conservationist Movement, 1925–1935," in Thomas Lekan and Thomas Zeller, eds., *Germany's Nature: New Approaches to Environmental History* (New Brunswick, N.J., 2005), 183–206; William Rollins, *A Greener Vision of Home: Cultural Politics and Environmental Reform in the German Hei-matschutz Movement, 1904–1918* (Ann Arbor, 1997); Thomas Lekan, *Imagining the Nation in Nature: Landscape Preservation and German Identity, 1885–1945* (Cambridge, Mass.,

2004). Article-length examples can be found in Colin Riordan, ed., *Green Thought in German Culture: Historical and Contemporary Perspectives* (Cardiff, 1997); Joachim Radkau and Frank Uekötter, eds., *Naturschutz und Nationalsozialismus* (Frankfurt, 2003); Christoph Mauch, ed., *Nature in German History* (New York, 2004); Lekan and Zeller, eds., *Germany's Nature*.

12. Cf. Geoff Eley, "Die deutsche Geschichte und die Widersprüche der Moderne: Das Beispiel des Kaiserreichs," in Frank Bajohr et al., eds., *Zivilisation und Barbarei: Die widersprüchlichen Potentiale der Moderne* (Hamburg, 1991), 17–65; Richard Evans, *Rereading German History: From Unification to Reunification, 1800–1996* (London, 1997); Geoff Eley and James Retallack, "Introduction" in idem, eds., *Wilhelminism and Its Legacies: German Modernities, Imperialism, and the Meanings of Reform, 1890–1930* (New York, 2003), 1–15; Jarausch and Geyer, *Shattered Past*; Hong, "Singular."

13. Cf. among others, Paul Weindling, *Health, Race, and German Politics Between National Unification and Nazism, 1870–1945* (Cambridge, 1989); Celia Applegate, *A Nation of Provincials: The German Idea of Heimat* (Berkeley, 1990); Alfons Labisch, *Homo hygienicus: Gesundheit und Medizin in der Neuzeit* (Frankfurt, 1992); Helmut W. Smith, *German Nationalism and Religious Conflict: Culture, Ideology, Politics, 1870–1914* (Princeton, 1995); Mark Roseman, ed., *Generations in Conflict: Youth Revolt and Generation Formation in Germany, 1770–1968* (Cambridge, 1995); Atina Grossman, *Reforming Sex: The German Movement for Birth Control and Abortion Reform, 1920–1950* (Oxford, 1995); Kathleen Canning, *Languages of Labor and Gender: Female Factory Work in Germany, 1850–1914* (Ithaca, N.Y., 1996); James Retallack, ed., *Saxony in German History: Culture, Society, and Politics, 1830–1933* (Ann Arbor, 2000); Pascal Grosse, *Kolonialismus, Eugenik, und bürgerliche Gesellschaft in Deutschland, 1850–1918* (Frankfurt, 2000); Abigail Green, *Fatherlands: State-Building and Nationhood in Nineteenth-Century Germany* (Cambridge, 2001); Lora Wildenthal, *German Women for Empire, 1884–1945* (Durham, N.C., 2001); Matti Bunzl and H. Glenn Penny, eds., *Worldly Provincialism: German Anthropology in the Age of Empire* (Ann Arbor, 2003); Dagmar Herzog, *Sex After Fascism: Memory and Morality in Twentieth-Century Germany* (Princeton, 2005).

14. Some of the many works that have uncovered this phenomenon of grassroots cultural activism include Geoff Eley, *Reshaping the German Right: Radical Nationalism and Political Change after Bismarck* (London, 1980); Richard Evans, ed., *Society and Politics in Wilhelmine Germany* (Totowa, N.J., 1981); David Blackbourn and Geoff Eley, *The Peculiarities of German History* (Oxford, 1984); Rüdiger vom Bruch, ed., *"Weder Kommunismus noch Kapitalismus": Bürgerliche Sozialreform in Deutschland vom Vormärz bis zur Ära Adenauer* (Munich, 1985); Vernon Lidtke, *The Alternative Culture: Socialist Labor in Imperial Germany* (Oxford, 1985); Robert Moeller, *German Peasants and Agrarian Politics, 1914–1924: The Rhineland and Westphalia* (Chapel Hill, N.C., 1986); David Blackbourn, *Populists and Patricians: Essays in Modern German History* (London, 1987); Ann T. Allen, *Feminism and Motherhood in Germany, 1800–1914* (New Brunswick, N.J., 1991); Geoff Eley, ed., *Society, Culture, and the State in Germany, 1870–1930* (Ann Arbor, 1996); Jochen-Christoph Kaiser and Wilfried Loth, eds., *Soziale Reform im Kaiserreich: Protestantismus, Katholizismus, und Sozialpolitik* (Stuttgart, 1997); David Barclay and Eric

Weitz, eds., *Between Reform and Revolution: German Socialism and Communism from 1840 to 1990* (New York, 1998); Diethart Kerbs and Jürgen Reulecke, eds., *Handbuch der deutschen Reformbewegungen, 1880–1933* (Wuppertal, 1999); Jan Palmowski, *Urban Liberalism in Imperial Germany: Frankfurt am Main, 1866–1914* (Oxford, 1999); Peter Lundgreen, ed., *Sozialgeschichte des Bürgertums* (Göttingen, 2000); Jean Quataert, *Staging Philanthropy: Patriotic Women and the National Imagination in Dynastic Germany, 1813–1916* (Ann Arbor, 2001); Kevin Repp, *Reformers, Critics, and the Path of German Modernity: Anti-Politics and the Search for Alternatives, 1890–1914* (Cambridge, Mass., 2001); Uwe Puschner, *Die völkische Bewegung im wilhelminischen Reich: Sprache—Rasse—Religion* (Darmstadt, 2001); Jennifer Jenkins, *Provincial Modernity: Local Culture and Liberal Politics in Fin-de-Siècle Hamburg* (Ithaca, N.Y., 2002). More specific emphases on the relationship between society and the fledgling welfare state and on contesting citizenship include Young-Sun Hong, *Welfare, Modernity, and the Weimar State, 1919–1933* (Princeton, 1998); David Crew, *Germans on Welfare: From Weimar to Hitler* (Oxford, 1998); Greg Eghighian, *Making Security Social: Disability, Insurance, and the Birth of the Social Entitlement State in Germany* (Ann Arbor, 2000); Geoff Eley, "Making a Place in the Nation: Meanings of 'Citizenship' in Wilhelmine Germany," in Eley and Retallack, eds., *Wilhelminism*, 16–30.

15. This has involved in part an investigation into the realities and perceptions of crisis as an unusually prominent characteristic of modern German culture. Cf. Detlev Peukert, *Die Weimarer Republik: Krisenjahre der klassischen Moderne* (Frankfurt, 1987); Anson Rabinbach, *The Human Motor: Energy, Fatigue, and the Origins of Modernity* (Berkeley, 1992), and *In the Shadow of Catastrophe: German Intellectuals Between Apocalypse and Enlightenment* (Berkeley, 1997); Steven Aschheim, *Culture and Catastrophe: German and Jewish Confrontations with National Socialism and Other Crises* (New York, 1996); Joachim Radkau, *Das Zeitalter der Nervosität: Deutschland zwischen Bismarck und Hitler* (Munich, 1998); Paul Betts and Greg Eghigian, eds., *Pain and Prosperity: Reconsidering Twentieth-Century German History* (Stanford, 2003); Jarausch and Geyer, *Shattered Past*.

16. Werner Sombart, *Das Proletariat* (Frankfurt, 1906), 21, and *Der moderne Kapitalismus* (Leipzig, 1902), 2:237, cited in Andrew Lees, *Cities Perceived: Urban Society in European and American Thought, 1820–1940* (Manchester, 1985), 213. Similarly conflicting views appeared in the influential sociology of Ferdinand Tönnies and Georg Simmel as well; and they persisted in sociological studies of urban society during the 1920s. Ferdinand Tönnies, *Gemeinschaft und Gesellschaft* (Berlin, 1887); Georg Simmel, "Die Großstädte und das Geistesleben" (1903), cited in Lees, *Cities*, 163–64; Bernhard Mewes, *Die erwerbstätige Jugend* (Berlin, 1929); Günther Dehn, *Proletarische Jugend: Lebensgestaltung und Gedankenwelt der großstädtischen Proletarierjugend*, 3d ed. (Berlin, 1933).

17. Jürgen Reulecke, *Geschichte der Urbanisierung in Deutschland* (Frankfurt, 1985), 9, 68, 74–81; David Crew, *Town in the Ruhr: A Social History of Bochum, 1860–1914* (New York, 1979); Hans J. Teuteberg and Clemens Wischermann, eds., *Wohnalltag in Deutschland, 1850–1914: Bilder, Daten, Dokumente* (Münster, 1985), 59; Nicholas Bullock, "Berlin," in M. Daunton, ed., *Housing the Workers: A Comparative History, 1850–1914* (London, 1990), 209; Tilman Harlander, ed., *Villa und Eigenheim: Suburbaner Städtebau*

in Deutschland (Ludwigsburg, 2001). By contrast, in 1870 there were fourteen cities in the United States with over 100,000 residents, increasing to fifty by 1910. This was a far slower rate of urbanization in a much less densely populated country. Campbell Gibson, "Population of the 100 Largest Cities and Other Urban Places in the United States, 1790–1990," www.census.gov/population/documentation/twps0027.

18. This has been true throughout the urbanizing world. See, for example, George Chauncey, *Gay New York: Gender, Urban Culture, and the Making of the Gay Male World, 1890–1940* (New York, 1994).

19. H. Breme, "Gutachten über sanitären Verhältnisse in der Emscherniederung in dem Distrikte," in H. Emmerich and F. Wolter, *Die Entstehungsgeschichte der Gelsenkirchener Typhusepidemie von 1901* (Munich, 1906), reprinted in Franz-Josef Brüggemeier and Thomas Rommelspacher, eds., *Blauer Himmel über der Ruhr: Geschichte der Umwelt im Ruhrgebiet, 1840–1990* (Essen, 1992), 146. On urban sanitation and public health, cf. Richard Evans, *Death in Hamburg* (Oxford, 1983); Labisch, *Homo hygienicus*; Peter Münch, *Stadthygiene im 19. und 20. Jahrhundert* (Göttingen, 1993). Histories of the modern German environment include Klaus-Georg Wey, *Umweltpolitik in Deutschland* (Opladen, 1982); Franz-Josef Brüggemeier and Thomas Rommelspacher, eds., *Besiegte Natur: Geschichte der Umwelt im 19. und 20. Jahrhundert* (Munich, 1987); Arne Andersen, ed., *Umweltgeschichte: Das Beispiel Hamburg* (Hamburg, 1990), and *Historische Technikfolgenabschätzung am Beispiel des Metallhüttenwesens und der Chemieindustrie, 1850–1933* (Stuttgart, 1996); Ulrike Gilhaus, *"Schmerzenskinder der Industrie": Umweltverschmutzung, Umweltpolitik, und sozialer Protest im Industriezeitalter in Westfalen, 1845–1914* (Paderborn, 1995); Jürgen Büschenfeld, *Flüsse und Kloaken: Umweltfragen im Zeitalter der Industrialisierung (1870–1918)* (Stuttgart, 1997); Beate Olmer, *Wasser: Zur Bedeutung und Belastung des Umweltmediums im Ruhrgebiet, 1870–1930* (Frankfurt, 1998); Gerhard Lenz, *Verlusterfahrung Landschaft: Über die Herstellung von Raum und Umwelt im mitteldeutschen Industriegebiet seit der Mitte des neunzehnten Jahrhunderts* (Frankfurt, 1999); Mark Cioc, *The Rhine: An Eco-Biography, 1815–2000* (Madison, 2002); Christoph Bernhardt and Geneviève Massard-Guilbaud, eds., *The Modern Demon: Pollution in Urban and Industrial European Societies* (Clermont-Ferrand, 2002).

20. Niedersächsiches Hauptstaatsarchiv, Hannover (hereafter NSHStAH), Hann. 174 Neustadt, Nr. 2492: "Bericht über die gemeinsame Versammlung des Deutschen Vereins für Wohnungsreform—Hannover vom 4. Mai 1912," 17–18; Deutscher Gewerkschaftsbund Augsburg, ed., *Spurensicherung: Beiträge zur fast vergessenen Geschichte Augsburgs* (Augsburg, 1985), 181–82; Reulecke, *Urbanisierung*, 69, 91–101; Teuteberg and Wischermann, *Wohnalltag*, 63; Franz-Josef Brüggemeier, "'Trautes Heim—Glück allein'? Arbeiterwohnen," in Wolfgang Ruppert, ed., *Die Arbeiter* (Munich, 1986), 117–26; Elizabeth Gransche and Franz Rothenbacher, "Wohnbedingungen in der zweiten Hälfte des 19. Jahrhunderts," *Geschichte und Gesellschaft* (1988), 64–95.

21. Staatsarchiv Hamburg (hereafter STAH), 122-3 264: "Der Leiter der Dienststelle des Bezirkswohnungskommissars, Bericht des 2. Februar 1921"; Bayerisches Hauptstaatsarchiv Munich (hereafter BayHStAM), MJu 5054: report by Dr. A. Wadler of the Staatskommissariat für Demobilmachung (November 22, 1919); Stadtarchiv Munich (hereafter

STM), Wohnungsamt 83a: "Bericht über die staatliche Wohnungsfürsorge in Bayern im Jahre 1919."

22. Siegfried Reck, *Arbeiter nach der Arbeit: Sozialhistorische Studie zu den Wandlungen des Arbeiteralltags* (Giessen, 1977), 85–94; Adelheid von Saldern, *Neues Wohnen: Wohnungspolitik und Wohnkultur im Hannover der Zwanziger Jahre* (Hannover, 1993).

23. NSHStAH, Hann. 174 Neustadt, Nr. 2492: Dr. Von Mangoldt, speech in Frankfurt entitled "Sozialpolitik und Wohnungsreform," quoted in "Bericht." Such concerns were common throughout Western Europe; cf. Nicholas Bullock and J. J. Read, *The Movement for Housing Reform in Germany and France, 1840–1914* (Cambridge, 1985).

24. Radkau, *Zeitalter*, 310. See also Anthony McElligott, *The German Urban Experience, 1900–1945* (London, 2001).

25. Anonymous, in *Vereins-Blatt für Freunde der natürlichen Lebensweise* (1882), quoted in Wolfgang Krabbe, *Gesellschaftsveränderung durch Lebensreform: Strukturmerkmale einer sozialreformerischen Bewegung im Deutschland der Industrialisierungsperiode* (Göttingen, 1974), 159. The best general study of *Lebensreform* remains Krabbe, *Lebensreform*, but see also Kristiana Hartmann, *Deutsche Gartenstadtbewegung* (Munich, 1976); Ulrich Linze, *Zurück, O Mensch, zur Mutter Erde: Landkommunen in Deutschland, 1890–1933* (Munich, 1983); Cornelia Regin, *Selbsthilfe und Gesundheitspolitik: Die Naturheilbewegung im Kaiserreich* (Stuttgart, 1995); Robert Jütte, *Geschichte der alternativen Medizin* (Munich, 1996); Eva Barlösius, *Naturgemäße Lebensführung: Zur Geschichte der Lebensreform um die Jahrhundertwende* (Frankfurt, 1997); Robert Proctor, *The Nazi War on Cancer* (Princeton, 1999); Klaus Wolbert, ed., *Die Lebensreform: Entwürfe zur Neugestaltung von Leben und Kunst um 1900* (Darmstadt, 2001); Michael Hau, *The Cult of Health and Beauty in Germany: A Social History, 1890–1930* (Chicago, 2003). *Lebensreform* ideas had emerged among Anglo-Saxon elites beginning in the late eighteenth century. Benjamin Franklin was a convinced practitioner of nudism, and Percy Shelley conceived of diet reform in England in the early nineteenth century. People practiced natural medicine, temperance, and vegetarianism in Victorian England and America. Cf., for instance, Bruce Haley, *The Healthy Body and Victorian Culture* (Cambridge, Mass., 1978); Stephen Nissenbaum, *Sex, Diet, and Debility in Jacksonian America* (Westport, Conn., 1980); James Whorton, *Crusaders for Fitness: The History of American Health Reformers* (Princeton, 1982).

26. Krabbe, *Lebensreform*, 144, 161.

27. Quoted in Radkau, *Zeitalter*, 315.

28. Hans Kampffmeyer, *Die Gartenstadtbewegung* (Leipzig, 1909), 98–99; Arne Andersen and Reinhard Falter, "'Lebensreform' und 'Heimatschutz,'" in Friedrich Prinz and Marita Kraus, eds., *München, Musenstadt mit Hinterhöfen: Die Prinzregentenzeit, 1886–1912* (Munich, 1988), 296.

29. Quoted in Horst Groschopp, *Zwischen Bierabend und Bildungsverein: Zur Kulturarbeit in der deutschen Arbeiterbewegung vor 1914* (Berlin, 1985), 63. Cf. Franz Walter, "Der Deutsche Arbeiter-Abstinenten-Bund," in Walter, Denecke, and Regin, *Lebensreformverbände*, 97–240; Michael Hübner, *Zwischen Alkohol und Abstinenz: Trinksitten und Alkoholfrage im deutschen Proletariat bis 1914* (Berlin, 1985).

30. Hermann Wolf, "Die Geschichte des Verbandes Volksgesundheit," *Volksgesundheit* (1928), 3–5, 22–24; Franz Walter and Cornelia Regin, "Der Verband der Vereine für Volksgesundheit," in Walter, Regin, and Denecke, *Lebensreformverbände*, 17–95; Bernhard Herrmann, *Arbeiterschaft, Naturheilkunde, und der Verband Volksgesundheit, 1880–1918* (Frankfurt, 1990).

31. Herrmann, *Arbeiterschaft*, 153–66.

32. Information in *Urania* 3 (1927), 64.

33. Lees, *Cities*, 11.

34. Reichsarbeitsminister Dr. Brauen, cited in *Frauenstimme* (May 15, 1924), no page number; Robert Whalen, *Bitter Wounds: German Victims of the Great War, 1914–1939* (Ithaca, N.Y., 1984), 40.

35. Peukert, *Weimarer Republik*, 266. Cf. also George Mosse, *Fallen Soldiers: Reshaping the Memory of the World Wars* (Oxford, 1990); Richard Bessel, *Germany After the First World War* (Oxford, 1993); Wolfgang Michalka, *Der Erste Weltkrieg: Wirkung, Wahrnehmung, Analyse* (Munich, 1994); Gerald Hirschfeld, Gerd Krumeich, and Irina Renz, eds., *"Keiner fühlt sich hier mehr als Mensch . . .": Erlebnis und Wirkung des Ersten Weltkriegs* (Frankfurt, 1996); Roger Chickering, *Imperial Germany and the Great War, 1914–1918* (Cambridge, 1998); Belinda Davis, *Home Fires Burning: Food, Politics, and Everyday Life in World War I Berlin* (Chapel Hill, N.C., 2000).

36. Cf. *Eldorado: Homosexuelle Männer und Frauen in Berlin, 1850–1950* (Berlin, 1984); Peter Alter, ed., *Im Banne der Metropolen: Berlin und London in den zwanziger Jahren* (Göttingen, 1993), 314–44; Adelheid von Saldern, "'Kunst für's Volk': Vom Kulturkonservatismus zur nationalsozialistischen Kulturpolitik," in Harald Welzer, ed., *Das Gedächtnis der Bilder* (Tübingen, 1995), 45–104, and "Überfremdungsängste: Gegen die Amerikanisierung der deutschen Kultur in den zwanziger Jahren," in Alf Lüdtke et al., eds., *Amerikanisierung: Traum und Alptraum im Deutschland des 20. Jahrhunderts* (Stuttgart, 1996), 213–44.

37. William Cronon, "Introduction," in idem, ed., *Uncommon Ground: Toward Reinventing Nature* (New York, 1995), 50–51.

38. Cf., for example, Raymond Williams, *The Country and the City* (Oxford, 1973); Carol MacCormack and Marilyn Strathern, eds., *Nature, Culture, and Gender* (Cambridge, 1980); Carolyn Merchant, *The Death of Nature: Women, Ecology, and the Scientific Revolution* (San Francisco, 1983); Keith Thomas, *Man and the Natural World: Changing Attitudes in England, 1500–1800* (Harmondsworth, 1984); D. G. Charlton, *New Images of the Natural in France: A Study in European Cultural History, 1750–1800* (Cambridge, 1984); Donald Worster, ed., *The Ends of the Earth: Perspectives on Modern Environmental History* (Cambridge, 1988), and *The Wealth of Nature: Environmental History and the Ecological Imagination* (Oxford, 1993); Ramachandra Guha, *The Unquiet Woods: Ecological Change and Peasant Resistance in the Himalaya* (Oxford, 1989); Thomas Laqueur, *Making Sex: Body and Gender from the Greeks to Freud* (Cambridge, Mass., 1990); John MacKenzie, ed., *Imperialism and the Natural World* (Manchester, 1990); William Cronon, *Nature's Metropolis: Chicago and the Great West* (New York, 1991); Londa Schiebinger, *Nature's Body: Gender in the Making of Modern Science* (Boston, 1993); Michael Bell, *Childerley:*

Nature and Morality in an English Village (Chicago, 1994); Donald Worster, *Under West-ern Skies: Nature and History in the American West* (Oxford, 1995); David Arnold, *The Problem of Nature: Environment, Culture, and European Expansion* (Cambridge, Mass., 1996); Richard White, *The Organic Machine: The Remaking of the Columbia River* (New York, 1996); Christoph Bernhardt, ed., *Environmental Problems in European Cities in the 19th and 20th Centuries* (Münster, 2001).

39. Quoted in Joachim Radkau, "Naturschutz und Nationalsozialismus—wo ist das Problem?" in Radkau and Uekötter, *Naturschutz*, 44.

40. "Runderlaß des Reichsforstmeisters vom 9. Juli 1940—I/II Nr. 3020—an die höheren Naturschutzbehörden, die Landforstmeister, Landesforstverwaltung usw.," re-printed in *Der märkische Naturschutz* (1940), 319.

Chapter 1

1. Desiderius Ehl von Ense, "Von der Körperseele," *Lachendes Leben* (1926), 8.

2. Adolf Koch, *Körperbildung—Nacktkultur* (Leipzig, 1924), 18.

3. See particularly Mosse, *Nationalism and Sexuality*.

4. See the following, which focus solely on right-wing nudists: Wilfried van der Will, "The Body Culture and the Body Politic as Symptom and Metaphor in the Transition of German Culture to National Socialism," in Brandon Taylor and Wilfried van der Will, eds., *The Nazification of Art* (Winchester, U.K., 1990), 14–52; Arnd Krüger, "Zwischen Sex und Zuchtwahl: Nudismus und Naturismus in Deutschland und Amerika," in Nor-bert Finzsch and Hermann Wellenreuther, eds., *Liberalitas* (Stuttgart, 1992), 343–65; Uwe Schneider, "Nacktkultur im Kaiserreich," in Uwe Puschner, ed., *Handbuch zur "Völk-ischen Bewegung," 1871–1918* (Munich, 1996), 411–35; Bernd Wedemeyer, "'Zum Licht': Die Freikörperkultur in der wilhelminischen Ära und der Weimarer Republik zwischen Völkischer Bewegung, Okkultismus, und Neuheidentum," *Archiv für Kulturgeschichte* (1999), 173–97. Two very recent books on the subject continue this tradition, both conflat-ing left- and right-wing nudist ideology and then focusing attention on the racism that was prominent on the right. The first book-length study of German nudism in English, Chad Ross, *Naked Germany: Health, Race, and the Nation* (Oxford, 2005), abounds in faulty generalizations and is sorely lacking in its analysis. Maren Möhring, *Marmorleiber: Körperbildung in der deutschen Nacktkultur (1890–1930)* (Cologne, 2004), is more theo-retically sophisticated and thorough, but it is marred by the author's commitment to a deterministic Foucauldian analysis. Both Ross and Möhring give scant attention to so-cialist nudism, choosing instead the teleological method that easily locates Nazi forerun-ners among the right-wing minority and then extending this view to the entirety of the movement. Georg Pfitzner, *Der Naturismus in Deutschland, Österreich, und der Schweiz* (Hamburg, 1964), and Dreßen, *Geschichte*, are detailed organizational chronicles, but they too focus mostly on bourgeois nudism. Somewhat more balanced but cursory stud-ies are Giselher Spitzer, *Der deutsche Naturismus: Idee und Entwicklung einer volkserzie-herischen Bewegung im Schnittfeld von Lebensreform, Sport, und Politik* (Ahrensburg, 1983); Michael Andritzky and Thomas Rautenberg, eds., *"Wir sind nackt und nennen uns Du": Von Lichtfreunden und Sonnenkämpfern—eine Geschichte der Freikörperkultur* (Giessen,

1989); Ulf Ziegler, *Nackt unter Nackten: Utopien der Nacktkultur, 1906–1942* (Berlin, 1990); Rolf Koerber, "Freikörperkultur," in Kerbs and Reulecke, *Handbuch*, 103–14. See also Karl Toepfer, *Empire of Ecstasy: Nudity and Movement in German Body Culture, 1910–1935* (Berkeley, 1997), and my review thereof in *Central European History* (2000), 145–47. On nudism elsewhere, see Francis and Mason Merrill, *Among the Nudists* (Garden City, N.Y., 1933); Fred Ilfeld and Roger Lauer, *Social Nudism in America* (New Haven, Conn., 1964); William Hartman, Marilyn Fithian, and Donald Johnson, *Nudist Society: An Authoritative, Complete Study of Nudism in America* (New York, 1970); Magnus Clarke, *Nudism in Australia* (Victoria, 1982); Ernst Eder, "Sonnenanbeter und Wasserratten: Körperkultur und Freiluftbadebewegung in Wiens Donaulandschaft, 1900–1939," *Archiv für Sozialgeschichte* (1993), 245–74.

5. Adolf Koch, "Freikörperkultur und Organisation," *Urania* (1929–30), 252; Krabbe, *Lebensreform*, 98, 150; Spitzer, *Naturismus*, 7, 139.

6. Dr. Hans Graaz, "Die körperliche und geistige Verfassung des deutschen Volkes," *Der nackte Mensch* (1928), 63.

7. R. Bergner, "Nacktkultur—Lebensreform—Proletariat," *Volksgesundheit* (1926), 87; Friedrich Weigelt, "Kleinkind, Schulkind, Pubertät," *Freie Körperkultur im Wort und Bild* (1929), 13.

8. Quoted in Adolf Koch, "Der Kampf um unsere Ideen in Hamburg," *Blätter der Körperkulturschule Adolf Koch* (1929), 65.

9. Heinrich Scham (pseudonym for Heinrich Pudor), *Nackende Menschen: Jauchzen der Zukunft* (Dresden, 1893), 17.

10. Krabbe, *Lebensreform*, 93, 147–49; Koerber, "Freikörperkultur," 105; Viktoria Schmidt-Linsenhoff, "Körperseele, Freilichtakt, und Neue Sinnlichkeit," in Andritzky and Rautenberg, *Wir sind nackt*, 124–29.

11. Heinrich Pudor, *Nackt-Kultur* (Berlin, 1906), 1:49, 1–2.

12. Ibid., 2:7–8, 3.

13. Richard Ungewitter, *Nacktheit und Kultur* (Stuttgart, c. 1907), 122.

14. Wedemeyer, "Zum Licht," 188.

15. Cited in Gerhard Hilbert, "Nacktkultur," *Glauben und Wissen* (1910), quoted in Krüger, "Zuchtwahl," 364–65.

16. Franz Walter, *Der Leib und sein Recht im Christentum* (Donauwörth, 1910), 434.

17. Spitzer, *Naturismus*, 118; Pfitzner, *Naturismus*, 26.

18. Spitzer, *Naturismus*, 120; Krabbe, *Lebensreform*, 148. The Federation's name from 1924 to 1926 was the Working Community of German Fighters for Light (*Arbeitsgemeinschaft der Bünde deutscher Lichtkämpfer*).

19. Spitzer, *Naturismus*, 120–21.

20. Staatsarchiv Munich (hereafter STAM), Pol. Dir. München 5934: police report of January 7, 1925; Staatsarchiv Leipzig (hereafter STAL), PPL-V 4475: Polizeipräsidium Leipzig to Adca, Postscheckamt, Arbeiterbank, Stadt- und Girokasse, Sparkasse Leipzig (September 8, 1933).

21. STAM, Pol. Dir. München 1172: file entitled "Bund der Lichtfreunde, 1924–1937"; Spitzer, *Naturismus*, 96.

22. Dietger Pforte, "Hans Surén: Eine deutsche FKK-Karriere," in Andritzky and Rautenberg, *Wir sind nackt*, 136.

23. Hans Surén, *Der Mensch und die Sonne* (Stuttgart, 1924), and *Deutsche Gymnastik* (Oldenburg, 1925), passim.

24. This assessment, based on a reading of Surén's Weimar texts, is in accord with Spitzer, *Idee*, 102–6. *Der Mensch und die Sonne* sold sixty-nine thousand copies in two years; it was revised and reprinted many times over the next fifteen years. The editors of *The Weimar Republic Sourcebook* base their argument that Surén was already protofascist in the 1920s on the revised sixty-first edition of *Der Mensch und die Sonne* that was published during the Third Reich. Kaes et al., eds., *Sourcebook*, 673–74.

25. Pforte, "Surén," 138.

26. For example, Walther Brauns, *Den Freien die Welt!* (Egestorf, 1926); *Nacktheit verjüngt* (Egestorf, 1930).

27. STAL, PPL-V 1481: revised statutes of *Freikörperkulturbund Leipzig*, 1926 and 1928.

28. Giselher Spitzer, "Die Adolf-Koch-Bewegung," in Hans-Joachim Teichler, ed., *Arbeiterkultur und Arbeitersport* (Clausthal, 1985), 78–79. Inexplicably, Ross is uncertain as to whether Koch was a socialist at all. Ross, *Naked Germany*, 58.

29. Adolf Koch, "Was Wir Wollen" (1924), reprinted in idem, *Der Kampf der FKK-Bewegung von 1920 bis 1930* (Leipzig, 1931), 18.

30. Spitzer, "Bewegung," 81; Walter and Regin, "Verband," 66–74.

31. STAL, PPL-V 1643: statutes of *Freie Menschen Leipzig, Gruppe für proletarische Lebensreform und Freikörperkultur* (June 19, 1928).

32. Spitzer, "Bewegung," 79.

33. "Nacktheit und Erziehung," *Vorwärts* (November 27, 1929), reprinted in Koch, *Kampf*, 21–22; stenographic report of Berlin city council (no date), reprinted in ibid., 5–7.

34. "Ein Skandal," *Deutsche Tageszeitung* (January 30, 1924), reprinted in Koch, *Kampf*, 3–4.

35. "Nacktheit und Erziehung," 22. Spitzer, "Bewegung," asserts without providing a source that Koch was "acquitted on all counts" but chose to leave the school service. It seems more likely that the *Vorwärts* article is correct, given that Koch himself reprinted it.

36. Spitzer, "Bewegung," 87, 91–92. Dieball was Koch's first wife.

37. Report on conference of November 1929, *Freie Körperkultur im Wort und Bild* (1929), 8–34.

38. *Blätter der Körperkulturschule Adolf Koch* (1929), 56.

39. Koch, *Körperbildung*, 211; Spitzer, *Naturismus*, 150.

40. Merrill and Merrill, *Among the Nudists*, 120–27, 137–45.

41. See, for instance, *Ideale Nacktheit* (Dresden, 1925, no author listed).

42. Ibid., 126.

43. Spitzer, "Bewegung," 87–88; Krabbe, *Lebensreform*, 149; Walter and Regin, "Verband," 61–64; Herrmann, *Verband*, 213.

44. Michael Andritzky, "Einleitung," in Andritzky and Rautenberg, *Wir sind nackt,*

8; Hermann Wolf, "Wie sind die Voraussetzungen glücklicher Ehen zu schaffen?" *Volksgesundheit* (1924), 51–52; George Bendix, *Frauenturnen, Spiel, und Sport* (Leipzig, 1924); H. Koch, "Einiges über Nacktkultur," *Rheinisches Land: Nachrichtenblatt des Gaues Rheinland des Touristenvereins "Die Naturfreunde"* (1926), 181; Kurt Hirche, "Die Rationalisierung des Erotischen und die Ehe," *Die Bundesgenossin* (June 19, 1929); Hermann Schmidt, "Die Stellung der Freikörperkultur in der Arbeitersportbewegung," *Volksgesundheit* (1932), 135; Adolf Koch, *In Natur und Sonne* (Berlin, 1949), 7; Michael Andritzky, "Berlin, Urheimat der Nackten," in Andritzky and Rautenberg, *Wir sind nackt*, 57.

45. Merrill and Merrill, *Among the Nudists*, 86–87.

46. See, e.g., Ross, *Naked Germany*, passim.

47. Anonymous article of September 1931 in the newspaper *Volksfreund* (Frankfurt/Oder), reprinted in Adolf Koch, *Wir sind nackt und nennen uns Du* (Leipzig, 1932), 49–50.

48. Quoted in Andritzky, "Berlin," 57.

49. Albrecht Kern, "Arbeit: Ein Beispiel von Wesen und Technik unserer Gymnastik," in Koch, *Wir sind nackt*, 81; Weigelt, "Kleinkind," 14.

50. Adolf Koch, "Proletarische Körperkultur," *Urania* (1926), 153–54.

51. Dr. Siegfried Kawerau, "Körperkultur und Familie," *Blätter der Körperkulturschule Adolf Koch* (1928), 37–38.

52. Viktor Noack, *Kulturschande: Die Wohnungsnot als Sexualproblem* (Berlin, 1925); Bruno Schwan, *Die Wohnungsnot und das Wohnungselend in Deutschland* (Berlin, 1929).

53. Else Hildebrandt, review of Hertha Riese, *Die sexuelle Not unserer Zeit* (Leipzig, 1927), *Bücherwarte* (1928), 20.

54. Victor Noack, "Wohnung und Geschlechtsleben—ein Staatsproblem," *Kulturwille* (1927), 51–52.

55. Ibid., 52.

56. See Alfons Labisch, "Die gesundheitspolitischen Vorstellungen der deutschen Sozialdemokratie von ihrer Gründung bis zur Parteispaltung (1863–1917)," *Archiv für Sozialgeschichte* (1976), 325–70.

57. Hermann Wagner, *Das Wesen der Geschlechtsliebe* (Jena, 1930), 62.

58. Ibid., 64.

59. See Grossmann, *Reforming Sex*.

60. Hans Graaz, "Freikörperkultur vom Standpunkt des Erziehers, vor allem des Sexualpädagogen aus," *Volksgesundheit* (March 1933), 41.

61. Adolf Koch, "Das Liebesleben der Jugend," *Jungsozialistische Blätter* (1926), 358.

62. Fritz Bauer, "Sexuelle Not und Freikörperkultur," *Der nackte Mensch* (1927), 16.

63. Wagner, *Wesen*, 71.

64. Quoted in Anon., "Unser Kampf in Bayern," *Blätter der Körperkulturschule Adolf Koch* (1929), 58.

65. Koch, "Liebesleben," 358.

66. Hermann Schmidt, "Zur Auflösung der Sparte freier Menschen im Verband Volksgesundheit," *Volksgesundheit* (1929), 76.

67. Ar., "Das Reich der Freien Menschen, Dresden," *Volksgesundheit* (1929), 185–86; *Vorwärts* (August 1931), reprinted in Koch, *Wir sind nackt*, 45–46; Spitzer, "Bewegung," 94.

68. Bergner, "Nacktkultur," 87.

69. Kawerau, "Körperkultur und Familie," 39.

70. "Ärztliches Gutachten" of January 14, 1924, reprinted in Koch, *Körperbildung*, 205.

71. Koch, *Körperbildung*, 83–84.

72. STAL, PPL-V 4378: file entitled "'Surenverein' zur Pflege von Nacktkultur, 1924"; STAM, Pol. Dir. München 1841: file entitled "Sonnenbund, Verein zur Pflege des Luft- und Sonnenbadens und neuzeitlicher Körperkultur, 1919–1931."

73. STAM, PDM 1172: "Ein öffentlicher Skandal" in *Bayerischer Kurier* (August 29, 1925).

74. Detlev Peukert, "Der Schund- und Schmutzkampf als 'Sozialpolitik der Seele,'" in *"Das war ein Vorspiel nur. . . . ": Bücherverbrennung in Deutschland 1933, Voraussetzungen und Folgen* (Berlin, 1983), 51–63.

75. Schulrat König, "Die Nacktkultur," *Weißes Kreuz: Zeitschrift für die Förderung sittlicher Reinheit unter Männern und jungen Männern* (1927), 12–20.

76. Ph. Küble, "Nacktkultur und Christentum," *Deutsche Jugendkraft* (1926), 2–7, quote from 4.

77. Quoted in Adolf Koch, "Der Kampf um unsere Ideen in Hamburg," *Blätter der Körperkulturschule Adolf Koch* (1929): 63–65.

78. Unidentified DNVP newspaper, quoted in Koch, *Wir sind nackt*, 7.

79. "Selchow gegen Berlin Moral," *Berliner 12 Uhr-Mittags-Zeitung* (September 1931), reprinted in Koch, *Wir sind nackt*, 51–53.

80. "Entschliessung der Freikörperkultur-Organisationen in Deutschland," *Freikörperkultur und Lebensreform* (1931), 85.

81. Quoted in Koch, *Wir sind nackt*, 21.

82. Hans Graaz, *Nacktkörperkultur* (Berlin, 1927), 16.

83. Hans Graaz, "Lebensreform—Kampf ums Dasein," *Volksgesundheit* (1928), 52; idem, *Nacktkörperkultur*, 21.

84. Bergner, "Nacktkultur," 87; Graaz, *Nacktkörperkultur*, 23; Wagner, *Wesen*, 70.

85. Adolf Koch, *Nacktheit, Körperkultur, und Erziehung* (Leipzig, 1929), 51–60, quoted in Spitzer, *Naturismus*, 149. On the relatively tolerant yet oftentimes unsteady attitudes of the Weimar left-wing parties toward homosexuality, see W. U. Eissler, *Arbeiterparteien und Homosexuellenfrage: Zur Sexualpolitik von SPD und KPD in der Weimarer Republik* (Berlin, 1980).

86. Graaz, *Nacktkörperkultur*, 23.

87. Koch, *Nacktheit*, 29–31, cited in Spitzer, *Naturismus*, 148.

88. Koch, *Wir sind nackt*, 29.

89. Fritz Ventzke, "Der Wechsel der Geschlechtsauffassung durch Nacktkultur," *Volksgesundheit* (1930), 255.

90. Hermann Schmidt, "Über den Einfluß der Freikörperkultur auf das Geschlechtsleben," *Urania* (1930–31), 222.

91. Cited in *Vorwärts* (November 1927) and reprinted in *Freie Körperkultur im Wort und Bild* (1929), 34.

92. Koch, *Wir sind nackt*, 27, 29.

93. Irmgard Koch, cited in Spitzer, "Bewegung," 92.

94. Ventzke, "Wechsel," 255.

95. Hermann Schmidt, "Zur Auflösung der Sparte Freier Menschen i. V.V.," *Volksgesundheit* (1929), 76.

96. These ideas abound in late Weimar nudism, e.g., Adolf Koch, "Proletarische Körperkultur," *Urania* (1926), 153; Hermann Schmidt, "Freikörperkultur als Grundzug für sozialistische Lebensgestaltung," *Urania* (1931–32), 253–54; Graaz, *Nacktkörperkultur*, passim.

97. Fritz Bauer, "Sexuelle Not und Freikörperkultur," *Der nackte Mensch* (1927), 17.

98. Möhring, *Marmorleiber*; Ross, *Naked Germany*.

99. Grossmann, *Reforming Sex*, passim.

100. *Gewerkschafts-Zeitung* (1928), 704; *Internationale Hygiene Ausstellung Dresden 1930* (Dresden, 1930).

101. Michael Schwartz has shown that the Federation for People's Health had a somewhat larger percentage of female members in Weimar than did the SPD—26.5 percent vs. 22 percent in the party itself. Many of these women were active advocates of eugenics, making the Federation a site of eugenicist influence in the labor movement. Michael Schwartz, *Sozialistische Eugenik: Eugenische Sozialtechnologien in Debatten und Politik der deutschen Sozialdemokratie, 1890–1933* (Bonn, 1995), 103–4. However, eugenicist definitions of female sexuality were sometimes contested in left-wing feminist movements. See Atina Grossmann, "Abortion and Economic Crisis: The 1931 Campaign Against Paragraph 218," in Renate Bridenthal, Atina Grossman, and Marion Kaplan, eds., *When Biology Became Destiny: Women in Weimar and Nazi Germany* (New York, 1984), 66–86.

102. Kurt Schadendorf, "Freikörperbewegung," *Volksgesundheit* (1931), 172.

103. Hans Graaz, "Die körperliche und geistige Verfassung des deutschen Volkes mit besonderer Berücksichtigung der proletarischen Schichten und unserer Aufgabe," *Der nackte Mensch* (1928), 65–66.

104. Graaz, *Nacktkörperkultur*, 8–9.

105. Hans Graaz, "Unsere Höhensonnen," *Blätter der Körperkulturschule Adolf Koch* (1928), 9.

106. John Toeplitz, "Rassenfragen," *Freie Körperkultur im Wort und Bild* (1929), 17–18.

107. Hildegard Wegscheider-Ziegler, "Das Recht auf den Körper," *Freie Körperkultur im Wort und Bild* (1929), 16–17.

108. Anon., "Vom heulenden Tod ins lachende Leben," *Volksgesundheit* (1932), 37–38, 49–50.

109. Koch, *Wir sind nackt*, 33.

110. Norbert Elias, *The Civilizing Process*, vol. I, *The History of Manners* (New York, 1978), 150.

111. Adolf Koch, "Vom Sinn der körperbildenden Arbeit," *Freie Körperkultur im Wort und Bild* (1929), 10–11.

112. Merrill, *Among the Nudists*, 137–43.

113. See Herzog, *Sex After Fascism*.

114. Spitzer, "Bewegung," 89–90.

115. Cited in "Die neuen preußischen Verordnungen gegen sittlichen Entartung" and "Ergänzung der Badepolizeiverordnung," *Volkswart* (1932), 148, 168.

116. NSHStAH, Hann. 174 Zellerfeld, Nr. 1302: "Runderlaß des preußischen Ministers des Innern des 3.3.1933: 'Bekämpfung der Nacktkulturbewegung.'"

117. Dreßen, *Geschichte*, 47.

118. STAL, PPL-V 1643: "Niederschrift über die für den 3. März 1933 einberufene außerordentliche Hauptversammlung im Stadtbad . . . des Vereins Freie Menschen e.V. Leipzig."

119. Bundesarchiv, Berlin-Lichterfelde (hereafter BArch), R15.01/26337: Adolf Koch to Oberregierungsrat Kerstins, Preußisches Ministerium des Innern (June 12, 1934); Spitzer, "Bewegung," 97–98, and *Naturismus*, 150.

120. Quoted in BArch, R15.01/26337: Adolf Koch, "Beschwerdeschrift" (August 27, 1934).

121. In contrast to the split between Socialists and Communists in the late Weimar *Naturfreunde* movement, there appears to have been no such political conflict within Weimar socialist nudism. Apparently the Communist Party made no attempt to infiltrate and undermine the nudist movement. Anon., "Vom heulenden Tod ins lachende Leben," 49.

122. BArch, R15.01/26337: Adolf Koch to Regierungsrat Linden, Reichsministerium des Innern (June 12, 1934), with attached statement of SA Motorbrigade Berlin-Brandenburg, Standarte M. 29; Koch to Kerstins. Graaz's book was entitled *Gesunde Mutter—schöne Kinder*; I have not been able to find a copy so do not know whether it contained negative eugenicism.

123. BArch, R15.01/26337: Adolf Koch, "Beschwerdeschrift" (August 27, 1934); Adolf Koch to Reichsminister des Innern Dr. Frick (August 27, 1934).

124. Quoted in Spitzer, "Bewegung," 98.

125. Spitzer, "Bewegung," 98; Dietger Pforte, "Zur Freikörperkultur-Bewegung im nationalsozialistischen Deutschland," in Andritzky and Rautenberg, *Wir sind nackt*, 145.

126. Spitzer, "Bewegung," 80, 99.

127. Horst Naftaniel, "Ein Jude spricht sich frei," *Helios* 35 (July 1953), reprinted at www.fkk-museum.de.

128. Wolfgang Krabbe, "'Die Weltanschauung der Deutschen Lebensreform-Bewegung ist der Nationalsozialismus': Zur Gleichschaltung einer Alternativströmung im Dritten Reich," *Archiv für Kulturgeschichte* (1989), 431–61, quote from 461.

129. It should be noted, however, that the Nazi Reich Sport Leader thought that the Weimar *Reichsverband* had "glided into pacifist-liberalist waters." BArch, R15.01/26337: Reichssportführer von Tschammer to Reichsminister des Innern (February 22, 1934).

130. STAL, PPL-V 4475: Der Führer der Gruppe III in der Fachsäule 11 des Reichssportführerringes (Bückmann) to alle Verein und Gemeinschaften der Deutschen Zeltlagerbewegung (January 14, 1934); BArch, R15.01/26337: Reichsportführer to Reichsminister des Innern (February 22, 1934); Carl Almenroeder, "Was ist geschehen? Was wird?" *Freikörperkultur und Lebensreform* (1933), 82.

131. Quoted in Dreßen, *Geschichte*, 48.

132. STAL, PPL-V 4475: Karl König and Erich Kaiser, Vorsitzende der Vereinigung für neuzeitliche und gesunde Lebensgestaltung e.V. to Politische Abteilung des Polizeipräsidiums (September 11, 1933); Dreßen, *Geschichte*, 48.

133. STAL, PPL-V 4457: Polizeipräsidium, Abt. IV to Kampfring für völkische Freikörperkultur, Reichsleitung (September 14, 1933).

134. Cited in Carl Almenroeder, "Minister Darré über die Freikörperkultur," *Deutsche Freikörperkultur* (1933), 39.

135. Landesarchiv Berlin (hereafter LAB), B Rep. 042 Acc. 2147/26419: Der Führer der Gruppe III in der Fachsäule 11 des Reichssportführerringes to the Amtgericht Berlin-Charlottenburg (January 31, 1934).

136. STAL, PPL-V 4475: Sächsischer Bund für Lebensreform to Polizeipräsidium Leipzig (December 15, 1933).

137. Quoted in BArch, R15.01/26337: Reichssportführer to Reichsminister des Innern (February 22, 1934).

138. BArch, R15.01/26337: Reichssportführer to Reichsminister des Innern (February 2, 1934).

139. Dreßen, *Geschichte*, 49.

140. STAL, PPL-V 4475: Polizeipräsidium Abt. 14 to Georg Fischer (December 12, 1933); "Bekämpfung der Nacktkulturbewegung" (March 12, 1934); Polizeipräsidium to Rat der Stadt Leipzig (April 12, 1934); Erich Kaiser to Georg Fischer, polizeilicher Treuhänder (April 16, 1934).

141. STAL, PPL-V 4475: Reichsleitung der NSDAP, Reichsamt für Gesundheitswesen to Reichsministerium des Innern (July 19, 1934).

142. NSHStAH, Hann. 174 Zellerfeld, Nr. 1302: Reichs- und Preußischer Minister des Innern to the Ober- und Regierungspräsidenten (July 8, 1935).

143. BArch, R15.01/26337: P. Büsch to Adolf Hitler (no date, c. 1933).

144. STAM, Gestapo 84: Bolte, "Wert der Freikörperkultur" (January 19, 1934). See also STAL, PPL-V 4475: report of Polizeipräsidium Leipzig, Abt. IV (April 6, 1934).

145. STAL, PPL-V 4475: "Aufnahmeantrag des Bundes für deutsche Leibeszucht" (no date); Polizeipräsidium L, Abt. IV, report of January 13, 1936.

146. Almenroeder, "Was ist geschehen?" 82; Karl Bückmann, "Ein Ostseelager mit Hindernissen," *Gesetz und Freiheit* (1935), 229; Anne Marie Koeppen, "Schönheit— gesunder Körper," *Gesetz und Freiheit* (1934), 109–11; Will Tschierschky, "Rassenaufartung und Freikörperkultur," *Deutsche Freikörperkultur* (1934), no page number.

147. STAM, Gestapo 84: Hans Surén, "Gutachten über Aufgaben, Ziele, und wahres Wesen einer Nordischen Freikörperkultur" (no date, probably 1934). Surén joined the NSDAP on May 1, 1933, and later that year he became a Sturmbannführer of the SS.

148. BArch, R15.01/26337: Reichssportführer to Reichsminister des Innern (February 22, 1934); Koerber, "Freikörperkultur," 109; Pforte, "Surén," 140. Surén was commander of a prisoner-of-war camp in southern France in 1940–41. He had some kind of unspecified trouble with the authorities late in the war. Based on his own false testimony and mistakes of the Allied denazification commission, Surén was acquitted by the commission and left with a large pension. He died in 1972. Pforte, "Surén," 137.

149. Surén, "Gutachten," no page number.

150. Koeppen, "Schönheit," 109.

151. Pforte, "Surén," 140.

152. Wilfried van der Will's argument that the concepts of total unity and national strength were common to both Nazi art and folkish nudism is suggestive in this regard. Van der Will, "Body Politic."

153. *Reichsgesetzblatt* I, 461 (July 10, 1942), quoted in Krüger, "Zuchtwahl," 354.

154. STAL, PPL-V 4475: membership list of *Bund für Leibeszucht e.V., Ortsgruppe Leipzig* (1943). Matthew Jefferies argues that there was no surge in the League's national membership following the decree, although he provides no concrete evidence for this point. If this is true, it may well be due to the increasing hardships of the war, which no doubt left little time or energy for nude bathing. Jefferies is certainly right in his more general claim that after the war, "Those who propagated naturism for ethical or ideological reason would increasingly find themselves outnumbered and outmaneuvered by people who considered naked sunbathing as nothing more than a leisure activity." Matthew Jefferies, "'For a Genuine and Noble Nakedness'? German Naturism in the Third Reich," *German History* (2006), 84. As nudism became more popular in postwar East and West Germany, it also became far less political.

155. Kurt Reichart, *Von Leibeszucht und Leibesschönheit* (Berlin, 1940), 9.

156. Clara Bohm-Schuch, "Die Stellung der Frau zur Nacktheit," *Freie Körperkultur in Wort und Bild* (1929), 9.

Chapter 2

1. Quoted in Levenstein, *Arbeiterfrage*, 373, 368.

2. Ibid., 359, 382, 374.

3. Ibid., 381.

4. Ibid., 376, 377.

5. Ibid., 363, 364, 379.

6. Ibid., 372, 380.

7. Engelbert Schramm, *Arbeiterbewegung und industrielle Umweltprobleme: Wahrnehmung und Theoriediskussion seit der zweiten Hälfte des 19. Jahrhunderts* (Frankfurt, 1989); Gilhaus, "*Schmerzenskinder der Industrie.*"

8. Horst Groschopp, *Zwischen Bierabend und Bildungsvereine: Zur Kulturarbeit in der deutschen Arbeiterbewegung vor 1914* (East Berlin, 1985), 45.

9. Historians neglected the TVNF before the 1980s, although there were some useful memoirs by former members, e.g., Heinrich Coblenz, *Geschichte der badischen Naturfreunde* (Karlsruhe, 1947); Emil Birkert, *Von der Idee zur Tat: Aus der Geschichte der Naturfreundebewegung* (Heilbronn, 1970). Since 1984 a number of German studies have been published: Jochen Zimmer et al., eds., *Mit uns zieht die neue Zeit: Die Naturfreunde* (Cologne, 1984); Wulf Erdmann and Klaus-Peter Lorenz, *Die grüne Lust der roten Touristen* (Hamburg, 1985); Jochen Zimmer and Wulf Erdmann, eds., *Hundert Jahre Kampf um die freie Natur: Eine illustrierte Geschichte der Naturfreunde* (Cologne, 1991); Viola Denecke, "Der Touristenverein 'Die Naturfreunde,'" in Walter et al., *Lebensreformverbände*, 241–91;

Manfred Pils, *"Berg frei": 100 Jahre Naturfreunde* (Vienna, 1994). These are primarily organizational histories. Analyses of ideology and practice have been few, notably article-length studies by Jochen Zimmer and Ulrich Linse and a dissertation by Hans-Christian Brinkschmidt. Linse and Zimmer both cast the *Naturfreunde* as a failure from the standpoint of progressive political and ecological values. The telos for their argument is the fruitless attempt by the organization's national leadership in spring 1933 to survive Nazi repression through "self-synchronization." The language of *Heimat* preservation and patriotism used in this appeal was, according to Linse and Zimmer, the logical outcome of the influx of reactionary "bourgeois" conservationist ideology into the Weimar TVNF. This thesis is founded on the erroneous view that both the *Heimat* concept and patriotism were innately reactionary. Linse and Zimmer also focus exclusively on the relatively conservative attitudes of national TVNF leaders in Nuremberg, which by no means characterized the entire movement. Furthermore, both scholars argue that the *Naturfreunde* largely failed to develop "truly socialist" forms of hiking and conservationism. Yet they are silent on what that would have entailed and fail to convince that such an alternative would have had a chance of surviving anywhere in the early twentieth century. Jochen Zimmer, "'Grüne Inseln im Klassenkampf'? Umweltschutzpolitik bei den Naturfreunden zwischen naturromantischer Ethik und sozialpolitischem Engagement," in Zimmer and Erdmann, *Kampf,* 37–62; Ulrich Linse, "Die 'freie Natur' als Heimat: Naturaneignung und Naturschutz in der älteren Naturfreundebewegung," in ibid., 63–77. (Curiously, Linse in another work argues that antimodernism like that found in the bourgeois conservationist movement had no chance in the TVNF, because the latter subscribed to a naively positive ideology of progress through the technological domination of nature. Ulrich Linse, *Ökopax und Anarchie: Eine Geschichte der ökologischen Bewegungen in Deutschland* [Munich, 1986], 54.) Hans-Christian Brinkschmidt, "Das Naturverständnis der Arbeiterbewegung am Beispiel der Naturfreunde" (Ph.D. diss., University of Frankfurt, 1998), is attentive to regional and political differences within the movement; but Brinkschmidt's analysis is also weakened by a static, and purely negative, concept of "bourgeois" ideology.

   10. Rob Burns and Wilfried van der Will, eds., *Arbeiterkulturbewegung in der Weimarer Republik,* 2 vols. (Frankfurt, 1982); Lidtke, *Alternative Culture*; Friedhelm Boll, ed., *Arbeiterkulturen zwischen Alltag und Politik: Beiträge zum europäischen Vergleich in der Zwischenkriegszeit* (Vienna, 1986); W. L. Guttsmann, *Workers' Culture in Weimar Germany* (New York, 1990); Lynn Abrams, *Workers' Culture in Imperial Germany* (London, 1992); Peter Lösche, ed., *Solidargemeinschaft und Milieu: Sozialistische Kultur- und Freizeitorganisationen in der Weimarer Republik,* 4 vols. (Berlin, 1990–93); Barclay and Weitz, *Between Reform and Revolution.* For a comparative history, see Geoff Eley, *Forging Democracy: The History of the Left in Europe, 1850–2000* (Oxford, 2002).

   11. Theodor Waechter, "Soziales Wandern," *Aufstieg* (1929), 1.

   12. On the dominant Marxist concept of nature, see Peter Coates, *Nature: Western Attitudes Since Ancient Times* (Berkeley, 1998), 149–51.

   13. Pils, *"Berg frei,"* 22–24. Karl Renner later became chancellor of the first Austrian republic from 1918 to 1920, and he was president of the second republic from 1945 until his death in 1950.

14. Georg Schmiedl, "Welche Gedanken haben mich bei der Gründung unseres Vereines geleitet?" *Der Naturfreund: Mitteilungen des TVNF in Wien* (1920), 69–70.

15. Jochen Zimmer, "Vom Walzen zum sozialen Wandern," in Albrecht Lehmann, ed., *Studien zur Arbeiterkultur* (Münster, 1984), 150–51; Hartmut Büsing et al., eds., *". . . damit wir allerorten der Erde Schönheit schau'n": Vom Arbeiterwanderclub "Die Naturfreunde" Rüstringen zum TVNF, Ortsgruppe Wilhelmshaven* (Wilhelmshaven, 1995), 15–16.

16. For the "embourgeoisement" thesis, see Günther Roth, *The Social Democrats in Imperial Germany: A Study in Working Class Isolation and National Integration* (New York, 1963), and the critiques in Richard Evans, ed., *The German Working Class, 1888–1933: The Politics of Everyday Life* (Totowa, N.J., 1982).

17. Auxiliaries were not included in the official membership statistics, so we have no idea how many there were.

18. Denecke, "Touristenverein," 242, 273; Augustin Upmann and Uwe Rennspiess, "Organisationsgeschichte der deutschen Naturfreundebewegung bis 1933," in Zimmer, ed., *Mit uns zieht die neue Zeit*, 70.

19. Coblenz, *Geschichte*, 14; Büsing et al., *Rüstringen*, 51–54; Denecke, "Touristenverein," 273.

20. Adolf Hanschen, "Wanderfahrt am 30. Juli 1916," reprinted in Büsing et al., *Rüstringen*, 20.

21. Günther Denzl, *75 Jahre Klause im Schindergraben der Münchner Naturfreunde* (Munich, 1987), 8.

22. A. E. George, "Was uns Not Tut," *Nordbayerischer Wanderer* (1923), 26.

23. "Denkschrift der Zentralkommission für Sport und Körperpflege an die Nationalversammlung," reprinted in *Arbeiter-Turn-Zeitung* (1919), 33.

24. Denecke, "Touristenverein," 242–43, 273–75, 285.

25. The number of *Naturfreunde* between fourteen and eighteen years of age is known only for the years after 1925. Between 1925 and 1928 this age group made up around 13 percent and fell to 11 percent beginning in 1929. Evidence indicates that there were also relatively large numbers of eighteen- to twenty-year-olds. Coblenz, *Geschichte*, 127; Zimmer, "Walzen," 158–59; Denecke, "Touristenverein," 280; *Statistisches Jahrbuch für den Staat Bayern* (Munich, 1930), 477. However, even these figures are not reliable, since a large number of youths were not registered as official members. On the *Naturfreundejugend* suborganization, see Heinz Hoffmann and Jochen Zimmer, eds., *Wir sind die grüne Garde: Geschichte der Naturfreundejugend* (Cologne, 1986).

26. Historische Kommission zu Berlin (hereafter HKB), NB457: TVNF, Reichsleitung to Allgemeiner Deutscher Gewerkschafts-Bund (July 19, 1926); Wulf Erdmann and Klaus-Peter Lorenz, "Baumeister der neuen Zeit: Das Naturfreundehäuserwerk entsteht," in Zimmer," *Zeit*," 141–83.

27. HKB, NB457: "Grundsteinlegung des Naturfreunde-Ferienheimes und der Jugendherberge Am Üdersee, veranstaltet vom TVNF Berlin-Brandenburg am 28. Oktober 1928"; Anon., *Das Naturfreundehaus auf dem Rohrberg bei Weissenburg in Bayern* (Nuremberg, 1925), 7–8.

28. BayHStAM, MK13977: TVNF Ortsgruppe Neustadt to Stadtverwaltung Neustadt (November 12, 1922), and TVNF Ortsgruppe Neustadt to Regierung der Pfalz (July 24, 1923).

29. Anon., "T.V. 'Die Naturfreunde,'" *Kulturwille* (1930), 8.

30. Denecke, "Touristenverein," 278–80; Erdmann and Lorenz, *Grüne Lust*, 74.

31. Mathilde Hürtgen, "Mädel und Bursche im Wandern," *Rheinisches Land* (1927), 78.

32. Burns and Will, *Arbeiterkulturbewegung*, 150.

33. Denecke, "Touristenverein," 276–77; Klaus-Michael Mallmann, *Kommunisten in der Weimarer Republik: Sozialgeschichte einer revolutionären Bewegung* (Darmstadt, 1996).

34. Quoted in "Protokoll der Gaukonferenz am 1. März 1925 zu Düsseldorf," *Der Naturfreund: Mitteilungsblatt für den Gau Rheinland des TVNF* (1925), 68.

35. Denecke, "Touristenverein," 257, 273–75. I have found no figures for 1932.

36. Karl Renner, "Der Arbeiter als Naturfreund und Tourist," *Der Naturfreund* (1926, orig. 1896), 3–4.

37. See Frederick Taylor, *The Principles of Scientific Management* (New York, 1911); Robert Brady, *The Rationalization Movement in German Industry* (Berkeley, 1933); Hans-Albert Wulf, *"Maschinenstürmer sind wir keine": Technischer Fortschritt und sozialdemokratische Arbeiterbewegung* (Frankfurt, 1987).

38. Fritz Endres, "Die ideellen und kulturellen Werte der Naturfreundebewegung," *Nordbayerischer Wanderer* (1930), 20; Karl Eckerlin, "Warum Arbeitersport- und Wanderbewegung?" *Aufstieg* (December 1929), 1–2; Gustav Riemann, "Der Kampf um unsere Freiheit," *Nord- und Ostdeutscher Wanderer* (1930), 51.

39. Adolf Lau, "Naturfreundschaft als Faktor des kulturellen Aufstieges," *Der Naturfreund: Mitteilungen des TVNF in Wien* (1926), 210.

40. Anon., "'Aufwärts!'" *Rheinisches Land* (1927), 149; Theo Müller, "Neue Kultur—Naturfreundschaft," *Rheinisches Land* (1926), 129.

41. Richard Kunze, "Kinokultur und richtiges Wandern," *Der Wanderfreund* (1920), 66.

42. Denecke, "Touristenverein," 248–49.

43. Anon., "Des Wanderns Einfluß auf die Nerven," *Touristen-Verein die Naturfreunde, Gau Mittelrhein-Main* (December 1921), no page numbers.

44. Walter Trojan, "Das Erlebnis des Zeitgeschehens," *Nordbayerischer Wanderer: Nachrichtenblatt des TVNF, Gau Nordbayern* (1925), 82.

45. Gustav Riemann, "Der Kampf um unsere Freiheit," *Nord- und Ostdeutscher Wanderer* (1930), 51.

46. Bruno Krause, "Wissenschaft und Klassenkampf," *Die Naturfreunde: Mitteilungsblatt für den Gau Rheinland des TVNF* (November 1924), 1.

47. Fritz Endres, "Vom Sinne des Wanderns," *"Berg frei": Mitteilungsblatt des TVNF, Gau Pfalz* (1922), no page numbers.

48. Bundesarchiv Berlin, Stiftung Archiv der Parteien und Massenorganisationen der DDR (hereafter SAPMO-BArch), RY22/V SUF/419: George, Steinberger, Burger (Reichsleitung) to TVNF, Gau Brandenburg (July 15, 1924).

49. Denecke, "Touristenverein," 244.

50. Cited in ibid., 250.

51. SAPMO-BArch, RY22/V SUF/419: Reichsleitung to Gau Brandenburg; Upmann and Rennspiess, "Organisationsgeschichte," 81–82; Denecke, "Touristenverein," 251.

52. BArch, R58/782: "Diskussionsgrundlage für die Regelung der Frage des Arbeiter-Wanderer-Bundes und des TVNF," in "Auszug aus Informationsblatt der KJD, Bezirk Nordbayern Nr. 5 vom 25.7.24," attached to Preußischer Minister des Innern to Polizeipräsidenten Abteilung XA (October 16, 1934).

53. SAPMO-BArch, RY22/V SUF/420: Herrmann Leupold, "Die Kultur des Proletariats und die Aufgaben der Naturfreundebewegung," *Gegen den Strom* (1924), 6–7, and Emil Jensen, "Die proletarische Kulturbewegung" in ibid., 9.

54. Jensen, "Kulturbewegung," 10.

55. Willy Buckpesch, "Der Wert des Jugendwanderns," *Luginsland: Touristen-Verein Die Naturfreunde, Gau Mittel-Rhein-Main* (1927), 56–57.

56. Mathilde Hürtgen, "Sollen wir Sport oder Kultur pflegen?" *Rheinisches Land* (1926), 151.

57. Werner Mohr, "Soziales Wandern," *Der Naturfreund: Mitteilungen des TVNF in Wien* (1930), 218.

58. Theo Müller, "Ein 'Berg frei' dem neuen Jahr!" *Die Naturfreunde: Mitteilungsblatt für den Gau Rheinland des TVNF* (January 1925), 1–2.

59. BayHStAM, MK13977: "Heimat und Wandern," *Fränkische Tagespost* (December 1, 1928).

60. K. M., "Die Gaukonferenz in Stuttgart," *Aufstieg* (March 1925), 1–3.

61. Coblenz, *Geschichte*, 26–27.

62. Denecke, "Touristenverein," 258.

63. Eco-Archiv im Archiv der Sozialen Demokratie der Friedrich-Ebert Stiftung, Bad Godesberg (hereafter eco-Archiv), Ortsgruppe Kuchen, *Wanderberichtsbuch*: "Tageswanderung am 4. März 1928."

64. Coblenz, *Geschichte*, 100–108.

65. Interview with Franz Bohne, reprinted in Zimmer, *Zeit*, 282.

66. Georg Glaser, *Geheimnis und Gewalt* (Stuttgart, 1953), quoted in Zimmer, "Walzen," 161.

67. Prof. Dr. Schomburg, "Soziales Wandern," *Der Naturfreund aus Gau Nordmark* (1932), 3–7.

68. In this version of evolution they were probably influenced less by Darwin than by Kropotkin's writings on symbiosis. See Coates, *Nature*, 147.

69. TVNF München, *Festschrift zum 25jährigen Bestehen* (Munich, 1930), 39.

70. Lutz Lerse, "Aus meinem Wanderbuch," *Der Naturfreund: Mitteilungen des TVNF in Wien* (1922), 82.

71. M. Frenzel, "Natur und Mensch," *Der Wanderfreund: Monatsschrift des Arbeiter-Wanderbundes "Naturfreunde"* (1920), 26.

72. Eco-Archiv, Ortsgruppe Kuchen, *Wanderberichtsbuch*: Eugen Bielforth, report of a hike on October 16, 1927.

73. Magistrat der Stadt Mörfelden-Walldorf, *Konrad*, 104–5; Erdmann and Lorenz, *Grüne Lust*.

74. Trojan, "Erlebnis," 82.

75. Lau, "Naturfreundschaft," 212.

76. For instance, Meyer, "Für den Naturschutz!" *Der Wanderfreund* (1922), 77. However, Linse has uncovered a minority strain of conservationism among some prominent left-wing German socialists. For example, during a 1912 debate in the Prussian House of Representatives over a proposed *Naturschutz* law, Karl Liebknecht spoke as follows: "It is unusually important that we recognize more and more the irreplaceable value of nature in all her beauty. . . . It is simple to dig up a forest, to drain a lake, to disfigure and ruin a landscape . . . but it is exceedingly difficult to repair any of those things. If we consider that nature needed hundreds, even thousands of years to create those natural features (*Naturdenkmäler*) that have delighted many generations, then we must acknowledge that any modern technological measures will fail to reverse these damages." Ulrich Linse, "Das Proletariat: Komplize kapitalistischer Naturzerstörung?" in Jost Hermand, ed., *Mit den Bäumen sterben die Menschen* (Cologne, 1993), 119–48, quote from 132.

77. Linse, "Freie Natur," 68–70.

78. STAL, PPL-V 708: "Satzungen des Gesamtvereins, beschlossen auf der 7. Hauptversammlung zu München, Pfingsten 1913."

79. Coates, *Nature*, 161–62; Peter Gould, *Early Green Politics: Back to Nature, Back to the Land, and Socialism in Britain, 1880–1900* (Brighton, 1988).

80. See, e.g., Albert Allinger, "Der sterbende Wald," *Rheinisches Land* (1926), 81–84.

81. Heinrich Gerbermann, "Naturfreunde und Natur- und Heimatkunde," *Der Naturfreund: Monatsschrift des Gaues Niedersachsen* (1928), 67.

82. Anon., "Der Sinn des Naturschutzes," *Rheinisches Land* (1926), 154.

83. SAPMO-BArch, RY 18/II 142/1: TVNF, "Schutz und Schonung der Natur" (c. 1921).

84. Markwart, "Der werdende Naturschutzpark in der Lüneburger Heide," *Der Naturfreund aus Gau Nordmark* (October 1924); Anon., "Zwei deutsche Naturschutzparke," *Nordbayerischer Wanderer* (1925), 135; Die Gauleitung, "Unsere Arbeit im Jahre 1926/27," *Nordbayerischer Wanderer* (1928), 50; Hans Peter Schmitz, "Naturschutz—Landschaftsschutz—Umweltschutz: Der TVNF als ökologisches Frühwarnsystem der Arbeiterbewegung," in Zimmer, *Zeit*, 184–204; Jochen Zimmer, "Kleine Chronik 'Naturschutz und Naturfreunde,'" in Zimmer and Erdmann, *Kampf*, 78–81.

85. "Um den Schutz der Natur," *Rheinisches Land* (1926), 137–39; Zimmer, "Inseln," 46.

86. Upmann and Rennspiess, "Organisationsgeschichte," 85; Peter Friedemann, "Die Krise der Arbeitersportbewegung am Ende der Weimarer Republik," in Friedhelm Boll, ed., *Arbeiterkulturen zwischen Alltag und Politik: Beiträge zum europäischen Vergleich in der Zwischenkriegszeit* (Vienna, 1986), 229–40.

87. "Die III. Reichsversammlung der Naturfreunde Deutschlands," *Der Naturfreund: Mitteilungen des TVNF in Wien* (1930), 228–29; W. Kober, "Die dritte Reichskonferenz in Dresden," *Aufstieg* (September 1930), 1–2; eco-Archiv, TVNF, Ortsgruppe Weissenburg

in Bayern: "Rundschreiben des TVNF Reichsleitung für Deutschland" (April 5, 1933), 3–4; Upmann and Rennspiess, "Organisationsgeschichte," 85–90; Denecke, "Touristenverein," 244, 254–55.

88. BArch, R58/782: "Rundschreiben Nr. 4 der Wandersparte der Roten Sporteinheit," quoted in TVNF Reichsleitung, "Anhang zum Rundschreiben an alle Ortsgruppen vom 3.2.1933: Abwehr kommunistischer Wühlarbeit," 3–4.

89. TVNF Reichsleitung, "Anhang zum Rundschreiben," 7.

90. "An alle Naturfreunde Württembergs!" *Arbeiter-Wanderer: Organ der oppositionellen Naturfreunde, Gau Württemberg* (1931); Upmann and Rennspiess, "Organisationsgeschichte," 77–88; Denecke, "Touristenverein," 244; SAPMO-BArch, SgY 2/V DF VIII/70: TVNF, Ortsgruppe Leipzig, "Für die Einheit" (c. 1930).

91. Denecke, "Touristenverein," 281.

92. STAL, PPL-V, 4404: testimony of former member Arno Fleischmann given to Polizeipräsidium Leipzig, Abteilung IV (May 17, 1935); E. D., "Gau-Konferenz 1932," *Der Naturfreund aus Gau Nordmark* (July 1932), 1–2.

93. TVNF Reichsleitung, "Anhang zum Rundschreiben," 8; BArch, R58/782: Polizeipräsident in Frankfurt to Gestapoamt (August 30, 1933).

94. Reprinted in Anon., "Die Nazis als Arbeiterfreunde," *Der Naturfreund: Mitteilungen des TVNF in Wien* (1931), 73.

95. "Das Naturfreundehaus in Maschen durch Nazis demoliert!" *Der Naturfreund aus Gau Nordmark* (May 1932), 7–8. See Donna Harsch, "The Iron Front: Weimar Social Democracy Between Tradition and Modernity," in Barclay and Weitz, *Between Reform and Revolution*, 251–74.

96. BArch, R58/782: TVNF, Reichsleitung für Deutschland to alle Ortsgruppenleitungen und Bezirksleitungen im TVNF Reichsgruppe Deutschland (March 16, 1933).

97. Coblenz, *Geschichte*, 136.

98. BArch, R58/782: TVNF Reichsleitung to Preussisches Ministerium des Innern in Berlin (March 24, 1933); eco-Archiv, TVNF, Ortsgruppe Weissenburg in Bayern: Rundschreiben of Reichsleitung (April 5, 1933).

99. BArch, R58/782: TVNF, Reichsleitung für Deutschland, "Denkschrift: Die Bedeutung der Naturfreunde-Bewegung und der Naturfreunde-Häuser für Volk, Staat, und Nation," 7.

100. Linse, "Freie Natur," 69–70.

101. A. C. Gé., "Frühling ohne Hoffnung?" *Der Wanderer* (March 1933), 18–19.

102. STAL, PPL-V 4404: Werner Mohr to Polizeipräsidium Leipzig (May 31, 1933).

103. Werner Mohr, "Soziales Wandern," *Der Naturfreund: Mitteilungen des TVNF in Wien* (1930), 217–18.

104. "Denkschrift," 6–8.

105. BayHStAM, MA 107384: Bayerischer Minister des Innern to Bayerische Staatskanzlei (June 17, 1933); BArch, R58/782: Staatspolizeistelle für die Regierungs-Bezirk Münster to Geheime Staatspolizeiamt in Berlin (July 28, 1933).

106. BArch, R58/782: Der Regierungspräsident in Düsseldorf to Preussischen Minister für Wissenschaft, Kunst, und Volksbildung in Berlin (August 14, 1933).

107. Steinberger was reestablished as postwar chairman of the TVNF, but he was tried and convicted for embezzling organizational funds in 1954. Christiane Dulk and Jochen Zimmer, "Die Auflösung des Touristenvereins 'Die Naturfreunde' nach dem März 1933," in Zimmer, *Zeit*, 116.

108. Hasso Spode, "'Der deutsche Arbeiter reist': Massentourismus im Dritten Reich," in Gerhard Huck, ed., *Sozialgeschichte der Freizeit* (Wuppertal, 1980), 296; *Festschrift zum Ersten Großdeutschen Wandertage* (Berlin, 1940), 1; "Zulassung der Zeitschrift 'Deutsches Wandern' durch die Politische Polizei Bayerns," reprinted in *Deutsches Wandern* (December, 1933), 3.

109. Leonhard Burger and Fritz Stremel, "Dem 'deutschen Wandern' auf dem Weg," *Deutsches Wandern* (December 1933), 2.

110. Erdmann, "Wandern," 25–27; Magistrat der Stadt Mörfelden-Walldorf, ed., *Konrad*, 107.

111. Eberhard Heuel, *Der umworbene Stand: Die ideologische Integration der Arbeiter im Nationalsozialismus, 1933–1935* (Frankfurt, 1989); Klaus-Michael Mallmann and Gerhard Paul, *Herrschaft und Alltag: Ein Industrierevier im Dritten Reich* (Bonn, 1991); Karl-Heinz Roth, *Facetten des Terrors: Der Geheimdienst der Deutschen Arbeiterfront und die Zerstörung der Arbeiterbewegung* (Bremen, 2000).

112. Alf Lüdtke, "Wo blieb die 'rote Glut'? Arbeitererfahrungen und deutscher Faschismus," in idem, ed., *Alltagsgeschichte* (Frankfurt, 1989), 224–82; Ulrich Herbert, *Hitler's Foreign Workers: Enforced Foreign Labor in Germany Under the Third Reich* (Cambridge, 1997).

113. Institut für Zeitgeschichte München (hereafter IfZ), Db 72.09: *Drei Jahre nationalsozialistische Gemeinschaft "Kraft durch Freude"* (Berlin, 1937), 4. See also Hermann Weiss, "Ideologie der Freizeit im Dritten Reich: Die NS-Gemeinschaft 'Kraft durch Freude,'" *Archiv für Sozialgeschichte* (1993), 289–304; Shelley Baranowski, *Strength Through Joy: Consumerism and Mass Tourism in the Third Reich* (Cambridge, 2004).

114. Quoted in Weiss, "Ideologie," 293.

115. Hasso Spode, "Die NS-Gemeinschaft 'Kraft durch Freude': Ein Volk auf Reisen?" in idem, ed., *Zur Sonne, zur Freiheit! Beiträge zur Tourismusgeschichte* (Berlin, 1991), 80.

116. Speech at the founding of the KDF (November 27, 1933), quoted in Weiss, "Ideologie," 294.

117. Helmut Urban, "Wandert mit 'Kraft durch Freude,'" *Arbeitertum* (February 15, 1935), 29.

118. Ibid. See also IfZ, Db 72.44: Anatol von Hübbenet, ed., *Ein Volk erobert die Freude* (Berlin, 1938).

119. Weiss, "Ideologie," 301.

120. IfZ, Db 72.14: Kraft durch Freude Gau Franken, Abt. Reisen Wandern Urlaub, *Jahresprogramm 1936* (Nuremberg, 1936), 28–29; IfZ, Db 72.09: *Fünf Jahre "Kraft durch Freude"* (Berlin, 1938), 35.

121. STAM, LRA 150944, folder 19: file entitled "Auflösung der Holzkirchener Naturfreunde."

122. BArch, R58/782: Leiter der Staatspolizeistelle Harburg-Wilhelmsburg to Geheime Staatspolizeistelle in Berlin (June 3, 1935).

123. Dulk and Zimmer, "Auflösung," 114.

124. On the postwar *Naturfreunde*, see Zimmer and Erdmann, *Kampf.*

Chapter 3

1. Romano Guardini, "Quickborn—Tatsachen und Grundsätze" (1922), reprinted in Werner Kindt, ed., *Grundschriften der deutschen Jugendbewegung* (Düsseldorf, 1963), 340. This chapter is a revised version of John Alexander Williams, "Ecstasies of the Young: Sexuality, the Youth Movement, and Moral Panic in Germany on the Eve of the First World War," *Central European History* (2001), 162–89 (© 2001 by Humanities Press, Inc. Reprinted with the permission of Cambridge University Press).

2. Jürgen Reulecke, "The Battle for the Young: Mobilizing Young People in Wilhelmine Germany," in Roseman, *Generations*, 97.

3. On generational relations, education, and youth subcultures in twentieth-century Germany, see Thomas Koebner et al., eds., *"Mit uns zieht die neue Zeit": Der Mythos Jugend* (Frankfurt, 1985); Detlev Peukert, *Jugend zwischen Krieg und Krise: Lebenswelten von Arbeiterjungen in der Weimarer Republik* (Cologne, 1987); Christa Berg, ed., *Handbuch der deutschen Bildungsgeschichte, Band IV: 1870–1918* (Munich, 1991); Roseman, *Generations*. Compare also Dick Hebdige, *Subculture: The Meaning of Style* (London, 1979); Dieter Dowe, ed., *Jugendprotest und Generationenkonflikt in Europe im 20. Jahrhundert* (Bonn, 1986); John Neubauer, *The Fin-de-Siècle Culture of Adolescence* (New Haven, Conn., 1992); David Fowler, *The First Teenagers: The Lifestyle of Young Wage-Earners in Interwar Britain* (Woburn, 1995); Giovanni Levi and Jean-Claude Schmitt, eds., *A History of Young People*, vol. II: *Stormy Evolution to Modern Times* (Cambridge, Mass., 1997); Axel Schildt and Detlef Siegfried, eds., *European Cities, Youth, and the Public Sphere in the Twentieth Century* (Hampshire, 2005); Mary Jo Maynes et al., eds., *Secret Gardens, Satanic Mills: Placing Girls in European History, 1750–1960* (Bloomington, Ind., 2005).

4. On *Jugendpflege*, see Hermann Giesecke, *Vom Wandervogel bis zur Hitlerjugend: Jugendarbeit zwischen Politik und Pädagogik* (Munich, 1981); Derek Linton, *"Who Has the Youth, Has the Future": The Campaign to Save Young Workers in Imperial Germany* (Cambridge, 1990). Linton in particular offers a detailed organizational study that shows how the state became interested in the project of "cultivating" the young; but he sees *Jugendpflege* primarily as an attempt to control young industrial workers. In fact, by 1914 youth cultivators' concept of adolescent socialization transcended class, and they were attempting to socialize *all* German adolescents between the ages of twelve and twenty.

5. Direct translation: "Wandering Birds." For many years historians tended to interpret this bourgeois youth movement simply as an antirational, antimodern forerunner of the Hitler Youth movement, e.g., Walter Laqueur, *Young Germany: A History of the German Youth Movement* (New Brunswick, N.J., 1984, orig. 1962); Stern, *Cultural Despair*; Harry Pross, *Jugend, Eros, Politik: Die Geschichte der deutschen Jugendverbände* (Bern, 1964); Mosse, *Nationalization*; Joachim Wolschke-Bulmahn, *Auf der Suche nach Arkadien: Zu Landschaftsidealen und Formen der Naturaneignung in der Jugendbewegung*

(Munich, 1990). More balanced early interpretations include Gerhard Ziemer and Hans Wolf, *Wandervogel und Freideutsche Jugend* (Bad Godesberg, 1961); Felix Raabe, *Die bündische Jugend* (Stuttgart, 1961). Recently the *Wandervögel* have undergone a reassessment by historians who have shown that the movement was not antimodern in any simple way, nor was there a straight path from the *Wandervögel* to fascist youth. See Ulrich Aufmuth, *Die deutsche Wandervogelbewegung unter soziologischem Aspekt* (Göttingen, 1979); Peter Stachura, *The German Youth Movement, 1900–1945* (New York, 1981); Joachim Knoll and Julius Schoeps, eds., *Typisch deutsch: Die Jugendbewegung* (Opladen, 1988); Marion de Ras, *Körper, Eros, und weibliche Kultur: Mädchen im Wandervogel und in der Bündischen Jugend, 1900–1933* (Pfaffenweiler, 1988); Irmgard Klönne, *Ich spring in diesem Ringe: Mädchen und Frauen in der deutschen Jugendbewegung* (Pfaffenweiler, 1990); Dietmar Schenk, *Die Freideutsche Jugend, 1913–1919/20* (Münster, 1991); Andreas Winnecken, *Ein Fall von Antisemitismus: Zur Geschichte und Pathogenese der deutschen Jugendbewegung vor dem Ersten Weltkrieg* (Cologne, 1991); Ulrich Herrmann, ed., *"Mit uns zieht die neue Zeit": Der Wandervogel in der deutschen Jugendbewegung* (Berlin, 2004).

6. Archiv der deutschen Jugendbewegung (hereafter AdJb), A2-104/8: Gertrud Bäumer, "Freideutsche Jugend" (1913), 7.

7. Klaus Tenfelde, "Großstadtjugend in Deutschland vor 1914," *Vierteljahrschrift für Sozial- und Wirtschaftsgeschichte* (1982), 182–218; Jürgen Reulecke, *Urbanisierung*, 76–77, and "Bürgerliche Sozialreformer und Arbeiterjugend im Kaiserreich," *Archiv für Sozialgeschichte* (1982), 299–329; Linton, *Youth*, 19–47.

8. Quoted in BayHStAM, MK 13963: "Jugendfürsorge der Fortbildungsschulen," *Das deutsche Handwerksblatt* (1908), 233. On *Jugendfürsorge*, see Detlev Peukert, *Grenzen der Sozialdisziplinierung: Aufstieg und Krise der deutschen Jugendfürsorge, 1878–1932* (Cologne, 1986); Edward Dickinson, *The Politics of German Child Welfare from the Empire to the Federal Republic* (Cambridge, Mass., 1996).

9. Edward Ross Dickinson, "Citizenship, Vocational Training, and Reaction: Continuation Schooling and the Prussian 'Youth Cultivation' Decree of 1911," *European History Quarterly* (1999), 115.

10. LAB, B Rep. 142-01/4988: Dr. Schmidt, speech at opening ceremony on March 5, 1911, reprinted in *Zweck und Einrichtung des städtischen Jugendheimes Stettin* (Stettin, 1911), 14–19.

11. Hertha Siemering, *Pflege der schulentlassenen weiblichen Jugend* (Berlin, 1914), 10–11.

12. STAL, PPL-V 3982: "Jahresbilanz der klerikalen Jugendbewegung," *Leipziger Volkszeitung* (December 21, 1912); "Umschau," *Jugendführung* (1914), 28–32; *Jugendpflege* (May 1914), 251; Josefine Dressel, *Entwicklung der weiblichen Jugendpflege in Bayern* (Munich, 1932).

13. Dr. H. Bertrams, "Staatsbürgerliche Schulung und katholische Jugendpflege," *Jugendführung* (1914), 37; Bischof Dr. Adolf Bertram, *Jugendpflege im Lichte katholischer Lebensauffassung* (Düsseldorf, 1914); STM, Wohlfahrt 1910: Rechenschafts-Bericht des Ledigenheimes Josephine Abelsches Arbeiterinnenheim (1909).

14. Erich Eberts, *Arbeiterjugend, 1904–1945* (Frankfurt, 1979), 23–52.

15. Quoted in Helmut Trotnow, *Karl Liebknecht* (Hamden, 1984), 75.

16. AdJb, A2-104/10: speech of May 11, 1914, by representative Wallbaum in steno-graphic report of the 77th meeting of the Prussian House of Representatives, 6624; Stachura, *Movement*, 101.

17. SAPMO-BArch, RY22/V SUF/110: Max Pechel, *Grundsätze und Leitfaden zur Förderung der Bildung der Arbeiterjugend* (Munich, 1913), 4–6.

18. Karl Retzlaw, "Die grausame Kleinstadt," in Wolfgang Emmerich, ed., *Proletarische Lebensläufe* (Reinbek, 1975), 2:70.

19. SAPMO-BArch, RY11/II 107/5: file entitled "Sozialistische Arbeiterjugend"; BayHStAM, MK 13963: file entitled "Sozialdemokratische Jugendpflege, 1907–1921."

20. LAB, Helene Lang Archiv: 1912 statutes of the *Deutscher Pfadfinder-Bund für junge Mädchen*; Karl Seidelmann, *Die Pfadfinder in der deutschen Geschichte* (Hannover, 1977). On Scouting elsewhere, see David Macleod, *Building Character in the American Boy: The Boy Scouts, YMCA, and Their Forerunners, 1870–1920* (Madison, 1983); Robert MacDonald, *Sons of the Empire: The Frontier and Boy Scout Movement* (Toronto, 1993).

21. Generalleutnant F. von Mülmann, "Unser Kaiser als Pfadfinder," *Der Pfadfinder* (1913), 98; W. Helfrich, "Sparta—deutsches Pfadfindertum," ibid., 258–59; Erich Mann, "Sprecht Deutsch!" *Der Pfadfinder* (1912), 159–60.

22. STAL, PPL-V 3982: "Jung-Deutschland," *Leipziger Volkszeitung* (October 1, 1911); *"Jungdeutschland": Bericht über die Vertrauensmännerversammlung des Bundes Jungdeutschland am 11. und 12. Dezember 1911* (Berlin, 1911), 3. See also Klaus Saul, "Der Kampf um die Jugend zwischen Volksschule und Kaserne: Ein Beitrag zur 'Jugendpflege' im wilhelminischen Reich, 1890–1914," *Militärgeschichtliche Mitteilungen* (1971), 97–143.

23. Linton, *Youth*, 159–63; Dickinson, "Citizenship," 137.

24. Quoted in Wallbaum speech of May 11, 1914 (AdJb, A2-104/10).

25. Quoted in STAL, PPL-V 3982: "Der Kampf um die Jugend," *Leipziger Neueste Nachrichten* (March 28, 1912).

26. STAL, PPL-V 3982: report of a session of the Saxon Diet in *Leipziger Tageszeitung* (April 20, 1912); Heinrich Hirtsiefer, ed., *Jugendpflege in Preußen* (Eberswalde, 1930), 7–8; Frank Zadach-Buchmeier, "Staatliche Jugendpflege in der kommunalen Praxis," in Adelheid von Saldern, ed., *Stadt und Moderne: Hannover in der Weimarer Republik* (Hamburg, 1989), 156.

27. STAL, PPL-V 3982: *Leipziger Volkszeitung* (February 17, 1913); *Jugendpflege* (May 1914), 251; Dickinson, "Citizenship," 113; Reulecke, "Battle," 96.

28. STAL, PPL-V 3982: "Eine 'brennende' Frage," *Leipziger Volkszeitung* (January 21, 1912).

29. Nicholas Stargardt, "German Childhoods: The Making of a Historiography," *German History* (1998), 5. On *Jugendkunde*, see Peter Dudek, *Jugend als Objekt der Wissenschaften* (Opladen, 1990); Johannes-Christoph von Bühler, *Die gesellschaftliche Konstruktion des Jugendalters* (Weinheim, 1990).

30. BayHStAM, MK 14970: Dr. Rudolf Schneider, *Pubertät und Auge* (Munich, 1911), 1.

31. Anson Rabinbach, *The Human Motor: Energy, Fatigue, and the Origins of Modernity* (Berkeley, 1992).

32. See Mosse, *Nationalism*, passim; Isabel Hull, *The Entourage of Kaiser Wilhelm II, 1888–1918* (Cambridge, 1982); James Steakley, "Iconography of a Scandal: Political Cartoons and the Eulenburg Affair in Wilhelmine Germany," in Martin Duberman et al., eds., *Hidden from History: Reclaiming the Gay and Lesbian Past* (New York, 1989), 233–63; Peter Jungblut, *Famose Kerle: Eulenburg—Eine wilhelminische Affäre* (Berlin, 2003). There was little public discussion of lesbianism in Germany during this era, a silence that reflected the dominance of men in the scandals, in the gay rights movement, and in society as a whole.

33. BayHStAM, MInn 73589: Prof. Dr. Max Gruber, "Ein flammender Weckruf gegen die geschlechtliche Zügellosigkeit," *Allgemeine Rundschau* (February 15, 1908), 99–100.

34. See James Steakley, *The Homosexual Rights Movement in Germany* (New York, 1975); John Fout, "Sexual Politics in Wilhelmine Germany: The Male Gender Crisis, Moral Purity, and Homophobia," in idem, ed., *Forbidden History: The State, Society, and the Regulation of Sexuality in Modern Europe* (Chicago, 1992), 259–92.

35. BayHStAM, MK 14847: file entitled "Sexuelle Aufklärung an den Mittelschulen, Band I, 1905–1926."

36. BayHStAM, MK 14847: "Die Fuldaer Bischofskonferenz über sexuelle Erziehung" (1914).

37. BayHStAM, MK 14847: Elternvereinigung München to Staatsministerium des Innern für Kirchen- und Schulangelegenheiten (January 31, 1911); protocol of 1,332nd meeting of the Munich school board (November 11, 1913); Dr. Matthäus Doell, "Sexualpädagogik und Elternhaus" (1913).

38. BayHStAM, MK 22898: Bayerischer Staatsminister des Innern to Staatsministerium des königlichen Hauses und des Äußern (November 11, 1910).

39. *Arbeiter-Jugend* (1910), 364.

40. See, e.g., SAPMO-BArch, RY11/II 107/4: H. F., "Ein Wort über die Schundliteratur," *Jugendheim: Mitteilungen für die arbeitende Jugend Neuköllns* (December 1912).

41. SAPMO-BArch, RY22/V SUF/110: R. Weimann, *Die Dresdner Arbeiter-Jugend und ihre Organisation* (Dresden, 1911), 41–42.

42. STAL, PPL-V 3982: "Um die weibliche Jugend," *Leipziger Tageszeitung* (June 11, 1912).

43. Dressel, *Entwicklung*; Linton, *Youth*, 165–85.

44. Quoted in Hirtsiefer, *Jugendpflege in Preußen*, 223.

45. STAM, PDM 3555: "Bericht über die Tätigkeit des Ortsausschusses für weibliche Jugendpflege München vom 2. Juli 1913 bis 31. Dezember 1914"; C. M., "Umschau," *Jugendführung* (1914), 29.

46. The emphasis on improving national health through exercise grew throughout Western civilization in the course of the nineteenth century. See, for instance, Norah March, *Towards Racial Health: A Handbook for Parents, Teachers, and Social Workers on the Training of Boys and Girls*, 4th ed. (London, 1920); Allen Guttmann, *Games and Empires: Modern Sports and Cultural Imperialism* (New York, 1994).

47. BayHStAM, MK 14847: Dr. K. Touton, *Über sexuelle Verantwortlichkeit* (Leipzig, 1908).

48. Eugen Doernberger, *Schülerwanderungen* (Munich, 1911); Gustav Chrosciel, *Wanderlust, ein Weg zur Kraft durch Freude* (Halle, 1912).

49. Anton Fendrich, *Der Wanderer* (Stuttgart, 1912), 50–51. The liberal youth cultivator Adele Schreiber also stressed the neutrality of nature enjoyment in STAL, PPL-V 3982: "Der Kampf der Parteien um die Jugend," *Leipziger Neueste Nachrichten* (March 31, 1912).

50. SAPMO-BArch, RY11/II 107/1: "Wanderregeln," *Rundschreiben der Zentralstelle für die arbeitende Jugend Deutschlands* (March 20, 1913), 22–24; SAPMO-BArch, RY22/V SUF/110: Max Pechel, *Grundsätze und Leitfaden zur Förderung der Bildung der Arbeiterjugend* (Munich, 1913), 18; and Weimann, *Dresdner*, 43.

51. Hertha Siemering, *Fortschritte der deutschen Jugendpflege von 1913 bis 1916* (Berlin, 1916), 9; Hauptausschuß für Leibesübungen und Jugendpflege, *Jahresbericht über das Geschäftsjahr 1911/1912* (Berlin, 1912); Martin Keilhacker, *Jugendpflege und Jugendbewegung in München von den Befreiungskriegen bis zur Gegenwart* (Munich, 1926), 171–72.

52. Wilhelm Münker, *Das deutsche Jugendherbergswerk: Seine Entstehung und Entwicklung bis 1933* (Bielefeld, 1944), 7–8. See also Heinrich Hassinger, *Vom Weg und Wesen, vom Wollen und Wirken der Jugendherbergen und des Jugendwanderns* (Hilchenbach, 1931); Ernst Enzensperger, *Von Jugendwandern und Bergsteigertum: Eine Geschichte des Bayerischen Jugendherbergwerkes* (Munich, 1951); Karl Götz, *Fünfzig Jahre Jugendwandern und Jugendherbergen, 1909–1959* (Detmold, 1959).

53. LAB, B Rep. 142-01/5166: Richard Schirrmann, "Aufruf zur Gründung von Jugendherbergen in der Eifel."

54. BayHStAM, MK 13973: Hauptausschuß für deutsche Jugendherbergen, ed., *Die deutschen Jugendherbergen, 1911–1919* (Hilchenbach, c. 1920); Karl Brossmer, "Jugendherbergen und Wanderheime," in Edmund Neuendorff, ed., *Die deutschen Leibesübungen* (Berlin, 1927), 587; Münker, *Jugendherbergswerk*, 9.

55. STAL, PPL-V 3982: "Geh. Medizinalrat von Strümpell über Jugendwandern," *Leipziger Neueste Nachrichten* (May 19, 1913); BayHStAM, MK 13973: Ortsausschuß München für Jugendalpenwanderungen, "Merkblatt für Führer" (1914), 7.

56. AdJb, A2-01: file entitled "Ur-Wandervogel (Stenographenverein; Gymnasium Steglitz)."

57. AdJb, A2-10/10: Friedrich W. Fulda, "Vom Mädchen-Wandervogel" (1912); Walter Fischer, "Das Wachstum des Wandervogels," *Wandervogel* (1913), 24; Ulfried Geuter, *Homosexualität in der deutschen Jugendbewegung* (Frankfurt, 1994), 320.

58. Gudrun Fiedler, "Beruf und Leben: Die Wandervogel-Idee auf dem Prüfstand," in Knoll and Schoeps, *Typisch deutsch*, 73.

59. Joseph von Eichendorff, *Aus dem Leben eines Taugenichts* (Berlin, 1826). *Wandervogel* publications often referred to this and to paeans to hiking by the likes of Goethe and Humboldt.

60. Aufmuth, *Wandervogelbewegung*, 130–37. See also Frank Trommler, "Modernität und die Kultur der Unproduktiven," *Jahrbuch des Archivs der deutschen Jugendbewegung* (hereafter *JADJB*) (1993–98), 159–80.

61. Ulrich Linse, "Lebensformen der bürgerlichen und der proletarischen Jugendbewegung," *JADJB* (1978), 49; Ras, *Körper*, 17.

62. Quoted in Ras, *Körper*, 43.

63. AdJb, A2-02: Hermann Hoffmann, "Hoch das Wandern," *Schülerwarte* (1898), 2–3, 15.

64. Ibid., 16.

65. Cited in AdJb, A2-104/1: Hans Wix, "Der Wandervogel am Scheidewege" (1914). Wolschke-Bulmahn, *Arkadien*, asserts that the bourgeois youth movement's landscape concept was escapist, antimodern, and illiberal. His study is based on a far too schematic and ahistorical concept of ideology, and his source analyses fail to convince.

66. Hans Breuer, "Herbstschau 1913," *Wandervogel* (1913), quoted in Ziemer and Wolf, *Wandervogel*, 17.

67. Recent years have brought several studies on the subject of sexuality in the *Wandervogel* movement. Historians who work on this subject, however, have tended to revert to the older general thesis according to which the youth movement between 1900 and 1933 was antimodern and politically either reactionary or quietist. They have argued that although the independent youth movement was ostensibly opposed to bourgeois norms, it faced the overwhelming pressures of bourgeois moral codes and of a masculinist and militarist ideology of national identity. The movement therefore attempted to divest its rhetoric and everyday practice of all the elements that might appear even slightly erotic. In most groups, the exclusively male league (*Männerbund*) became the preferred form. These measures, according to most interpretations, stunted the sexual development of members. See Mosse, *Nationalism*; Ulrich Linse, "'Geschlechtsnot der Jugend': Über Jugendbewegung und Sexualität," in Koebner et al., *Mit uns*, 245–309; Friedhelm Musall, "'Es ist doch auch ein mönchisches Leben . . .': Adoleszenz und Sexualität in der frühen Jugendbewegung," *JADJB* (1986–87), 271–94; Nicolaus Sombart, "Männerbund und Politische Kultur in Deutschland," in Knoll and Schoeps, *Typisch deutsch*, 155–76. All of these authors argue that arrested sexual development paralleled the allegedly stunted *political* development of bourgeois youths in the movement. Their evident purpose is to buttress a negative judgment of the youth movement for its supposed unwillingness to confront the problems of industrial modernity. This thesis, in fact, is a new permutation of a much earlier critique of the movement by contemporary youth cultivators and left-wing commentators, all of whom dismissed the *Wandervögel* for their alleged immaturity, emotionalism, and/or effeminacy. See Max Hodann, "Das erotische Problem in der bürgerlichen Jugendbewegung" (1916), reprinted in idem, *Bub und Mädel* (Leipzig, 1924), 108–15; Elisabeth Busse-Wilson, *Die Frau und die Jugendbewegung* (Hamburg, 1920); Fritz Jungmann, "Autorität und Sexualmoral in der freien bürgerlichen Jugendbewegung," in Max Horkheimer, ed., *Studien über Autorität und Familie* (Paris, 1936), 669–705. The postwar study that kept this early critique alive was Pross, *Jugend, Eros, Politik*. It is interesting to note that the Nazis also dismissed the *Wandervogel* tradition along these lines, as will be shown in Chapter 5. Given the historical provenance of this critique, a reevaluation is in order. To date, only Geuter has undertaken it, in his excellent *Homosexualität*.

68. Geuter, *Homosexualität*, 38–44, 49–58.

69. Willie Jahn, speech of October 10, 1913, reprinted in Kurtis and Joachim Pieper, "Die Hanstein Tagung," *Jung-Wandervogel* (1913), 163–64.

70. Hans Blüher, *Die deutsche Wandervogelbewegung als ein erotisches Phänomen: Ein Beitrag zur Erkenntnis der sexuellen Inversion* (Prien, 1922, orig. Berlin, 1912), 85. See also Geuter, *Homosexualität*, 67–117.

71. Quoted in Blüher, *Wandervogelbewegung*, 40.

72. Ibid., 81.

73. The *Jung-Wandervögel* and *Alt-Wandervögel* kept their hikes strictly segregated by gender; and although the WVEV allowed some coed hiking, single-sex hikes were still the rule. Commentators asserted that segregated hikes would preserve essentially different gender characteristics. Any coed hiking that did occur drew the suspicion of outside observers. One conservative Leipzig newspaper, for instance, wrote vaguely that it led to "abuses" and should be stopped. STAL, PPL-V 3982: "Jugendpflege," *Allgemeine Zeitung* (February 16, 1913). See also AdJb, A2-10/10: file entitled "Diskussionen über das Mädchenwandern."

74. AdJb, A2-08/2: "Die Bundesleitung des Wandervogels e.V. an sämtliche Herren Schulleiter."

75. Quoted in Geuter, *Homosexualität*, 94.

76. Georges Barbizon, "Die treibenden Kräfte," *Der Anfang* (1913), 1. For the organizational history of the *Anfang* Circle, see Klaus Laermann, "Der Skandal um den *Anfang*," in Koebner et al., *Mit uns*, 360–81; Philip Lee Utley, "Radical Youth: Generational Conflict in the *Anfang* Movement, 1912–1914," *History of Education Quarterly* (1979), 207–28, and "Schism, Romanticism, and Organization: *Anfang*, January–August 1914," *Journal of Contemporary History* (1999), 109–24.

77. Gustav Wyneken, "Zwei Briefe zum Freideutschen Jugendtag," *Jung-Wandervogel* (1913), 174, "Wandervogel und Freie Schulgemeinde" in ibid., 179, and *Die neue Jugend: Ihr Kampf um Freiheit und Wahrheit in Schule und Elternhaus, in Religion und Erotik* (Munich, 1914), 46–47.

78. Ardor (pseudonym for Benjamin), "Erfahrung," *Der Anfang* (1913), 169; Herbert Blumenthal, "Von der Mission der Jugend," ibid., 134.

79. D. A., "Bericht über den ersten Freideutschen Jugendtag," ibid., 193–98.

80. M. G. Grünling, "Das Land eurer Kinder!" ibid., 239.

81. Ernst, "Nacktheit—Wahrheit!" ibid., 138–40; Friederich Mono, "Unsere Geselligkeit," ibid., 200–210.

82. Herbert Blumenthal, "Erotik," ibid., 167.

83. See *Freideutsche Jugend: Zur Jahrhundertfeier auf dem Hohen Meissner* (Jena, 1913); Gustav Mittelstraß, ed., *Freideutscher Jugendtag*, 2d ed. (Hamburg, 1919); Winfried Mogge, "Der Freideutsche Jugendtag 1913," in Jürgen Reulecke and Winfried Mogge, eds., *Hoher Meissner 1913* (Cologne, 1988), 33–62.

84. Gertrud Prellwitz, "Die Ehe und die neue Zeit," *Freideutsche Jugend*, 153–54.

85. Ludwig Klages, "Mensch und Erde," ibid., 95–105. On Klages, see Rohkrämer, *Moderne*.

86. AdJb, A2-104/1: flyer entitled "Freideutscher Jugendtag" (Fall 1913).

87. Gertrud Prellwitz, "Was ist Vaterlandsliebe?" *Freideutsche Jugend*, 150–53.

88. Paul Natorp, "Aufgaben und Gefahren unserer Jugendbewegung," ibid., 121–34.

89. "Gustav Wynekens Rede auf dem 'Hohen Meissner' am Morgen des 12. Oktobers," in Mittelstraß, *Jugendtag*, 34.

90. Ibid., 38. The belligerently nationalist, racist speech by a representative of the Austrian *Wandervögel* at the festival contrasted sharply to the language of patriotism described here (Schenk, *Freideutsche Jugend*, 72). Unfortunately, there is no reliable evidence on the reception of the various speeches and essays written in conjunction with the festival. Thus, no conclusions can be drawn about the popularity of these competing types of nationalism among the youth movement rank and file.

91. Gustav Wyneken, "Reformphilistertum oder Jugendkultur?" *Freideutsche Jugend*, 167.

92. Quoted in "Feuerrede Knud Ahlborns," in Mittelstraß, *Jugendtag*, 29.

93. Untitled article in the Progressive Party newspaper *Frankfurter Zeitung* (October 14, 1913), reprinted in Reulecke and Mogge, *Hoher Meissner*, 315.

94. Franz Pfemfert, "Die Jugend spricht!" *Die Aktion* (October 11, 1913), reprinted in ibid., 330–31.

95. "Zwei Jugendtagungen," *Hamburger Nachrichten* (October 14, 1913), reprinted in ibid., 337.

96. "Freideutsche Jugend," *Reichsbote* (October 15, 1913), reprinted in ibid., 339.

97. *"Jugendkultur": Dokumente zur Beurteilung der "modernsten" Form "freier" Jugenderziehung, von einem bayerischen Schulmann* (Munich, 1914).

98. *Verhandlungen der Kammer der Abgeordneten des bayerischen Landtags, XXXVI. Landtagsversammlung, II. Session im Jahre 1913/1914* (Munich, 1914), 133.

99. Quoted in ibid., 136.

100. Ibid., 134.

101. BayHStAM, MK 15003: *Neues Münchener Tagesblatt* (January 30, 1914), and *Bayerischer Kurier* (February 1–2 and February 7, 1914).

102. *Verhandlungen der Kammer*, 137.

103. Ibid., 172.

104. Anon., "Zum Kampf gegen die freideutsche Jugendbewegung und gegen die neue Jugendkultur," *Münchener Post* (February 8–10, 1914).

105. Quoted in "Der Protest der freideutschen Jugend," *Münchener Post* (February 1, 1914), and in BayHStAM, MK 15003: *München-Augsburger Abendzeitung* (February 10, 1914).

106. Quoted in BayHStAM, MK 15003: *Bayerischer Kurier* (March 12, 1914).

107. BayHStAM, MK 15003: Königliche Polizeidirektion München to Königliches Staatsministerium des Innern für Kirchen und Schulangelegenheiten (February 16, 1914).

108. Laermann, "Skandal," 373.

109. Quoted in *Die Marburger Tagung der Freideutschen Jugend* (Hamburg, 1914), 28. See also Schenk, *Freideutsche Jugend*, 70–81.

110. Akademisches Comité für Schulreform, "Die Zukunft der FDJ," *Der Anfang* (July 1914), 96.

111. Quoted in Laermann, "Skandal," 365.

112. AdJb, A2-104/10: stenographic report of the 77th meeting of the Prussian House of Representatives, 6624, 6556, 6560, 6583–84.

113. Evidence from Bavaria and Saxony is found in BayHStAM, MK 15003: file entitled "Höhere Lehranstalten: 'Jungdeutsche Jugendkultur,' 1913–1924."

114. BayHStAM, MK 15003: Hans Bormann, "Zur Wandervogel-Bewegung," *Kölnische Volkszeitung* (June 5, 1914).

115. BayHStAM, MK 15003: Dr. Hoffmann, "Falsche Bahnen," *Allgemeine Rundschau* (February 21, 1914), E. Grünholtz, "Das Grundproblem der modernen Erziehungsreformbestrebungen," *Literarische Beilage der kölnischen Volkszeitung* (July 23, 1914), and Bormann, "Bewegung."

116. Alfred Odin, "Die Soldaten," *Wandervogel* (1919), 111–12; Gudrun Fiedler, *Jugend im Krieg: Bürgerliche Jugendbewegung, Erster Weltkrieg, und sozialer Wandel, 1914–1923* (Cologne, 1989), 43. The secondary sources disagree on the casualty statistics. The lowest number of ten thousand appears in Fiedler, *Krieg*, 238. The highest, fifteen thousand, appears in AdJb, A2-11/7: Rudolf Kneip, "Der Feldwandervogel 1914/1918" (unpublished typescript, 1963). This statistical discrepancy stems from the organizational complexities of the youth movement itself. Neither Kneip nor Fiedler make clear, for example, whether their statistics include soldiers from the older student groups in the *Freideutsche Jugend*.

117. Studies arguing that adults used *Geländespiele* to indoctrinate the *Wandervögel* in militant nationalism include Joachim Wolschke-Bulmahn, "Kriegsspiel und Naturgenuß: Zur Funktionalisierung der bürgerlichen Jugendbewegung für militärische Ziele," *JADJB* (1986–87), 251–69; Christoph Schubert-Weller, "'Die Sendung der jungen Generation': Von der Militarisierung zur Verstaatlichung," *JADJB* (1988–92), 37–76. Fiedler argues against taking the games too seriously in *Krieg*, 40. This position is supported by contemporary *Wandervogel* sources, e.g., Hanna Diehl, "Kriegsspiel in der Davert," *Wandervogel: Monatsschrift für deutsches Jugendwandern* (1914), 233–35. Even the socialist youth cultivator Heinrich Schulz argued that "war games" had been around for a long time and were generally harmless. Heinrich Schulz, "Die Wandlungen der militärischen Jugenderziehung," *Arbeiter-Jugend* (1916), 41–42.

118. Robert Wohl, *The Generation of 1914* (Cambridge, Mass., 1979), 47; Mosse, *Nationalism*, 116.

119. At least during the early phase of the war, there were few significant differences between the rhetoric of the WVEV and that of other independent youth movement organizations. The exception was the *Anfang* Circle, most of whom took up an antiwar position. For a comprehensive analysis of the youth movement's changing reactions to the war, see Fiedler, *Krieg*.

120. AdJb, A2-11/6: *Kriegsflugblatt* (1914).

121. Edmund Neuendorff, "Brüder und Schwestern!" *Wandervogel: Monatsschrift für deutsches Jugendwandern* (1914), 258; Willi Maschke, "Die Wandervögel in der Kriegszeit" and "Amtliches," *Wandervogel, Kriegsheft für Schlesien* (December 1914), 4–7, 14.

122. Hans Freimark, "Sonnenwende," *Wandervogel, Kriegsheft für Schlesien* (July 1915), 53–54; Rudolf Zwetz, "Vor dem Auszug," *Wandervogel* (1914), 273; Mutter Anna-

Karoline, "Liebe Söhne und Töchter, die Ihr Wandervögel seid!" *Wandervogel, Kriegsheft für Schlesien* (February 1915), 15.

123. Geuter also comes to this conclusion in *Homosexualität*, 103–8, 138–48.

124. Otto Weniger, 1915 letter from the front, quoted in Fiedler, *Krieg*, 42.

125. Quoted in ibid., 50.

126. Quoted in ibid., 52.

127. Uwe-K. Ketelsen, "'Die Jugend von Langemarck': Ein Poetisch-politisches Motiv der Zwischenkriegszeit," in Koebner et al., *Mit uns*, 68–96.

Chapter 4

1. This analysis does not attend to Protestant, Catholic, or Jewish *Jugendpflege*, but see Paul Hastenteufel, *Jugendbewegung und Jugendseelsorge: Geschichte und Probleme der katholischen Jugendarbeit im 20. Jahrhundert* (Munich, 1962); Irmtraud Götz von Olenhusen, *Jugendreich, Gottesreich, Deutsches Reich: Junge Generation, Religion, und Politik, 1928–1933* (Cologne, 1987); Jutte Hetkamp, *Die jüdische Jugendbewegung in Deutschland, 1913–1933* (Essen, 1991); John A. Williams, "Giving Nature a Higher Purpose: Back-to-Nature Movements in Weimar Germany" (Ph.D. diss., University of Michigan, 1996); Tilmann Eysholdt, *Evangelische Jugendarbeit zwischen "Jugendpflege" und "Jugendbewegung"* (Cologne, 1997).

2. Dr. August Hornesser, "Der Einfluß des Krieges auf die Erziehbarkeit der Jugend," in Wilhelm Müller, ed., *Wie Deutschlands Jugend den Weltkrieg erlebt* (Dresden, 1918), 146.

3. Otto Baumgarten, "Der sittliche Zustand des deutschen Volkes unter dem Einfluß des Krieges" in idem, ed., *Geistige und sittliche Wirkungen des Krieges in Deutschland* (Stuttgart, 1927), 76.

4. Reports from local groups in *Der Feldmeister* (1917), 31–32; Siemering, *Fortschritte*, 46ff.; Heinrich Schulz, "Die proletarische Jugendbewegung," in Hertha Siemering, ed., *Die deutschen Jugendpflegeverbände: Ihre Ziele, Geschichte, und Organisation* (Berlin, 1918), 1:435.

5. Hauptausschuß für Leibesübungen und Jugendpflege, *Jahresbericht über das Geschäftsjahr 1914/1915* (Berlin, 1916), 10–11.

6. BayHStAM, MK 13963: Zentralstelle für die arbeitende Jugend Deutschlands to Preußischer Eisenbahnminister (May 12, 1916); Preußischer Minister der öffentlichen Arbeiten to Zentralstelle für die arbeitende Jugend Deutschlands (September 17, 1916).

7. Anon., "Unsere Bewegung im zweiten Kriegsjahr," *Arbeiter-Jugend* (1916), 153–54; Stachura, *Movement*, 104.

8. STAH, III-2 CIII 13: Stellvertretendes Generalkommando XI, in Kassel, "Erweiterung der Verordnung gegen die Zuchtlosigkeit der Jugendlichen" (January 1, 1916).

9. STAH, III-2 CIII 13: Stellvertretendes Generalkommando XI, in Kassel, announcement accompanying the ban on youth in bars after 6:00 P.M. (October 1, 1915).

10. Elsa von Liszt, "Die Verwahrlosung der Jugend im Weltkrieg," in Müller, *Deutschlands Jugend*, 135–37.

11. Elizabeth Tobin, "War and the Working Class: The Case of Düsseldorf, 1914–1918," *Central European History* (1985), 265–73; Elisabeth Domansky, "Politische Dimensionen

von Jugendprotest und Generationenkonflikt in der Zwischenkriegszeit in Deutschland," in Dowe, *Jugendprotest*, 116–26; Volker Ullrich, "Everyday Life and the German Working Class, 1914–1918," in Roger Fletcher, ed., *Bernstein to Brandt: A Short History of German Social Democracy* (Baltimore, 1987), 61.

12. Quoted in *Arbeiter-Jugend* (1915), 55.

13. SAPMO-BArch, RY11/II 107/4: "Antrag an die Zentralstelle für der arbeitende Jugend Deutschlands" (October 17, 1915); SAPMO-BArch, RY11/II 107/6: file entitled "Sozialistische Arbeiterjugend, 1916"; Anon., "Experimente in unserer Jugendbewegung," *Arbeiter-Jugend* (1916), 81–82; Anon., "Ein wilder Verein," ibid., 89–90.

14. STAH, III-2 AII, 197: file entitled "Bekämpfung sozialdemokratischer Jugendorganisationen und ihrer Aktivitäten, September 1915–Juni 1918"; Staatsarchiv Augsburg (hereafter STAA), 10/32: file entitled "Politische Arbeiterbewegung."

15. STAA, 10/32: Bayerisches Kriegsministerium to Herrn stellvertretenden Kommandierenden General des I.II.III. Armeekorps (February 22, 1918); BayHStAM, MK 13963: decree of Ober-Militärbefehlshaber in Berlin (June 30, 1917).

16. Davis, *Home Fires Burning*; Klaus Tenfelde, "Linksradikale Strömungen in der Ruhrbergarbeiterschaft, 1905–1919," in Hans Mommsen und Ulrich Borsdorf, eds., *Glück auf, Kameraden: Die Bergarbeiter und ihre Organisationen in Deutschland* (Cologne, 1979), 199ff.

17. Friedrich Bauermeister, *Vom Klassenkampf der Jugend* (Jena, 1916), 15.

18. AdJb, A2-104/4: "Rundbrief an Wandervögel" (Spring 1918).

19. AdJb, A2-104/4: manifesto of November 10, 1918, reprinted in flyer entitled "An die Freideutsche Jugend" (Spring 1919).

20. AdJb, A2-104/8: Otger Gräff, "Die Freideutsche Jugend" (1918); Hermann Buddensieg, *Vom Geist und Beruf der freideutschen Jugendbewegung* (Lauenburg, 1924), 24–37.

21. By the early 1920s, the many *bündische* youth organizations had arranged themselves broadly into two branches: a small, far-right-wing sector that was vehemently antirepublican, radically nationalist, and anti-Semitic and/or anti-Slavic; and a much larger moderate to conservative sector. See Werner Kindt, ed., *Die deutsche Jugendbewegung, 1920 bis 1933: Die bündische Zeit* (Düsseldorf, 1974).

22. Elizabeth Domansky, "Militarization and Reproduction in World War I Germany," in Eley, *Society*, 427–64.

23. Stadtarchiv Augsburg (hereafter STA), 10, 3737: Dr. Oskar Winger, "Die Beeinflussung des Fortpflanzungswillens durch den Krieg," *Das neue Deutschland* (1916), 179, and Deutsche Gesellschaft für Bevölkerungspolitik, Ortsgruppe Augsburg, "Aufruf" (1915).

24. BayHStAM, MK 14847: Dr. Rosenthal to Bayerisches Ministerium für Unterricht und Kultus (June 1917), and Deutsche Gesellschaft zur Bekämpfung der Geschlechtskrankheiten to Staatssekretär des Innern (February 14, 1918).

25. Many state authorities agreed with this diagnosis of sexual degeneration, for instance, BayHStAM, MK 14847: Bayerisches Ministerium des Innern zu Regierungen der deutschen Freistaaten außer Preußen (February 17, 1919). Nevertheless, historians have found no conclusive evidence to confirm that prostitutes were spreading VD to large numbers of youths or that premarital sex increased.

26. Dr. Martin Chotzen, "Die Gefahren der Entwicklungsjahre," in *Einführung in die Sexualpädagogik* (Berlin, 1921), 74–90. I have found no evidence to confirm Chotzen's assertion; indeed, the existing evidence about adolescent misbehavior indicates no increase in the number of boys who were accused of homosexual activity under Paragraph 175. For instance, figures on the 1,212 adolescents in Leipzig who were caught committing crimes in the year 1918 include only one boy accused of "unnatural fornication." Stadtarchiv Leipzig (hereafter STL), Verkehrsamt Nr. 927: "Jahresbericht der Zentrale für Jugendfürsorge in Leipzig über das Jahr 1918."

27. See Hans-Georg Stümke, *Homosexuelle in Deutschland: Eine politische Geschichte* (Munich, 1989).

28. Hans Blüher, *Die Rolle der Erotik in der männlichen Gesellschaft*, 2 vols. (Berlin, 1917–1919); STAM, PDM 3772: report on Blüher's speech of July 2, 1920.

29. BayHStAM, MK 14847: "Denkschrift der Schulkommission des ärztlichen Vereins München: Über die außerordentliche Gefahren, welche die Jugendbewegung in den letzten Jahren gezeitigt hat" (January 1920).

30. LAB, B Rep. 142/01, 2854: "Aus dem Verhandlungsbericht der Vereinigung der Direktoren der höheren Schulen der Provinz Hannover," quoted in *Äußerungen von Fachgelehrten über die pädagogische und volkshygienische Bedeutung der Bestrebungen der "Zentrale für sexuellen Jugendschutz"* (Berlin, c. 1925).

31. STAM, RA57867: "Ortspolizeiliche Vorschriften, betreffend Zulassung Jugendlicher zu Filmvorstellungen" (March 13, 1921), and Polizeidirektion report of November 15, 1921.

32. BArch, R43 I/1980: quoted in Preußischer Minister für Volkswohlfahrt to sämtliche Herren Regierungspräsidenten und den Herrn Oberpräsidenten in Charlottenburg (February 8, 1923); Peukert, "Sozialpolitik der Seele."

33. Quoted in Peukert, *Grenzen*, 22. On Weimar-era welfare aimed specifically at helping poor working youths, see Peukert, *Grenzen*; Peter Stachura, *The Weimar Republic and the Younger Proletariat* (New York, 1989); Elizabeth Harvey, *Youth and the Welfare State in Weimar Germany* (Oxford, 1993).

34. BArch, R36/2030: file entitled "Ortsausschuß für Jugendpflege, 1921–36"; LAB, B Rep. 142-01/144: file entitled "Vorbildung und Anstellung von Jugendpflegern, 1918–31"; LAB, B Rep. 142-01/2549: file entitled "Bericht über die Tätigkeit des Bielefelder Jugendamtes auf dem Gebiet der Jugendpflege und -bewegung, 1926–27"; Giesecke, *Wandervogel*, 142–44; Zadach-Buchmeier, "Praxis," 155–80.

35. Quoted in Hirtsiefer, *Jugendpflege in Preußen*, 3–4.

36. Quoted in Zadach-Buchmeier, "Jugendpflege," 160.

37. Jean-Jacques Rousseau, *The Social Contract* (London, 1968, orig. 1761), 64.

38. NSHStAH, Hann. 122a, Nr. 4490: "Erlaß betreffend die militärische Vorbereitung der Jugend während des mobilen Zustandes" (August 16, 1914).

39. NSHStAH, Hann. 122a, Nr. 4490: Kriegsministerium to die stellvertretenden Generalkommandos des I., II., IV.–XI., XVII., XX., und XXI. Armeekorps (August 19, 1914), and Stellvert. Generalkommando X. Armeekorps to die Bezirkskommandos des X. Armeekorps (September 7, 1914); Wilhelm Flitner, "Der Krieg und die Jugend," in Baumgarten, *Wirkungen*, 277–78.

40. Freiherr von der Goltz, quoted in *Jugendführung* (1914), 161.

41. NSHStAH, Hann. 122a, Nr. 4490: "Richtlinien für die militärische Vorbildung der älteren Jahrgänge der Jugendabteilungen während des Kriegszustandes" (August 1914).

42. SAPMO-BArch, RY11 107/1: "Zur Frage der militärischen Jugenderziehung," in *Rundschreiben der Zentralstelle für die arbeitende Jugend Deutschlands* (March 10, 1916); *Jugendführung* (1914), 223–28; Siemering, *Fortschritte*, 54.

43. Oberfeldmeister Schönfeld, "Der Pfadfinder im Kriege," *Der Feldmeister* (1917), 27; Reichsfeldmeister Major Bayer, "Wir Pfadfinder und die Jugendwehr," ibid., 51.

44. Richard Nordhausen, "Mobilisierung der Jugend," *Der Tag* (September 6, 1914), and "Lassen wir die Stunde nicht ungenützt," *Der Tag* (October 17, 1914); Dr. Otto Braun, "Staatszwanges in der Jugendbewegung," *Der Tag* (November 21, 1914), all quoted in *Jugendführung* (1914), 158–59.

45. Linton, *Youth*, 191; Siemering, *Fortschritte*, 51; Flitner, "Krieg," 278–79.

46. STAM, PDM 4554: Bayerischer Wehrkraftverein, Ortsgruppe München to Herrn Geschäftsführer Schnell (May 22, 1916).

47. Siemering, *Fortschritte*, 42, 45.

48. Quoted in Flitner, "Krieg," 280.

49. BayHStAM, MK 13974: "Amtsblatt des Bayerischen Ministeriums für Unterricht und Kultus . . . über die Beteiligung von Schülern an Vereinen" (December 29, 1923).

50. Ernst Enzensperger, *Der Jugendwanderführer* (Munich, 1930), 28; Anon., "Jugendpflege in Bayern," *Der Führer* (1926), 7–8.

51. Generalpräses Mosterts, "Ziel und Grenzen des Ausschusses der deutschen Jugendverbände," *Ratgeber für Jugendvereinigungen* (1922), 128–29.

52. Mewes, *Jugend*, 98–99, 152–58.

53. See, e.g., BayHStAM, MK 13844: Lieutenant Colonel Hörl, speech entitled "Leibeserziehung—Dienst am Volk," in "Niederschrift über die Konferenz am 12. Juli 1927 in Altdorf."

54. F. Müller, "Pfadfinder und Jugendbewegung," *Der Feldmeister* (1919), 14.

55. On Weimar socialist *Jugendpflege*, see Heinrich Eppe, *Selbsthilfe und Interessenvertretung: Die sozial- und jugendpolitischen Bestrebungen der sozialdemokratischen Arbeiterjugendorganisationen, 1904–1933* (Bonn, 1983); Cornelius Schley, *Die Sozialistische Arbeiterjugend Deutschlands* (Frankfurt, 1987).

56. W. Dahrendorf, "Der Arbeiter-Jugendbund," *Junge Menschen* (1919), 39.

57. Johannes Schult, "Jugend und Sozialismus," in Emil Müller, ed., *Das Weimar der arbeitenden Jugend* (Berlin, 1920), 53, 55.

58. *Unser Weg: Bericht des Verbandes der Sozialistischen Arbeiterjugend über das Jahr 1923* (Berlin, 1924), 4.

59. Heinrich Schulz, "Sozialdemokratische Kulturarbeit," *Arbeiter-Bildung* (1920), 98.

60. P. Lindemann, "Gedanken eines Heimgekehrten," *Wandervogel: Monatsschrift für deutsches Jugendwandern* (1920), 22; Robert Bel-gran, "Wandervogel und Kultur," *Das Rautenfähnlein der Wandervögel in Bayern* (1919), 25–26.

61. Robert Bel-gran, "Wandervogel und Philistertum," *Das Rautenfähnlein der Wandervögel in Bayern* (1919), 62, and idem, "Wandervogel und Kultur," 25–26.

62. Karl Sonntag, "Zwei Wege," *Der Weiße Ritter* (1919–20), 101.

63. For example, a 1924 essay in a socialist journal asserted, "Same-sex feelings of love have been strongly promoted by the *Wandervogel* movement. Adolescent boys incline toward other boys, girls toward other girls, and when boys and girls associate, they see each other only as comrades." A. Scholte, "Über die derzeitigen Anschauungen von der gleichgeschlechtlichen Liebe und ihre Ursachen," *Volksgesundheit* (1924), 85.

64. Adjb, A2-152/1: Oswald Matthias, "Kritik des Bundeslagers des Bundes Deutscher Neupfadfinder auf dem Eierhauk in der Rhön, Sommer, 1924."

65. Ras, *Körper*, 58. See also Elizabeth Heinemann, "Gender Identity in the *Wandervogel* Movement," *German Studies Review* (1989), 249–70; Elizabeth Harvey, "Serving the Volk, Saving the Nation: Women in the Youth Movement and the Public Sphere in Weimar Germany," in James Retallack and Larry E. Jones, eds., *Elections, Mass Politics, and Social Change in Modern Germany: New Perspectives* (Cambridge, 1992), 201–21; Geuter, *Homosexualität*.

66. BArch, R36/2071: file entitled "Verein Museum für Leibesübungen e.V., 1927–1933."

67. Quoted in Horländer, "Die Leibesübungen, ein Mittel zum Wiederaufbau unserer Volkskraft," *Die Willenskraft* (June 15, 1922), 3.

68. As one essayist in the SPD newspaper *Vorwärts* explained, exercise is a "natural and superbly effective method of alleviating these drives," for it "absorbs energies that would otherwise be directed toward achieving erotic relief (*Entladung*)." F. W., "Laßt Jugend Sport treiben," *Vorwärts* (February 24, 1928).

69. Julius Deutsch, *Sport und Politik* (Berlin, 1928); Helmut Wagner, *Sport und Arbeitersport* (Berlin, 1931).

70. Bier, *Pflege der Leibesübungen*, 15–16.

71. Münker, *Jugendherbergswerk*, 12.

72. The board of the Bavarian district branch of the Federation, for instance, was composed of professors; members of various boards of education; school administrators and teachers; the state Minister for Education and Culture; the mayor of Munich; members of the Bavarian medical association; a lawyer; an architect; and representatives from *Jugendpflege* groups, sporting clubs, women's associations, and independent youth groups. BayHStAM, MInn 72884: "Jahres-Bericht 1930, Landesverband Bayern für Jugendwandern und Jugendherberge." Nor did the Federation have any qualms about working with the labor movement. The General Association of German Unions (ADGB) helped to erect and equip hostels at the local and district levels. BayHStAM, MK 13973: Anon., "Arbeiterschaft und Jugendherbergen," *Nachrichtendienst über Jugendwandern und Jugendherbergen* (March 1920); Anon., "Gewerkschaften und Jugendherbergsverband," *Gewerkschafts-Zeitung* (1933), 268–69.

73. STAH, iii-i Cl. Vii Lit. H*e* No. 9 vol. 6: Hamburger Ausschuß für Jugendherbergen e.V., *Warum braucht Deutschland Jugendherbergen?* (Hamburg, 1925).

74. STL, Jugendamt Nr. 45, Band I: statutes of the Verband für deutsche Jugendherbergen, Ortsgruppe Leipzig e.V. (no date); STAH, iii-i Cl. Vii Lit. H*e* No. 9 vol. 6: "Das gesundheitliche Wert der Ferienwanderungen—Feststellungen vom Stadtschularzt

Dr. Röder, Berlin" (flyer, c. 1925); Anon., "Unser Ziel" (no date), quoted in Münker, *Jugendherbergswerk*, 65.

75. BayHStAM, MK 13973: Ernst Enzensperger, "Jugendwandern-Jugendherbergen," *Verzeichnis der Jugendherbergen* (Hilchenbach, c. 1922).

76. STAM, LRA München 20081: Reichsminister des Innern to Preussischen Minister des Innern, die obersten Jugendwohlfahrtsbehörden der Länder, . . . die deutsche Reichsbahn-Gesellschaft Hauptverwaltung in Berlin (no date); Ernst Enzensperger, "Jugendwandern und Jugendherbergen," *Gesundheitswacht* (April 1926), 5–6; Münker, *Jugendherbergswerk*, 51–54. On the many ways in which the hostels were funded, see ibid., 30–36.

77. Anon., "Wildes Wandern," *Jugendpflege: katholische Monatsschrift zur Pflege der schultentlassenen Jugend* (1915–16), 382.

78. Anon., "Wildes Wandern," *Arbeiter-Jugend* (1918), 8.

79. "Grundsätze für staatlich unterstützte Jugendwanderungen außerhalb der Schulzeit" (July 2, 1923), quoted in Giesecke, *Wandervogel*, 156–57.

80. BayHStAM, MK 13979: quoted in Reichsministerium des Innern to Bayerisches Ministerium für Unterricht und Kultus (December 4, 1923).

81. Richard Schirrmann, "Wie stehts um die Jugendherbergen?" *Der Führer* (March 1925), no page numbers; BayHStAM, MK 13978: rules of order developed in 1926 by the Landesverband Bayern für Jugendwandern und Jugendherberge; Studiendirektor Schneller, "10 Gebote für Wanderer," quoted in Münker, *Jugendherbergswerk*, 53.

82. STAH, III-I Cl. VII Lit H e No. 9 vol. 6: Reichsverband für deutsche Jugendherbergen, "Die deutschen Städte und Gemeinden und das werdende Reichsherbergsnetz" (1925), 8–9.

83. Enzensperger, *Jugendwanderführer*, 6.

84. See Hermann Altrock, "Leibesübungen und Heimatpflege," in *Handbuch der Heimaterziehung* (Berlin, 1924), 5:87–97; Heinrich Hassinger, *Vom Weg und Wesen, vom Wollen und Wirken der Jugendherbergen und des Jugendwanderns* (Hilchenbach, 1931), 29.

85. BArch, Reichsministerium für die besetzten Gebiete, Abt. I, 691–94, 704: files entitled "Sport und Wandern, 1921–1927" and "Heimatpflege"; BayHStAM, MK 13823 and MK 13975: files entitled "Turn- und Sportvereine im besetzen Gebiet, 1922–1925" and "Jugendherbergen im Grenzgebiet des Bayerischen Waldes, 1923–1933"; BayHStAM, MK 13978: Deutscher Rhein e.V. to Reichsministerium für die besetzten Gebiete (June 15, 1925).

86. BayHStAM, MK 13974: Jugendherberge Weiskirchen, guest book (1928).

87. Fritz Müller-Marquardt, *Das Wandern* (Leipzig, 1927), 47–48.

88. NSHStAH, Hann. 174 Zellerfeld, Nr. 4579: file entitled "Jugendwandern—Jugendherbergen, 1931–1936"; BArch, R58/461: file entitled "Sozialistische Arbeiterjugend"; Hans Hackmack, *Arbeiterbewegung und sexuelle Frage* (Berlin, 1920), 6–9; Maria Fellner, "Vom Wandern der Mädchen," *Das Bayernland* (1931), 374–75.

89. Müller-Marquardt, *Wandern*, 32; Fritz Brather, *Schülerwanderungen: Eine Zielweisung zur geistigen, künstlerischen, und sittlichen Bereicherung auf Wanderfahrten* (Leipzig, 1922), 12; BayHStAM, MK 13870: Ernst Enzensperger, "Vorschläge für die

Ausbildung von Führern von Jugendwandergruppen" (October 17, 1922); Enzensperger, *Jugendwanderführer,* 15.

90. Schönbrunn, *Jugendwandern,* 12.

91. Ibid., 134–35.

92. Ernst Kemmer, *Volksnot und Jugendwandern* (Munich, 1922), 5, 11, 17.

93. Schönbrunn, *Jugendwandern,* 12, 29, 90.

94. See Michel Foucault, *Discipline and Punish: The Birth of the Prison* (New York, 1979), and *The History of Sexuality,* vol. I: *An Introduction* (New York, 1980).

95. Schönbrunn, *Jugendwandern,* 71, 136.

96. Müller-Marquardt, *Wandern,* 13.

97. Ibid., 23, 44–45.

98. Johannes Schult, *Das Jugendproblem in der Gegenwart* (Berlin, 1924), 80.

99. Hermann Sendelbach, "Wanderschaft," *Kulturwille* (1925), 129–30.

100. Anon., "Höre, Wanderer!" *Der eifrige Jugendbündler: Mitteilungen der Arbeiterjugendvereine in den Elbgemeinden* (1922–23), no page numbers. Wolschke-Bulmahn, *Arkadien,* mistakenly argues that the socialist youth movement was indifferent to nature conservation. There is plentiful evidence to the contrary, e.g., Johann Charlet, "Was wir beim Wandern lernen können," *Arbeiter-Jugend* (1921), 130; Heinrich Schöps, "Naturschutz und Naturschutzparke," *Arbeiter-Jugend* (1927), 235–36.

101. Münker, *Jugendherbergswerk,* 43–44, 85.

102. Hildegard Jüngst, *Die jugendliche Fabrikarbeiterin* (Paderborn, 1929), 92; Hubert Jung, *Das Phantasieleben der männlichen werktätigen Jugend* (Münster, 1930), 28; Lisbeth Franzen-Hellersberg, *Die jugendliche Arbeiterin* (Tübingen, 1932), 92; Emilie Düntzer, *Die gesundheitliche und soziale Lage der erwerbstätigen weiblichen Jugend* (Berlin, 1933), 36–38.

103. The numbers have been rounded off. "Winter sports" included sledding, ice skating, and snowshoeing. "Other" included tennis, hockey, golf, and horseback riding. Dinse's survey was well balanced along gender and professional lines. Some 30 percent of the respondents were unskilled workers, 13 percent male apprentices, 11 percent upper-school students, and 26 percent "other"—that is, primarily female salespeople, shop employees, dressmakers, servants, and household apprentices.

104. Quoted in Dehn, *Proletarische Jugend,* 173.

105. Quoted in Dinse, *Freizeitleben,* 96.

106. Quoted in Dehn, *Proletarische Jugend,* 178.

107. Quoted in Carl Stockhaus, *Die Arbeiterjugend zwischen 14 und 18 Jahren* (Wittenberg, 1926), 65.

108. Quoted in ibid., 66.

Chapter 5

1. Peukert, *Jugend,* 30.

2. Maike Bruhns, "'Bauvolk der kommenden Welt': Arbeiterjugendbewegung," in *Vorwärts—und nicht vergessen: Arbeiterkultur in Hamburg um 1930* (Berlin, 1982), 175; Peukert, *Weimarer Republik,* 235.

3. Dick Geary, "Jugend, Arbeitslosigkeit, und politischer Radikalismus am Ende der Weimarer Republik," *Gewerkschaftliche Monatshefte* (1983), 304–9; Peukert, *Jugend*, 30–56; Stachura, *Proletariat*, 94–103.

4. Elisabeth Domansky and Ulrich Heinemann, "Jugend als Generationserfahrung: Das Beispiel der Weimarer Republik," *SOWI: Zeitschrift für Geschichte, Politik, Wirtschaft* (1984), 16–17; Jürgen Reulecke, "Jugend und 'junge Generation' in der Gesellschaft der Zwischenkriegszeit," in Christa Berg, ed., *Handbuch der deutschen Bildungsgeschichte, Band V (1918–1945)* (Munich, 1989), 86–110.

5. Donna Harsch, *German Social Democracy and the Rise of Nazism* (Chapel Hill, N.C., 1993), 129.

6. Larry E. Jones, "German Liberalism and the Alienation of the Younger Generation in the Weimar Republic," in Larry E. Jones and Konrad Jarausch, eds., *In Search of a Liberal Germany* (New York, 1990), 319–20.

7. Josef Goebbels, quoted in Hans Mommsen, "Generationskonflikt und Jugendrevolte in der Weimarer Republik," in Koebner et al., *Mit uns*, 59.

8. Thomas Childers, *The Nazi Voter* (Chapel Hill, N.C., 1986); Jürgen Falter, *Hitlers Wähler* (Munich, 1991).

9. As Detlev Peukert showed in his *Weimarer Republik*, this late Weimar trend toward authoritarianism was common among elites whose range of possible actions was becoming ever more restricted.

10. STL, Jugendamt Nr. 91: Anon., "Unsere Arbeit im Zeichen der Wirtschaftskrise," *Geschäfts-Bericht des Ortsausschusses Leipzig der Jugendverbände für die Zeit vom 1. April 1931 bis 31. März 1932*; STL, Jugendamt Nr. 45, Band I: Gau Sachsen im Reichsverband für Deutsche Jugendherbergen to Oberbürgermeister Dr. Goerdeler (January 23, 1931); Otto Reise, "Gefährdet das Zeltlagerwesen das Jugendherbergswerk?" *Das Junge Deutschland* (1931), 247; Münker, *Jugendherbergswerk*, 36.

11. Dinse, *Freizeitleben*, 101–2; Giesecke, *Wandervogel*, 140.

12. Alois Funk, *Film und Jugend* (Munich, 1934), 48.

13. Hirtsiefer, *Jugendpflege in Preußen*, 19, 226–27. Some 55 percent of girls and 68 percent of boys in Berlin went to the movies according to Funk, *Film und Jugend*, 49.

14. See Chapter 4, Table 4.2.

15. For example, the number of visitors to hostels in the Hannover area who went to an elementary or secondary school fell from 49 to 34 percent in 1932. The number of "others under twenty," who were most likely working-class youths, grew from 32 to 42 percent in the same period. The number of visitors over twenty also rose from 18 to 24 percent, another probable indicator of the influx of unemployed workers. NSHStAH, Hann. 174 Zellerfeld, Nr. 4579: Jahresbericht 1932 des Reichsverbandes für Deutsche Jugendherbergen, Gau Hannover (March 1933). The number of local subsidiaries of the Federation had reached 1,117 by 1932. There were 128,199 adult members and 2,760 hostels. Münker, *Jugendherbergswerk*, 29.

16. Quoted in Münker, *Jugendherbergswerk*, 89.

17. NSHStAH, Hann. 174 Zellerfeld, Nr. 4579: Vereinigung für Jugendwohlfahrt im Regierungsbezirk Hildesheim to Herren Vorsitzenden der Arbeitsämter im Reg.-Bezirk

Hildesheim, die Herren Landräte als Vorsitzende der Kreisausschüsse für Jugendpflege, die Herren Kreisjugendpfleger, die Jugendämter im Reg.-Bez. Hildesheim (July 9, 1931).

18. Hirtsiefer, *Jugendpflege in Preußen*, 19.

19. Quoted in STL, Jugendamt Nr. 313: *Leipziger Neueste Nachrichten* (September 15, 1932).

20. BayHStAM, MK 13828: Reichsminister des Innern to Reichskuratorium für Jugendertüchtigung (November 23, 1932). On organization, see BArch, R36/2013: "Erziehung zur Wehrhaftigkeit," *Börsen-Zeitung* (September 15, 1932), and "Militarisierung der Jugendpflege," *Vorwärts* (September 15, 1932); BayHStAM, MK 13828: Reichsminister des Innern to Landesregierungen (September 15, 1932).

21. BArch, R36/2013: "Organisierter Wehrsport," *Berliner Tageblatt* (September 15, 1932).

22. BayHStAM, MK 13828: Reichskuratorium für Jugendertüchtigung, "Entwurf! Richtlinien für die Ausbildung im Geländesport" (October 1932).

23. Kerl, "Pfingstlager in Bayern," *Der Pfadfinder* (1925), 183.

24. SAPMO-BArch, RY11/II 107/9: Sozialistische Arbeiterjugend Unterbezirk Döbeln to alle Ortsgruppen (July 29, 1929); STAM, PDM 5988: report of April 30, 1927.

25. Heinrich Voggenreiter, ed., *Deutsches Spielhandbuch, 2. Teil: Geländespiele/Scharkämpfe* (Potsdam, 1930), 14.

26. BayHStAM, MK 13828: "Richtlinien," 6.

27. Gerhard Wahrig, ed., *dtv-Wörterbuch der deutschen Sprache* (Munich, 1978), 336.

28. SAPMO-BArch, RY11/II 107/3: Verband der Sozialistischen Arbeiterjugend Deutschlands, Hauptvorstand (Erich Ollenhauer), Rundschreiben Nr. 49/1932 (October 5, 1932); BayHStAM, MK 13832: Reichsminister des Innern to Landesregierungen (October 22 and November 7, 1932).

29. Eric Michaud, "Soldiers of an Idea: Young People Under the Third Reich," in Levi and Schmitt, *History*, 2:263.

30. NSHStAH, Hann. 174 Zellerfeld, Nr. 4538: Der Regierungs-Präsident, Abt. für Kirchen und Schulen to die Landräte und Oberbürgermeister des Bezirks als Vorsitzende der Kreis- und Stadtausschüsse für Jugendpflege (November 27, 1933).

31. AdJb, A2-02: Stadtjugendpfleger Kaiser, "Beiträge zur Steglitzer Heimatwoche," *Steglitzer Anzeiger* (April 14, 1934); Josepha Fischer, *Die Mädchen in den deutschen Jugendverbände* (Leipzig, 1933), 24.

32. Giesecke, *Wandervogel*, 190.

33. NSHStAH, Hann. 174 Zellerfeld, Nr. 4538: protocol of a meeting of the district committee in Clausthal-Zellerfeld (January 9, 1934), Kreisfrauenschaftsleitung Clausthal-Zellerfeld, "Meine Erfahrungen, über den Mißerfolg des von der Regierung angeordneten Zusammenschlusses Nichtorganisierter weiblicher Jugend in der Stadt Clausthal-Zellerfeld" (December 13, 1934), and Bürgermeister Clausthal-Zellerfeld to Landrat des Kreises Zellerfeld (November 21, 1935).

34. STL, Jugendamt Nr. 91: "Grundsätze für die körperliche Beziehung der Jugend außerhalb der Schule," cited in *Zentralblatt* (May 1935), and *Sächsisches Verwaltungsblatt 1936, Teil I, Nr. 7*, 32.

35. IfZ, Db 44.76: Ernst Schlünder, "Die körperliche Erziehung in der Hitlerjugend," *Wille und Macht* (July 15 / August 1, 1936), 11.

36. Quoted in Arno Klönne, *Jugend im Dritten Reich: Die Hitler-Jugend und ihre Gegner* (Düsseldorf, 1982), 181.

37. STAM, PDM 6074: "Ein Mahnruf!" *Bayerischer Kurier* (February 17, 1933).

38. Unpublished letter from Ludwig Wolker to the dioceses, quoted in Olenhusen, *Jugendreich*, 75.

39. "Kardinal Pacelli in seiner Botschaft an die Jungmänner," *Der Jungführer* (1934), 7.

40. Double memberships in Catholic *Jugendpflege* groups and the *Hitler-Jugend* were not allowed, nor were organized Catholics allowed into the German Labor Front. See BArch R58/232: file entitled "Das katholische Vereinswesen: Die Organisation der katholischen Jugendvereine. Sonderbericht des SD-Hauptamtes, September, 1935." On the persecution of Catholic youth, see Klönne, *Jugend*, 183–87; Barbara Schellenberger, *Katholische Jugend und Drittes Reich: Die Geschichte des Katholischen Jungmännerverbandes, 1933–1939* (Mainz, 1975); Evi Kleinöder, "Verfolgung und Widerstand der katholischen Jugendvereine," in Martin Broszat et al., eds., *Bayern in der NS-Zeit* (Munich, 1979), 2:175–236.

41. "Anordnung des Reichsführers SS Himmler als Stellvertreter Chef und Inspekteur der preußischen Geheimen Staatspolizei und politischen Polizeikommandeur," in Matthias von Hellfeld and Arno Klönne, eds., *Die betrogene Generation: Jugend in Deutschland unter dem Faschismus* (Cologne, 1985), 49–50.

42. Quoted in Klönne, *Jugend*, 195.

43. IfZ, Fa 119/1: Geheime Staatspolizei, Staatspolizeileitstelle München to alle Staatspolizeistellen, Bezirksämter, Stadtkommissare (November 27, 1936).

44. STAM, LRA Freising 116520: Gestapo document of January 25, 1938, entitled "Auflösung katholischer Jugendverbände." None of these accusations were completely false. There had been an increase in banned practices of group exercise after 1935, and Catholic youths in many locales went so far as to distribute copies of Pius XI's forbidden anti-Nazi encyclical *Mit brennender Sorge* in 1937. Klönne, *Jugend*, 188–90.

45. Fischer, *Mädchen*, 10.

46. The groups incorporated were the *Deutsche Freischar, Freischar junger Nation, Geusen, Deutscher Pfadfinderbund, Ringgemeinschaft deutscher Pfadfinder, Ring deutscher Pfadfindergaue, Deutsches Pfadfinderkorps,* and *Freischar evangelischer Pfadfinder.*

47. AdJb, A2-54/1: Vizeadmiral von Trotha, "Leitsätze des Großdeutschen Bundes" (April 3, 1933).

48. AdJb, A2-54/3: Erich Küsel to Baldur von Schirach (May 11, 1933); AdJb, A2-54/1: Vizeadmiral a.D. von Trotha to Herrn Reichskanzler (April 29, 1933), and Vizeadmiral a.D. von Trotha to Adolf Hitler (May 22, 1933).

49. AdJb, A2-54/3: *Der deutsche Sturmtrupp* (May 1, 1933), quoted in "Verunglimpfungen der bündischen Jugend durch die Presse"; AdJb, A2-54/1: Anon., "Vernichtet die Bünde," *Junge Nation* (May 1933), quoted in Vizeadmiral a.D. von Trotha to Herrn Reichspräsidenten Generalfeldmarschall von Hindenburg (June 23, 1933).

50. AdJb, A2-54/1: Staatssekretär in der Reichskanzlei to Vizeadmiral a.D. von Trotha (June 1, 1933).

51. AdJb, A2-54/1: Adolf Hitler to Reichspräsidenten Hindenburg (June 15, 1933).

52. AdJb, A2-54/1: Vizeadmiral a.D. von Trotha to Herrn Reichspräsidenten Generalfeldmarschall von Hindenburg (June 23, 1933).

53. Klönne, *Jugend*, 81ff.

54. See Matthias von Hellfeld, *Bündische Jugend und Hitlerjugend: Zur Geschichte von Anpassung und Widerstand, 1930–1939* (Cologne, 1987).

55. Jürgen Zarusky, "Jugendopposition," in Wolfgang Benz et al., eds., *Lexikon des deutschen Widerstandes* (Frankfurt, 1994), 105–6.

56. One such leader, the communist sympathizer and head of the *Deutsche Jungenschaft 1.11.*, Eberhard Koebel, called on his twenty-five hundred followers in 1933 to join the HJ collectively as a kind of elite secret order. Members of Koebel's group exposed Hans Scholl to *bündische* ideas while he was in the HJ in the mid-1930s, thereby undermining the Nazis' influence on the young man. Scholl later was a founding member of the student resistance movement in Munich, the White Rose. The political police and Gestapo did their utmost to root out *"Jungenschaft* cells" of Koebel's followers in the HJ. See IfZ, Fa 119/1: Bayerische Politische Polizei to sämtliche Polizeidirektionen (June 4, 1935); Zarusky, "Jugendopposition," 105; Stachura, *Movement*, 61–62. Another subversive *bündische* group was the *Nerother Wandervögel* with about seven hundred members led by Robert Oelbermann. Stefan Krolle, *"Bündische Umtriebe": Die Geschichte des Nerother Wandervogels vor und unter dem NS-Staat* (Münster, 1986).

57. For example, Ro., "Bund und Bundesopfer," *Der Jungführer* (1935), 226–29.

58. Anon., "Jugend-Gegenwarts-Romantik," *Hitler-Jugend* (1928), 140.

59. Baldur von Schirach, *Die Hitler-Jugend: Idee und Gestalt* (Leipzig, 1934), 53.

60. Ibid., 13–15.

61. IfZ, Db 44.76: Friedrich Hymmen, "Vom Hohen Meissner nach Potsdam?" *Wille und Macht* (June 15, 1935), 13–19.

62. IfZ, Db 44.76: G. Mögling, "Bündische Jugend ist heute Bolshewismus," *Wille und Macht* (August 15, 1935), 16–19.

63. Rundschreiben Nr. 71 der Gestapo an alle Außenstellen (April 17, 1936), in Hellfeld and Klönne, *Generation*, 52, my italics.

64. Geoffrey Giles, "The Institutionalization of Homosexual Panic in the Third Reich," in Gellately and Stoltzfus, *Outsiders*, 233–50.

65. STAM, LRA 146308: file entitled "Erfassung der homosexuellen Personen (mit Personalien) im Landkreis Erding, 1934–1936"; Manfred Herzer, "Hinweise auf das schwule Berlin in der Nazizeit," in Michael Bollé, ed., *Eldorado: Homosexuelle Männer und Frauen in Berlin, 1850–1950* (Berlin, 1984), 47.

66. "Staatsfeinde sind auszumerzen!" *Informationsdienst* (June 20, 1938), quoted in Robert Proctor, *Racial Hygiene: Medicine Under the Nazis* (Cambridge, Mass., 1988), 212–13.

67. Decree of October 10, 1936, quoted in Hans-Georg Stümke, "From the 'People's Consciousness of Right and Wrong' to 'The Healthy Instincts of the Nation': The Persecution of Homosexuals in Nazi Germany," in Michael Burleigh, ed., *Confronting the Nazi Past* (New York, 1996), 159.

68. Arno Klönne, ed., *Jugendkriminalität und Jugendopposition im NS-Staat, kommentierter Nachdruck des Lageberichts der Reichsjugendführung "Kriminalität und Gefährdung der Jugend" vom 1.1.1941* (Münster, 1981), 113. The oppositional *Nerother Wandervögel,* for example, were subjected to this law. Their leader, Robert Oelbermann, was arrested in 1936, and in 1941 he was murdered in Dachau bearing the pink triangle. See Krolle, *"Umtriebe."*

69. The most useful studies of the Hitler Youth include Klönne, *Jugend;* Gerhard Rempel, *Hitler's Children: The Hitler Youth and the SS* (Chapel Hill, N.C., 1989); Dagmar Reese, *"Straff, aber nicht stramm—herb aber nicht derb": Zur Vergesellschaftung von Mädchen durch den Bund Deutscher Mädel im sozialkulturellen Vergleich zweier Milieus* (Weinheim, 1989); Hermann Langer, *"Im gleichen Schritt und Tritt": Die Geschichte der Hitlerjugend in Mecklenburg von den Anfängen bis 1945* (Rostock, 2001); Michael Buddrus, *Totale Erziehung für den totalen Krieg: Hitlerjugend und nationalsozialistische Jugendpolitik* (Munich, 2003); Michael Kater, *Hitler Youth* (Cambridge, Mass., 2004).

70. Another example is the incorporation of 235,000 Austrian and Sudeten German groups in 1938. Klönne, *Jugend,* 23, 32.

71. BArch, R36/2014: "Gesetz über die Hitlerjugend vom 1.12.1936," *Reichsgesetzblatt* (1936).

72. Klönne, *Jugend,* 71–81, 123, quote from 77.

73. Quoted in Hellfeld and Klönne, *Generation,* 189.

74. Baldur von Schirach, speech of November, 1933, quoted in Reese, *Straff,* 69; Albrecht Möller, *Wir werden das Volk: Wesen und Forderung der Hitler-Jugend* (Breslau, 1935), 118–19. See also IfZ, Db 44.02: "Lehr- und Stundenplan für dreiwöchige Führerlehrgänge an den HJ.-Führerschulen," in *Verordnungsblatt der Reichsjugendführung (Sonderdruck) Nr. 7, Abteilung E und S* (Berlin, 1934), 3–11, and Abteilung Schulung, ed., *Schulungsplan der Hitler-Jugend* (Berlin, 1934).

75. Quoted in Hellfeld and Klönne, *Generation,* 189, and in Elfriede Zill, "Die körperliche Schulung im BDM," in Hilde Munske, ed., *Mädel im Dritten Reich* (Berlin, 1936), 25.

76. Klönne, *Jugend,* 140.

77. Willi Hofmeister, *Leibesübungen und Geländesport als Erlebnis und Verpflichtung: Zur Neugestaltung des Schulturnens in der deutschen Volksschule,* 2d ed. (Leipzig, 1941), 9.

78. Wilhelm Münker, *Geschichte des Jugendherbergswerkes von 1933 bis 1945* (Bielefeld, 1946), 7.

79. Speech of April 10, quoted in Münker, *Geschichte,* 7, Lauterbacher's first name and the audience not specified.

80. Münker, *Geschichte,* 8–9.

81. Ernst Enzensperger, "Die Bayerischen Jugendherbergen unter der Führung der Hitler-Jugend," *Das bayerische Jugendherbergswerk* (May 8, 1933), 8; BayHStAM, MK 13992: Landesverband Bayern für Jugendwandern und Jugendherberge to Ministerium für Unterricht und Kultus (June 9, 1933).

82. See Münker, *Geschichte,* 57–97.

83. Ibid., 23; Max Kochkämpfer, *Herbergen der neuen Jugend* (Berlin, 1937).

84. Münker, *Geschichte*, 20. Münker gives no date for this decision.

85. IfZ, Db 44.34: DOBl. RJf IV/11 vom 15.5.1936, reprinted in Reichsjugendführung Personalamt-Überwachung, *Richtlinien für den Hitler-Jugend Streifendienst, Teil IV: Anhang—Sammlung von Gesetzen und Dienstbestimmungen vom 1. Juni 1938* (Berlin, 1938), 77, and Reichsjugendführung Personalamt-Überwachung, *Richtlinien für den Hitler-Jugend Streifendienst, Teil I vom 1. Juni 1938* (Berlin, 1938), 24–25, 35–36. Schirach established the *Streifendienst* in late 1933 as a method of self-surveillance by Hitler Youth members. There were some fifty thousand members by 1935. Klönne, *Jugend*, 262; Kater, *Hitler Youth*, 62. In addition to seeking out nonconforming youths, *Streifendienst* units were entrusted with controlling the behavior of the Hitler Youth. Their official duties were (1) checking HJ identification papers, (2) surveillance of trips by HJ members, (3) surveillance of HJ camps, (4) observation of the public behavior of HJ and BDM members, (5) surveillance of all HJ and BDM *Heime*, and (6) surveillance of youth hostels. Der Leiter der Personalabteilung im Gebiet Ruhr-Niederrhein 10 Düppe, Bannführer, "Die Aufgaben des HJ-Streifendienstes" (October 1937), reprinted in Hellfeld and Klönne, *Generation*, 301–3.

86. IfZ, Db 44.34: RB. RJf 41/II vom 26.11.1937, reprinted in Reichsjugendführung Personalamt-Überwachung, *Richtlinien, Teil IV*, 71; Münker, *Geschichte*, 20–23.

87. BArch, R36/2014: NSDAP Reichsjugendführung to Deutscher Gemeindetag (August 3, 1937).

88. See, e.g., STL, Jugendamt Nr. 335: Urteil des I. Senats des Volksgerichtshofs vom 28. 10. 1938.

89. Klönne, ed., *Jugendkriminalität*; Detlev Peukert, *Die Edelweißpiraten* (Cologne, 1983); Matthias von Hellfeld, *Edelweißpiraten in Köln* (Cologne, 1983); Wilfried Breyvogel, *Piraten, Swings, und Junge Garde: Jugendwiderstand im Nationalsozialismus* (Bonn, 1991); Birgid Ratzlaff, *Arbeiterjugend gegen Hitler* (Werther, 1993); Klönne, *Jugend*, 143–213.

90. Reprinted in Klönne, *Jugend*, 197.

91. Ibid.

92. "Wandern verboten!" and "Unterbindung des wilden Wanderbetriebes," reprinted in Hellfeld and Klönne, *Generation*, 317–19.

93. IfZ, Db 44.34: RB. RJf 29/II vom 6.8.1937, reprinted in Reichsjugendführung Personalamt-Überwachung, *Richtlinien, Teil IV*, 68.

94. IfZ, Db 44.34: RB. RJf 20/I vom 5.6.1936, reprinted in Reichsjugendführung Personalamt-Überwachung, *Richtlinien für den Hitler-Jugend Streifendienst, Teil IV: Anhang—Sammlung von Gesetzen und Dienstbestimmungen vom 1. Juni 1938* (Berlin, 1938), 59.

95. Reichsverband für deutsche Jugendherbergen, ed., *Fahrt: Erlebnisberichte deutscher Jungen und Mädel* (Berlin, 1938), no page number, my italics.

96. Heinrich Hauser, "Die Arbeitslosen," *Die Tat* (1933), 76, reprinted in Anton Kaes et al., eds., *The Weimar Republic Sourcebook* (Berkeley, 1994), 84.

97. IfZ, Db 44.34: DOBl. RJf Sonderdruck 7/37 vom 10.5.1937, and RB. RJf 4/III vom 4.2.1938, reprinted in Reichsjugendführung Personalamt-Überwachung, *Richtlinien für den Hitler-Jugend Streifendienst, Teil IV: Anhang—Sammlung von Gesetzen und Dienstbestimmungen vom 1. Juni 1938* (Berlin, 1938), 59–60, 66.

98. *Der ewige Jude* (1940 film directed by Fritz Hippler); Anon., *Die Wanderung und Verbreitung der Juden in der Welt* (Essen, 1938). See Wolfgang Wippermann, *Wie die Zigeuner: Antisemitismus und Antiziganismus im Vergleich* (Berlin, 1997).

99. Unnamed periodical of April 1937, quoted in Münker, *Geschichte*, 81.

100. IfZ, Fa 119/1: Bayerische Politische Polizei to alle Polizeidirektionen (January 10, 1936). (These rules applied nationwide.) On the Jewish youth movement, see Walter Angress, *Between Fear and Hope: Jewish Youth in the Third Reich* (New York, 1988).

101. IfZ, Db 44.42: Anon., "Jungvolkführer, das geht Dich an!" *Die Jungenschaft* (May 1935), 1.

102. STAM, PDM 6839: "Auszug aus dem Büchlein *Hammerschläge, Schriftenreihe der HJ 'Jungvolk'"*; Dr. Gerhard Ramlow, *Deutsche Jungens auf Fahrt* (Berlin, 1934), 10; Alfred Oberstadt, "Unsere Fahrt," in Reichsverband für deutsche Jugendherbergen, *Fahrt*, no page numbers.

103. Anon., "Wir bilden eine Gemeinschaft," in Gerda Zimmermann and Gretel Both, eds., *Jungmädels Welt, Heim, und Zelt* (Leipzig, 1934), 285; Johannes Rodatz, *Erziehung durch Erleben: Der Sinn des Deutschen Jugendherbergwerkes*, 2d ed. (Berlin, 1936), 17.

104. Zill, "Schulung," 27.

105. Oberstadt, "Unsere Fahrt," no page numbers.

106. Rodatz, *Erziehung*, 53.

107. See, e.g., IfZ, Db 44.42: Anon., "Lager im masurischen Waldsee," *Die Jungenschaft* (May 1935), 11–14.

108. Möller, *Wir werden*, 82.

109. Reichsjugendführung der NSDAP, "Der Dienst der Pflicht-Hitler-Jugend, Jahrgang 1923" (1941), reprinted in Hellfeld and Klönne, *Generation*, 205.

110. "NS-Weltanschauung im HJ-Lager," reprinted in Hellfeld and Klönne, *Generation*, 115–20.

111. BayHStAM, MK 13979: "Denkschrift des Ortsausschuß München für Jugendalpenwanderungen über organisatorische Notwendigkeiten im deutschen Jugendwandern" (1923).

Chapter 6

1. Konrad Guenther, *Die Heimatlehre vom Deutschtum und seiner Natur* (Leipzig, 1932), 12; BayHStAM, MK 51147: Konrad Guenther, "Naturschutz als Lehrfach," paraphrased in *Bayerische Staatszeitung und Bayerischer Staatsanzeiger* (December 10, 1930). My thanks to Sandra Chaney and Frank Uekötter for generously sharing their research with me during the final stage of revising this chapter.

2. Konrad Guenther, *Deutsches Naturerleben* (Stuttgart, 1935).

3. Bergmann, *Agrarromantik*, 361. See also Hermann Bausinger, "Zwischen Grün und Braun: Volkstumsideologie und Heimatpflege nach dem Ersten Weltkrieg," in Hubert Cancik, ed., *Religions- und Geistesgeschichte der Weimarer Republik* (Düsseldorf, 1982), 215–29; Linse, *Ökopax*; Michael Wettengel, "Staat und Naturschutz, 1906–1945: Zur Geschichte der Staatlichen Stelle für Naturschutz in Preußen und der Reichsstelle für Naturschutz," *Historische Zeitschrift* (1993), 355–99; Joachim Wolschke-Bulmann and

Gert Gröning, *Die Liebe zur Landschaft, Teil III: Der Drang nach Osten* (Munich, 1987). These arguments for straightforward continuities between pre-1933 and Nazi-era conservation were probably a necessary stage in the historiography, given that the postwar conservationist movement tended to whitewash its relationship with Nazism, e.g., Walther Schoenichen, *Naturschutz, Heimatschutz: Ihre Begründung durch Ernst Rudorff, Hugo Conwetz, und ihre Vorläufer* (Stuttgart, 1954); Hans Klose, *Fünfzig Jahre Staatlicher Naturschutz: Ein Rückblick auf den Weg der deutschen Naturschutzbewegung* (Gießen, 1957).

4. Anna Bramwell, *Ecology in the Twentieth Century* (New Haven, Conn., 1989), and *The Fading of the Greens* (New Haven, Conn., 1994); Alston Chase, *In a Dark Wood: The Fight over Forests and the New Tyranny of Ecology* (Boston, 1995).

5. John Muir, "The Wild Parks and Forest Reservations of the West," *Atlantic Monthly* (January 1898), 15, quoted in Thomas Dunlap, *Nature and the English Diaspora: Environment and History in the United States, Canada, Australia, and New Zealand* (Cambridge, 1999), 106.

6. John R. Short, *Imagined Country: Society, Culture, and Environment* (London, 1991); Kenneth Olwig, *Nature and the Body Politic: From Britain's Renaissance to America's New World* (Madison, Wis., 2002).

7. Quoted in Kenneth Olwig, "Reinventing Common Nature: Yosemite and Mount Rushmore—A Meandering Tale of a Double Nature," in Cronon, *Uncommon Ground*, 393.

8. Raymond Dominick, *The Environmental Movement in Germany: Prophets and Pioneers, 1871–1971* (Bloomington, Ind., 1992); Andreas Knaut, *Zurück zur Natur! Die Wurzeln der Ökologiebewegung* (Greven, 1993); Danny Trom, "Natur und nationale Identität: Der Streit um den Schutz der 'Natur' um die Jahrhundertwende in Deutschland und Frankreich," in Etienne François et al., eds., *Nation und Emotion* (Göttingen, 1995), 178–206; Williams, "Chords," and "Protecting Nature"; Karl Ditt, "Naturschutz zwischen Zivilisationskritik, Tourismusförderung, und Umweltschutz: USA, England, und Deutschland, 1860–1970," in Matthias Frese and Michael Prinz, eds., *Politische Zäsuren und Gesellschaftlicher Wandel im 20. Jahrhundert* (Paderborn, 1996), 499–533, and "Die Anfänge der Naturschutzgesetzgebung in Deutschland und England, 1935/49," in Radkau and Uekötter, *Naturschutz*, 107–44; Rollins, *Greener Vision*; Franz-Josef Brüggemeier, *Tschernobyl, 26. April 1986: Die ökologische Herausforderung* (Munich, 1998); Kiran Patel, "Neuerfindung des Westens—Aufbruch nach Osten: Naturschutz und Landschaftsgestaltung in den Vereinigten Staaten von Amerika und in Deutschland, 1900–1945," *Archiv für Sozialgeschichte* (2003), 191–221; Friedemann Schmoll, *Erinnerungen an die Natur: Die Geschichte des Naturschutzes im Kaiserreich* (Frankfurt, 2004); Lekan, *Imagining*. Cross sections of recent scholarship that investigate the relationship between conservation and Nazism are Radkau and Uekötter, *Naturschutz*, and Franz-Josef Brüggemeier et al., eds., *How Green Were the Nazis? Nature, Environment, and the Nation in the Third Reich* (Athens, Ohio, 2005). The most thoroughly researched works on *Naturschutz* under the Third Reich are Willi Oberkrome, *"Deutsche Heimat": Nationale Konzeption und regionale Praxis von Naturschutz, Landschaftsgestaltung, und Kulturpolitik in Westfalen-Lippe und Thüringen (1900–1960)* (Paderborn, 2004); and Frank Uekötter, *The Green and*

the Brown: A History of Conservation in Nazi Germany (Cambridge, 2006). Thanks to Uekötter for sending me a copy of his book during my final revision in Berlin in the fall of 2006. Unavailable to me at the time of writing were Brüggemeier et al., *How Green*, and Oberkrome, *Deutsche Heimat*; but see my reviews of both at www.h-net.org/reviews in 2006 and 2007.

9. Some significant exceptions—that is, conservationists who clung to a Romantic and anti-industrialist viewpoint—may be found on the regional level, as Thomas Lekan demonstrates in *Imagining*.

10. Ernst Rudorff, *Heimatschutz* (Berlin, 1926, orig. 1897), 53, 74.

11. See Jürgen Kocka, ed., *Bürger und Bürgerlichkeit im 19. Jahrhundert* (Göttingen, 1987).

12. On the *Deutscher Bund Heimatschutz*, which had about thirty thousand members by 1914, see NSHStAH, Hann. 122a, Nr. 4481: file entitled "Der Bund Heimatschutz und dessen Zweigvereine, 1906–1942"; Knaut, *Zurück zur Natur*; Rollins, *Greener Vision*. On preservationism in general, see Applegate, *Nation of Provincials*; Alon Confino, *The Nation as a Local Metaphor: Württemberg, Imperial Germany, and National Memory, 1871–1918* (Chapel Hill, N.C., 1997); Rudy Koshar, *Germany's Transient Pasts: Preservation and National Memory in the Twentieth Century* (Chapel Hill, N.C., 1998).

13. Quoted in Sieferle, *Fortschrittsfeinde*, 167.

14. Quoted in Linse, *Ökopax*, 23. See Norbert Borrmann, *Paul Schultze-Naumburg, 1869–1949* (Essen, 1989).

15. Quoted in Gesellschaft der Freunde des Deutschen Heimatschutzes, ed., *Der deutsche Heimatschutz* (Munich, 1930), 187–88.

16. Rollins, *Greener Vision*.

17. NSHStAH, Hann. 174 Zellerfeld, Nr. 3522: "Schutz der Natur und Bund Naturschutz" (1909).

18. Rollins, *Greener Vision*, attempts without success to cast the *Heimatschutz* movement as socially and politically progressive. See my review of Rollins in *Central European History* (1999), 345–49. On nature aesthetics in European conservationism, see Olwig, "Reinventing," 379–408; James Winter, *Secure from Rash Assault: Sustaining the Victorian Environment* (Berkeley, 1999); James Sievert, *The Origins of Nature Conservation in Italy* (New York, 2000); Robert Lambert, *Contested Mountains: Nature, Development, and Environment in the Cairngorms Region of Scotland, 1880–1980* (Cambridge, 2001). See also Richard Grove, *Green Imperialism: Colonial Expansion, Tropical Island Edens, and the Origins of Environmentalism* (Cambridge, 1995); Douglas Weiner, *A Little Corner of Freedom: Russian Nature Protection from Stalin to Gorbachev* (Berkeley, 1999); Ramachandra Guha, *Environmentalism: A Global History* (New York, 2000).

19. Ulrich Linse, "'Der Raub des Rheingoldes': Das Wasserkraftwerk Laufenberg," in Ulrich Linse et al., *Von der Bittschrift zur Platzbesetzung: Konflikte um technische Großprojekte* (Berlin, 1988), 11–62.

20. Ludwig Bolgiano, "Isartal und Isartalverein," *Das Bayernland* (1925), 435–38; Karl Berchtold, "Der Isartalverein und sein Arbeitsgebiet," *Das Bayernland* (1927), 449–54.

21. The vast majority were schoolteachers, professors, lawyers, doctors, forestry

experts, and writers, with a small percentage of aristocrats. BayHStAM, MK 51192: file entitled "Lehrgänge für Naturdenkmalpflege veranstaltet von der Staatlichen Stelle für Naturdenkmalpflege in Preußen, 1924–1927"; STAM, LRA München 19702: file entitled "Naturschutz, Allgemeines 1909–1945"; Knaut, *Zurück zur Natur!*

22. Karl Ditt, "Die Anfänge der Naturschutzgesetzgebung in Deutschland und England 1935/49," in Radkau and Uekötter, *Naturschutz*, 113.

23. Hugo Conwentz, *Die Gefährdung der Naturdenkmäler und Vorschläge zu ihrer Erhaltung* (Berlin, 1904), quote from 82.

24. Ministerium der geistlichen und Unterrichts-Angelegenheiten, "Grundsätze für die Wirksamkeit der Staatlichen Stelle für Naturdenkmalpflege in Preußen" (Oktober 2, 1906), reprinted in Hugo Conwentz, *Merkbuch für Naturdenkmalpflege und verwandte Bestrebungen* (Berlin, 1918), 97–99.

25. Eduard von Reuter, "Über die Organisation des Naturschutzes in Bayern," *Beiträge zur Naturdenkmalpflege* (1926), 427–28; BayHStAM, MK 14475: Bayerisches Ministerium des Innern to Ministerium für Unterricht und Kultus (February 7, 1924). The quote from a meeting of participating Bavarian ministries is in Arne Andersen and Reinhard Falter, "'Lebensreform' und 'Heimatschutz,'" in Friedrich Prinz and Marita Kraus, eds., *München, Musenstadt mit Hinterhöfen: Die Prinzregentenzeit* (Munich, 1988), 299.

26. There were only occasional exceptions. The president of Hannover province in Prussia, for example, called in 1912 for the preservation of the landscape through "considerate planning of transportation routes" and directed his underlings to solicit input from conservationists during the planning of new roads. It seems doubtful that local authorities put this directive into practice, however, given the dominant ethos that technological progress should always take precedence over *Naturschutz*. NSHStAH, Hann. 174 Zellerfeld, Nr. 3522: Regierungs-Präsident in Hildesheim to the Herren Landräte (July 13, 1912).

27. See, e.g., Prof. Dr. Bestelmeyer, "Die künstlerische Gestaltung von Ingenieurbauten," *Mitteilungen des Landesvereins Sächsischer Heimatschutz* (1911–12), 90–104.

28. Quoted in Schoenichen, *Naturschutz*, 279.

29. Verein Naturschutzpark, *Der erste deutsche Naturschutzpark in der Lüneburger Heide* (Stuttgart, 1912); Dominick, *Movement*, 53–55.

30. BayHStAM, MK 14475: "Denkschrift für die Errichtung eines Naturschutzgebietes am Königsee," *Blätter für Naturschutz und Naturpflege* (May 1920); BayHStAM, MK 40501: Bayerischer Landesausschuß für Naturpflege, *Jahresbericht XI–XVIII (1916–1923)*; Reinhard Falter, "Achtzig Jahre 'Wasserkrieg': Das Walchenseekraftwerk," in Linse et al., *Bittschrift*.

31. NSHStAH, Hann. 174 Zellerfeld, Nr. 3522: Staatliche Stelle für Naturdenkmalpflege in Preußen, "Über die Notwendigkeit der Schaffung von Moorschutzgebieten" (1916), quoted in "Sicherung von Naturdenkmälern bei der bevorstehenden Kultivierung der Ödländereien. Denkschrift überreicht von der Staatlichen Stelle für Naturdenkmalpflege in Preußen" (1919), 2. The fact that conservationists would agitate against feeding the undernourished population is yet another indicator of their elitism.

32. Applegate, *Nation of Provincials*, 108–19; Willi Oberkrome, "'Kerntruppen' in

'Kampfzeiten': Entwicklungstendenzen des deutschen Naturschutzes im Ersten und Zweiten Weltkrieg," *Archiv für Sozialgeschichte* (2003), 228–32; Lekan, *Imagining*, 74–85.

33. Quoted in Schoenichen, *Naturschutz*, 257.

34. Dr. Hans Klose and Dr. M. Hilzheimer, "Zur Einführung," *Naturdenkmalpflege und Naturschutz in Berlin und Brandenburg* (1929), 3; statutes of the *Volksbund Naturschutz*, reprinted in ibid., 30; Anon., "Fünf Jahre Volksbund Naturschutz!" *Naturschutz* (1927), 230–35; Dominick, *Movement*, 84.

35. NSHStAH, Hann. 174 Zellerfeld, Nr. 3522: "Sicherung von Naturdenkmälern bei der bevorstehenden Kultivierung der Ödländereien: Denkschrift überreicht von der Staatlichen Stelle für Naturdenkmalpflege in Preußen" (1919).

36. BayHStAM, MK 14475: Bayerisches Ministerium des Innern to Ministerium für Unterricht und Kultus (September 24, 1921).

37. For instance, STAM, LRA München 19708: *Isartalverein* and *Bund Naturschutz in Bayern* to Bezirksamt München-Land (December 16, 1924), requesting woodland protection in the Isar Valley, and Bezirksamt to *Isartalverein* and *BNB* (May 12, 1926). On the size of *Naturdenkmäler*, see Ditt, "Anfänge," 114.

38. Ditt, "Anfänge," 114–16.

39. Bernd Weisbrod, "The Crisis of Bourgeois Society in Interwar Germany," in Richard Bessel, ed., *Fascist Italy and Nazi Germany* (Cambridge, 1996), 23–39, quote from 29.

40. BayHStAM, MK 40501: *Bayerischer Landesausschuß für Naturpflege, Jahresbericht XI–XVIII (1916–1923)*.

41. See, e.g., Walther Schoenichen, "Die Verrummelung der Natur," *Naturschutz* (1929–30), 132–37, 157–65.

42. Konrad Guenther, *Der Naturschutz* (Stuttgart, 1919, orig. Freiburg, 1912), iii–iv, 13.

43. Anon., "Fünf Jahre," 231.

44. The Forest Association eventually managed to convince President von Hindenburg to join by presenting itself as a "border watch" against the Czechs, whose sinister purpose, they claimed, was to smuggle in foreign influence under the seemingly harmless guise of tourism. BayHStAM, MInn 73602: Wugg Retzer to the son of President von Hindenburg (April 16, 1932); BayHStAM, MK 51152: Reichminister des Innern to Ministerialrat Sperr (January 26, 1925).

45. BayHStAM, MK 14930: Reichsschulkonferenz 1920, Leitsätze über Schule und Heimat (June 16, 1920); "Leitsätze der 5. Tagung des Reichsschulausschusses vom 27. bis 29.4.1922," quoted in Klaus Goebel, "Der Heimatkundeunterricht in den deutschen Schulen," in Edeltraud Klueting, ed., *Antimodernismus und Reform: Zur Geschichte der deutschen Heimat bewegung* (Darmstadt, 1991), 98.

46. Eduard Spranger, "Der Bildungswert der Heimatkunde," in *Handbuch der Heimaterziehung* (1923), 20–21.

47. Anon., "Fünf Jahre," 231; BayHStAM, MK 51166: "Kurze Darlegung der Entstehung des Nordbayerischen Verbandes für Heimatpflege und Heimatforschung" (c. 1925).

48. BayHStAM, MK 51152: Der Kreistag des Kreises Schwaben und Neuburg to Landesamt für Denkmalpflege München (November 16, 1929).

49. Spranger, "Bildungswert," 7.

50. Quoted in Hugo Conwentz, *Heimatkunde und Heimatschutz in der Schule* (Berlin, 1922), 5–6.

51. Heinrich Hassinger, "Heimat und Volk," *Wandern und Schauen* (November 1929), 3.

52. Ibid., 4.

53. BayHStAM, MK 51147: Richard Weinmann to Bayerisches Ministerium für Unterricht und Kultus (September 29, 1930). In addition to the influential conservationists Werner Lindner and Walter Schoenichen, the GFDHS counted among its members high-ranking governmental ministers and legislative figures; several clergymen of both the Protestant and Catholic churches; lawyers and members of the judiciary; professors; authors; journalists; aristocrats; museum directors; industrialists; military officers; and even Konrad Adenauer, then mayor of Cologne. Introduction to GFDHS, *Heimatschutz*, 6–8.

54. Karl Wagenfeld, "Industrie und Volkstum," in ibid., 73.

55. See, e.g., Karl Wagenfeld, "Heimatschutz Volkssache," *Heimatschutz* (Winter 1925–26), 1. More research is needed on the extent of anti-Semitism, both overt and latent, in conservationism between 1920 and 1940. Friedemann Schmoll, "Die Verteidigung organischer Ordnungen: Naturschutz und Antisemitismus zwischen Kaiserreich und Nationalsozialismus," in Radkau and Uekötter, *Naturschutz*, 169–82, is suggestive but fails to provide strong evidence that anti-Semitism was latent throughout conservation discourse during the 1920s. I have found examples only in Wagenfeld's writings, though this of course does not mean that anti-Semitism might not have been latent in other conservationists.

56. Eugen Fischer, "Mensch und Familie," in GFDHS, *Heimatschutz*, 35. Fischer, the Catholic director of the *Kaiser Wilhelm Institut für Anthropologie, menschliche Erblehre und Eugenik* in Berlin, coauthored the standard eugenics textbook of the 1920s, Erwin Baur, Eugen Fischer, and Fritz Lenz, *Grundriss der menschlichen Erblichkeitslehre und Rassenhygiene* (Munich, 1921).

57. Karl Hahm, "Heimatschutz und Heimatpflege," in GFDHS, *Heimatschutz*, 90.

58. Karl Giannoni, "Heimat und Volkserziehung," in ibid., 60.

59. Anton Helbok, "Mensch und Volk," in ibid., 17.

60. Regional *Heimat* and conservation organizations often retained their emphasis on the local homeland. See Applegate, *Nation of Provincials*; Lekan, *Imagining*. Still, they came under increasing pressure in the early 1930s to conform their rhetoric to the nationalist conception of *Heimat*.

61. This trend did not go completely uncontested, and there are rare examples of conservationists who offered relatively sophisticated ecological analyses in favor of natural diversity. See, for instance, Heinrich Kraft, "Natur und Mensch," in GFDHS, *Heimatschutz*, 9–11.

62. Guenther, *Naturschutz*, 3, 111, 275; Konrad Guenther, "10 Leitsätze für den Deutschen und seine Heimatnatur," *Naturschutz* (1926), 319–20.

63. Guenther, *Heimatlehre*, 8, 16.

64. Giannoni, "Volkserziehung," 57.

65. It is also evident in various writings concerning the rational exploitation of natural resources, e.g., Alfons Diener von Schönberg, "Des deutschen Waldes Not," *Mitteilungen des Landesvereins sächsischer Heimatschutz* (1932), no page numbers.

66. Paul Schultze-Naumburg, *Die Entstellung unseres Landes*, 3d ed. (Meiningen, 1909), 70–71.

67. Walther Schoenichen, "Aus der Entwicklung der Naturdenkmalpflege," in GFDHS, *Heimatschutz*, 226.

68. Richard Weinmann, *Von der Kulturmission der Heimatarbeit* (Windsheim, 1932), 15. Lekan, *Imagining*, implies that regional *Heimatschutz* organizations retained the earlier meaning of "landscape care" even into the Nazi era and used it to resist the state's destruction of the landscape. The point is well taken; but there is also evidence that at least some regional conservationists followed national leaders in advocating "cultivation." One Bavarian, for example, announced that humanity has a "natural right to dig the signs of his existence, culture, and civilization into the landscape." Georg Wolf, "Industriebauten in der Landschaft," *Blätter für Naturschutz und Naturpflege* (1929), 38.

69. Hans Schwenkel, "Gegner des Heimatschutzes," *Naturschutz* (1930–31), 27; Friedrich Hassler, "Heimatschutz und Technik," in GFDHS, *Heimatschutz*, 186; Carl Fuchs, "Heimatschutz und Volkswirtschaft," in ibid., 152.

70. Dominick, *Movement*, 114. Frank Uekötter has recently criticized an earlier version of my argument about the basic change in conservationist ideology in late Weimar (presented in Williams, "Protecting Nature"). Uekötter maintains that I underestimate the organizational and ideological complexity of late Weimar conservationism and thus make an unconvincing assertion about general ideological change: "It seems highly unlikely that a large, disparate, and structurally conservative group like the conservationists could uniformly change their perception of nature within a few years. The publications Williams cites could scarcely have produced such a dramatic shift, and it seems doubtful that any kind of treatise could have led to such a fundamental change of mind" (Frank Uekötter, "Green Nazis? Reassessing the Environmental History of Nazi Germany," *German Studies Review* [2007], 269). This critique is based on a fundamental misunderstanding of my argument. Nowhere do I assert that *every* conservationist underwent the same transformation; nor do I ever maintain that certain texts caused the change. Instead, my position on the conservationist texts discussed here is that they gave expression to the changing ideology. I do not think that Uekötter can effectively deny that there was an important shift in conservationist thinking in the late 1920s and early 1930s, despite the organizational variety of the movement.

71. Ibid., 96–102; Wettengel, "Naturschutz," 379–81.

72. Thomas Lekan, "Regionalism and the Politics of Landscape Preservation in the Third Reich," *Environmental History* (1999), 391ff. Yet there is evidence of considerable state concern regarding regionalist organizations. For instance, the president of Lower Saxony in early 1934 pointed to the existence of local *Heimat* organizations as a threat to the centralization of the state's power. See NSHStAH, Hann. 174 Fallingbostel, Nr. 2/3: Regierungspräsident Niedersachsens to the Oberpräsidealen in Hannover (December 2,

1934). Leaders of regional *Heimatschutz* organizations sometimes used the centralizing impetus against their competitors, denouncing as traitors any individuals or groups that insisted on the continued celebration of the regional homeland. See, for example, the documentation of Richard Weinmann's attack against the president of the Franconian League for the latter's "one-sided stress on the tribal idea" in BayHStAM, MK 51166: file entitled "Heimatpflege und Heimatforschung. Nordbayerischer Verband in Nürnberg, 1925–1939." For a list of some of the many organizations in the *Reichsbund*, which allegedly contained over 4 million people by early 1934, see Anon., "Grundlage und Aufbau des Reichsbundes Volkstum und Heimat," *Volkstum und Heimat* (1934), 18–19.

73. STAM, LRA Wolfratshausen 41918: Dr. R. Wiesend, "Die Kulturaufgaben des Landbürgermeisters im neuen Reiche," reprint from *Blätter für Naturschutz und Naturpflege* (November 1933).

74. Walther Schoenichen, *Naturschutz im Dritten Reich* (Berlin, 1934), 2–3.

75. Konrad Guenther, "Die Heimat der deutschen Frau: Naturverbundenheit als Erbe der Vorfahren," *Unser Vaterland: Monatsschrift für alle Deutschen* (1933), 1–19.

76. Quoted in BayHStAM, MK 51195: Bayerischer Landesausschuß für Naturpflege and Bayerischer Landesverein für Heimatschutz to Staatsministerium für Wirtschaft (February 4, 1935). I do not know when exactly Hitler expressed this sentiment.

77. Schoenichen, *Reich*, 1, 5. Schoenichen's writings in the Third Reich are also interesting in that they sometimes attempted to combine fundamentally incompatible elements of neo-Romantic nature worship and social darwinism. He glorified natural diversity at the same time as he idealized the homogeneity and "purity" of the German race. See especially Walther Schoenichen, *Urwaldwildnis in deutschen Landen: Bilder vom Kampf des deutschen Menschen mit der Urlandschaft* (Berlin, 1934). For an analysis of Schoenichen's writings on "primeval wilderness," see Ludwig Fischer, "Die 'Urlandschaft' und ihr Schutz," in Radkau and Uekötter, *Naturschutz*, 183–206. Anna Bramwell, *Richard Walther Darré and Hitler's "Green Party"* (Abbotsbrook, U.K., 1985), attempts to show that Darré led a "green wing" of the Nazi Party. In an effective rebuttal, Gesine Gerhard shows that the concept of *Boden* had no specific ecological meaning for Darré; rather, it was a metaphor for peasant "rootedness" and "settledness." These characteristics were, in turn, preconditions for "Nordic blood." The concept of nature itself hardly appears in Darré's writings, although he had a "very limited" interest in organic farming. Gesine Gerhard, "Richard Walther Darré—Naturschutzer oder 'Rassenzüchter'?" in Radkau and Uekötter, *Naturschutz*, 257–72. See also Mark Bassin, "Blood or Soil? The *Völkisch* Movement, the Nazis, and the Legacy of Geopolitik," in Brüggemeier et al., *How Green*, 204–42.

78. Lekan, *Imagining*, 153 ff.

79. Dr. Ilse Waldenburg, "Naturschutz einst und jetzt," *Volkstum und Heimat* (1936), 99.

80. Schoenichen, *Reich*, 75–77.

81. Of eighteen prominent conservationists surveyed by Dominick, only Paul Schultze-Naumburg joined the NSDAP before 1933, and nine joined afterward, including Schoenichen in March 1933. On party membership, see Dominick, *Movement*, 81–115.

Interestingly, Hans Klose never joined the NSDAP, yet he played a prominent role in the Third Reich. As Uekötter points out, Klose's story shows that "one did not have to be an ideological fanatic to cooperate with the Nazis" (*Green*, 208). Schultze-Naumburg is well known to historians of Weimar culture for his hatred of avant-garde modernism. Raging against the Bauhaus, Schultze-Naumburg contrasted "traditional German" architecture from around 1800 to that of "nomads of the metropolis," such as Walter Gropius. Around the time of his entry into the Nazi *Kampfbund für Deutsche Kultur* in 1928, his attack on modernism began to include a vile demonization of people with mental and physical handicaps. See Paul Schultze-Naumburg, *Kunst und Rasse* (Berlin, 1928).

82. Schoenichen, *Reich*, i.

83. BayHStAM, MK 40501: Bund Naturschutz in Bayern to Bayerisches Staatsministerium für Unterricht und Kultus (May 4, 1933); Schoenichen, *Reich*, i.

84. Schoenichen, *Reich*, 5, 81–84; Walther Schoenichen, *Taschenbuch der in Deutschland geschützen Tiere* (Berlin, 1939), iv.

85. Klose was "honorary adviser on *Naturschutz*" in the Reich Forestry Office at the time.

86. On the law's relationship to previous Prussian laws and decrees, see BayHStAM, StK 7511: "Vorläufige Begründung zum Entwurf eines Naturschutzgesetzes" (February 1935), sent by Reichsjustizminister Gürtner to Länderregierungen, Reichsjustizministerium Abteilungen in Hamburg, Dresden, Munich, Stuttgart, Oberlandesgerichtspräsidenten in Darmstadt und Braunschweig. On the complicated history of the law and Göring's role, see Edeltraud Klueting, "Die gesetzlichen Regelungen der nationalsozialistischen Reichsregierung für den Tierschutz, den Naturschutz, und den Umweltschutz," in Radkau and Uekötter, *Naturschutz*, 92–97; Charles Closmann, "Legalizing a *Volksgemeinschaft*: Nazi Germany's Reich Nature Protection Law of 1935," in Brüggemeier et al., *How Green*, 18–42; Uekötter, *Green*, 61–69.

87. BayHStAM, MK 51183: Reichsnaturschutzgesetz (June 26, 1935), 1.

88. BayHStAM, StK 7511: "Vorläufige Begründung zum Entwurf eines Naturschutzgesetzes" (February 1935); BayHStAM, Reichsstatthalter 667: "Verordnung zur Durchführung des Reichsnaturschutzgesetzes" (October 31, 1936).

89. "Verordnung zur Durchführung," 1.

90. Werner Weber and Walther Schoenichen, *Das Reichsnaturschutzgesetz vom 26. Juni 1935* (Berlin, 1936), 31.

91. Considerable uncertainty remains over the increase in the number of *Naturschutzgebiete* under the Nazis. According to the best estimates, by 1940 some four hundred conservation areas had been added to the approximately four hundred that already existed in 1932. I have yet to find any reliable numbers for the war years. See Gert Gröning, "Naturschutz und Nationalsozialismus," in Klaus-Peter Lorenz, ed., *Politische Landschaft—die andere Sicht auf die natürliche Ordnung* (Duisburg, 2002), 159–87; Klueting, "Regelungen," 101. According to Uekötter, this confusion arose because conservationists were drowning in the bureaucratic red tape spawned by hundreds of local projects and therefore were not able to compile accurate lists. This would explain why not even Hans Klose was willing to give specific numbers in "Fünf Jahre Reichsnaturschutzgesetz,"

Der märkische Naturschutz (October 1940), 317–24, and "Von unserer Arbeit während des Krieges und über Nachkriegsaufgaben," *Naturschutz* (April 1944), 2–5. The reader is reminded that Hitler himself called on July 9, 1940, for continued public access to all existing conservation areas and parks, probably with the intention of giving citizens the sense that despite the war, things were going fine (see Introduction). This may have boosted local wartime conservation efforts. However, I would infer from the little existing evidence that the number of protected areas added during the war was not very impressive. We are left only with the impressions gleaned from the lists, in regional *Naturschutz* journals, of newly protected monuments and areas. According to a 1942 issue of the Brandenburg conservation journal, for example, three new conservation areas had recently been established and several towns had protected "monuments," such as old trees. However, seven towns had removed similar monuments from protection. *Der märkische Naturschutz* (April 1942), 19.

92. Uekötter, *Green*, 142.

93. Dr. Ilse Waldenburg, "Ein Blick in das Reichsnaturschutzbuch," *Volkstum und Heimat* (1936), 299–301; Klueting, "Regelungen," 99–104.

94. BayHStAM, StK 7511: Der Reichs- und Preußische Arbeitsminister to (a) die Landesregierungen (Sozialverwaltungen), (b) den Herrn Reichskommissar für das Saarland (March 22, 1938); BayHStAM, Reichsstatthalter 667: "Beachtung des P. 20 des Reichsnaturschutzgesetz. All.Bfg. 8 d. Rfm. u. Pr. Lfm. vom 22.1.1938."

95. Hans Klose admitted as much late in the war. He looked forward to a postwar era in which "[we will] return to a time when we no longer come up against polite refusals. 'Dear friend, what you are asking for is under the circumstances unimportant.' (Less friendly: 'YOU have problems!')." Klose, "Arbeit," 3.

96. Uekötter, *Green*, 144. With a couple of important exceptions, there is a striking lack of clear evidence that the indemnity clause was used in specific negotiations with property owners. Uekötter interprets this lack as a sign that conservationists shied away from a clause that they may well have considered unfair. The state had no such compunctions when it refused to compensate a mining company after declaring the Hohenstoffeln mountain in Baden a protected area in 1939. Ibid., 85–99.

97. Waldenburg, "Naturschutz," 98.

98. Quoted in Weber and Schoenichen, *Reichsnaturschutzgesetz*, 31.

99. BayHStAM, Reichsstatthalter 667: "Beachtung des P. 20 des Reichsnaturschutzgesetz. Allgemeine Befugnis 8 des Reichsforstmeisters und Preußischen Landesforstmeisters vom 22.1.1938"; "Zweite Verordnung zur Änderung und Ergänzung der Naturschutzverordnung," in *Reichsgesetzblatt Teil I vom 1. April 1940* (March 16, 1940); Klueting, "Regelungen," 99.

100. BayHStAM, MK 51195: Bund Naturschutz in Bayern to Bayerisches Staatsministerium für Unterricht und Kultus (February 19, 1936); Bayerisches Staatsministerium für Wirtschaft to Firma Kraftzug-Bedarf H. Krienes & Co. (May 6, 1936).

101. BayHStAM, Reichsstatthalter 667: Georg Priehäusser and Fritz Doehling to Reichsforstmeister Göring (January 15, 1936), "Antrag auf Schaffung des 'Reichsnaturschutzgebietes Bayrischer Wald,'" and Bayerischer Ministerpräsident, Landesforstwaltung

to Herrn Reichsforstmeister (July 9, 1936); BayHStAM, StK 7511: Reichsstatthalter in Bayern, Planungsreferat to the Bayerische Landesstelle für Naturschutz, München (January 26, 1939). For other, more detailed case studies, see Uekötter, *Green*, 83–136.

102. NSHStAH, Hann. 174 Zellerfeld, Nr. 3522: Walther Schoenichen, *Aufforstung? Jawohl! Aber mit Bedacht!* (Berlin, 1934), and Alwin Seifert, "Die Gefährdung der Lebensgrundlagen des dritten Reiches durch die heutigen Arbeitsweisen des Kultur- und Wasserbaus" (August 13, 1935); Walther Schoenichen, *Appell der deutschen Landschaft an den Arbeitsdienst* (Berlin, 1933), 3–8.

103. Quoted in Wettengel, "Naturschutz," 386. See also Heinrich Rübner, *Deutsche Forstgeschichte, 1933–1945: Forstwirtschaft, Jagd, und Umwelt im NS-Staat* (St. Katharinen, 1985); Michael Imort, "'Eternal Forest—Eternal Volk': The Rhetoric and Reality of National Socialist Forest Policy," in Brüggemeier et al., *How Green*, 43–72.

104. Klueting, "Regelungen," 88–92; Brüggemeier, *Tschernobyl*, 167–72; Uekötter, *Green*, 167–83.

105. Werner Lindner, "Heimatraum als Grundlage gesunden Volkstums," *Volkstum und Heimat* (1935), 89–90.

106. David Blackbourn, "'Die Natur als historisch zu etablieren': Natur, Heimat, und Landschaft in der modernen deutschen Geschichte," in Radkau and Uekötter, *Naturschutz*, 68.

107. Ditt, "Anfänge," 123–24.

108. See Dietmar Klenke, "Autobahnbau und Naturschutz in Deutschland: Eine Liaison von Nationalpolitik, Landschaftspflege und Motorisierungsvision bis zur ökologischen Wende der siebziger Jahre," in Frese and Prinz, *Zäsuren*, 465–98; Thomas Zeller, *Straße, Bahn, Panorama: Verkehrswege und Landschaftsveränderung in Deutschland von 1930 bis 1990* (Frankfurt, 2002).

109. Guenther, *Naturerleben*; Walther Schoenichen, "'Das deutsche Volk muß gereinigt werden': Und die deutsche Landschaft?" *Naturschutz* (1932–33), 205. The extent of anti-Semitism in conservationist rhetoric under the Third Reich still needs research. Friedhelm Schmoll alleges a strong current of anti-Semitism in the conservationists' attacks on billboards; yet he appears to have read the 1930s sources selectively. Although Schoenichen and some others blamed the "disfigurement of the landscape through billboards" on "Jewish poison" (cited in Schmoll, "Verteidigung," 177–80), there are other sources in which such arguments are conspicuously absent, e.g., Anon., "Volkstumsarbeit rückt vor! Die Säuberung des deutschen Heimatbildes schreitet fort!" *Volkstum und Heimat* (1934), 206; NSHStAH, Hann. 174 Zellerfeld, Nr. 3522: Dr. Hartmann, Provinzialkommissar für Naturschutz in Hannover, Entwurf für einen "Leitfaden zum Reichsnaturschutzgesetz" (November 13, 1936). The fact that conservationists continued to see billboards as a problem into the late 1930s suggests that even after Aryanization, they perceived capitalism itself as the enemy. But it is also likely that their anti-Semitism increased in the course of the 1930s.

110. BayHStAM, MWi 2675: Karl Stauder to Bayerisches Staatsministerium (July 30, 1933).

111. BayHStAM, MWi 2675: Anon., untitled statement (p. 24103), and Staatskanzlei des Freistaates Bayern to Bezirksamt Ebermannstadt (February 2, 1934).

112. Cited in Patel, "Neuerfindung," 219.

113. See Mechthild Rössler and Sabine Schleiermacher, eds., *Der "Generalplan Ost":
Hauptlinien der nationalsozialistischen Planungs- und Vernichtungspolitik* (Berlin, 1993);
Klaus Fehn, "'Lebensgemeinschaft von Volk und Raum': Zur nationalsozialistischen
Raum- und Landschaftsplanung in den eroberten Ostgebieten," in Radkau and Uekötter,
Naturschutz, 207–24.

114. Reprinted in Rössler and Schleiermacher, *Generalplan Ost*, 136–47.

115. Oberkrome, "Kerntruppen," 236.

116. Quoted in Fehn, "Lebensgemeinschaft," 207.

117. Brüggemeier, *Tschernobyl*, 174.

118. Radkau, "Problem," 53–54.

119. See Zygmunt Baumann, *Modernity and the Holocaust* (Ithaca, N.Y., 1989).

120. Blackbourn, "Natur," 72.

121. Only after the destruction of the Third Reich did a more humane conservationism emerge in Germany, but it must be recognized that the RNSG helped lay the
groundwork for the large network of nature and landscape preserves that exists today.
On conservation after 1945, see Sandra Chaney, "Visions and Revisions of Nature: From
the Protection of Nature to the Invention of the Environment in the Federal Republic of
Germany, 1945–1975" (Ph.D. diss., University of North Carolina, 1997, revised and forth-
coming from Berghahn books as *Nature of the Miracle Years: Conservation in West Germany, 1945–1975*); Frank Uekötter, *Naturschutz im Aufbruch: Eine Geschichte des Naturschutzes in Nordrhein-Westfalen, 1945–1980* (Frankfurt, 2004); Franz-Josef Brüggemeier
and Jens Engels, *Natur- und Umweltschutz nach 1945: Konzepte, Konflikte, Kompetenzen*
(Frankfurt, 2005); Uekötter, *Green*, 184–201.

Conclusion

1. STAH, III-1 Cl. Vii Lit. He No. 9 vol. 6: Hamburger Ausschuß für Jugendherbergen, *Warum braucht Deutschland Jugendherbergen?* (Hamburg, 1925), 1.

2. Jarausch and Geyer, *Shattered Past*, 23–24.

3. David Arnold, *The Problem of Nature: Environment, Culture, and European Expansion* (Cambridge, Mass., 1996), 185.

4. Hans Gerth and C. Wright Mills, eds., *From Max Weber* (New York, 1958), 155.

5. Eugen Fischer, *Der völkische Staat, biologisch gesehen* (Berlin, 1933), 14–15.

6. Adolf Hitler, *Mein Kampf*, trans. Ralph Manheim (Boston, 1971, orig. 1925),
391–93.

7. Adolf Lau, "Naturfreundschaft als Faktor des kulturellen Aufstieges," *Der Naturfreund: Mitteilungen des TVNF in Wien* (1926), 210.

German Archives and Periodicals Consulted

Archival Files

Archiv der deutschen Jugendbewegung, Burg Ludwigstein: A2-01, 02, 05, 08, 10, 11, 54, 104, 130, 152, 170; Julius Groß Fotoarchiv.

Bayerisches Hauptstaatsarchiv, Munich: MA 15558, 92394, 107384; MInn 71799, 72884, 73589, 73591, 73602, 73766, 73882, 79902; MJu 5054, 17612; MK 13814, 13823, 13828, 13832, 13833, 13844, 13845, 13846, 13848, 13870, 13874, 13875, 13953, 13961, 13963, 13964, 13973, 13974, 13975, 13977, 13978, 13979, 13988, 13992, 13998, 14009, 14012, 14474, 14475, 14847, 14930, 14970, 15003, 15027, 15274, 22898, 40451, 40491, 40500, 40501, 41625, 41639, 41641, 51147, 51152, 51166, 51183, 51192, 51195; MWi 1930, 2675, 2779, 8032; Reichsstatthalter 667; StK 7511.

Bundesarchiv Berlin-Lichterfelde: R15.01/26337; R36/2013, 2014, 2023, 2030, 2071; R43 I/1980; R58/232, 461, 630, 774, 782.

Bundesarchiv Berlin-Lichterfelde, Stiftung Archiv der Parteien und Massenorganisationen der DDR: RY11/II 107/1, 107/4, 107/5, 107/6, 107/9; RY18/I 2/710/8; RY18/II 142/1; RY22/V SUF/110, 418, 419, 420; SgY 2/V DF VII/104; SgY 2/V DF VIII/70.

eco-Archiv im Archiv der Sozialen Demokratie der Friedrich-Ebert Stiftung, Bad Godesberg: TVNF, Ortsgruppe Kuchen. *Wanderberichtsbuch*; TVNF, Ortsgruppe Weissenburg in Bayern.

Historische Kommission zu Berlin: NB457.

Institut für Zeitgeschichte, Munich: Db 44, 72; Fa 119, 215; MA 1496.

Landesarchiv Berlin: B Rep. 042 Acc. 2147/26419, 26797, 26894; B Rep. 142-01/144, 2549, 2854, 4028, 4988, 5166; Helene Lang Archiv.

Niedersächsisches Hauptstaatsarchiv, Hannover: Hann. 80 Lüneburg III, Abteilung XVI, Nr. 317; Hann. 122a, Nr. 4481, 4490; Hann. 174 Fallingbostel, Nr. 2/3; Hann. 174 Neustadt, Nr. 2492; Hann. 174 Zellerfeld, Nr. 1302, 3522, 4538, 4579; Hann. 180 Hann. E1, Nr. 323/1; Hann. 310 IIA, Nr. 29; Hann. 1749 Hann. I, Nr. 137.

Staatsarchiv Augsburg: 10/32; BA Donauwörth 9705; NSD 43, 112/3; NSDAP Gau Schwaben, HJ-Gebiet Schwaben 24, 27, 108.

Staatsarchiv Hamburg: III-1 Cl. Vii Lit. H*e* No. 9 vol. 5. Conv. I; III-1 Cl. Vii Lit. H*e* No. 9 vol. 6; III-2 AII p. 197; III-2 CIII 13; 122-3 264; 131-4 1934 A XI/105.

Staatsarchiv Leipzig: PPL-V 708, 981, 1481, 1643, 3656, 3982, 4302, 4315, 4378, 4404, 4457, 4475, 4494, 4495.

Staatsarchiv Munich: Gestapo 84; LRA 146308; LRA 150944, folders 19 and 20; LRA Freising 116520; LRA Fürstenfeldbrück 10072, 10073; LRA Garmisch-Partenkirchen 61800, 61802; LRA München 19702, 19703, 19708, 19709, 20081; LRA Wolfratshausen 41918; PDM 1172, 1841, 3555, 3772, 4554, 5774, 5934, 5936, 5976, 5988, 6074, 6839, 6840; RA 57867.

Stadtarchiv Augsburg: 10, 1211; 10, 3737; 10, B1/32; V2 883, 1827.

Stadtarchiv Leipzig: Jugendamt Nr. 45, 91, 311, 313, 335; Verkehrsamt Nr. 927, 1068, 1532.

Stadtarchiv Munich: Amt für Leibesübungen 107, 213, 272; Wohlfahrt 83a, 1910, 3442, 4085, 4086, 4627; Wohnungsamt 83a.

Periodicals

Der Alpenfreund: Touristische Halbmonatsschrift für das deutsche Alpengebiet. Munich, 1920–23.

Alt-Wandervogel: Monatsschrift für deutsches Jugendwandern. Göttingen, 1913.

Der Anfang: Zeitschrift der Jugend. Berlin/Vienna, 1913–14.

Arbeit: Zeitschrift des Arbeiterwanderbundes Naturfreunde. Berlin, 1909–?

Arbeiter-Bildung: Monatsschrift für die Arbeiterbildungsausschüsse und Bildungsorgan für Jungsozialisten. Berlin, 1920–28.

Arbeiter-Jugend: Organ für die geistigen und wirtschaftlichen Interessen der jungen Arbeiter und Arbeiterinnen. Berlin, 1909–33.

Arbeitertum: Blätter für Theorie und Praxis der Nationalsozialistischen Betriebszellen-Organisation. Amtliches Organ der Deutschen Arbeitsfront. Berlin, 1934–35.

Arbeiter-Turn-Zeitung. Leipzig, 1919–33.

Arbeiter-Wanderer: Organ der oppositionellen Naturfreunde, Gau Württemberg. Stuttgart, 1931–32.

Archiv für Bevölkerungspolitik, Sexualethik und Familienkunde. Berlin, 1931–34.

Aufstieg: Nachrichten der Naturfreunde Gau Schwaben. Stuttgart, 1921–33.

Das bayerische Jugendherbergswerk: Nachrichtenblatt des Landesverbandes Bayern für Jugendwandern und Jugendherbergen Gau Bayern im D.J.H.e.V. Munich, 1927–36.

Bayerischer Heimatschutz. Munich, 1929–36.

Das Bayernland: Illustrierte Halbmonatsschrift für Bayerns Land und Volk. Munich, 1919–33.

Beiträge zur Naturdenkmalpflege. Berlin, 1926.

"Berg frei": Mitteilungsblatt des TVNF, Gau Pfalz. Mainz, 1922.

Der Bergwanderer: Nachrichtenblatt des Gaues Südbayern des TVNF. Munich, 1921–23. After 1923 entitled *Südbayerischer Wanderer: Nachrichtenblatt des Gaues Südbayern des TVNF, München*. Munich, 1923–29.

Blätter der Arbeitsgemeinschaft des Bundes für Freie Schulgemeinden. Berlin, 1919.

Blätter der Körperkulturschule Adolf Koch. Leipzig, 1928–31.

Blätter für Naturschutz und Naturpflege. Munich, 1919–35.

Die Bücherwarte: Zeitschrift für sozialistische Buchkritik. Berlin, 1926–33.

Deutsche Freischar. Potsdam, 1928–33.

Deutsche Jugendkraft: Zeitschrift für willenstärkende Leibesübungen und vernunftsgemässe Gesundheitspflege. Düsseldorf, 1921–30.

Deutsches Wandern: Monatsschrift für Deutsches Heimatwandern und Bergsteigen, Landschaft und Volkstum, Skilaufen, Wasserwandern, Reisen. Nuremberg, 1933–34.

Deutschwandervogel: Blätter des Bündnisses. Kassel, 1921–28.

Der Eifrige Jugendbündler: Mitteilungen der Arbeiterjugendvereine in den Elbgemeinden. Hamburg, 1922–23.

Der Feldmeister: Führerzeitung und Bundesblatt des Deutschen Pfadfinderbundes. Beilage zu "Der Pfadfinder." Leipzig/Berlin, 1912–23.

Fichte Wandersparte: Mitteilungsblatt für die Gruppen Leipzig und Brandis. Leipzig, 1930–33.

Frauenstimme. Berlin, 1924.

Die Frauenwelt: Beilage zum Vorwärts. Berlin, 1924–27.

Freie Körperkultur im Wort und Bild. Leipzig, 1929.

Das Freie Wort: SPD Diskussionsorgan. Berlin, 1929–33.

Freikörperkultur und Lebensreform: Zeitschrift des Reichsverbandes für Freikörperkultur e.V. (RFK). Berlin, 1929–33. Retitled *Deutsche Freikörperkultur. Zeitschrift für Rassenpflege, naturgemässe Lebensweise und Leibesübungen* (1933–34), *Gesetz und Freiheit* (1934–36), and *Deutsche Leibeszucht* (1937–43).

Frohe Fahrt: Monatsschrift für wandernde Arbeiter und Arbeiterinnen. Heilbronn, 1921–31.

Der Führer: Monatsschrift für Führer und Helfer in der Arbeiterjugendbewegung. Berlin, 1921–33.

Die Genossin: Informationsblätter für weibliche Funktionäre der SPD. Berlin, 1924–32.

Die Gesellschaft: Internationale Revue für Sozialismus und Politik. Berlin, 1924–33.

Gesundheitswacht: Zeitschrift für Gesundheits- und Körperpflege. Munich, 1926–32.

Gewerkschafts-Zeitung: Organ des ADGB. Berlin, 1891–1933.

Die Glocke: Sozialistische Wochenschrift für Politik, Finanzwirtschaft und Kultur. Berlin, 1915–25.

Der Greif: Nachrichtenblatt der deutschen Wandervogelgemeinschaft. Berlin, 1920–26.

Die grüne Fahne: Monatsschrift für jugendliche Weltanschauung. Leipzig, 1924–25.

Handbuch der Heimaterziehung. Berlin, 1923–24.

Hauptausschuß zur Förderung von Leibesübungen und Jugendpflege in Groß-Berlin, Jahresbericht über das Geschäftsjahr. Berlin, 1912–16.

Heimatschutz: Mitteilungen des Deutschen Bundes Heimatschutz. Bremen, 1925–26.

Hitler-Jugend: Kampfblatt schaffender Jugend. Plauen, 1928–29.

Jahrbuch der Leibesübungen für Volks- und Jugendspiele. Im Auftrag des Deutschen Reichsausschusses für Leibesübungen. Berlin, 1928.

Jahrbuch der Münchner Gewerkschaftsbewegung. Munich, 1925–29.

Jahrbuch des Allgemeinen Deutschen Gewerkschaftsbundes. Berlin, 1925.

Jahrbuch des Alpenfreundes. Munich, 1923–24.

Jahresberichte des Isartalvereins. Munich, 1915–37.

Jugend und Arbeitersport. Berlin, 1925–33.

Jugendblätter des Zentralverbandes der Angestellten. Berlin, 1924–31.

Jugend-Führer: Mitteilungen für die Leiter der Jugendabteilungen in den Gewerkschaften. Berlin, 1928–30, 1932.

Die Jugendführerin in katholischen Mädchenvereinen. Düsseldorf, 1931–32.

Jugendführung: Zeitschrift für Jünglingspädagogik und Jugendpflege. Düsseldorf, 1914–33.

Die Jugendherberge: Zeitschrift des Verbandes für Deutsche Jugendherbergen. Hilchenbach, 1919–34.

Jugendpflege: katholische Monatsschrift zur Pflege der schulentlassenen Jugend. Munich, 1913–26.

Jugendpflege im Regierungsbezirk Aurich. Aurich, 1923–25.

Jugend-Stimme: Mitteilungsblatt der Sozialistischen Arbeiterjugend Frankens. Nuremberg, 1924–26.

Der Jugendverein: Ratgeber und Korrespondenzblatt für die Vorstände und Mitarbeiter im katholischen Jünglingsvereinigungen. Düsseldorf, 1919–27.

Das junge Deutschland: Stimmen vom Willen und Weg der deutschen Jugend. Überbündische Zeitschrift des Reichsausschusses der deutschen Jugendverbände. Berlin, 1924–36.

Junge Menschen: Blatt der deutschen Jugend. Hamburg, 1919–27.

Die junge Schar: Blätter für die Jüngeren der katholischen abstinenten Jugend der Werktätigen. Frankfurt, 1926–33.

Das junge Volk: Zeitschrift des jungen Deutschland. Plauen, 1919–29.

Jungenblatt im Quickborn. Burg Rothenfels, 1929–31.

Der Jungfrauenverein: Organ des Zentralverbandes der katholischen Jungfrauenvereinigungen Deutschlands. Bochum, 1921–22.

Der Jungführer: Führerzeitschrift und amtliches Mitteilungsblatt. Düsseldorf, 1934–37.

Die Jungmannschaft: Halbmonatsschrift für katholische junge Männer. Munich, 1918–21.

Jungvolk am Niederrhein: Mitteilungsblatt der Sozialistischen Arbeiterjugend. Duisburg, 1925–28.

Jungvolk vom Bau: Jugendblatt des Deutschen Baugewerksbundes. Hamburg, 1925–30.

Jungwacht: Zeitschrift der katholischen Jugendvereine. Düsseldorf, 1919–34.

Jung-Wandervogel: Zeitschrift des Bundes für Jugendwandern "Jung-Wandervogel." Berlin, 1913–19.

Der Kranz: Halbmonatsschrift für die katholische Mädchenwelt. Organ der katholischen Jungfrauenverein Westdeutschlands. Mönchen-Gladbach, 1928–33.

Kulturwille. Leipzig, 1924–33.

Luginsland: Touristen-Verein Die Naturfreunde, Gau Mittel-Rhein-Main. Koblenz, 1927.

Metallarbeiter-Jugend: Wochenblatt des deutschen Metallarbeiter-Verbandes. Berlin, 1923–31.

Mitteilungen des Bundes für Heimatschutz in Württemberg und Hohenzollern. Stuttgart, 1922.

Mitteilungen des Landesvereins Sächsischer Heimatschutz. Dresden, 1911–35.

Mitteilungsblatt des Gaues Brandenburg im TVNF. Berlin, 1920–25.

Die Münchener Post. Munich, 1914.

Nachrichtenblatt für Naturdenkmalpflege. Berlin, 1925–32.

Nachrichtenblatt für Rheinische Heimatpflege: Organ für Heimatmuseen, Denkmalpflege, Archivberatung, Natur- und Landschaftsschutz. Düsseldorf, 1929–32.

Der nackte Mensch. Leipzig, 1927–28.

Naturdenkmalpflege und Naturschutz in Berlin und Brandenburg. Berlin, 1929–37; continued as *Der märkische Naturschutz: Mitteilungen aus Berlin u. d. Mark Brandenburg.* Berlin, 1938–42.

Der Naturfreund: Bezirk an der Saale. Halle, 1919–?

Der Naturfreund: Gau Thüringen. Jena, 1920–?

Der Naturfreund: Mitteilungen des TVNF in Wien. Vienna, 1905–33.

Der Naturfreund: Monatsschrift des Gaues Niedersachsen. Hannover, 1922–?

Der Naturfreund aus Gau Nordmark. Hamburg, 1920–32.

Die Naturfreunde: Mitteilungsblatt für den Gau Rheinland des TVNF. Cologne, 1920–26.

Die Naturfreunde: Mitteilungsblatt Gau Mittelrhein-Main, Frankfurt am Main. Frankfurt, 1920–29.

Naturfreunde-Jahrbuch. Nuremberg/Vienna, 1926–33.

Naturschutz: Zeitschrift für die gesamten Gebiete des Naturschutzes, Naturdenkmalpflege und verwandte Bestrebungen. Nachrichtenblatt des Volksbundes Naturschutz. Berlin, 1925–44.

Neue Blätter für den Sozialismus. Berlin, 1931–33.

Die Neue Zeit. Berlin, 1883–1923.

Nord- und Ostdeutscher Wanderer: Monatsschrift der Gaue Brandenburg-Pommern, Niedersachsen und Schlesien des TVNF, Zentrale Wien; beginning 1930 entitled *Der Wanderer: Monatsschrift der Gaue Brandenburg, Niederhessen, Niedersachsen, Rheinland, Schlesien, Westfalen;* beginning 1931 entitled *Der Wanderer: Monatsschrift der Reichsleitung und der Gaue Brandenburg, Niederhessen, Niedersachsen, Nordbayern, Rheinland, Saar, Schlesien, Westfalen.* Hannover and Nürnberg, 1929–1933.

Der Pfad: Ein Merkblatt für die Jugend. Burg Rothenfels, 1924.

Der Pfadfinder: Jugendzeitung des deutschen Pfadfinderbundes. Leipzig, 1912–30.

Die Pfadfinderin: Zeitschrift des Bundes deutscher Pfadfinderinnen. Bamberg, 1924.

Proletarier-Jugend: Sozialistische Jugendzeitschrift. Leipzig 1920–22.

Ratgeber für Jugendvereinigungen. Berlin, 1919–23.

Das Rautenfähnlein der Wandervögel in Bayern. Ansbach, 1919–20.

Rheinisches Land: Nachrichtenblatt des Gaues Rheinland im TVNF e.V. Düsseldorf, 1926–28.

Der rote Wanderer. Berlin, 1923–?

Der sozialistische Arzt. Berlin, 1926–32.

Sozialistische Bildung: Monatsschrift des Reichsausschusses für sozialistische Bildungsarbeit. Berlin, 1929–33.

Sozialistische Monatshefte: Internationale Revue des Sozialismus. Berlin, 1897–1933.

Stimmen der Jugend. Düsseldorf, 1921–32.

Touristen-Verein die Naturfreunde, Gau Mittelrhein-Main. Frankfurt, 1921.

Urania: Monatshefte für Naturkenntnis und Gesellschaftslehre. Jena, 1924–32.

Volksgesundheit. Dresden, 1919–33.

Volkstum und Heimat: Blätter für nationalsozialistische Volkstumsarbeit und Lebensgestaltung. Berlin, 1934–36.

Volkswart: Monatsschrift des Verbands zur Bekämpfung der öffentlichen Unsittlichkeit. Cologne, 1908, 1929–32.

Vorwärts. Berlin, 1919–33.

Die Wacht: Zeitschrift katholischer Jungmänner. Düsseldorf, 1918–33.

Der Wanderfreund: Monatsschrift des Arbeiter-Wanderbundes "Naturfreunde." Berlin, 1919–23.

Wandern und Schauen: Mittelrheinischer Heimatblätter. Mainz, 1925–33.

Wandervogel: Fahrtenblatt für Ems-Weserland. Bremen, 1914.

Wandervogel: Monatsschrift für deutsches Jugendwandern. Hartenstein, 1908–27.

Wandervogel, Kriegsheft für Schlesien. Görlitz, 1914–15.

Weibliche Jugend: Fachschrift für weibliche Jugendpflege. Zeitschrift für den Verband der Berufsarbeiterinnen der Inneren Mission. Berlin, 1919–34.

Der Weiße Ritter: Bund Deutscher Neupfadfinder. Unabhängige überbündische Führerzeitung. Regensburg, 1919–26.

Weißes Kreuz: Zeitschrift für die Förderung sittlicher Reinheit unter Männern und jungen Männern. Cologne, 1926–29.

Der westdeutsche Naturfreund: Nachrichten der Gaue Rheinland und Westfalen im TVNF. Essen, Düsseldorf, 1920–30.

Die Willenskraft: Diözesanverband katholischer Jugendvereinigungen Pfalz. Landau, 1921–27.

Zwiespruch: Unabhängige Zeitung für die Wanderbünde, Nachrichtenblatt der Wandervogelämter und Anzeiger unseres wirtschaftlichen Lebens. Halle, 1919.

Bibliography

Abrams, Lynn. *Workers' Culture in Imperial Germany*. London: Routledge, 1992.

Altenberger, Erich, ed. *Natur, Wandern, Waldfest*. Waldenburg: Altenberger, 1929.

Amt für Leibesübungen des Bayerischen Wandervogels, ed. *Leibesübungen*. Lichtenfels: Schulze, 1926.

Andersen, Arne, ed. *Umweltgeschichte: Das Beispiel Hamburg*. Hamburg: Ergebnisse, 1990.

Andersen, Arne, and Helmut Konrad, eds. *Ökologie, Technischer Wandel, und Arbeiterbewegung*. Vienna: Europaverlag, 1990.

Andresen, Sabine. *Mädchen und Frauen in der bürgerlichen Jugendbewegung*. Berlin: Beltz, 2003.

Andritzky, Michael, and Thomas Rautenberg, eds. *"Wir sind nackt und nennen uns Du": Von Lichtfreunden und Sonnenkämpfern—eine Geschichte der Freikörperkultur*. Giessen: Anabas, 1989.

Applegate, Celia. *A Nation of Provincials: The German Idea of Heimat*. Berkeley: University of California Press, 1990.

Astel, Karl, ed. *Jahns Erbe: Wege des jungen Deutschen*. Augsburg: Bärenreiter, 1925.

Aufmuth, Ulrich. *Die deutsche Wandervogelbewegung unter soziologischem Aspekt*. Göttingen: Vandenhoeck und Ruprecht, 1979.

Ausstellung "Das Wunder des Lebens" Berlin, 1935. Berlin: Reichsausschuß für Volksgesundheitsdienst, 1935.

Bajohr, Frank, ed. *Zivilisation und Barbarei: Die widersprüchlichen Potentiale der Moderne*. Hamburg: Christians, 1991.

Bajohr, Stefan. *Vom bitteren Los der kleinen Leute: Protokolle über den Alltag Braunschweiger Arbeiterinnen und Arbeiter, 1900–1933*. Cologne: Bund, 1984.

Baranowski, Shelley. *Strength Through Joy: Consumerism and Mass Tourism in the Third Reich*. Cambridge: Cambridge University Press, 2004.

Barclay, David, and Eric Weitz, eds. *Between Reform and Revolution: German Socialism and Communism from 1840 to 1990*. New York: Berghahn, 1998.

Barlösius, Eva. *Naturgemässe Lebensführung: Zur Geschichte der Lebensreform um die Jahrhundertwende.* Frankfurt: Campus, 1997.

Bauermeister, Friedrich. *Vom Klassenkampf der Jugend.* Jena: Diederichs, 1916.

Baumgarten, Otto, ed. *Geistige und sittliche Wirkungen des Krieges in Deutschland.* Stuttgart: Deutsche Verlagsanstalt, 1927.

Die Bedeutung der Jugendheime für die Jugendpflege: Bericht über die Sitzung des Landesbeirats für Jugendpflege, Jugendbewegung, und Leibesübungen vom 7. Mai 1929. Berlin: Decker, 1929.

Behler, Phillip. *Psychologie des Berufsschülers: Ein Beitrag zur Industriepädagogik.* Cologne: Du Mont Schauburg, 1928.

Benz, Wolfgang, ed. *Lexikon des deutschen Widerstandes.* Frankfurt: Fischer, 1994.

Bergmann, Klaus. *Agrarromantik und Großstadtfeindschaft.* Meisenheim: Hain, 1970.

Bernett, Hajo, ed. *Nationalsozialistische Leibeserziehung: Eine Dokumentation ihrer Theorie und Organisation.* Schorndorff: Hofmann, 1966.

Bessel, Richard. *Germany After the First World War.* Oxford: Oxford University Press, 1993.

Bier, August. *Die Pflege der Leibesübungen—ein Mittel zur Rettung des deutschen Volkes aus seiner Erniedrigung.* Munich: Lehmanns, 1920.

Blüher, Hans. *Die deutsche Wandervogelbewegung als erotisches Phänomen: Ein Beitrag zur Erkenntnis der sexuellen Inversion.* 6th ed. Prien: Kampmann & Schnabel, 1922. (Orig. pub. 1912.)

Blumtritt, Max. *Rationalisierung und Arbeitersport.* Leipzig: Oldenburg, 1922.

Boll, Friedhelm, ed. *Arbeiterkulturen zwischen Alltag und Politik: Beiträge zum europäischen Vergleich in der Zwischenkriegszeit.* Vienna: Europa-Verlag, 1986.

Bollé, Michael, ed. *Eldorado: Homosexuelle Männer und Frauen in Berlin, 1850–1950.* Berlin: Frölich und Kaufmann, 1984.

Bondy, Curt. *Die proletarische Jugendbewegung in Deutschland mit besonderer Berücksichtigung der Hamburger Verhältnisse.* Lauenburg: Adolf Saal, 1922.

Borrmann, Norbert. *Paul Schultze-Naumburg, 1869–1949.* Essen: Bacht, 1989.

Bramwell, Anna. *Ecology in the Twentieth Century: A History.* New Haven, Conn.: Yale University Press, 1989.

Brather, Fritz. *Schülerwanderungen: Eine Zielweisung zur geistigen, künstlerischen, und sittlichen Bereicherung auf Wanderfahrten.* Leipzig: Quelle und Meyer, 1922.

Bräuer, Martin. *Unser Wandern: Ratschläge und Winke zur sozialen und kulturellen Schauen.* Berlin: Arbeiter-Jugend-Verlag, 1925.

Brauns, Friedrich, and W. Leibenow, eds. *Wandern und Schauen: Gesammelte Aufsätze von Frank Fischer.* Hartenstein: Greifenverlag, 1921.

Bridenthal, Renate, Atina Grossman, and Marion Kaplan, eds. *When Biology Became Destiny: Women in Weimar and Nazi Germany.* New York: Monthly Review Press, 1984.

Brinkschmidt, Hans-Christian. "Das Naturverständnis der Arbeiterbewegung am Beispiel der Naturfreunde." Ph.D. diss., University of Frankfurt, 1998.

Brüggemeier, Franz-Josef. *Tschernobyl, 26. April 1986: Die ökologische Herausforderung.* Munich: DTV, 1998.

Brüggemeier, Franz-Josef, Mark Cioc, and Thomas Zeller, eds. *How Green Were the Nazis? Nature, Environment, and Nation in the Third Reich.* Athens: Ohio University Press, 2005.

Brüggemeier, Franz-Josef, and Thomas Rommelspacher. *Blauer Himmel über der Ruhr: Geschichte der Umwelt im Ruhrgebiet 1840–1990.* Essen: Klartext, 1992.

———, eds. *Besiegte Natur: Geschichte der Umwelt im 19. und 20. Jahrhundert.* Munich: Beck, 1987.

Buddrus, Michael. *Totale Erziehung für den totalen Krieg: Hitlerjugend und nationalsozialistische Jugendpolitik.* 2 vols. Munich: Saur, 2003.

Burns, Rob, and Wilfried van der Will, eds. *Arbeiterkulturbewegung in der Weimarer Republik.* 2 vols. Frankfurt: Suhrkamp, 1982.

Büsing, Hartmut, Ernst Neumann, and Bernhard Rohde, eds. *". . . damit wir allerorten der Erde Schönheit schau'n": Vom Arbeiterwanderclub "Die Naturfreunde" Rüstringen zum Touristenverein "Die Naturfreunde" Ortsgruppe Wilhelmshaven e.V.* Wilhelmshaven: Reihe "Arbeiter- und Gewerkschaftsbewegung in Rüstringen und Wilhelmshaven," 1995.

Charlet, Johannes. *Heimatwandern: Ein Buch für die Jugend.* Berlin: Arbeiter-Jugend-Verlag, 1925.

Classen, Walther. *Die deutsche Familie und der Krieg.* Munich: Callwey, 1916.

Coates, Peter. *Nature: Western Attitudes Since Ancient Times.* Berkeley: University of California Press, 1998.

Coblenz, Heinrich. *Geschichte der badischen Naturfreunde.* Karlsruhe: Landesgruppe Baden des TVNF, 1947.

Confino, Alon. *The Nation as a Local Metaphor: Württemberg, Imperial Germany, and National Memory, 1871–1918.* Chapel Hill: University of North Carolina Press, 1997.

Conti, Christoph. *Abschied vom Bürgertum: Alternative Bewegungen in Deutschland von 1890 bis heute.* Reinbek: Rowohlt, 1984.

Conwentz, Hugo. *Die Gefährdung der Naturdenkmäler und Vorschläge zu ihrer Erhaltung.* Berlin: Börntraeger, 1904.

———. *Heimatkunde und Heimatschutz in der Schule.* Berlin: Borntraeger, 1922.

———. *Merkbuch für Naturdenkmalpflege und verwandte Bestrebungen.* Berlin: Borntraeger, 1918.

Cronon, William, ed. *Uncommon Ground: Toward Reinventing Nature.* New York: Norton, 1995.

Davis, Belinda. *Home Fires Burning: Food, Politics, and Everyday Life in World War I Berlin.* Chapel Hill: University of North Carolina Press, 2000.

Dehn, Günther. *Proletarische Jugend: Lebensgestaltung und Gedankenwelt der großstädtischen Proletarierjugend.* 3d ed. Berlin: Furche, 1933.

Denecke, Viola. *Die Arbeitersportgemeinschaft: Eine kulturhistorische Studie über die Braunschweiger Arbeitersportbewegung in den zwanziger Jahren.* Duderstadt: Mekke, 1990.

Deutsch, Julius. *Sport und Politik: Im Auftrage der sozialistischen Arbeiter-Sport-Internationale.* Berlin: Dietz Nachfolger, 1928.

Dickinson, Edward Ross. "Citizenship, Vocational Training, and Reaction: Continuation Schooling and the Prussian 'Youth Cultivation' Decree of 1911." *European History Quarterly* (1999), 109–47.

Dinse, Robert. *Das Freizeitleben der Großstadtjugend: 5000 Jungen und Mädchen berichten.* Eberswalde: Müller, 1932.

Ditt, Karl. "Naturschutz zwischen Zivilisationskritik, Tourismusförderung, und Umweltschutz: USA, England, und Deutschland, 1860–1970." In Matthias Frese and Michael Prinz, eds., *Politische Zäsuren und Gesellschaftlicher Wandel im 20. Jahrhundert,* 499–533. Paderborn: Schöningh, 1996.

———. "The Perception and Conservation of Nature in the Third Reich." *Planning Perspectives* (2000), 161–87.

Dominick, Raymond. *The Environmental Movement in Germany: Prophets and Pioneers, 1871–1971.* Bloomington: Indiana University Press, 1992.

Dowe, Dieter, ed. *Jugendprotest und Generationenkonflikt in Europa im 20. Jahrhundert: Deutschland, England, Frankreich, und Italien im Vergleich.* Bonn: Neue Gesellschaft, 1986.

Dressel, Josefine. *Entwicklung der weiblichen Jugendpflege in Bayern.* Munich: Bayerischer Landesausschuß der deutschen Jugendverbände, 1932.

Dreßen, Karl. *Geschichte des Naturismus: Von der Nacktheit über die Nacktkultur zum Naturismus.* Antwerp: Internationale Naturisten-Föderation, 1995.

Dudek, Peter. *Jugend als Objekt der Wissenschaften: Geschichte der Jugendforschung in Deutschland und Österreich 1890–1933.* Opladen: Westdeutscher Verlag, 1990.

Düntzer, Emilie. *Die gesundheitliche und soziale Lage der erwerbstätigen weiblichen Jugend.* Berlin: Schoetz, 1933.

Eberts, Erich. *Arbeiterjugend, 1904–1945: Sozialistische Erziehungsgemeinschaft—politische Organisation.* Frankfurt: dipa, 1979.

Eder, Klaus. *Die Vergesellschaftung der Natur: Studien zur sozialen Evolution der praktischen Vernunft.* Frankfurt: Suhrkamp, 1988.

Ehrenthal, Günther. *Die Deutsche Jugendbünde: Ein Handbuch ihrer Organisation und ihrer Bestrebungen.* Berlin: Zentral-Verlag, 1929.

Einführung in die Sexualpädagogik. Berlin: Mittler, 1921.

Einweihung des Naturfreundehauses der Ortsgruppe Kelheim im Hammertal am 7. September 1924. Kelheim: TVNF, Ortsgruppe Kelheim, 1924.

Eley, Geoff, ed. *Society, Culture, and the State in Germany, 1870–1930.* Ann Arbor: University of Michigan Press, 1996.

Eley, Geoff, and James Retallack, eds. *Wilhelminism and Its Legacies: German Modernities, Imperialism, and the Meanings of Reform, 1890–1930.* New York: Berghahn, 2003.

Emmerich, Wolfgang, ed. *Proletarische Lebensläufe.* 2 vols. Reinbek: Rowohlt, 1975.

Engelhardt, Viktor. *An der Wende des Zeitalters: Individualistische oder sozialistische Kultur?* Berlin: Arbeiter-Jugend-Verlag, 1925.

———. *Der Mann in der Jugendbewegung.* Berlin: Arbeiter-Jugend-Verlag, 1924.

Enzensperger, Ernst. *Der Jugendwanderführer: Taschenbuch zur Vorbereitung und zum Nachschlagen.* Munich: Pössenbacher, 1930.

————. *Von Jugendwandern und Bergsteigertum: Eine Geschichte des Bayerischen Jugend-herbergwerkes.* Munich: Deutsches Jugendherbergswerk, Landesverband Bayern, 1951.

Eppe, Heinrich. *Selbsthilfe und Interessenvertretung: Die sozial- und jugendpolitischen Bestrebungen der sozialdemokratischen Arbeiterjugendorganisationen, 1904–1933.* Bonn: Die Falken, 1983.

Erdmann, Wulf, and Klaus-Peter Lorenz. *Die grüne Lust der roten Touristen.* Hamburg: Junius, 1985.

Fendrich, Anton. *Der Wanderer.* Stuttgart: Franckh's Sportverlag, 1912.

Festschrift zum 25jährigen Bestehen der Ortsgruppe München des Touristenverein "Die Naturfreunde." Munich: Ortsgruppe München, 1930.

Fiedler, Gudrun. *Bürgerliche Jugendbewegung, Erster Weltkrieg, und sozialer Wandel, 1914–1923.* Cologne: Verlag Wissenschaft und Politik, 1989.

Fikenscher, Friedrich, ed. *Volkhafter Heimatunterricht: Ein Neuaufbau der Heimatkunde.* 2d ed. Ansbach: Prögel, 1942.

Fischer, Eugen. *Der völkische Staat, biologisch gesehen.* Berlin: Junker und Dünnhaupt, 1933.

Fischer, Josepha. *Die Mädchen in den deutschen Jugendverbände: Stand, Ziele und Aufgaben.* Leipzig: Voigtländer, 1933.

Fout, John, ed. *Forbidden History: The State, Society, and the Regulation of Sexuality in Modern Europe.* Chicago: University of Chicago Press, 1992.

Franken, Paul. *Vom Werden einer neuen Kultur: Aufgaben der Arbeiter-Kultur- und Sport-organisationen.* Berlin: Laub, 1930.

Franzen-Hellersberg, Lisbeth. *Die jugendliche Arbeiterin: Ihre Arbeitsweise und Lebens-form.* Tübingen: Mohr, 1932.

Frecot, Janos, Johann Geist, and Diethart Kerbs. *Fidus, 1868–1948: Zur ästhetischen Pra-xis bürgerlicher Fluchtbewegungen.* Munich: Rogner and Bernhard, 1972.

Die Freideutsche Jugend im Bayerischen Landtag. Hamburg: Saal, 1914.

Fritz, Michael, Benno Hafeneger, Peter Krahulec, and Ralf Thaetner. *". . . und fahr'n wir ohne Wiederkehr": Ein Lesebuch zur Kriegsbegeisterung junger Männer. Band 1: Der Wandervogel.* Frankfurt: Brandes und Apsel Verlag, 1990.

Fröhbrodt, Käte. *Arbeitermädel! Wir rufen Dich!* Berlin: Arbeiter-Jugend-Verlag, 1930.

Frohn, Hans-Werner. *Arbeiterbewegungskulturen in Köln, 1890 bis 1933.* Essen: Klartext, 1997.

Fulda, Leopold, ed. *Im Lichtkleid! Stimmen für und gegen das gemeinsame Nacktbaden von Jungen und Mädchen im Familien und Freundeskreise.* Rudolstadt: Greifenverlag, 1921.

Funk, Alois. *Film und Jugend: Eine Untersuchung über die psychischen Wirkungen des Fil-mes im Leben der Jugendlichen.* Munich: Reinhardt, 1934.

Gauger, Gerda, ed. *Mädel im Freizeitlager.* Potsdam: Voggenreiter, 1936.

Gellately, Robert, and Nathan Stoltzfus, eds. *Social Outsiders in Nazi Germany.* Prince-ton: Princeton University Press, 2001.

Gesellschaft der Freunde des Deutschen Heimatschutzes, ed. *Der deutsche Heimatschutz: Ein Rückblick und Ausblick.* Munich: Kastner and Callwey, 1930.

Gesundheitsbehörde Hamburg, ed. *Hygiene und Soziale Hygiene in Hamburg.* Hamburg: Gesundheitsamt der Hansestadt Hamburg, 1928.

Geuter, Ulfried. *Homosexualität in der deutschen Jugendbewegung.* Frankfurt: Suhrkamp, 1994.

Giese, Fritz, and Hedwig Hagemann. *Weibliche Körperbildung und Bewegungskunst.* Munich: Bruckmann, 1920.

Giesecke, Hermann. *Vom Wandervogel bis zur Hitlerjugend: Jugendarbeit zwischen Politik und Pädogogik.* Munich: Juventa, 1981.

Gilhaus, Ulrike. *"Schmerzenskinder der Industrie": Umweltverschmutzung, Umweltpolitik, und sozialer Protest im Industriezeitalter in Westfalen, 1845–1914.* Paderborn: Schöningh, 1995.

Goebbels, Joseph, and Artur Axmann. *Die deutsche Jugend im Kriege.* Berlin: Eher, 1942.

Götz, Karl. *Fünfzig Jahre Jugendwandern und Jugendherbergen, 1909–1959.* Detmold: Deutsches Jugendherbergswerk, 1959.

Götz von Olenhusen, Irmtraud. *Jugendreich, Gottesreich, Deutsches Reich: Junge Generation, Religion und Politik 1928–1933.* Cologne: Verlag Wissenschaft und Politik, 1987.

Graaz, Hans. *Nacktkörperkultur.* Berlin: Der Syndikalist, 1927.

Großklaus, Götz, and Ernst Oldemeyer, eds. *Natur als Gegenwelt: Beitrag zur Kulturgeschichte der Natur.* Karlsruhe: Von Loeper, 1983.

Grossmann, Atina. *Reforming Sex: The German Movement for Birth Control and Abortion Reform, 1920–1950.* Oxford: Oxford University Press, 1995.

Grotjahn, Alfred. *Soziale Hygiene, Geburtenregelung und das Problem der körperlichen Entartung.* Leipzig: Kröner, 1918.

Gstettner, Peter. *Die Eroberung des Kindes durch die Wissenschaft: Aus der Geschichte der Disziplinierung.* Reinbek: Rowohlt, 1981.

Guenther, Konrad. *Deutsches Naturerleben.* Stuttgart: Steinkopf, 1935.

———. *Die Heimatlehre vom Deutschtum und seiner Natur.* Leipzig: Voigtländer, 1932.

———. *Der Naturschutz.* Stuttgart: Franckh, 1919. (Orig. pub. 1912.)

———. *Rasse und Heimat.* Berlin: Hillger, 1935.

Guha, Ramachandra. *Environmentalism: A Global History.* New York: Longman, 2000.

Guttsmann, W. L. *Workers' Culture in Weimar Germany.* New York: Berg, 1990.

Haenisch, Konrad. *Sozialdemokratische Kulturpolitik: Rede im Preußischen Abgeordnetenhaus am 5.6.1918 über Fragen der Schulpolitik.* Berlin: Arbeiter-Jugend-Verlag, 1918.

Hartwig, Theo. *Wanderlust und Bergfreude.* Vienna: Czerny, 1927.

Hassinger, Heinrich. *Vom Weg und Wesen, von Wollen und Wirken der Jugendherbergen und des Jugendwanderns.* Hilchenbach: Reichsverband für deutsche Jugendherbergen, 1931.

Hau, Michael. *The Cult of Health and Beauty in Germany: A Social History, 1890–1930.* Chicago: University of Chicago Press, 2003.

Hellfeld, Matthias von. *Bündische Jugend und Hitlerjugend: Zur Geschichte von Anpassung und Widerstand, 1930–1939.* Cologne: Verlag Wissenschaft und Politik, 1987.

Hellfeld, Matthias von, and Arno Klönne, eds. *Die betrogene Generation: Jugend in Deutschland unter dem Faschismus.* Cologne: Pahl-Rugenstein, 1985.

Helwig, Werner. *Die blaue Blume des Wandervogels: Vom Aufstieg, Glanz, und Sinn einer Jugendbewegung.* Heidenheim: Südmarkverlag, 1980. (Orig. pub. 1960.)

Hentschel, Hermann. *Naturschutz in Ostwestfalen-Lippe von den Anfängen bis zum Landschaftsgesetz.* Detmold: Lippischer Heimatbund, 1987.

Hepp, Corona. *Avantgarde, moderne Kunst, Kulturkritik, und Reformbewegungen nach der Jahrhundertwende.* Munich: DTV, 1987.

Hermand, Jost. *Grüne Utopien in Deutschland: Zur Geschichte des ökologischen Bewußtseins.* Frankfurt: Fischer, 1991.

———, ed. *Mit den Bäumen sterben die Menschen: Zur Kulturgeschichte der Ökologie.* Cologne: Böhlau, 1993.

Hermes, Gertrud. *Die geistige Gestalt des marxistischen Arbeiters und die Arbeiterbildungsfrage.* Tübingen: Mohr, 1926.

Herrmann, Bernhard. *Arbeiterschaft, Naturheilkunde, und der Verband Volksgesundheit, 1880–1918.* Frankfurt: Lang, 1990.

Herrmann, Ulrich, ed. *"Mit uns zieht die neue Zeit": Der Wandervogel in der deutschen Jugendbewegung.* Berlin: Juventa, 2004.

Herzog, Dagmar. *Sex After Fascism: Memory and Morality in Twentieth-Century Germany.* Princeton: Princeton University Press, 2005.

Hirtsiefer, Heinrich. *Jugendpflege in Preußen: Aus Anlaß des 10jährigen Bestehens des Ministeriums für Volkswohlfahrt.* Eberswalde: Müller, 1930.

HJ erlebt Deutschland: Die Großfahrten der sächsischen Hitlerjugend. Berlin: Teubner, 1935.

Hodann, Max. *Sexualpädagogik: Erziehungshygiene und Gesundheitspädagogik. Gesammelte Aufsätze und Vorträge, 1916–1927.* Rudolstadt: Greifenverlag, 1928.

Hoffmann, Heinz, and Jochen Zimmer, eds. *Wir sind die grüne Garde: Geschichte der Naturfreundejugend.* Cologne: Klartext, 1986.

Hoffmann, Hermann. *In Freude Wandern.* Burg Rothenfels: Deutsches Quickbornhaus, 1918.

Hofmeister, Willi. *Leibesübungen und Geländesport als Erlebnis und Verpflichtung: Zur Neugestaltung des Schulturnens in der deutschen Volksschule.* Leipzig: Klinkhardt, 1941. (Orig. pub. 1935.)

Hübbenet, Anatol von. *Die NS-Gemeinschaft "Kraft durch Freude."* Berlin: Junker und Dünnhaupt, 1939.

———. *Das Taschenbuch "Schönheit der Arbeit."* Berlin: DAF, 1938.

———, ed. *Ein Volk erobert die Freude.* Berlin: DAF, 1938.

Huck, Gerhard, ed. *Sozialgeschichte der Freizeit.* Wuppertal: Hammer, 1980.

Hümmeler, Hans. *Jugend an der Maschine.* Freiburg: Herder, 1932.

Jaensch, Walter. *Leibesübungen und Körperkonstitution.* Berlin: Metzner, 1935

Jarausch, Konrad, and Michael Geyer. *Shattered Past: Reconstructing German Histories.* Princeton: Princeton University Press, 2003.

Jauch, Dr. Bernhard. *Moderne Jugendpflege: Kurze Orientierung über die gegenwärtigen Jugendpflegeprobleme und der heutigen Stand der Jugendorganisationen in Deutschland.* Freiburg: Herder, 1915.

Jefferies, Matthew. "'For a Genuine and Noble Nakedness'? German Naturism in the Third Reich." *German History* (2006), 62–84.

Jung, Hubert. *Das Phantasieleben der männlichen werktätigen Jugend: Ein Beitrag zur Psychologie und Pädagogik der Reifezeit.* Münster: Helios, 1930.

"Jungdeutschland": Bericht über die Vertrauensmännerversammlung des Bundes "Jungdeutschland" am 11. und 12. Dezember 1911 (Auszug aus dem Stenogramm). Berlin: Königliche Hofbuchdruckerei von E. S. Mittler & Sohn, 1911.

Jungdeutschland im Dritten Reich: Jahrbuch der Jugend im neuen Deutschland Nr. II. Munich: Kress und Hornung, 1935.

Kaes, Anton, Martin Jay, and Edward Dimendberg, eds. *The Weimar Republic Sourcebook.* Berkeley: University of California Press, 1994.

Kampffmeyer, Hans. *Die Gartenstadtbewegung.* Leipzig: Teubner, 1909.

Kater, Michael. *Hitler Youth.* Cambridge, Mass.: Harvard University Press, 2004.

Kautsky, Karl. *Vermehrung und Entwicklung in Natur und Gesellschaft.* Stuttgart: Dietz Nachfolger, 1910.

Keilhacker, Martin. *Jugendpflege und Jugendbewegung in München von den Befreiungskriegen bis zur Gegenwart.* Munich: Bayerland, 1926.

Kemmer, Ernst. *Volksnot und Jugendwandern.* Munich: Gesundheitswacht, 1922.

Kerbs, Diethart, and Jürgen Reulecke, eds. *Handbuch der deutschen Reformbewegungen, 1880–1933.* Wuppertal: Hammer, 1999.

Kindt, Werner, ed. *Die deutsche Jugendbewegung, 1920 bis 1933: Die bündische Zeit.* Düsseldorf: Diederichs, 1974.

———, ed. *Grundschriften der deutschen Jugendbewegung.* Düsseldorf: Diederichs, 1963.

Klein, Emil, ed. *Die Hitlerjugend im neuen Staat.* Diessen: Huber, 1933.

Klönne, Arno. *Jugend im Dritten Reich: Die Hitler-Jugend und ihre Gegner.* Düsseldorf: Diederichs, 1982.

———, ed. *Jugendkriminalität und Jugendopposition im NS-Staat, kommentierter Nachdruck des Lageberichts der Reichsjugendführung "Kriminalität und Gefährdung der Jugend" vom 1.1.1941.* Münster: Lit, 1981.

Klönne, Irmgard. *Ich spring in diesem Ringe: Mädchen und Frauen in der deutschen Jugendbewegung.* Pfaffenweiler: Centaurus, 1990.

Klueting, Edeltraud, ed. *Antimodernismus und Reform: Zur Geschichte der deutschen Heimatbewegung.* Darmstadt: WBG, 1991.

Knaut, Andreas. *Zurück zur Natur! Die Wurzeln der Ökologiebewegung.* Greven: Gilda, 1993.

Kneip, Rudolf. *Jugend in der Weimarer Zeit: Handbuch der Jugendverbände, 1919–1938.* Frankfurt: dipa, 1974.

Knoll, Joachim, and Julius Schoeps, eds. *Typisch deutsch: Die Jugendbewegung.* Opladen: Leske und Budrich, 1988.

Koch, Adolf. *In Natur und Sonne.* Berlin: Weiss, 1949.

———. *Der Kampf der FKK-Bewegung von 1920 bis 1930.* Leipzig: Oldenburg, 1931.

———. *Körperbildung, Nacktkultur: Anklagen und Bekenntnisse, gesammelt von Adolf Koch.* Leipzig: Oldenburg, 1924.

———. *Wir sind nackt und nennen uns Du.* Leipzig: Oldenburg, 1932.

Koebner, Thomas, Rolf-Peter Janz, and Frank Trommler, eds. *"Mit uns zieht die neue Zeit": Der Mythos Jugend.* Frankfurt: Suhrkamp, 1985.

Krabbe, Wolfgang. *Gesellschaftsveränderung durch Lebensreform: Strukturmerkmale einer sozialreformerischen Bewegung im Deutschland der Industrialisierungsperiode.* Göttingen: Vandenhoeck und Ruprecht, 1974.

———. "'Die Weltanschauung der Deutschen Lebensreform-Bewegung ist der Nationalsozialismus': Zur Gleichschaltung einer Alternativströmung im Dritten Reich." *Archiv für Kulturgeschichte* (1989), 431–61.

Krolle, Stefan. *"Bündische Umtriebe": Die Geschichte des Nerother Wandervogels vor und unter dem NS-Staat.* Münster: Lit-Verlag, 1986.

Krüger, Arnd. "Zwischen Sex und Zuchtwahl: Nudismus und Naturismus in Deutschland und Amerika." In Norbert Finzsch and Hermann Wellenreuther, eds., *Liberalitas: Festschrift für Erich Angermann zum 65. Geburtstag,* 343–65. Stuttgart: Steiner, 1992.

Kühn, Fritz. *Die Arbeitersportbewegung: Ein Beitrag zur Klassengeschichte der Arbeiterschaft.* Münster: Lit, 1981. (Orig. pub. 1922.)

Labisch, Alfons. *Homo hygienicus: Gesundheit und Medizin in der Neuzeit.* Frankfurt: Campus, 1992.

Lager-Ordnung für das Hochland Lager 1935. Munich: Eher, 1935.

Landesverein Sächsischer Heimatschutz. *Heimatschutz und neue Baugesinnung.* Dresden: Landesverein Sächsischer Heimatschutz, 1931.

Langer, Hermann. *"Im gleichen Schritt und Tritt": Die Geschichte der Hitlerjugend in Mecklenburg von den Anfängen bis 1945.* Rostock: Koch, 2001.

Langewiesche, Dieter. "Politik—Gesellschaft—Kultur: Zur Problematik von Arbeiterkultur und kulturelle Arbeiterorganisationen in Deutschland nach dem I. Weltkrieg." *Archiv für Sozialgeschichte* (1982), 359–402.

Laqueur, Walter. *Young Germany: A History of the German Youth Movement.* New Brunswick, N.J.: Transaction, 1984. (Orig. pub. 1962.)

Lauffer, Otto. *Heimat und Vaterland.* Hamburg: Hartung, 1932.

Lees, Andrew. *Cities Perceived: Urban Society in European and American Thought, 1820–1940.* Manchester, U.K.: Manchester University Press, 1985.

Lehmann, Albrecht, ed. *Studien zur Arbeiterkultur.* Münster: Coppenrath, 1984.

Lehmann, Albrecht, and Klaus Schriewer, eds. *Der Wald—ein deutscher Mythos? Perspektiven eines Kulturthemas.* Berlin: Reimer, 2000.

Lekan, Thomas. *Imagining the Nation in Nature: Landscape Preservation and German Identity, 1885–1945.* Cambridge, Mass.: Harvard University Press, 2004.

———. "Regionalism and the Politics of Landscape Preservation in the Third Reich." *Environmental History* (1999), 384–404.

Leo, Heinrich. *Jungdeutschland: Wehrerziehung der deutschen Jugend.* Berlin: Jungdeutschlandbund, 1912.

Levenstein, Adolf. *Die Arbeiterfrage: Mit besonderer Berücksichtigung der sozialpsychologischen Seite des modernen Großstadtbetriebes und der psychophysischen Einwirkungen auf die Arbeiter.* Munich: Reinhardt, 1912.

Levi, Giovanni, and Jean-Claude Schmitt, eds. *A History of Young People*. Vol. II: *Stormy Evolution to Modern Times*. Cambridge, Mass.: Harvard University Press, 1997.

Lidtke, Vernon. *The Alternative Culture: Socialist Labor in Imperial Germany*. Oxford: Oxford University Press, 1985.

Lindner, Werner. *Heimatschutz im neuen Reich*. Leipzig: Seemann, 1934.

Linse, Ulrich. *Ökopax und Anarchie: Eine Geschichte der ökologischen Bewegungen in Deutschland*. Munich: DTV, 1986.

Linse, Ulrich, Reinhard Falter, Dieter Rucht, and Winfried Kretschmer. *Von der Bittschrift zur Platzbesetzung: Konflikte um technische Großprojekte*. Berlin: Dietz Nachfolger, 1988.

Linton, Derek. *"Who Has the Youth, Has the Future": The Campaign to Save Young Workers in Imperial Germany*. Cambridge: Cambridge University Press, 1990.

Lorenz, Klaus-Peter, ed. *Politische Landschaft: Die andere Sicht auf die natürliche Ordnung*. Duisburg: Trikont, 2002.

Magistrat der Stadt Mörfelden-Walldorf, ed. *"Der Konrad, der hat die Mandoline gespielt und ich die Gitarre": Eine kulturgeschichtliche Ausstellung zur Naturfreundebewegung der Weimarer Republik am Beispiel der Ortsgruppe Mörfelden*. Mörfelden-Walldorf: Magistrat der Stadt, 1992.

Mallwitz, Artur. *Jugendpflege durch Leibesübungen*. Berlin: Schoetz, 1919.

Die Marburger Tagung der Freideutschen Jugend. Hamburg: Saal, 1914.

McElligott, Anthony. *The German Urban Experience, 1900–1945*. London: Routledge, 2001.

Merrill, Francis, and Mason Merrill. *Among the Nudists*. Garden City, N.Y.: Garden City Publishing, 1933.

Mewes, Bernhard. *Die erwerbstätige Jugend*. Berlin: De Gruyter, 1929.

Mittelstraß, Gustav, ed. *Freideutscher Jugendtag 1913*. 2d ed. Hamburg: Saal, 1919.

Möhring, Maren. *Marmorleiber: Körperbildung in der deutschen Nacktkultur (1890–1930)*. Cologne: Böhlau, 2004.

Möller, Albrecht. *Wir werden das Volk: Wesen und Forderung der Hitler-Jugend*. Breslau: Hirt, 1935.

Monitor, Gottlieb. *Katholik und moderne Körperkultur*. Munich: Seitz, 1926.

Mosse, George. *Fallen Soldiers: Reshaping the Memory of the World Wars*. Oxford: Oxford University Press, 1990.

———. *Nationalism and Sexuality: Middle-Class Morality and Sexual Norms in Modern Europe*. Madison: University of Wisconsin Press, 1985.

Mühlbach, Ernst. *Glück und Tragik der Vererbung*. Jena: Urania, 1926.

Müller, Emil. *Die Arbeiter-Jugend und ihre Welt: Ein Buch, das alte und junge Arbeiter zusammenführen soll*. Magdeburg: Pfannkuch, 1913.

———. *Das Weimar der arbeitenden Jugend*. Berlin: Arbeiter-Jugend-Verlag, 1920.

Müller, Johannes. *Jugend erwache! Es geht um Dich!* Berlin: Dietz Nachfolger, 1932.

Müller, Wilhelm, ed. *Wie Deutschlands Jugend den Weltkrieg erlebt*. Dresden: Mitteldeutsche Verlagsanstalt, 1918.

Müller-Gaisberg, G. *Volk nach der Arbeit*. Berlin: Schmidt, 1936.

Müller-Marquardt, Fritz. *Das Wandern.* Leipzig: Quelle und Meyer, 1927.

Münker, Wilhelm. *Das deutsche Jugendherbergswerk: Seine Entstehung und Entwicklung bis 1933.* Bielefeld: Deutscher Heimat-Verlag, 1944.

———. *Geschichte des Jugendherbergswerkes von 1933 bis 1945.* Bielefeld: Deutscher Heimat-Verlag, 1946.

Munske, Hilde, ed. *Mädel im Dritten Reich.* Berlin: Freiheitsverlag, 1936.

Natorp, Paul. *Hoffnungen und Gefahren unserer Jugendbewegung.* Jena: Diederichs, 1914.

Der Naturfreund. Vienna: Touristenverein "Die Naturfreunde," 1926. (Orig. pub. 1896.)

Das Naturfreundehaus auf dem Rohrberg bei Weissenburg in Bayern. Nuremberg: Touristenverein "Die Naturfreunde," 1925.

Naturfreunde-Liederbuch Berg Frei! Nuremberg: Reichsleitung des TVNF, 1930.

Der neue Mensch: Volksgemeinschaft, Volkserneuerung, Lebensreform. Berlin: Poppe, 1934.

Neuendorff, Edmund, ed. *Die deutschen Leibesübungen: Großes Handbuch für Turnen, Spiel und Sport.* Berlin: Andermann, 1927.

Neuloh, Otto, and Wilhelm Zilius. *Die Wandervögel: Eine empirisch-soziologische Untersuchung der frühen deutschen Jugendbewegung.* Göttingen: Vandenhoeck und Ruprecht, 1982.

Nitzsche, Max. *Bund und Staat, Wesen und Formen der bündischen Ideologie.* Würzburg: Triltsch, 1942.

Noack, Viktor. *Das soziale Sexualverbrechen: Wohnungsnot und Geschlechtsnot. Ein Kampfwort auch für die Jugend.* Stuttgart: Pöttmann, 1932.

Nordbayerischer Verband für Heimatforschung und Heimatpflege e. V. Windsheim—Monatsberichte. Windsheim: Delp, 1931–33.

Oberkrome, Willi. "'Kerntruppen' in 'Kampfzeiten': Entwicklungstendenzen des deutschen Naturschutzes im Ersten und Zweiten Weltkrieg." *Archiv für Sozialgeschichte* (2003), 228–32.

Pahmeyer, Peter, and Lutz van Spankeren. *Die Hitlerjugend in Lippe (1933–1939).* Bielefeld: Aisthesis, 1998.

Pallaske, Christoph. *Die Hitlerjugend der Freien Stadt Danzig, 1926–1939.* Münster: Waxmann, 1999.

Patel, Kiran. "Neuerfindung des Westens—Aufbruch nach Osten: Naturschutz und Landschaftsgestaltung in den Vereinigten Staaten von Amerika und in Deutschland, 1900–1945." *Archiv für Sozialgeschichte* (2003), 191–221.

Petzina, Dietmar, ed. *Fahne, Fäuste, Körper: Symbolik und Kultur der Arbeiterbewegung.* Essen: Klartext, 1986.

Peukert, Detlev. *Grenzen der Sozialdisziplinierung: Aufstieg und Krise der deutschen Jugendfürsorge 1878 bis 1932.* Cologne: Bund, 1986.

———. *Inside Nazi Germany: Conformity and Opposition in Everyday Life.* New Haven, Conn.: Yale University Press, 1987.

———. *Jugend zwischen Krieg und Krise: Lebenswelten von Arbeiterjungen in der Weimarer Republik.* Cologne: Bund, 1987.

———. *Max Webers Diagnose der Moderne.* Göttingen: Vandenhoeck und Ruprecht, 1989.

―――. "Der Schund- und Schmutzkampf als 'Sozialpolitik der Seele.'" In Hermann Haarmann, Walter Huder, and Klaus Siebenhaar, eds., *"Das war ein Vorspiel nur . . .": Bücherverbrennung in Deutschland 1933, Voraussetzungen und Folgen*, 51–63. Berlin: Medusa, 1983.

―――. *Die Weimarer Republik: Krisenjahre der klassischen Moderne.* Frankfurt: Suhrkamp, 1987.

Peukert, Detlev, and Jürgen Reulecke, eds. *Die Reihen fast geschlossen: Beiträge zur Geschichte des Alltags unterm Nationalsozialismus.* Wuppertal: Hammer, 1981.

Pfitzner, Georg. *Der Naturismus in Deutschland, Österreich, und der Schweiz.* Hamburg: Danehl, 1964.

Piechowski, Paul. *Proletarischer Glaube: Die religiöse Gedankenwelt der organisierten deutschen Arbeiterschaft nach sozialistischen und kommunistischen Selbstzeugnissen.* Berlin: Furche, 1928.

Pils, Manfred. *"Berg frei": 100 Jahre Naturfreunde.* Vienna: Verlag für Gesellschaftskritik, 1994.

Plenge, Johann. *Antiblüher—Affenbund oder Männerbund?* 2d ed. Hartenstein: Greifenverlag, 1920. (Orig. pub. 1917.)

Pörtner, Rudolf, ed. *Alltag in der Weimarer Republik: Erinnerungen an eine unruhige Zeit.* Düsseldorf: Econ, 1990.

Präsidium des Kartells jüdischer Verbindungen in Berlin, ed. *Jüdische Jugend.* Berlin: Kartell jüdischer Verbindungen, 1922.

Proctor, Robert. *The Nazi War on Cancer.* Princeton: Princeton University Press, 1999.

Projektgruppe Arbeiterkultur Hamburg, ed. *"Vorwärts—und nicht vergessen": Arbeiterkultur in Hamburg um 1930.* Berlin: Frölich und Kaufmann, 1982.

Pross, Harry. *Jugend, Eros, Politik: Die Geschichte der deutschen Jugendverbände.* Bern: Scherz, 1964.

Pudor, Heinrich (pseudonym Heinrich Scham). *Nackende Menschen: Jauchzen der Zukunft.* Dresden: Verlag der Dresdner Wochenblätter, 1896. (Orig. pub. 1893.)

―――. *Nackt-Kultur.* 3 vols. Berlin: Selbstverlag, 1906–7.

Puschner, Uwe, Walter Schmitz, and Justus Ulbricht, eds. *Handbuch zur "Völkischen Bewegung," 1871–1918.* Munich: Sauer, 1996.

Raabe, Felix. *Die bündische Jugend.* Stuttgart: Brentanoverlag, 1961.

Rabinbach, Anson. *The Human Motor: Energy, Fatigue, and the Origins of Modernity.* Berkeley: University of California Press, 1992.

Radbruch, Gustav. *Kulturlehre des Sozialismus: Ideologische Betrachtungen.* Berlin: Dietz, 1922.

Radkau, Joachim. *Das Zeitalter der Nervosität: Deutschland zwischen Bismarck und Hitler.* Munich: Hanser, 1998.

Radkau, Joachim, and Frank Uekötter, eds. *Naturschutz und Nationalsozialismus.* Frankfurt: Campus, 2003.

Ras, Marion de. *Körper, Eros, und weibliche Kultur: Mädchen im Wandervogel und in der Bündischen Jugend, 1900–1933.* Pfaffenweiler: Centaurus, 1988.

Reck, Siegfried. *Arbeiter nach der Arbeit: Sozialhistorische Studie zu den Wandlungen des Arbeiteralltags.* Giessen: Agos, 1977.

Reese, Dagmar. *"Straff, aber nicht stramm—herb aber nicht derb": Zur Vergesellschaftung von Mädchen durch den Bund Deutscher Mädel im sozialkulturellen Vergleich zweier Milieus.* Weinheim: Beltz, 1989.

Reichart, Kurt. *Von Leibeszucht und Leibesschönheit.* Berlin: Verlag Deutsche Leibeszucht, 1940.

Reichsverband für deutsche Jugendherbergen, ed. *Fahrt: Erlebnisberichte deutscher Jungen und Mädel.* Berlin: Limpert, 1938.

———. *Schafft uns Jugendherbergen.* Berlin: Universum, 1934.

Renn, Ortwin. "Die alternative Bewegung: Eine historisch-soziologische Analyse des Protestes gegen die Industriegesellschaft." *Zeitschrift für Politik* (1985), 153–94.

Repp, Kevin. *Reformers, Critics, and the Path of German Modernity: Anti-politics and the Search for Alternatives, 1890–1914.* Cambridge, Mass.: Harvard University Press, 2001.

Reulecke, Jürgen. *Geschichte der Urbanisierung in Deutschland.* Frankfurt: Suhrkamp, 1985.

———. "Jugend und 'junge Generation' in der Gesellschaft der Zwischenkriegszeit." In Christa Berg, ed., *Handbuch der deutschen Bildungsgeschichte, Band V (1918–1945),* 86–110. Munich: Beck, 1989.

Reulecke, Jürgen, and Adelheid Gräfin zu Castell Rüdenhausen, eds. *Stadt und Gesundheit: Zum Wandel von "Volksgesundheit" und kommunaler Gesundheitspolitik im 19. und frühen 20. Jahrhundert.* Stuttgart: Steiner, 1991.

Reulecke, Jürgen, and Winfried Mogge, eds. *Hoher Meissner 1913: Der I. Freideutsche Jugendtag in Dokumenten, Deutungen, und Bildern.* Cologne: Verlag Wissenschaft und Politik, 1988.

Richter, Paul. *Aufgaben und Ziele der "Naturfreunde": Rede auf der Hauptversammlung in Bregenz.* Vienna: Happisch, 1932.

Riordan, Colin, ed. *Green Thought in German Culture: Historical and Contemporary Perspectives.* Cardiff: University of Wales Press, 1997.

Ritter, Gerhard A., and Klaus Tenfelde. *Arbeiter im deutschen Kaiserreich, 1871–1914.* Bonn: Dietz, 1992.

Rodatz, Johannes. *Erziehung durch Erleben: Der Sinn des Deutschen Jugendherbergwerkes.* 2d ed. Berlin: Limpert, 1936.

Rohkrämer, Thomas. *Eine andere Moderne? Zivilisationskritik, Natur, und Technik in Deutschland, 1880–1933.* Paderborn: Schöningh, 1999.

Rollins, William. *A Greener Vision of Home: Cultural Politics and Environmental Reform in the German Heimatschutz Movement, 1904–1918.* Ann Arbor: University of Michigan Press, 1997.

Roseman, Mark, ed. *Generations in Conflict: Youth Revolt and Generation Formation in Germany, 1770–1968.* Cambridge: Cambridge University Press, 1995.

Ross, Chad. *Naked Germany: Health, Race, and the Nation.* Oxford: Berg, 2005.

Rössler, Mechthild, and Sabine Schleiermacher, eds. *Der "Generalplan Ost": Hauptlinien der nationalsozialistischen Planungs- und Vernichtungspolitik.* Berlin: Akademie-Verlag, 1993.

Roth, Lutz. *Die Erfindung des Jugendlichen.* Munich: Juventa, 1983.

Rudorff, Ernst. *Heimatschutz: Im Auftrag des Deutschen Bundes für Heimatschutz neu bearbeitet von Paul Schultze-Naumburg.* Berlin: Bernmühler, 1926. (Orig. pub. 1897.)

Saldern, Adelheid von. "Arbeiterkulturbewegung in der Zwischenkriegszeit." In Friedhelm Boll, ed., *Arbeiterkultur im europäischen Vergleich*, 29–70. Munich: Beck, 1986.

———. "Massenfreizeitkultur im Visier: Ein Beitrag zu den Deutungs- und Einwirkungsversuchen während der Weimarer Republik." *Archiv für Sozialgeschichte* (1993), 21–58.

———, ed. *Stadt und Moderne: Hannover in der Weimarer Republik*. Hamburg: Ergebnisse, 1989.

Saul, Klaus. "Der Kampf um die Jugend zwischen Volksschule und Kaserne: Ein Beitrag zur 'Jugendpflege' im wilhelminischen Reich, 1890–1914." *Militärgeschichtliche Mitteilungen* (1971), 97–143.

Schaxel, Julius. *Das Geschlecht: Seine Erscheinungen—seine Bestimmung—sein Wesen bei Tier und Mensch*. Jena: Urania, 1926.

———. *Das Weltbild der Gegenwart und seine gesellschaftlichen Grundlagen*. Jena: Urania, 1932.

Schellenberger, Barbara. *Katholische Jugend und Drittes Reich: Die Geschichte des Katholischen Jungmännerbundes, 1933–1939*. Mainz: Grünewald, 1975.

Scheller, Thilo. *Geländespiele für die deutsche Jugend*. Leipzig: Quelle und Meyer, 1933.

Schenk, Dietmar. *Die Freideutsche Jugend, 1913–1919/20*. Münster: Lit, 1991.

Schirach, Baldur von. *Die Hitler-Jugend: Idee und Gestalt*. Leipzig: Koehler und Amelang, 1934.

Schley, Cornelius. *Die sozialistische Arbeiterjugend Deutschlands*. Frankfurt: dipa, 1987.

Schmidt, Heinrich. *Der Kampf ums Dasein*. Jena: Urania, 1930.

Schmoll, Friedemann. *Erinnerungen an die Natur: Die Geschichte des Naturschutzes im Kaiserreich*. Frankfurt: Campus, 2004.

Schneider, Bernhard. *Daten zur Geschichte der Jugendbewegung unter besonderer Berücksichtigung des Pfadfindertums, 1890–1945*. Münster: Lit, 1990.

Schoenichen, Walther. *Appell der deutschen Landschaft an den Arbeitsdienst*. Berlin: Neumann, 1933.

———. *Naturschutz, Heimatschutz: Ihre Begründung durch Ernst Rudorff, Hugo Conwetz, und ihre Vorläufer*. Stuttgart: WVG, 1954.

———. *Naturschutz im Dritten Reich: Einführung in Wesen und Grundlagen zeitgemässer Naturschutz-Arbeit*. Berlin: Bernmühler, 1934.

———. *Taschenbuch der in Deutschland geschützten Tiere*. Berlin: Bermühler, 1939.

———. *Urwaldwildnis in deutschen Landen: Bilder vom Kampf des deutschen Menschen mit der Urlandschaft*. Berlin: Neumann, 1934.

———. *Die Verrummelung der Natur*. Berlin: Naturschutz-Verlag, 1930.

———. *Zauber der Wildnis in deutscher Heimat*. Berlin: Neumann, 1935.

———, ed. *Wege zum Naturschutz*. Breslau: Staatliche Stelle für Naturdenkmalpflege in Preußen, 1926.

Schomburg, Emil. *Der Wandervogel: Seine Freunde und seine Gegner*. Wolfenbüttel: Zwiesler, 1917.

Schomburg, Emil, and G. Koetschau, eds. *Das Wandervogel-Buch*. Oranienburg: Wandervogel e.V., 1917.

Schönbrunn, Walter. *Jugendwandern als Reifung zur Kultur*. Berlin: Hensel, 1927.

Schramm, Engelbert. "Historische Umweltforschung und Sozialgeschichte des 19. und 20. Jahrhunderts." *Archiv für Sozialgeschichte* (1987), 439–55.

Schult, Johannes. *Das Jugendproblem in der Gegenwart*. Berlin: Arbeiter-Jugend-Verlag, 1924.

Schultze-Naumburg, Paul. *Aufgabe des Heimatschutzes*. Munich: Callwey, 1908.

———. *Die Gestaltung der Landschaft durch die Menschen*. 2d ed. Munich: Callwey, 1922. (Orig. pub. 1915–17.)

———. *Die Kultur des weiblichen Körpers als Grundlage der Frauenkleidung*. Jena: Diederichs, 1922. (Orig. pub. 1903.)

———. *Kunst aus Blut und Boden*. Leipzig: Seemann, 1934.

Schwan, Bruno. *Die Wohnungsnot und das Wohnungselend in Deutschland*. Berlin: Heymanns, 1929.

Schwartz, Michael. *Sozialistische Eugenik: Eugenische Sozialtechnologien in Debatten und Politik der deutschen Sozialdemokratie, 1890–1933*. Bonn: Dietz Nachfolger, 1995.

Sick, Ludwig. *Das Recht des Naturschutzes*. Bonn: Röhrscheid, 1935.

Sieferle, Rolf-Peter. *Fortschrittsfeinde? Opposition gegen Technik und Industrie von der Romantik bis zur Gegenwart*. Munich: Beck, 1984.

Sieferle, Rolf-Peter, and Helga Breuninger, eds. *Natur-Bilder: Wahrnehmungen von Natur und Umwelt in der Geschichte*. Frankfurt: Campus, 1999.

Siemering, Hertha, ed. *Die deutschen Jugendpflegeverbände: Ihre Ziele, Geschichte und Organisation*. 2 vols. Berlin: Zentralstelle für Volkswohlfahrt, 1918.

———. *Fortschritte der deutschen Jugendpflege von 1913 bis 1916*. Berlin: Verlag Julius Springer, 1916.

———. *Pflege der schulentlassenen weiblichen Jugend*. Berlin: Heymanns, 1914.

Solger, Friedrich. *"Die Heimat als Lebenseinheit": Sonderdrück aus* Naturschutz *XIV:11*. Berlin: Neumann, 1934.

Spitzer, Giselher. "Die Adolf-Koch-Bewegung." In Hans-Joachim Teichler, ed., *Arbeiterkultur und Arbeitersport*, 77–103. Clausthal-Zellerfeld: Deutsche Vereinigung für Sportwissenschaft, 1985.

———. *Der deutsche Naturismus*. Ahrensburg: Czwalina, 1983.

Spode, Hasso, ed. *Zur Sonne, zur Freiheit! Beiträge zur Tourismusgeschichte*. Berlin: Verlag für universitäre Kommunikation, 1991.

Sprondel, Walter. "Kulturelle Modernisierung durch antimodernistischen Protest: Der lebensreformerische Vegetarismus." *Kölner Zeitschrift für Soziologie und Sozialpsychologie* (1986), 314–30.

Stachura, Peter. *The German Youth Movement, 1900–1945*. New York: St. Martin's, 1981.

———. *The Weimar Republic and the Younger Proletariat*. New York: St. Martin's, 1989.

Stählin, Wilhelm. *Fieber und Heil in der Jugendbewegung*. Hamburg: Hanseatische Verlagsanstalt, 1922.

Stern, Fritz. *The Politics of Cultural Despair: A Study in the Rise of the Germanic Ideology*. Berkeley: University of California Press, 1961.

Stollberg, Gunnar. "Die Naturheilvereine im Deutschen Kaiserreich." *Archiv für Sozialgeschichte* (1988), 287–306.

Straesser, Charly. *Jugendgelände: Ein Buch vom neuen Menschen.* Rudolstadt: Greifenverlag, 1926.

Stremmel, Ralf. *"Gesundheit—unser einziger Reichtum?" Kommunale Gesundheits- und Umweltpolitik 1800–1945 am Beispiel Solingen.* Solingen: Stadtarchiv Solingen, 1993.

Surén, Hans. *Deutsche Gymnastik.* Oldenburg: Stalling, 1925.

———. *Der Mensch und die Sonne.* Stuttgart: Dieck, 1924.

Sywottek, Arnold. "Freizeit und Freizeitgestaltung: Ein Problem der Gesellschaftsgeschichte." *Archiv für Sozialgeschichte* (1993), 1–20.

Tenfelde, Klaus. "Großstadtjugend in Deutschland vor 1914." *Vierteljahrschrift für Sozial- und Wirtschaftsgeschichte* (1982), 182–218.

———, ed. *Arbeiter im 20. Jahrhundert.* Stuttgart: Klett-Cotta, 1991.

Teuteberg, Hans, ed. *Stadtwachstum, Industrialisierung, Sozialer Wandel: Beiträge zur Erforschung der Urbanisierung im 19. und 20. Jahrhundert.* Berlin: Duncker and Humblot, 1986.

Teuteberg, Hans J., and Clemens Wischermann, eds. *Wohnalltag in Deutschland, 1850–1914: Bilder, Daten, Dokumente.* Münster: Coppenrath, 1985.

Theologus Christianus. *Nacktkultur? Darf und soll der Mensch Nackt leben?* Munich: Seitz, 1926.

Thurnwald, Richard. *Die neue Jugend.* 2 vols. Leipzig: Quelle und Meyer, 1927.

Tiletschke, Frigga, and Christel Liebold. *Aus grauer Stadt Mauern: Bürgerliche Jugendbewegung in Bielefeld, 1900–1933.* Bielefeld: Verlag für Regionalgeschichte, 1995.

Toepfer, Karl. "Nudity and Modernity in German Dance, 1910–30." *Journal of the History of Sexuality* (1992), 58–108.

Touristenverein "Die Naturfreunde": Denkschrift zum sechzigjährigen Bestehen. Zürich: Zentralausschuß der Naturfreunde-Internationale, 1955.

Treziak, Ulrike. *Deutsche Jugendbewegung am Ende der Weimarer Republik: Zum Verhältnis von bündischer Jugend und Nationalsozialismus.* Frankfurt: dipa, 1986.

Trom, Danny. "Natur und nationale Identität: Der Streit um den Schutz der 'Natur' um die Jahrhundertwende in Deutschland und Frankreich." In Etienne François, Hannes Siegrist, and Jakob Vogel, eds., *Nation und Emotion: Deutschland und Frankreich im Vergleich im 19. und 20. Jahrhundert,* 178–206. Göttingen: Vandenhoeck und Ruprecht, 1995.

Ueberhorst, Horst. *Frisch, frei, stark, treu: Die Arbeitersportbewegung in Deutschland, 1893–1933.* Düsseldorf: Dorst, 1973.

———, ed. *Arbeitersport- und Arbeiterkulturbewegung im Ruhrgebiet.* Opladen: Westdeutscher Verlag, 1989.

Uekötter, Frank. *The Green and the Brown: A History of Conservation in Nazi Germany.* Cambridge: Cambridge University Press, 2006.

Ulmer Naturfreundehaus im kleinen Lautertal bei Herrlingen. Ulm: TVNF, Ortsgruppe Ulm, 1927.

Ungewitter, Richard. *Aus Entartung zur Rassenpflege.* Stuttgart: Selbstverlag, 1934.

———. *Die Nacktheit in entwicklungsgeschichtlicher, gesundheitlicher, moralischer und künstlerischer Beleuchtung.* Stuttgart: Selbstverlag, c. 1907.

———. *Nacktheit und Kultur.* Stuttgart: Selbstverlag, c. 1907.

———. *Nacktheit und Moral: Wege zur Rettung des deutschen Volkes.* Stuttgart: Selbstverlag, 1925.

———, ed. *Deutschlands Wiedergeburt durch Blut und Eisen.* Stuttgart: Selbstverlag, 1916.

Usborne, Cornelie. *The Politics of the Body in Weimar Germany: Women's Reproductive Rights and Duties.* Hampshire: Macmillan, 1992.

Vesper, Will, ed. *Deutsche Jugend.* Berlin: Limpert, 1934.

Voggenreiter, Heinrich, ed. *Deutsches Spielhandbuch, II. Teil: Geländespiele/ Scharkämpfe.* Potsdam: Voggenreiter, 1930.

———. *Taschenbuch für den deutschen Jugendführer.* Potsdam: Voggenreiter, 1933.

Vondung, Klaus, ed. *Das Wilhelminische Bildungsbürgertum.* Göttingen: Vandenhoeck and Ruprecht, 1976.

Wagener, Hermann. *Der jugendliche Industriearbeiter und die Industriefamilie: Beiträge zur Psychologie der Reifezeit. Ein Beitrag zur Schulung und Erziehung des Arbeiternachwuchses.* Münster: Münsterverlag, 1931.

Wagner, Helmut. *Sport und Arbeitersport.* Berlin: Gutenberg, 1931.

Walter, Franz. *Der Leib und sein Recht im Christentum.* Donauworth: Auer, 1910.

Walter, Franz, Viola Denecke, and Cornelia Regin. *Sozialistische Gesundheits- und Lebensreformverbände.* Bonn: Dietz, 1991.

Wandersport: Eine Anleitung für Wandern und Geländespiel. Diessen: Huber, 1932.

Weber, Werner, and Walther Schoenichen. *Das Reichsnaturschutzgesetz vom 26. Juni 1935.* Berlin: Bermühler, 1936.

Wedemeyer, Bernd. "'Zum Licht': Die Freikörperkultur in der wilhelminischen Ära und der Weimarer Republik zwischen Völkischer Bewegung, Okkultismus, und Neuheidentum." *Archiv für Kulturgeschichte* (1999), 173–97.

Weindling, Paul. *Health, Race, and German Politics Between National Unification and Nazism, 1870–1945.* Cambridge: Cambridge University Press, 1989.

Weinmann, Richard. *Von der Kulturmission der Heimatarbeit.* Windsheim: Delp, 1932.

Weiss, Hermann. "Ideologie der Freizeit im Dritten Reich: Die NS-Gemeinschaft 'Kraft durch Freude.'" *Archiv für Sozialgeschichte* (1993), 289–304.

Weissler, Sabine, ed. *Fokus Wandervogel: Der Wandervogel und seine Beziehungen zu den Reformbewegungen vor dem Ersten Weltkrieg.* Marburg: Jonas, 2001.

Wenz, Eugen. *Kein Nacktkultus! Wahre und falsche Kultur, oder der Nacktkultus und seine Auswüchse der Erotismus und Feminismus vor dem Forum der sittlichen Vernunft.* Lorch: Rohr, 1911.

Wettengel, Michael. "Staat und Naturschutz 1906–1945: Zur Geschichte der Staatlichen Stelle für Naturschutz in Preußen und der Reichsstelle für Naturschutz." *Historische Zeitschrift* (1993), 355–99.

Wey, Klaus-Georg. *Umweltpolitik in Deutschland: Kurze Geschichte des Umweltschutzes in Deutschland seit 1900.* Opladen: Westdeutscher Verlag, 1982.

Wildt, Dieter. *Sonnenkult: Von der vornehmen Blässe zum nahtlosen Braun.* Düsseldorf: ECON, 1987.

Wildung, Fritz. *Arbeitersport.* Berlin: Bücherkreis, 1929.

Will, Wilfried van der. "The Body Culture and the Body Politic as Symptom and Metaphor in the Transition of German Culture to National Socialism." In Brandon Taylor and Wilfried van der Will, eds., *The Nazification of Art*, 14–52. Winchester, U.K.: Winchester Press, 1990.

Will, Wilfried van der, and Rob Burns. *Arbeiterkulturbewegung in der Weimarer Republik.* 2 vols. Frankfurt: Suhrkamp, 1982.

Willett, John. *Art and Politics in the Weimar Republic.* New York: Pantheon, 1978.

Williams, John A. "'The Chords of the German Soul Are Tuned to Nature': The Movement to Preserve the Natural *Heimat* from the Kaiserreich to the Third Reich." *Central European History* (1996), 339–84.

———. "Ecstasies of the Young: Sexuality, the Youth Movement, and Moral Panic in Germany on the Eve of the First World War." *Central European History* (2001), 162–89.

———. "Giving Nature a Higher Purpose: Back-to-Nature Movements in Weimar Germany, 1918–1933." Ph.D. diss., University of Michigan, 1996.

———. "Protecting Nature Between Democracy and Dictatorship: The Changing Ideology of the Bourgeois Conservationist Movement, 1925–1935." In Thomas Lekan and Thomas Zeller, eds., *Germany's Nature: New Approaches to Environmental History*, 183–206. New Brunswick, N.J.: Rutgers University Press, 2005.

———. "Steeling the Young Body: Official Attempts to Control Youth Hiking in Germany, 1913–1938." *Occasional Papers in German Studies* 12 (July 1997), 1–54.

Winnecken, Andreas. *Ein Fall von Antisemitismus: Zur Geschichte und Pathogenese der deutschen Jugendbewegung vor dem Ersten Weltkrieg.* Cologne: Verlag Wissenschaft und Politik, 1991.

Wolbert, Klaus, ed. *Die Lebensreform: Entwürfe zur Neugestaltung von Leben und Kunst um 1900.* 2 vols. Darmstadt: Häusser, 2001.

Woldt, Richard. *Die Lebenswelt des Industriearbeiters.* Leipzig: Quelle und Meyer, 1926.

Wolf, Benno. *Das Recht der Naturdenkmalpflege in Preußen.* Berlin: Borntraeger, 1920.

Wolschke-Bulmahn, Joachim. *Auf der Suche nach Arkadien: Zu Landschaftsidealen und Formen der Naturaneignung in der Jugendbewegung und ihrer Bedeutung für die Landespflege.* Munich: Minerva, 1990.

Wolschke-Bulmahn, Joachim, and Gert Gröning. *Die Liebe zur Landschaft, Teil III: Der Drang nach Osten.* Munich: Minerva, 1987.

Wulf, Hans-Albert. *"Maschinenstürmer sind wir keine": Technischer Fortschritt und sozialdemokratische Arbeiterbewegung.* Frankfurt: Campus, 1987.

Wyneken, Gustav. *Eros.* Lauenburg: Saal, 1924.

———. *Der Gedankenkreis der Freien Schulgemeinde.* Jena: Diederichs, 1914.

———. *Der Krieg und die Jugend.* Munich: Steinicke, 1915.

———. *Die neue Jugend: Ihr Kampf um Freiheit und Wahrheit in Schule und Elternhaus, in Religion und Erotik.* Munich: Steinicke, 1914.

———. *Was ist Jugendkultur?* Munich: Steinicke, 1913.

Zeller, Thomas. *Straße, Bahn, Panorama: Verkehrswege und Landschaftsveränderung in Deutschland von 1930 bis 1990.* Frankfurt: Campus, 2002.

Zentralstelle für Volkswohlfahrt. *Wohnungsaufsicht und Wohnungspflege: Ein Leitfaden.* Berlin: Heymanns, 1918.

Ziegler, Ulf. *Nackt unter Nackten: Utopien der Nacktkultur, 1906–1942.* Berlin: Nishen, 1990.

Ziemer, Gerhard, and Hans Wolf. *Wandervogel und Freideutsche Jugend.* Bad Godesberg: Voggenreiter, 1961.

Zimmer, Jochen, ed. *Mit uns zieht die neue Zeit: Die Naturfreunde—zur Geschichte eines alternativen Verbandes in der Arbeiterkulturbewegung.* Cologne: Pahl-Rügenstein, 1984.

Zimmer, Jochen, and Wulf Erdmann, eds. *Hundert Jahre Kampf um die freie Natur: Eine illustrierte Geschichte der Naturfreunde.* Cologne: Pahl-Rügenstein, 1991.

Zimmermann, Gerda, and Gretel Both, eds. *Jungmädels Welt, Heim, und Zelt.* Leipzig: Seybold, 1934.

Zinzinger, Hugo. *Das deutsche Mädel bei Übung und Spiel im Gelände, auf Schulwanderungen, und im Schullandheim.* Berlin: Limpert, 1936.

Index

9 780804 700153